AFTER HOMICIDE

CLARENDON STUDIES IN CRIMINOLOGY

Published under the auspices of the Institute of Criminology, University of Cambridge, the Mannheim Centre, London School of Economics, and the Centre for Criminological Research, University of Oxford.

GENERAL EDITORS: DAVID DOWNES AND PAUL ROCK
(London School of Economics)

EDITORS: ANTHONY BOTTOMS AND TREVOR BENNETT
(University of Cambridge)

ROGER HOOD, RICHARD YOUNG AND LUCIA ZEDNER
(University of Oxford)

Recent titles in this series:

Prisons and the Problem of Order
SPARKS, BOTTOMS, and HAY

The Local Governance of Crime
CRAWFORD

Policing the Risk Society
ERICSON and HAGGERTY

Crime in Ireland 1945–95: Here be Dragons
BREWER, LOCKHART, and RODGERS

Sexed Work: Gender, Race and Resistance in a Brooklyn
Drug Market
MAHER

Law in Policing: Legal Regulation and Police Practices
DIXON

Private Security and Public Policing
JONES and NEWBURN

Forthcoming titles:

Negotiating Domestic Violence: Police, Criminal Justice and Victims
HOYLE

Violent Racism
BOWLING

AFTER HOMICIDE

Practical and Political Responses to Bereavement

PAUL ROCK

CLARENDON PRESS OXFORD
1998

Oxford University Press, Great Clarendon Street, Oxford OX2 6DP

Oxford New York

Athens Auckland Bangkok Bogotá Buenos Aires Calcutta
Cape Town Chennai Dar es Salaam Delhi Florence Hong Kong Istanbul
Karachi Kuala Lumpur Madrid Melbourne Mexico City Mumbai
Nairobi Paris São Paolo Singapore Taipei Tokyo Toronto Warsaw
and associated companies in
Berlin Ibadan

Oxford is a registered trade mark of Oxford University Press

Published in the United States
by Oxford University Press Inc., New York

British Library Cataloguing in Publication Data
Data available

Library of Congress Cataloguing-in-Publication Data
Rock, Paul Elliot.
After homicide: practical and political responses to bereavment / Paul Rock
p. cm.
Includes bibliographical references and index.
1. Murder victims' families—Services for—Great Britain.
4. Bereavement—Psychological aspects.
5. Homicide—Psychological aspects. I. Title.
HV6535.G4R53 1998 362.88—dc21 98–3017
ISBN 0–19–826795–9

1 3 5 7 9 10 8 6 4 2

Typeset by Pure Tech India Limited, Pondicherry, India.
Printed in Great Britain
on acid-free paper by
Biddles Ltd., Guildford and King's Lynn

For Bob and Julia Scott

General Editors' Introduction

The *Clarendon Studies in Criminology* series was inaugurated in 1994 under the auspices of centres of criminology at the Universities of Cambridge and Oxford and the London School of Economics. There was a view that criminology in Britain and elsewhere was flowing with interesting work and that there was scope for a new dedicated series of scholarly books. In particular, there was a recognition that authors of research monographs, the life-blood of any subject, face growing difficulties in publishing their work. The intention, declared Roger Hood, its first general editor, was 'to provide a forum for outstanding work in all aspects of criminology, criminal justice, penology, and the wider field of deviant behaviour.' We trust that that intention has been fulfilled. Some twenty titles have already been published, covering policing; prisons and prison administration; gender and crime; the media reporting of crime news, and much else; and others will follow.

Among the most momentous changes in this field over the past two decades have been the rise of victim consciousness and of consciousness of victimisation. Paul Rock is at the very forefront of the analysis and documentation of these developments. He has already to his credit a trilogy of important studies on the subject of policy and practice regarding victims of crime – *A View From The Shadows* (1986), on the making of victim support policy in Canada; *Helping Victims of Crime* (1990) on the rise of the victim support movement in Britain; and *The Social World of an English Crown Court* (1993) on the changing shape of court procedures regarding victims. It should be stressed that these studies, particularly the first, achieve an insight into actual processes of law and policy-making all too rare in the field of social policy and administration, let alone criminology and criminal justice studies.

His long involvement in the practical and organisational contexts of victim support prepared him uniquely well for the challenge of the research and writing of *After Homicide*. The 'secondary victims' of homicide are an exceptionally traumatised group of people who have generated an unusually intense set of networks and organisations of marked diversity. It took great interpersonal skill as well as the rapport born of genuine sympathy for him to become accepted as an authentic medium for their views, beliefs and histories. The result is an anatomy of pain, painstakingly wrought: the mixture of grief, anger, bitterness and loss which seems to be unassuagable; followed, for some, by survivors' guilt when the ebbing of emotion is equated with betrayal. In a sense, the history of *Support After Murder and Manslaughter* (SAMM), *Parents of Murdered Children* (POMC) and other groups founded to express the needs of the families and friends of victims of homicide, is a refusal to be blanked by History, and a stand against the reduction of unique lives to the status of a statistic. This book makes plain the need to understand that response, not as blind, emotive reaction but as a demand for a role, recognition and redress.

David Downes

Preface

Introduction

Work on this book was prompted by a general and long-standing interest in policy-making for victims of crime, on the one hand, and, on the other, by a more specific awareness that things seemed to be stirring in the politics of victims of homicide and violence in the mid-1990s.[1] I had been invited to the launch of SAMM (Support After Murder and Manslaughter) in September 1994, and to a Conference on Justice for Victims that was to take place in February 1995, and I sensed that more must be happening out of immediate sight. A little questioning made it plain that a spate of new organizations, collectively identified by some as the 'angry victims', had been launched within only a few months of one another. There had been the births of Citizens Against Crime, the Gemma and Oliver Graham Memorial Foundation, the North of England Victims Association, the Manwaring Trust, Victims Fight Back, and Justice for Victims in 1993; and of The Zito Trust, HURT (Help Untwist Rape Trauma), the Victims of Crime Trust, MAMAA (Mothers Against Murder and Aggression[2]), SAMM, the United Survivors Forum, PETAL, (People Experiencing Trauma and Loss), Families of

[1] England and Wales were not the only countries in which those shifts and stirrings were taking place at that time. For example, in this (and in earlier episodes) there were marked similarities between the phasing and substance of the histories of the politics of victims in Canada and in the United Kingdom. Just as the 'secondary victims' or 'survivors of homicide' were becoming prominent in England and Wales, they were gaining visibility in Canada. 'In March [1997],' wrote a consultant who had been commissioned to report to Ontario's Ministry of the Attorney-General, 'I became aware from several sources that there was a need in Toronto for services to families and friends of homicide victims...' (E. White; 'Interim Report re Possible Services for Families and Friends of Homicide Victims', MS, 31 May 1997). Her report was to be part of a larger review of the Victim Witness Assistance Program's provision of services to homicide survivors. What I report in this book has its echoes elsewhere.

[2] MAMAA was founded as a response to the murder of James Bulger in Liverpool. It 'was set up to try and bring about changes that may save other children dying;' and it campaigns, *inter alia*, for 'Time to Fit the Crime', the better vetting of those who

Murdered Children, Victim of Crime, Respond ('for adults with learning disabilities who had been sexually abused'), and others in 1994. To be sure, many of those organizations were small and ephemeral, little more than a name and an aspiration, and they manifestly failed to thrive. Others were more robust. But the advent of so many new bodies in such a brief period did signify that something intriguing was afoot. Perhaps they represented the beginnings of a new social movement and a new identity.

Indeed, so new are the groups, and so ill-defined is the role of the bereaved in the context of crime and criminal justice, that their members have yet to agree fully on an accepted description of themselves, using the words 'victim', 'secondary victim', and 'survivor' more or less interchangeably. Deborah Spungen, an American who is herself a survivor and a member of the American organization Parents of Murdered Children, also used the words 'hidden victims', 'invisible victims', and 'co-victims' to describe the bereaved[3] but I have not encountered those words in use in England. I have elected principally to employ the word 'survivor' in this book because it incurs a smaller risk of ambiguity and confusion than 'victim' when it denotes the relatives of homicide victims. It does read oddly at first, implying, as it does, that one has escaped an attempt on one's own life rather than suffered through the loss of another's. It almost certainly borrows from the language of other support groups, and groups for the victims of the holocaust, rape, incest, and domestic violence, in particular, who prefer 'survivor', with its connotations of resilience, to 'victim', with its implications of passivity and defeat. 'Survivor' seems to be emerging as the approved term for the new role and identity, and it does seem to have international currency. When a new group was formed in New Orleans at the beginning of the 1990s, for instance, it also chose to call itself 'Survive'.[4]

After Homicide is an analysis of those new events and identities. It describes the collective responses of bereaved people to the aftermath of violent death. More particularly, it concentrates upon the birth, development and organization of a family of self-help and campaigning groups that emerged in and about the last decade and

work with children; and the widespread installation of 'Stranger Danger' signs (MAMAA, 'Putting Children First', Shirley, Croydon, 1997).

[3] *Homicide: The Hidden Victims* (Sage, Thousand Oaks, Calif., 1997).

[4] See H. Prejean, *Dead Man Walking* (Vintage, New York, 1994), ch 11.

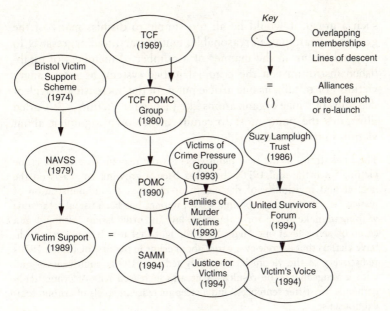

Fig. A The evolution of the principal groups covered in the book

whose rough configuration is displayed in Fig. A. It examines them as attempts to give institutional expression to interpretations of grief, and it understands those attempts, in their turn, as deeply implicated in a very special and potent phenomenology of mourning. Violent death inflicts a profound disjuncture between the past and present of those who grieve, and people often look back upon their former selves as if they were, in effect, strangers in some other life.[5]

Yeats once said that man created death and life,[6] and it is precisely that process of construction that *After Homicide* studies. It looks at victims' organizations striving to re-assert meaning and control in a world that has been turned upside down. There are distinctive symbolic procedures at work which must be understood before the politics and practices of those groups become transparent. Without

[5] So it was that, after the death of her son in a road crash, after the belittling of that death by a criminal justice system that labelled it simply a motoring offence, and by others who called it an 'accident', the founder of RoadPeace, Brigitte Chaudhry, said 'I knew that I couldn't go back to any normal life at all.'

[6] 'Death and life were not
Till man made up the whole . . .' (*The Tower*, 1926)

such a grasp, it would be all too simple to dismiss many of the groups as marginal, unreasonable, unnecessary, and aggressive; to despatch them, in the manner of a number of members of established institutions in the criminal justice system, as mere 'angry victims'; or to talk, as one article put it, of the 'increasingly strident demands of fringe organizations like Justice for Victims . . .'[7] Carlen illustrates the point most forcefully in her own argument about victims in the United Kingdom:[8]

The final strand in the new punitiveness is the rise and rise of the crime victim. Since the mid-1970s there has been a growing emphasis on the neglect and invisibility of the victim of crime in the administration of justice. The trumpeting of crime victim wrongs has been useful to anyone wishing to make an electoral appeal on law and order issues. Although at a common-sense level one might have thought that it is because crimes do have victims that anyone ever cared about crime in the first place, the 1970s rediscovery of the victim has certainly fed into 1990s punitiveness—and with a vengeance! The results? A greatly increased fear of crime, daily demands for stiffer sentences, and a steep increase in levels of criminological nonsense . . .[9]

The new organizations have evidently been given short shrift, yet they do deserve attention and understanding from criminologists and others. Criminology and sociology are replete with areas marked *terra incognita*, and the homicide survivors' organizations are amongst them.[10] I believe that they represent something very new and extraordinary on the political margins of criminal justice, and that there is interest and use in exploring their history.[11] They are certainly the first appreciable groups of victims who have

---

[7] S. Casey, 'Victims' Rights', *Oxford Today,* Hilary 1995, (Vol 7, No 2), 24.

[8] For comparable doubts about the politics of the new groups in America, see B. Shapiro, 'Victims & Vengeance', *The Nation*, 10 Feb 1997, esp 12.

[9] P. Carlen, *Jigsaw: a political criminology of youth homelessness* (Open University Press, Buckingham, 1996), 53.

[10] See, for example, the claims made about the neglect of homicide survivors in A. Amick-McMullan *et al*, 'Family Survivors of Homicide Victims: Theoretical Perspectives and an Exploratory Study', *Journal of Traumatic Stress* (1989, Vol 2, No 1); and about self-help groups for the bereaved in T. Walter, *The Revival of Death* (Routledge, London, 1994), 129. There are, however, a small number of manuals designed to help those who help grieving parents, particularly in America, where homicide is so abundant. See, for instance, B. Conrad, *When a Child Has Been Murdered: Ways You Can Help the Grieving Parents* (Baywood Publishing, Amityville, New York), forthcoming.

[11] I certainly would not pretend that studying them could be justified by their wider political significance: they are unlikely to exercise a major influence on criminal

organized themselves explicitly *as* and *for* victims in England and Wales.[12] Some, and SAMM especially, have accomplished much. Despite besetting organizational contradictions and dilemmas, they have suceeded in comforting, consoling, and reducing the alienation of those whose lives have been devastated.

Yet the symbolic processes implicated in their mourning are not easy to comprehend. They are exceptional responses to exceptional events and they set the bereaved apart. Survivors themselves claim that one can never appreciate their significance unless one has been bereft as they have. The chemical furnace of grief is simply too powerful. At its core are not just commonplace reactions to disagreeable experiences, but a mass of turbulent emotional and physical sensations which are at once individual and collective, cognitive and somatic, thought and felt, expressible and inexpressible, clear and confused.

The life-world of the survivors is quite singular. They have been forced to define chaotic events in uncommon and uncomfortable ways; and they have sought to restore order to disorder, driven by a great demiurge to found new organizations, and moved by a dialectic that yields distinct and unstable institutional forms. They have worked with a form of analogical reasoning that leads to the making of very specific comparisons and demands and a reiterating process of social fusion, fission, and separation. There are nagging contradictions within their groups, but organizational controls are weak and tensions persist.

Politically, survivors have actively challenged the very idea of what it is to be a 'victim', arguing, as they do, that, as 'secondary'

justice policy-making in the near future. Homicide is a relatively rare event in England and Wales, the organizations are not numerous, populous, or well-connected, and their accompanying politics have been muted in proportion. Only very fitfully, when there is talk about restoring capital punishment, does homicide itself become at all politically salient. But that talk is becoming less frequent, and it has tended to be instigated by people and groups (such as Members of Parliament and the Prison Officers Association) who are more central to Government.

[12] Victim Support, the main body in the field, had its origins in NACRO, the National Association for the Care and Resettlement of Offenders, a voluntary organization for offenders, and there is no expectation that its volunteers and staff will have been victims in any significant existential sense themselves. The founders of women's refuges and rape crisis centres neither cared for the word 'victim' nor identified their problems within a context set by the criminal justice system. I deal with those issues in my *Helping Victims of Crime: The Home Office and the Rise of Victim Support in England and Wales* (Clarendon Press, Oxford, 1990).

or 'indirect' victims,[13] they are also entitled to claim a symbolic role and stake in crime and criminal justice. They have demanded greater information, support, recognition, and respect, and it is a demand that might indeed eventually bring about a limited redrafting of the ends, boundaries, and recipients of criminal justice. They are unusually driven and unusually harrowed, and policy-makers, practitioners, and politicians have found it impracticable to deny them an audience. Yet, all too often (but not invariably), the experiential chasm between the bereaved and the professional, between the hot discourse of the campaigner and the cool reasonableness of the official, has subverted the possibility of effective communication, and those audiences have broken up in confusion, accomplishing little.

In short, activist survivors deploy styles of sense-making and organizing which are *sui generis*, and they repay deconstruction, not only because they are consequential and would otherwise be lost and obscure to criminology,[14] but also because it is right that the survivors themselves should, in effect, testify before a wider, public audience.[15]

This book attempts what probably defies final realisation, to report in words a cluster of experiences and behaviour that defy words. A psychiatrist closely attached to some of the groups, Colin Murray-Parkes, advised me that the one thing I should never say in my meetings with their members was 'I understand,' because it could never be true. *After Homicide* must at best be an outsider's reconstruction of another's very unfamiliar world, a rational analysis of that which is neither wholly rational nor analytic. I shall dilate on the problems that posed later in this preface.

---

[13] Many, indeed, would not qualify the term 'victim' at all, but refer to themselves simply as 'victims'.

[14] I have been mindful of McCall and Wittner's observation that it is easy enough for some truths to get lost in criminology and sociology: 'The experiential knowledge of subordinate people...is kept submerged by positivist methodologies which assume that social scientists know enough to ask the questions that yield meaningful explanations of society and social life.' M. McCall and J. Wittner, 'The Good News about Life History', in H. Becker and M. McCall (eds), *Symbolic Interaction and Cultural Studies* (University of Chicago Press, Chicago, 1990), 47.

[15] It certainly seemed to be the case that a number of the people I came to know confided in me precisely because they assumed there was a tacit contract that I would help them to make their needs more widely known, and I am quite content to honour that obligation.

Confronted with such a special life-world, it is proper to turn to the methods of 'thick description'.[16] Thick description is achieved by adopting a restricted focus, piling detail on detail, and using primary and secondary documents, observation and interview, to furnish a minute, densely-textured, and many-layered analysis of the relations between actions, situations, and interpretations. It is only thus that an unusual site can be reconstructed. 'Thick description,' Sofsky argued, 'succeeds to the extent that it expands the understanding of a strange and alien world.'[17]

To animate that description, I have leaned on a version of sociological phenomenology that requires a blend of distance and intimacy, analysis and appreciation, for its exercise. Powdermaker called it being both 'stranger and friend'.[18] There is a need for intellectual distance because effective inquiry requires a heightened anthropological sensitivity to the strange, arbitrary, and problematic characteristics of social life; and for intimacy, because description is intended to catch some part of the inner, lived experience of others, the part identified by Wolcott as 'sense-and-meaning-making',[19] which allows one to understand something of their behaviour.

Being at once near and far has its problems. The two states are contradictory and symbiotic, and each requires the discipline of the other. Appreciation certainly should not and cannot be the same as conversion. Indeed, the reflexive procedures of sociology (and of the sociology of homicide survivors' organizations in particular) continually reinforce a sensation of one's own otherness. But it would have been difficult to remain altogether dispassionate in the face of the manifest pain suffered by survivors. Des Pres wrote in the introduction to his own book on holocaust survivors that 'I could not take a stance of detachment, could not be "clinical" or "objective" in the way now thought proper... On the other hand, to allow feeling much play when speaking of atrocity is to border on hysteria...'[20] Just so with this book. It would probably not be helpful

[16] C. Geertz, *The Interpretation of Culture* (Basic Books, New York, 1973).

[17] W. Sofsky, *The Order of Terror* (Princeton University Press, Princeton, New Jersey, 1997), 14.

[18] H. Powdermaker, *Stranger and friend: The way of an anthropologist* (W.W. Norton, New York, 1966).

[19] H. Wolcott, 'Making a Study "More Ethnographic"', in J. Van Maanen (ed), *Representation in Ethnography* (Sage, Thousand Oaks, Calif., 1995), 85.

[20] T. Des Pres, *The Survivor: An Anatomy of Life in the Death Camps* (Oxford University Press, Oxford, 1976), p. vi.

to look too closely at the strictness of the parallels between the experiences of homicide survivors and holocaust survivors, but I did find Des Pres's comments pertinent. In its own fashion, *After Homicide* tries to follow *The Survivor* in being neither partisan and proselytising, on the one hand, nor wholly detached, on the other. It would certainly have appeared incongruous, tasteless, and unconstructive to avoid graphic language when attempting to reconstitute some of the most poignant experiences which men and women can endure.

History and methods

I have always been fortunate in my relations with Victim Support, the largest voluntary organization for victims in Britain, and Helen Reeves, its Director, allowed me to use it once more as a point of embarkation for research. Apart from having had a long tradition of hospitality to academic research on victims, a growing commitment to supporting the families of homicide victims, and a new connection with SAMM and the principle of self-help, Victim Support was itself curious about the new organizations that were cropping up all around it. Its environment was changing in ways as yet little understood. So it was that Tim Gustafson—the national co-ordinator of Victim Support's Crown Court Witness Service programme, and my mentor in an earlier piece of research—presented me to Jane Cooper, the new co-ordinator of Victim Support's affiliate, the new SAMM. She too proved to be most helpful and supportive, acting as one of my prime contacts, and she introduced me to others in SAMM, and to David Howden, its then Chairman, in particular. David Howden, in his turn, was open and sympathetic, and he and Jane Cooper proceeded to steer me towards a series of events to consider and people to meet. Hence, by the end of 1994, I had started on what was to become a three year period of fieldwork, interviewing,[21] reading, and observing the private deliberations and

---

[21] Eighty five taped interviews (and many more untaped conversations) were held with the principals of this history, including all the founders, co-ordinators, and chairmen of SAMM; the officers of Victim Support with chief responsibility for SAMM; Home Office officials who had had dealings with SAMM, Justice for Victims and the other new organizations; members of Justice for Victims; members of Victim's Voice and its major constituent groups—RoadPeace, the Suzy Lamplugh Trust, and Disaster Action; officers of the charities responsible for funding SAMM; members of

public gatherings of SAMM, Justice for Victims, Victim's Voice, and other, associated organizations.[22] There was one very practical consequence of my beginning in this way. Because my base had been firmly established in the largest of the new groups, it was inevitable that SAMM became the centrepiece of the history that was to come.

Not knowing much about SAMM and its environment at first, I was obliged to advance little by little and in common-sense fashion.[23] I sought to discover the names of the people and organizations who formed the past and the present of the new archipelago of victims' groups, using familiar contacts to pass me on to others as yet unfamiliar; I endeavoured to find out what records and information were held by whom; and I tried to ascertain how the emerging history and relations of the new organizations appeared from the standpoint of the occupants of each position. At such a very early stage, when the terrain lying before me lacked detail, almost any new piece of information had to be treated simultaneously as a datum that might be interesting in its own right, as a possible guide to fresh retrospective and prospective readings of the other data that adjoined it, and as a signpost to yet further questions to explore. I had, as it were, set out as a map-maker, hoping to chart the major configurations of the new politics, and necessarily mindful that those configurations were not fixed but changing. It was evident not only that they were evolving fast, but also that their appearance was itself shifting as I came to learn more and discovered new questions to put.

Meaning was thus emergent and unstable, continually being reformulated as new items appeared. There was a dialectic in

the Bar Council, the Crown Prosecution Service, Liberty and others who had had meetings with SAMM and Justice for Victims; those responsible for Victim Support's homicide training programme and victim support volunteers who had supported the families of homicide victims; Members of Parliament; journalists; television producers who had made programmes on the new groups; psychiatrists who had provided professional expertise to the groups; practitioners and leaders of groups in North America; and others. The only people who did not consent to meet me were Government ministers.

[22] I attended the general meetings of SAMM that took place during the period of my research; meetings of SAMM local groups; and meetings of POMC chapters in the United States. In addition, I marched with Justice for Victims from the Home Office to the Law Courts, attended a memorial service for the victims of homicide, and observed meetings of Victim's Voice.

[23] See 'A Natural History of Research on Policy-Making', in N. Fielding (ed), *Actions and Structures: Research Methods and Social Theory* (Sage, London, 1988).

which, over time, I came to learn something of the history of SAMM and the other new groups, as well as something of its narrators and narratives. And those narratives, in their turn, had to be set within interpretive frames which they had helped to create, becoming topics and resources, matters to explain and be explained.

By the middle of 1996, I was receiving extended commentaries on events in train from their various protagonists; I had access to papers; and I had become something of a confidant to a number of the principals. I felt that I had become well enough entrenched to grasp some significant themes in what Gubrium would have called the structured logic-in-use[24] of the new politics of homicide.

It was about that time, in the summer of 1996, that I quit the field in England to take up a term's fellowship in the United States, and I decided to use that break to mark the effective conclusion of the substantive history traced in this book. I had acquired enough materials for a book and my leaving England coincided with some minor benchmarks in the development of the organizations. For example, SAMM, the central group, had had a climactic Annual General Meeting in May; and Ron Rodgers, its new chairman (eventually to be its new paid co-ordinator) had entered office in June, inaugurating a new regime. Perhaps those were not outstanding turning-points, but they did serve as a convenient, if somewhat arbitrary, sign that the opening phase of the new politics had come to an end.[25] It is for that reason that *After Homicide* will concentrate on the birth and infancy of a social movement that took its first steps in the last days of a Conservative Government under John Major, the Prime Minister, and Michael Howard, the Home Secretary. That Government fell from power on 1 May 1997 to be succeeded by a Labour administration, but this history cannot cover the events that then began to unfold.

Whilst a Fellow at the Center for Advanced Study in the Behavioral Sciences at Stanford in northern California, I sought out organizations similar to those I had studied in England: POMC (Parents of Murdered Children), Citizens Against Homicide, Justice for Murder Victims, Crime Victims United, and Families and Friends of Murder Victims. Coupled with meetings in Ontario in November 1995 with officers of CAVEAT (Canadians Against

---

[24] J. Gubrium, *Analyzing Field Reality* (Sage, Newbury Park, Calif., 1988), 13.

[25] However, on my return I did catch up with the principal events that had elapsed in my absence.

Violence Everywhere Advocating its Termination) and with staff of the Victim–Witness Program and the director of Bereaved Families of Ontario in August 1997, those brief excursions into the history and politics of North American groups offered a useful comparative gloss on English developments. In particular, they seemed to point to structural alternatives to the embedded contradictions that were then tearing the English groups apart.

At the Center, I gave a paper on trauma and the social organization of survivors' groups, and Sander Gilman and other Fellows suggested I might find it profitable to explore the relatively extensive and searching writings on holocaust survivors. There are obvious and profound differences between homicide and the massive scale, intensity, and barbarism of what happened in the holocaust, but there is also a set of instructive affinities between the two populations of survivors (and with other groups, such as the survivors of those killed in war[26] or in prisoner of war camps). Members of both populations, for example, believe that their histories have alienated them from the everyday world; both believe that they can be understood only by those who have suffered as they have done; both claim to be stigmatised in the eyes of others; both evince a desire to testify on behalf of the dead who cannot speak for themselves; and both have problems in grappling with memories of an unspeakable past. At a late stage, therefore, I was introduced to a number of analogies on which I shall draw as the argument of this book develops. My interest in doing so will be instrumental, focusing on the phenomenology of grief rather than on the larger structural properties of holocaust survivors' organizations. In an already lengthy exploratory study, it is probably best to retain a steady gaze on the subject at hand instead of ranging too widely.

On my return from the United States at the very end of 1996, I did attempt to ascertain whether there had been any significant shifts in the trends which I had discerned in the broad history of survivors' groups. There had not. *Inter alia*, I attended the annual general meeting of SAMM in May 1997 and spoke to the organization's new chairman and co-ordinator, and it did appear that the course that had been set in the early 1990s was being followed still, that the dialectic which I described was still at work.

---

[26] See, for example, L. Shamgar-Handelman, *Israeli War Widows: Beyond the Glory of Heroism* (Bergin and Garvey, Massachusetts, 1986).

A first draft of this book was completed by the summer of that year and was circulated to the principals who had bulked large in it. It was distributed as a matter of courtesy and propriety: prior warning and discussion were necessary lest people who had suffered in the past were to suffer needlessly again from an unheralded and very public disclosure of their affairs. As important, perhaps, subjecting my analysis to the scrutiny of those whose actions it covers would not only correct error and add an invaluable extra interpretive layer to thick description but also go some way to meet a test of phenomenological adequacy. After all, this book is a description of other people's life-worlds. It is an interpretation of interpretations, a scheme of 'constructs of the constructs made by actors on the social scene',[27] and its success will pivot in part on whether those principals endorse what is said.

One issue does warrant mention. I had not expected at the outset that I would confront problems in gaining access to information. My links with Victim Support were sound, and SAMM itself had been established as a charity to 'promote and support research into the effects of murder and manslaughter on society'.[28] Yet the SAMM/Victim Support Steering Committee resolved at the beginning that I should not be allowed to observe its meetings[29] and that confidential information should be withheld from minutes before I received them.[30] After attending a number of meetings of Victim's Voice (a nascent federation of new groups), an attempt was made to exert editorial control over what I could write.[31] Again, for example, I had to supply written proofs of my good faith before being allowed to talk to the founder of a small group in California. There was a palpable guardedness which I had not encountered before in earlier research.

Those checks were unexpected because I had not been troubled by restrictions on research for a long while. Indeed, I had had

---

[27] A. Schutz, 'Common-Sense and Scientific Interpretations of Human Action', in *Collected Papers* (Martinus Nijhoff, The Hague, 1964), 6.

[28] Co-ordinator's workplan—SAMM Project, June 1995.

[29] Minutes of meeting of 25 Jan 1995.

[30] Minutes of meeting of 1 Mar 1995. I have been told that, in any event, those minutes were very circumspect (as almost the minutes of any committee are). They were circulated to all members of SAMM and they omitted many observations made at what were often animated meetings.

[31] *Inter alia*, I was invited to agree to a condition that 'Victim's Voice must have editorial control, **PRIOR TO PUBLICATION,** of any material which the observer

something of a charmed run in obtaining access to delicate materials (including, for instance, Cabinet papers in Canada and Home Office and Prison Department papers in England) without adverse consequences or difficulties. The new obstructions to knowledge prompted reflection, Read aright, they became data which could illuminate facets of the new politics of homicide.

First, like all groups,[32] SAMM, Victim's Voice, and the others had their private and public faces, and there was an understandable reluctance to allow the stranger in. It was a reluctance that was especially stressed in the case of the new organizations because, as I shall show, their meetings could be fraught and emotional, riven by an abiding anger which is one of the most distinctive traits of bereavement after violent death.[33] A member of SAMM reflected, 'almost everybody goes through a destructive [phase]—it's so bad that you can't make a sensible point of anything because you are so angered.'[34] I was told later that a great part of the hesitation about allowing me in flowed from a reluctance to bare so many raw emotions and divisions before an outsider.

Second, there is a gulf traced between insiders and outsiders, the bereaved and the unafflicted, those who are 'like us' and those who are 'not like us' (and, as one who was not myself bereaved, I could not but be an outsider). Some survivors placed no trust in the claims to expertise and authority of professionals claiming a specialist knowledge of death and bereavement. The expert was held to possess the inauthentic understanding and weak motivation of one who had never personally been bereaved by homicide (one member of Victim's Voice said to applause at a meeting, 'we're all here because we've been represented by so-called experts in the field and they've let us down!') And there was a companion reluctance to open a small, secure, and private world to interlopers (another

wishes to use from knowledge gained at a Victim's Voice Meeting' (letter of 19 Jan 1996, emphasis in the original). After some discussion, in which Mike McConville of the University of Warwick played a most supportive part, that condition was withdrawn.

[32] See S. Blackman, *Youth: Positions and Oppositions* (Avebury, Aldershot, 1995), 32.

[33] See C. Murray-Parkes, 'Psychiatric Problems Following Bereavement by Murder or Manslaughter', *British Journal of Psychiatry* (1993, Vol 162), 52, and G. Getzel and R. Masters, 'Serving Families who Survive Homicide Victims', *Social Casework* (Mar 1984, Vol 65, No 3), 141.

[34] Interview. Any further unascribed quotations should be assumed to stem from interviews or observation.

member said, 'I wish we could do it all on our own and say "sod off" to everyone else!'). At first, and, in one instance, at the end, I was yet another interloper to be repelled.

Third (and as I shall again show) members of the groups tended to have had unhappy experiences with journalists, authors, and others who wished to write and broadcast about them. At their meeting in January 1996, for example, members of Victim's Voice talked about how they had been bruised in the past and how necessary it was to defend children who were no longer able to defend themselves. They were the victims of assault by false representation. Eventually, to be sure, I did receive privy information about the new groups (although I never was to attend the meetings of the SAMM/Victim Support Steering Committee), but the obstructions were telling and, in one case, quite damaging.

One other problem complicated the presentation of the analysis offered in this book. It will become apparent that the politics of the new victims' groups were often marked by division and rancour, and that one of the prime targets of that rancour was Victim Support, the principal voluntary organization serving survivors. To be sure, praise was often heaped on Victim Support and its volunteers, and Victim Support was widely commended for its role in furthering the development of SAMM in the 1990s. But there was criticism as well, especially from the angrier victims. Whilst I could freely reproduce that criticism, Victim Support's Code of Practice requires that information about help offered to individuals is normally confidential. In circumstances where none of the criticism has been the subject of a formal complaint to the Scheme concerned, Victim Support was not willing to make details public, and an imbalance resulted.

In the event, it was apparent that the wariness I had encountered at the outset had not been wholly dispelled. Although most approved what was written, I had not satisfied everyone, and I came to be reminded quite forcibly of Denzin's aphorism that 'Those we study have their own understandings of how they want to be represented.'[35] One woman survivor, prominent in the politics of the new organizations, reflected after reading a draft, 'I can imagine it is very difficult to produce a text that will satisfy the need of the groups to be "honoured", given the emotional and political experiences they have faced. Good luck!'

[35] N. Denzin, *Interpretive Ethnography* (Sage, Thousand Oaks, Calif., 1997), p. xiii.

Writing alienates and objectifies experience and the very act of reading their own accounts of traumatic bereavement and organizational dilemmas proved distressing to a number. In one instance, I was told that reproducing a misleading and damaging account of a murder that had already been published in *Marie Claire*, a popular magazine, caused anguish to the victim's parents and, after discussion, the passage was deleted. I had made it plain that the account had been presented only to demonstrate just how the mass media can deform narratives, but I could well appreciate how unwelcome its reappearance was. In another instance, a group wrote discontentedly, 'It seems obvious...that we misunderstood [what] Mr Rock's motives were in attending our meetings. He was obviously more interested in looking at group dynamics and the efforts of a number of people sever[e]ly traumatised in the past, to form an organization....' It was as if the analysis of group dynamics was somehow improper.

I suppose I should never have imagined it could be otherwise but, to those who want passion and advocacy, sociology can appear to be a distancing discipline, the sociologist a stranger, and print a cool medium. I had in effect stumbled across the phenomenological paradox that a signifier can never be the same as the thing signified, that charged experiences are transformed with description.[36] Ironically, that paradox was to confirm one of the prime theses of this book, that survivors claim an existential understanding which is different in kind from other forms of knowledge, but it was none the less a source of difficulty. The problem for the survivors is, of course, that existential understanding must stay silent if it is to remain true to itself: an inauthentic voice may be better than none.

Victim's Voice—formerly the United Survivors' Forum, a confederation of some of the new groups, the body that had raised objections to what its members conceived to be my 'negative' analysis of their 'group dynamics'; of the slow progress they were making; of the logic on which they proceeded and the dilemmas which they faced—were so pressing that I should not publish an account of their doings, that I decided, on balance, not to include the chapter

---

[36] William James reflected '...what does *thinking about* the experiences of... people come to, compared to directly and personally feeling it as they feel it? The philosophers are dealing in shades while those who live and feel know truth.' (*Pragmatism* (Longmans, New York, 1949), 30).

centred on them at all. I could, of course, have published and been damned, but the ethics of the matter seemed to militate against such a choice. The organization had still not been formally launched by the time I quit the field, three years after its conception; it had yet to make an impact on the politics of victims; members of many substantial organizations in its environment knew nothing of it; and its absence from this book does not materially affect the flow of my argument. But it is a pity that its members were not prepared to withstand an outsider's scrutiny.

The scheme of this book

The new organizations could have justified the writing of any number of books, but, applying Occam's Razor, I decided to restrict myself to a single thread of argument. I have already argued that the examination of a novel and unusual area of social life by a lone investigator requires a steady gaze. This is not, for instance, a general work about the social structure of homicide or the conduct of homicide investigations and trials. Neither is it a broad study of grief after homicide or of all the new projects undertaken by Victim Support and other bodies. It is not a minute chronology of every single stage of a history. It is not a comparative analysis of organizing. Rather, it explores broad themes in the opening phases of the evolution of a very particular social movement established by and for the bereaved.[37]

The book's analytic focus is on organizations and organizing and it will be guided as much by the interest of what transpired as by the mere size of the institutions analysed. Its empirical focus will be on changing associations within a particular configuration of victims and between that configuration and the criminal justice system, and it will raise questions not only about the rights, identities, and relations of victims but also about the beginnings of the new social movement which they fostered, its objectives, methods, and contradictions. The new victims' organizations combine features that are quite distinctively their own with familiar structural predicaments.

---

[37] I was not drawn to consider whether organizers and joiners are 'dissimilar' to those who mourn without resorting to the new groups. That would have been a quite different (albeit interesting) study, and one that would have been difficult to pursue. The groups themselves have compiled only the most rudimentary data about their

Just as in the 'environmental movement', the Women's Liberation Movement, the Gay Movement, and even the movement championing women police officers,[38] homicide survivors have been riven by schisms about proper styles of representation and presentation, the appropriateness of formal and informal styles of organizing, the virtues of confrontation or negotiation, and the utility of working inside or outside the 'system'. Just as in those other movements, homicide survivors have often appeared to be as much occupied by warring with factions within their own world as with turning outwards to face a larger audience of public agencies and Government.[39]

The book is organized into three main parts: an examination of the criminology and victimology of homicide in England and Wales; a constitutive analysis of the phenomenology of grief, in which there is a prolonged exploration of bereavement after violent death; and a history of the emergence of the new organizations (and of the growth of SAMM, the principal organization, in particular).

Accordingly, I shall begin in Chapter 1 with a brief review of some of the conventional academic arguments about the principal features of the demography and incidence of homicide. I shall then change style and, in the chapters that follow, focus on reproducing the practical reasoning of a succession of pivotal people as they mobilised a joint response to the problems left behind in the wake of murder and manslaughter. I shall show that what criminologists and practitioners in England and Wales have tended to dismiss as a statistically small, contained, and morally equivocal problem is viewed by many of those most intimately affected as a cataclysmic event which throws their life into utter disorder. Homicide can lead to a fervid quest for control and understanding; to a new moral economy; a new experience of time, risk, and sociation; and a consuming urge to restore order through social and political action. As a third step, I shall move to demonstrate how that reasoning was to be fed into the manufacture and evolution of self-help and campaigning organizations in the 1980s and 1990s, and,

own membership; they define their members simply by identifying those who receive their newsletters; and it would have been beyond my resources to find and interview anything like a 'representative' sample of non-joiners.

[38] See J. Brown, 'European Policewomen; A Comparative Research Perspective', *International Journal of the Sociology of Law* (1997, Vol 25, No 1).

[39] I am grateful to Bridget Hutter for this point.

simultaneously, I shall attempt to record how the actions of other institutions, and the survivors' reactions to those actions, affected what was accomplished. The analytic centre will be occupied in Chapters 5, 6 and 9 by the evolution of the largest and most important of those new organizations, SAMM (Support After Murder and Manslaughter), which was born as POMC (Parents of Murdered Children), within another organization, TCF (The Compassionate Friends). About that centre were to be found a number of vigorous, embryonic groups that pressed in on SAMM, pointed to alternative futures and affected its course. The most active of those groups, Justice for Victims, will be discussed in Chapters 7 and 8. And, finally, there will be a continuous running analysis of more abstract issues as they surfaced in the tracing of that history, issues that touch, for example, on the part played by emotion, or on the so-called mind–body problem. But let me turn first to the criminology and victimology of homicide in England and Wales.

Acknowledgements

Empirical research incurs debts. This book could not have been written without the generosity of the principals whose lives and actions it describes, and I am deeply grateful to them for their patience, kindness and candour in talking to me, often more than once and at length, and for giving me access to papers and meetings. I would like especially to thank Helen Peggs, Helen Reeves and Ann Viney of Victim Support; Jane Cooper, the first co-ordinator of SAMM, and successive chairmen of SAMM, David Howden, Frank Green, Ron Rodgers and John Davis; Ann Robinson and June Patient, the co-founders of POMC; Joan Bacon, Pat Green, Derek Rogers, Sandra Sullivan and Ann Virgin of Justice for Victims; Ian Chisholm and Christine Stewart of the Home Office; Andrew Puddephatt of Liberty; Jillian Tallon of TCF; Jayne Zito of The Zito Trust, and all the other people whose names will appear in the text that follows.

Those voices would have been mute had it not been for the work of transcribing hours of interview tapes, and I am grateful to Amanda Francis, Elaine Meagher and Seeta Persaud for performing that unthankful job. I am grateful to David Driver for giving me access to the library of *The Times*; to Glennys Howarth for introducing me to the burgeoning writting on death and bereavement on which she is so expert; to Colin Scott, Michael Zander and Lucia Zedner for helpful advice about legal rights; to Helen Peggs for advice about the mass media's treatment of victim issues; to Coline Covington for guidance about Jung's conception of the shadow; to Andri Soteri for carrying out a statistical exercise whose mechanics I had forgotten; to Susan Lee for introducing me to survivors' groups in Ontario; and to Amanda Goodall who was highly enterprising in investigating the connections between the new survivors' organizations and the mass media that are discussed in Chapter 7. I am also most grateful for the funding supplied by the Social Research Division of the London School of Economics and by STICERD, the Suntory Toyota International Centre for Economics and Related Disciplines.

In 1996, I spent a term as a Fellow at the Center for Advanced Study in the Behavioral Sciences, Stanford, California and I would like to thank Bob Scott, Neil Smelser and the Center for inviting me to such a stimulating and hospitable place; to the other Fellows, and Carol Delaney, Sander Gilman and Gary Marx, in particular, for their ideas; and for the financial support provided by the National Science Foundation Grant SBR-9022192. Andrew Moss of the University of California, San Francisco, was as thought-provoking as ever, and it was a joy talking to him.

Finally, I would like to thank Joan Bacon, Stan Cohen, Jane Cooper, Coline Covington, David Downes, Glennys Howarth, Bridget Hutter, Michael Naish, June Patient, Helen Peggs, Gill Pennicard, Ann Robinson, Sandra Sullivan, Anne Viney, Margaret Watson and Jayne Zito for their comments on earlier drafts of this book.

Contents

Figures

Tables

Abbreviations

BMA	British Medical Association
C4	The Criminal Policy Division of the Home Office
CADD	Campaign against Drinking and Driving, founded in May 1985
CPS	Crown Prosecution Service
DSS	Department of Social Security
FOMC	Families of Murdered Children
TCF	The Compassionate Friends
MP	Member of Parliament
NABS	National Association of Bereavement Services
NACRO	National Association for the Care and Resettlement of Offenders
NAVSS	National Association of Victim Support Schemes, later changed to Victim Support
NCVO	National Council of Voluntary Organisations
Number 10	Number 10 Downing Street, the official residence of the Prime Minister
OBE	Order of the British Empire
PETAL	People Experiencing Trauma and Loss
POMC	Parents of Murdered Children
PTSD	Post-Traumatic Stress Disorder
SAMM	Support After Murder and Manslaughter

Dramatis Personae

Bacon, Joan	Member of Justice for Victims and SAMM
Black, Norman	Vice-Chair of SAMM; Chair of SAMM, June 1996 (on Rodgers becoming co-ordinator)
Chaudhry, Brigitte	Founder RoadPeace, 1991
Cooper, Jane	Co-ordinator, Camden Victim Support; Project Development Officer, Families of Murder Victims Project, 1987; Project Officer, Victim Support 1990–4; Development Officer, SAMM, 1994–6
Davis, John	Fourth chair of SAMM, November 1996–November 1997
Fuller, Ruth	Member of POMC committee; SAMM volunteer
Gerrard, Neil	Labour MP for Walthamstow
Green, Frank	Second Chair of SAMM, 1995
Green, Pat	Co-founder of SAMM Merseyside, 1995
Hines, David	Founder of NEVA, 1993
Howard, Michael	Conservative Home Secretary, 1993–7
Howden, David	Last Chair of POMC; first Chair, SAMM, 1994
Lamplugh, Diana and Paul	Co-founders, Suzy Lamplugh Trust, 1986, and Victim's Voice, 1994
McConville, Michael	Professor of Law, University of Warwick
Maclean, David	Conservative Home Office Minister, 1993–7.
Palm, Jill	Second co-ordinator of POMC
Patient, June	Essex County Secretary, TCF; co-founder POMC, 1984

Peggs, Helen	Press Officer, Victim Support
Pennicard, Gill	Third co-ordinator of POMC
Puddephatt, Andrew	Director, Liberty
Renhard, David	Chairman of TCF, 1986–9
Reeves, Helen	Director, Victim Support
Robinson, Ann	Essex County Secretary, TCF; co-founder POMC, 1984
Rodgers, Ron	Vice-Chair of SAMM, April 1995; Chair of SAMM, 1996; co-ordinator, June 1996
Rogers, Derek	Member of Justice for Victims, Victim's Voice and SAMM
Stephens, Simon	Assistant chaplain, Coventry and Warwickshire Hospital; founder TCF, 1969
Sullivan, Sandra	Member of Justice for Victims, Victim's Voice, and SAMM
Tallon, Jillian	Secretary, TCF
Viney, Anne	Assistant Director, Victim Support
Virgin, Ann	Member of Justice for Victims, Victim's Voice, and SAMM.
Watson, Margaret and James	Founders of Families of Murdered Children, 1991
Whent, Peter	Detective Superintendent and Victim Support Liaison Officer, Essex Police, 1988
Zito, Jayne	Founder of The Zito Trust, 1994

1

Homicide in England and Wales

It is best to begin by setting the scene, and I shall do so by rehearsing some of the occasionally contradictory arguments which authorities have advanced to make sense of criminal homicide in England and Wales.[1]

Definitions

Criminal homicide is not a single entity in law, and its subdivisions have been shaped by strong moral and instrumental imperatives. Murder, especially, has been set apart from any other form of homicide as an abhorrent act which violates the principle of the sanctity of life and which must be awarded its own distinctive penalty. In the moral language of jurisprudence and Government,[2] it tends to be represented as the most heinous of all crimes (indeed, the word 'heinous' seems to have been reserved especially to describe that one offence). Murder, wrote the Law Commission, should 'be regarded as a special *category* of act, requiring special treatment from the rest of the law of homicide'.[3] Justice, the United Kingdom branch of the International Commission of Jurists, captured its extraordinary standing when it declared that murder 'has a unique place in the law of England not only because it is the most heinous crime in the criminal calendar but also

---

[1] Events are volatile and may well change. I can deal only with the state of affairs as it existed in late 1996 and early 1997 when I was writing.

[2] The Prison Governors Association observed that, in 1991, 'the House of Lords, with the support of many related professional and pressure groups, held the view that the mandatory life sentence should be abolished. But the House of Commons agreed with the Government's belief that murder is a "uniquely heinous" crime which is best punished by a mandatory life sentence.' Evidence to the Committee on the Penalty for Homicide.

[3] Law Commission; primary evidence submitted to the House of Lords Select Committee on Murder, Manslaughter and Life Imprisonment, 1989, 38.

because it is the most serious crime for which the sentence is fixed by law.'[4]

Following Sir Edward Coke,[5] the Crown Prosecution Service defined murder as a common law offence committed 'where a person of sound mind[6] unlawfully[7] kills any reasonable creature[8] in being and under the Queen's peace with intent to kill or cause grievous bodily harm, the death following within a year and a day'.[9] 'The mental element is fundamental in the definition of crime', observed the Criminal Law Revision Committee in its report on *Offences Against the Person*,[10] and it is that mental element—the element of intent, premeditation, and wilfulness—that distinguishes murder; makes it exceptionally reprehensible; justifies the imposition of special punishment;[11] and prescribes legal defences at trial. Only two absolute defences can be offered to a charge of murder:[12] insanity, which is attached to the principle of a defect of reason under the M'Naghten rules;[13] and self-defence,[14] which is pinned on to the issue of unlawfulness.

---

[4] Justice; Evidence to House of Lords Select Committee on Murder, Manslaughter and Life Imprisonment, 1989, 1.

[5] 3 Co Inst 47.

[6] There is a presumption in law that a child under the age of 10 cannot form the necessary intention to commit a crime.

[7] All killing is unlawful unless it falls under the advance of justice (for example, a lawful execution), the prevention of crime or in effecting an arrest, or in time of war when committed by the armed services.

[8] A 'reasonable creature' is a person who has been born and is still alive. See Criminal Law Revision Committee; 'Offences Against the Person', Fourteenth Report, Cmnd 7844 (HMSO, London, 1980), 14.

[9] Submissions by the Crown Prosecution Service to the House of Lords Select Committee on Murder and Life Imprisonment, 1989, 3.

[10] Fourteenth Report, Cmnd 7844 (London, HMSO, 1980), 4.

[11] In Britain and America, legal doctrine holds, in the words of Judge Bazelon in the *Durham* case, that 'Our collective conscience does not allow punishment where it cannot impose blame' (quoted in N. Morris, *The Brothel Boy and Other Parables of Law* (Oxford University Press, New York, 1992), 126).

[12] Duress, for instance, is not a valid defence.

[13] The rules promulgated in 1843, and named after a man who attempted to assassinate Sir Robert Peel, laid down that 'to establish a defence on the ground of insanity, it must be clearly proved that, at the time of the committing of the act, the party accused was labouring under such a defect of reason, from disease of the mind, as not to know the nature and quality of the act he was doing, or, if he did know it, that he did not know he was doing what was wrong.'

[14] S 3 Criminal Law Act 1967. Self-defence requires that the defendant was personally threatened by someone proximate to him and that he or she used reasonable (rather than excessive) force to prevent a crime.

Murder and manslaughter have been continually redefined around that pivotal issue of culpability. Section 2 of the 1957 Homicide Act for instance, introduced the defence of 'diminished responsibility'[15] and convictions for manslaughter followed under that section 'in circumstances that would previously have resulted in convictions for murder'.[16] Murder may now be reduced to voluntary manslaughter where there was provocation,[17] diminished responsibility[18] or complicity in a suicide pact;[19] and to involuntary manslaughter where there was deemed to be an unlawful killing without the intent to kill, that is, where there was gross negligence, a dangerous act or recklessness.

The distribution of homicides between murder, Section 2 manslaughter, and other forms of manslaughter in England and Wales over time is set out in Fig. 1.1. It may be seen that just over 30 per cent of the homicides brought to trial were decided at court to be murder. To be sure, that decision is not simple—intent is not easy to prove—and it may well reflect judgements about the moral worth of the defendant and his victim, tactical judgements about the prospects of securing a conviction, and the success of defences mobilised around the vexed question of a sound mind, rather than some ontologically absolute distinction between classes of behaviour. Indeed, although

[15] The section reads: 'Where a person kills or is a party to the killing of another, he shall not be convicted of murder if he was suffering such abnormality of mind (whether arising from a condition of arrested or retarded development of mind or any inherent causes or induced by disease or injury) as substantially impaired his mental responsibility for his acts and omissions in doing or being a party to the killing.'

[16] *Background Paper No 263: Homicide Statistics*, Statistical Section, House of Commons Library Research Division, Dec 1990, 3.

[17] S 3 Homicide Act 1957. Originally restricted to cases where violence was actually offered to the killer by the person killed, where a husband discovered his wife in the act of adultery, and where a father discovered his son being sodomised (see G. Slapper, 'When provoked was a male word', *The Times*, 16 Jan 1996), provocation is now understood to be by things done or said, or both together, sufficient to make a 'reasonable man' lose his self-control. It is currently a contentious matter. Under the so-called 'battered women's defence', it is being claimed that provocation does not have to be immediate or substantial but the climax of a long history of abuse. See 'Justice for Emma Humphreys?', *Childright*, Mar 1993, No 4.

[18] Borrowing heavily from the M'Naghten rules, S 2(1) Homicide Act 1957 reads: 'Where a person kills or is a party to a killing of another, he shall not be convicted of murder if he was suffering from such abnormality of mind (whether arising from a condition of arrested or retarded development of mind or any inherent causes or induced by death or injury) as substantially impaired his mental responsibility for his acts and omissions in doing or being a party to the killing.'

[19] S 4 Homicide Act 1957.

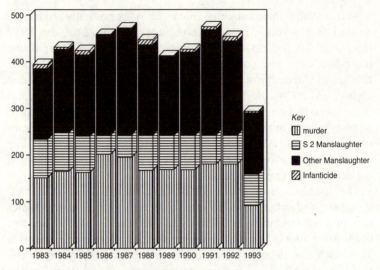

Fig. 1.1   Homicides in England and Wales: 1983–93

most suspects (87 per cent in 1993[20]) are initially indicted for murder, if found guilty, they are most likely to be convicted of manslaughter or infanticide (60 per cent were so convicted in that year).

A number of lawyers and penal reformers hold that the law of homicide presents difficulties of application and consistency. For example, a conviction for murder can ensue even when the killer intended only to injure his or her victim. The results of action cannot always be foreseen by the perpetrator,[21] and the onus has been effectively placed on the jury to ascertain how probable it was that there would have been certain harm or death. The M'Naghten rules require psychiatrists and expert witnesses to testify in bad faith and within the framework of an antiquated theory of mind to which almost no one would now subscribe.[22] And, under the 'year and a day rule', the determination of the cause or causes of death can become ever more elusive as the gap lengthens between injury and death. Whether a death is treated as murder may depend as much on the rapidity of the response of the emergency services, and the

[20] See *Criminal Statistics England and Wales 1993*, Cm 2680 (HMSO, London, 1994), 74.
[21] See T. Hadden, 'Offences of Violence: The Law and the Facts', *The Criminal Law Review* (1968), 533.
[22] See R. Smith, *Trial by Medicine* (Edinburgh University Press, Edinburgh, 1981).

efficacy of medical techniques and skills, as on the killer's culpability or intentionality (after all, life-support machines can sustain a semblance of life for very long periods[23]).

The penalty for homicide

The precise calibration, justification, and management of the punishments for killing have long concentrated the minds of people who work in and about the criminal justice system. Determining and applying the proper penalty has been the one problem of homicide that has received sustained attention in England and Wales. That penalty not only stands out as the most severe punishment that can be imposed, serving as a vivid demonstration of the role and power of government,[24] but it touches intimately on the creditability of trial procedures; the deterrent, retributive, and expressive functions of the law; and, above all, on what is typically addressed as the question of 'the sanctity of life'.[25] Compressed within debates about capital punishment and life imprisonment are a mass of much larger political and religious disputes about life, death, and the limits of civil authority.

Before 1957, all convicted murderers aged eighteen or over (apart from pregnant women) were sentenced to death (148 were executed between 1946 and 21 March 1957, when the Act came into force[26]). Between 1957 and 1965 some convicted murderers only were sentenced to death[27] (and 29 were executed during that period). Although the public scaffold was abolished in 1868, hangings were always highly dramatic events, attended by formal and informal rituals inside and outside the prison, and reported and elaborated descriptively in newspapers, broadsheets, and drama. Magical properties were associated with the hangman, his ropes, and the

[23] See B. Mitchell, *Murder and Penal Policy* (Macmillan, London, 1990), 21.
[24] See M. Foucault, *Discipline and Punish: The Birth of the Prison* (Allen Lane, Harmondsworth, 1977).
[25] See G. Williams, *The Sanctity of Life and the Criminal Law* (Faber and Faber, London, 1958).
[26] *Background Paper No 209: Homicide Statistics*, House of Commons Library Research Division, Mar 1988, 2.
[27] S 5 of the 1957 Act laid down *inter alia* that the death penalty should be retained for murder done in the course or furtherance of theft; by shooting or by causing an explosion; in the course or for the purpose of resisting, avoiding, or preventing a lawful arrest; of a police officer acting in the course of his or her duty; or of a prison officer by a prisoner.

corpses of the men and women he executed. It may be supposed that all that terrifying iconography helped not only to impress the awfulness of murder on popular symbolism in Britain[28] (and elsewhere[29]) but also made it difficult for reformers, politicians, and officials to think outside the confines of the almost obsessive British preoccupation with the abolition of capital punishment, the 'most important theme in post-war penal reform'.[30]

After 1965,[31] a mandatory sentence of life imprisonment[32] replaced the death penalty for murder,[33] and, by the end of June 1994, 3192 prisoners were serving life sentences in England and Wales, of whom 82 per cent had been convicted of murder, and 7 per cent of manslaughter and other offences of homicide.[34]

In the event, of course, a life sentence will not always require a prisoner to spend the rest of his lifetime in prison. The Criminal Justice Act of 1991 introduced a scheme by which the trial judge sets a tariff period for 'retribution and deterrence' when passing sentence. In a practice direction in February 1993, the Lord Chief Justice determined that such a period should always be fixed save only in 'the very exceptional case where the judge considers that the offence is so serious that detention for life is justified by the seriousness of the offence alone'. In the ordinary case, inmates serving discretionary life sentences come before the Parole Board at the end of the tariff period to resolve whether, when, and on what conditions they should be released on licence. Weighing with the

---

[28]   See J. Lofland *The Dramaturgy of State Executions* (Patterson Smith, Montclair, New Jersey, 1977).

[29]   See F. Zimring and G. Hawkins, *Capital Punishment and the American Agenda* (Cambridge University Press, Cambridge, 1986).

[30]   T. Morris, *Crime and Criminal Justice since 1945* (Blackwell, Oxford, 1989), 78.

[31]   The Murder (Abolition of Death Penalty) Act came into effect experimentally on 9 Nov 1965 and was made permanent from 16 Dec 1969.

[32]   It should be noted that that was the only such mandatory sentence at the time, a continuing mark of the seriousness with which murder was regarded, and an attempt to supply suitably consequential symbolic compensation for the abolition of the death penalty,

[33]   That change had been foreshadowed when, in 1861, it was determined that the death penalty could be commuted to life imprisonment and, in 1948, there was a power to release lifers on licence.

[34]   The population of life sentence prisoners has been steadily increasing, and there is a growing problem of ageing prisoners, particularly in Leyhill. The number of 'lifers' has risen from 140 in 1957, to 1137 in 1975, 1999 in 1985 and 2795 in 1990 (NACRO Briefing 'Life Sentence Prisoners', Feb 1991.)

Board will be the question of whether continued detention is necessary for the protection of the public, but the Home Secretary may choose to reverse the Parole Board's decision, even if no risk is thought to be offered to society, for reasons of 'public confidence' or 'public acceptability'.[35] The frequency with which the Home Office has overruled the Parole Board in homicide cases has increased: in 1981, for example, 4 out of the 147 recommendations (or 2.7 per cent) were overturned; in 1984, the number was 10 out of 112 (9 per cent); in 1987, 23 out of 147 (16 per cent); and in 1990, 35 out of 138 (25 per cent).[36]

The notorious or sadistic murderer, terrorist, killer of police and prison officers, and the murderer who used firearms in the course of robbery, can usually expect to serve a minimum of 20 years imprisonment, and some, like Myra Hindley and Rosemary West[37]—double deviants indeed, women who murdered children—may well never leave prison. In early 1997, 24 life prisoners had been informed by the Home Secretary that they would never be released,[38] although the capacity of one Home Secretary to bind the decisions of his successors is moot. The period will be less than 20 years for other offenders, but it has nevertheless been increasing steadily: murderers sentenced to a life sentence and released in 1981, for instance, had served an average period of 10 years; in 1986, 11 years; in 1990, 12 years; and, in 1994, 15 years.

Many life prisoners (and Victim Support[39] and survivors' groups[40]) maintain that the methods by which the date of release

[35] This section is based on 'The Mandatory Life Sentence', submissions by the Penal Affairs Consortium to the House of Commons Home Affairs Committee in Dec 1994 and Jan 1996, Penal Affairs Consortium, London, 1996.

[36] Answer to written parliamentary question, 22 May 1991.

[37] See London *Evening Standard*, 29 July 1997.

[38] See *The Times*, 5 Feb 1997.

[39] Victim Support remarked that 'As the majority of murders occur within social or familiar networks, the issues arising from release in relation to the surviving members/friends of the deceased can be very complex and can often engender strong feelings of anxiety, fear and anger. . . . It is therefore recommended that relevant procedures are built into the system to ensure that . . . [t]he victim's family are asked whether. . . they wish to be informed, at the appropriate time, of the offender's release date.' Memorandum by Victim Support to Select Committee on Murder and Life Imprisonment, HL Paper 20-xxiii (HMSO, London, 1988), 493.

[40] On 5 Dec 1994, a 'victim helpline' was instituted by the Assisted Prison Visits unit of the Prison Service. Victims and victims' families could use the helpline to communicate their anxieties about the proposed temporary release or home leave of a prisoner or about unwanted letters or telephone calls. Further, instructions to

is set are so secretive that they mystify and frustrate those most directly affected. Prisoners wrote to the Lane Committee on the Penalty for Homicide[41] to protest, *inter alia*, that: 'The very indeterminacy of the sentence can only increase the insecurity that the lifer feels, due to anxiety...', and that: 'The indeterminate sentence can produce, terrible affects upon people, never knowing when they may be getting out, they fear for their sanity, never seeing any light at the end of the tunnel, they have nothing to work for.' It was their complaint too that they had been transformed by the Home Secretary into 'political prisoners' and 'political pawns'.

The victim's family and friends may also deplore secretiveness. David Howden, then Chair of Parents of Murdered Children, told the House of Lords Select Committee on Murder and Life Imprisonment on 5 June 1989 that: 'If my daughter's killer was sentenced to life I would much rather know it was going to be 20 years, although I do not think that is enough, but I would rather know. My wife has said to me on many occasions, "I don't want to be around in this country when he gets out". I do not know what we are going to do....People ask you all the time, "Where is he, when is he coming out" and you do not know.'

The criminology of homicide

Homicide is portrayed differently in the empirically-driven language of the scholar and practitioner. Presenting their arguments as if they were a deliberate counterweight to the strong moral condemnation of murder as the most detestable of all crimes, and prompted by an undoubted antipathy to hanging and indeterminate sentences of imprisonment, British criminologists have tended to describe murder as statistically uncommon, socially contained, and morally equivocal, a mundane problem whose gravity has been somewhat overblown by popular and press misconceptions centred on the reporting of egregious cases.

Consider Terence Morris and Louis Blom-Cooper, two prominent scholars with an uncommon interest in homicide and the debate

Governors CI 43/1992 and IG 70/1994 required the position and views of known victims and the community to be fully assessed before the granting of home leave or temporary release (written answers 25 Nov 1994). However, the length of the tariff still remains secret.

[41]   I am grateful to Lord Lane for allowing me to see submissions to the committee.

about capital punishment. Morris and Blom-Cooper wrote in 1964: 'Although murder is regarded as a serious crime in this country, it can hardly be said to be a serious social problem.... In this country murder is overwhelmingly a domestic crime in which men kill their wives, mistresses and children, and women kill their children.'[42]

Theirs has been a vein of reasoning which has survived intact. Thirty years on, the report of the Prison Reform Trust's Committee on the Penalty for Homicide, a committee on which Terence Morris served and which Lord Lane, a former Lord Chief Justice chaired, embodied very much the same kind of sentiment:

We are acutely concerned about the attitude of the public in general. Not unnaturally the general public base their views on the information which they receive from the media. The media focus attention upon the high profile murders; they are, generally speaking, not concerned with the more humdrum, less newsworthy killings, many of which would not be regarded by the ordinary law person as true murder at all.[43]

In 1997, again, Morris and Blom-Cooper wrote to *The Times* to applaud the observations of a law lord who had declared that the law of homicide 'is permeated by anomaly, fiction, misnomer and obsolete reasoning'.[44] In sum, at least two criminologists would argue, homicide has been mystified and its importance has been exaggerated. Murder and manslaughter should not really be considered a major problem in England and Wales.

The consequence has been an intellectual neglectfulness. A rare event has been rarely analysed unless it has been set within the frame of an abolitionist politics of the death penalty. So few murders and manslaughters are committed, so analytically commonplace are they assumed to be, so few are the criminologists who might study them, and possibly so loath are those scholars to become entangled with a subject that appears to be riddled with an unappealing politics of retribution, that homicide has

[42] T. Morris and L. Blom-Cooper, *A Calendar of Murder: Criminal Homicide in England since 1957* (Michael Joseph, London, 1964), 277, 280.

[43] *Report*, Committee on the Penalty for Homicide (Prison Reform Trust, London, 1993), 6.

[44] Letter to *The Times* published on 10 Oct 1997. The quotation which they recited was from a judgment of Lord Mustie in the House of Lords.

not actually been copiously investigated in England and Wales.[45] One must make do with what little British criminology of homicide there is.

Incidence and distribution

The research that does exist is spattered with numbers, and my own synopsis must be spattered too. Criminologists would say, first, that murder is uncommon, and there certainly are relatively few homicides in England and Wales. In 1987, for instance, a rate of 0.7 homicides per 100,000 population was one of the very smallest recorded internationally: being, for example, roughly a third that of Canada and Australia (2.0); half that of Norway (1.4); and a twelfth that of the United States (8.6).[46] For male victims, the rate of 0.6 homicides per 100,000 in 1992 was again very low, a mere one fiftieth that of Mexico, one fortieth that of the Russian Federation, one twenty-fifth that of the United States, and half or less than half that of Sweden, Switzerland, the Netherlands, France, Denmark, Germany, and Spain.[47]

Homicide in England and Wales, in short, is something of an infrequent and idiosyncratic crime with its own patterns and etiology. Fig. 1.2 and 1.3[48] make it clear that, although the number of homicides may have risen, it has not grown as steeply or inexorably as the rough and ready indices of other offences or of the total figure of offences of violence recorded by the police[49] over the same period

[45] To be sure, almost all British criminological studies tend to open with such a complaint, but it is none the less valid. The first edition of the authoritative 1259 page *Oxford Handbook of Criminology* (Oxford University Press, Oxford, 1994), for example, contained no chapter or index entry on homicide, manslaughter, or murder, although the second edition, published with new content in 1997, did include an examination of homicide within a larger chapter on 'Violent Crime' by Michael Levi. In the United States, by contrast, where homicide is rife and a major threat to life, Wolfgang claimed some time ago that it was the crime most frequently researched of all. M. Wolfgang, preface to *Studies in Homicide* (Harper and Row, New York, 1967), p. vii.

[46] *Background Paper No 209*, House of Commons Library Research Division, London, Mar. 1988.

[47] Based on E. Leyton, *Men of Blood: Murder in Modern England* (Constable, London, 1995), 22.

[48] Based on *Criminal Statistics England and Wales 1993* (HMSO, London, 1993), Table 4.1, p. 76.

[49] Figures *recorded* by the police are not the same as those experienced or reported by victims—the three rates can vary quite independently of one another, making such

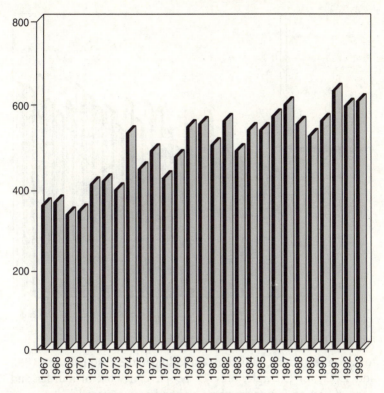

Fig. 1.2   Homicides in England and Wales: 1967–93

(Fig. 1.4).[50] Indeed, so very unusual is it, so far does it lie outside the boundaries of commonplace behaviour, that some have argued that its small numbers must necessarily include a much larger *proportion* of grossly abnormal forms of killing, including serial and mass murders.[51] (However, there have been only thirteen identified British multiple killers in the last 120 years.[52]) Those who kill tend not

comparisons most rudimentary. There appears to be general confidence that the reporting and recording rates for homicide are very high, indeed 100 per cent, although there are dissenting voices which claim that a number of homicides do go undetected each year, and particularly deaths from poisoning. See J. Havard, *The Detection of Secret Homicide* (Macmillan, London, 1960).

[50] Based on *Criminal Statistics England and Wales 1992*, (HMSO, London, 1993).
[51] See D. Canter *et al*, 'A case for special agents?', *Policing Today*, Apr. 1996, 25, and E. Leyton *Compulsive Killers* (Washington Mew Books, New York, 1986), 23.
[52] *The Times*, 2 Jan 1995.

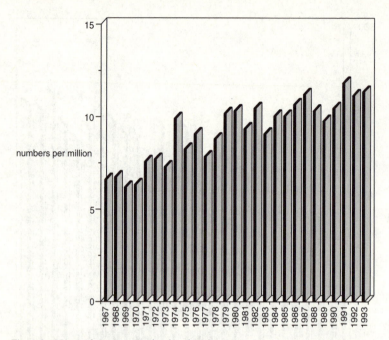

Fig. 1.3   Homicide rates in England and Wales: 1967–93

to have a record of convictions for killing in the past: between 1983 and 1993, for example, only 12 people convicted of murder and none of Section 2 manslaughter had had such a record.[53]

The methods of violence commonly employed by Englishmen (and women) are probably a material influence in producing such a low figure. Compare the methods prevalent in England and Wales with those in America. Estimates of gun ownership in those countries are inevitably inexact, but there may have been some two million guns in private possession in Britain in 1995, half of them unlicensed.[54] There were about 223 million guns 'available to the general public'[55] in America in the same year.

---

[53] *Criminal Statistics England and Wales 1993*, 89.

[54] The figure was reported to have been offered by the Government's Firearms Consultative Committee. One million of those guns were illegally owned, and they included some 190,000 pump-action shotguns, 60,000 unlicensed shotguns, 400,000 handguns and 120,000 rifles (The *Sunday Times*, 23 July 1995). Since that time, of course, the private ownership of handguns has become illegal in the United Kingdom.

[55] *Bureau of Justice Statistics Selected Findings: Guns Used in Crime* (US Department of Justice, Washington DC, 1995) and P. Cook and J. Ludwig, 'Guns in

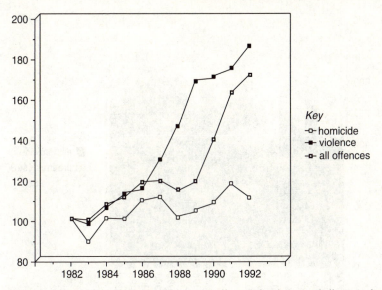

Fig. 1.4   Trends in recorded rates of homicide, offences of violence, and all criminal offences: 1982–92

There are conflicting assessments of the scale of the risk of being victimised by violent crime in those countries.[56] However, leaning on large national crime surveys, it may be said that the risk of being violently assaulted in England and Wales was very roughly 40 per cent that of America,[57] and it less frequently entailed firearms. According to the British Crime Survey, only 1 per cent of victims of violence in England and Wales had faced

America: National Survey on Private Ownership and Use of Firearms' (National Institute of Justice, Washington DC, May 1997).

[56] I have in mind a small international crime survey of some 2,300 respondents in each of a number of countries. That International Crime Victims Survey of 1996 suggested that the rates of violence in the United States and England and Wales were quite comparable (see P. Mayhew and J. van Dijk, *Criminal Victimisation in Eleven Industrialised Countries* (Ministry of Justice, The Hague, 1997), 2–3). If those rates are comparable in that fashion, it would yet further strengthen my argument.

[57] Based on a comparison between an estimated rate of just under 20 offences per 1,000 households/individuals in Table A2.2 of the 1992 British Crime Survey (HMSO, London, 1993, 112) and a rate of 51.1 given by the American National Crime Victimization Survey in Table 1 of *Criminal Victimization 1993* (Bureau of Justice Statistics Bulletin, Washington, DC, 1995). There is the problem that it is difficult to contrast different crime surveys. In Pat Mayhew's term, they do 'not mesh'. For example, the US figures include items such as threats of violence which are not covered by their English and Welsh counterpart.

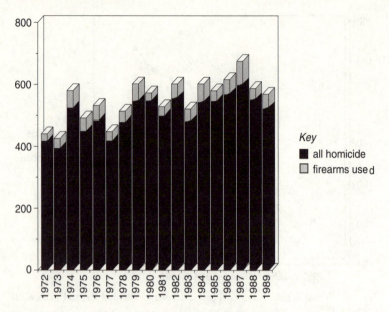

Fig. 1.5   The use of firearms in homicides in England and Wales: 1972–89

an offender with a firearm with all its hazards in 1995. The 1993
National Crime Survey for the United States estimated that 29 per
cent of victims of violent crime had been so confronted. The most
frequent means of killing in England and Wales was the use of a
sharp instrument (33 per cent) or a blunt instrument (12 per cent),
strangulation (18 per cent), hitting and kicking (15 per cent)[58]—but
not the gun. Fig. 1.5 shows that only 7 per cent of the 600 homicides
recorded by the police each year in England and Wales involved
firearms.[59] In the United States, by contrast, 70 per cent of the
24,526 homicides in 1993 were committed with firearms.[60] The
use of guns does make a difference to the outcome of violent
encounters.[61]

[58] Aggregated figures for 1978–82 taken from B. Mitchell, *Murder and Penal
Policy* (n 23 above), 64.

[59] *Background Paper No 263: Homicide Statistics*, House of Commons Library
Research Division, Dec. 1990, 15.

[60] *Bureau of Justice Statistics Selected Findings: Guns Used in Crime* (n 55 above).

[61] To be sure, other differences must be invoked as well. One of them appears to be
the greater heterogeneity of the American population. See H. Hansmann and
J. Quigley, 'Population Heterogeneity and the Sociogenesis of Homicide', *Social
Forces*, Sept. 1982, Vol. 61, No. 1.

The very endorsement of physical force also makes a difference, and there is a more general argument that points to the impact of cultural proscriptions on violence. Drawing on Norbert Elias's thesis of the civilising process,[62] for instance, the Canadian social anthropologist, Elliott Leyton, contended that a low rate of killing may be explained by the remarkably early pacification of the manners of the English, a 'programmed internalisation of shame and fear',[63] that led to a decline of the masculine tradition of honour, feud, and revenge that is so conducive to homicide.[64] It is only amongst the residuum, as yet undisciplined, that violence is still practised on a significant scale. The consequence, Leyton claimed, is that murder 'is [now] an extremely rare event, statistically insignificant compared to all other causes of death. A population of close to 50 million has fewer than 600 murders each year; fewer than 600 personal catastrophes out of 48 million relatively peaceful lives, a malfunction rate that designers of any mechanical or electronic systems might envy.'[65]

Ironically, perhaps, what Elias and Leyton would call a civilised society, Nils Christie would define as a society in which conceptions of honour had collapsed, in which there was little 'social capital' to be lost, the good opinions of others serve as a less effective disciplining force, and where there was less of a stake in conformity. The consequent loss of social cohesion can pose its own problems of crime and disorder.[66]

The criminological demography of homicide

If the first argument of the criminologist and practitioner is that homicide is infrequent in England and Wales, the second is that its victims and perpetrators seem to be concentrated in discrete homogeneous clusters within the larger population, and that their peculiar demographic structure repays interest. People tend to kill and be

---

[62] N. Elias, *The Civilizing Process* (Blackwell, Oxford, 2 Vols, 1978, 1982).

[63] E. Leyton, *Men of Blood: Murder in Modern England* (n 47 above), 9.

[64] For a description of the close links between honour and violence in Chicano gangs in Chicago, see R. Horowitz, *Honor and the American Dream* (Rutgers University Press, New Brunswick, NJ, 1983).

[65] ibid.

[66] N. Christie, *Hvor tett et samfunn? How tightly knit a society?* (Universitetsforlaget, Oslo, 1982).

killed by those with whom they have an intimate social connection. Jock Young wrote:

What is murder really like? When you bolt your doors at night to keep yourself safe from strangers you are locking yourself up with all those people most likely to do you harm...What does your likely murderer look like? If you pick up a mirror and look into it, you will see the image of your most likely attacker. He will be of the same class as you, of the same ethnic group, probably the same age, a member of your own social circle— dressing like you with the same accent and habits. Despite all the talk of inter-racial attacks, he will be the same colour as you...[67]

The demographic facts are stark. Homicide is not a random event but an act contingent on gender, age, class, and space. First consider gender. The population of murderers is disproportionately male: in 1991, for instance, 379 men, but only 22 women, were convicted of murder, and 275 men, but only 19 women, were convicted of manslaughter in the Crown Court of England Wales.[68]

The population of victims is also gendered, reflecting, in part, different patterns of sociability, where men spend more time with people outside their family and home, and women spend more time with family and female friends in domestic settings.[69] Victims, it follows, are more often male and they tend to be killed in places[70] and at times[71] where they are at risk of violence from other males, and from single males especially.[72] Lower class men, the men least touched by the civilising process, are killed in the defence of honour and personal reputation[73] in the boisterous and competitive world of the public house and street. In 1991, again, 36 per cent of 343 male

[67] J. Young, 'Murder Most English', *Time Out*, Jan. 14–21 1987, No 856, 5.
[68] *Criminal Statistics England and Wales: Supplementary tables 1991 Vol 2, Proceedings in the Crown Court* (Home Office, London, 1993), 7.
[69] See L. Maher, *Sexed Work* (Clarendon Press, Oxford, 1997), 33.
[70] For America, see M. Wolfgang, 'Homicide: Behavioral Aspects', *Encyclopedia of Crime and Justice*, Vol. 2 (The Free Press, New York, 1983), 853.
[71] See P. Mayhew *et al, The 1992 British Crime Survey* (HMSO, London, 1993), 81.
[72] B. Mitchell, *Murder and Penal Policy* (n 23 above), 47.
[73] Of America, Daly and Wilson write, if 5 Sept. 1980 'was a typical Friday, then about 100 Americans died at the hands of their fellow citizens. Most of the victims were men, and almost all were killed by men. Most of the victims, like most of the offenders, were nobodies, unpropertied and unmarried, little educated, often unemployed. Most of the homicides were not committed in the course of robbery, but instead arose out of arguments or insults or rivalries. Most of the victims were acquainted with their killers. Only a handful were related to them.' M. Daly and M. Wilson, *Homicide* (Aldine de Gruyter, New York, 1988) 124.

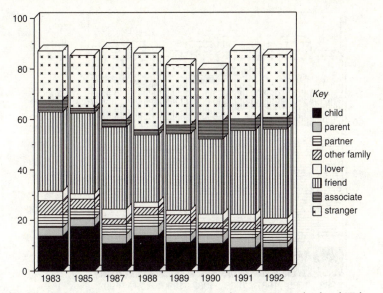

Fig. 1:6   Relationship of male victims to principal suspects in England and Wales: 1983–92.

victims were murdered by friends or other associates; and 30 per cent by strangers. Only 8 per cent were killed by their spouses or lovers, and 15 per cent by other members of their family.

Women are at risk from their male partners and relatives[74] in the private sphere of the home.[75] Of 288 female victims in 1991, 41 per cent were killed by their spouses or lovers; 20 per cent by members of their family; 17 per cent by friends or other associates; and only 14 per cent by strangers[76] (and Figs 1.6 and 1.7 show that those proportions are quite stable over time[77]).

[74] B. Mitchell, *Murder and Penal Policy* (n 23 above), 47.
[75] In America, Gelles observes, 'the home or apartment [is] the arena of family combat, and . . . certain spatial locations in the home [are] frequently battlegrounds.' R. Gelles, *The Violent Home* (Sage, Newbury Park, Calif, 1987), 96. For the Canadian data, see M. Wilson and M. Daly, 'Spousal Homicide', *Juristat Service Bulletin*, Vol 14, no 8, Mar. 1994. 47 per cent of the 544 Canadian homicides with a 'known location' occurred in the victim's residence in 1995 ('Homicide in Canada—1995', Statistics Canada, Ottawa, 1996, 15).
[76] *Digest 2: Information on the Criminal Justice System in England and Wales* (Home Office Research and Statistics Department, London, 1993), 15. The proportions for 1993 were very comparable: see 'Domestic Violence Factsheet' (Home Office Research and Statistics Department, London, 1995).
[77] Based on *Criminal Statistics England and Wales 1992* (HMSO, London, 1993), 79. It is interesting that, in the United States, where murder is much more common,

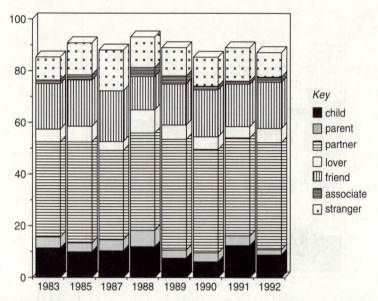

Fig. 1.7   Relationship of female victims to principal suspects in England and Wales: 1983–92

Homicide is contingent on age. The most vulnerable group of all is that of children under 1 year old[78] (41 per million were killed on average between 1983 and 1993 although it seems that the strengthening of child protection work has led to a decline in the suspicious deaths of babies and young children[79]). Those between 1 and 5 years were killed at the rate of 9.7 per million; between 5 and under 16 at a rate of 3.5; between 16 and under 30 at a rate of 13.5; between 30 and under 50 at a rate of 12.3; between 50 and under 70 at a rate of 8.8; and 70 and over at a rate of 8.1.

Figure 1.8 shows how the risks associated with gender and age intertwine. There are two particularly exposed groups, the first being that of the very young who are in the power of their parents.

murder within the family forms a smaller proportion of the whole than stranger murder (*Special Report: National Crime Victimization Survey, August 1995*, Bureau of Justice Statistics, Washington DC, 1995). It is as if the disciplining etiquette of public life is still stronger in the United Kingdom.

[78] Based on *Criminal Statistics England and Wales*, 83.
[79] See C. Pritchard, 'Re-Analysing Children's Homicide and Undetermined Death Rates as an Indication of Improved Child Protection', *British Journal of Social Work*, 1993, Vol. 23, 648.

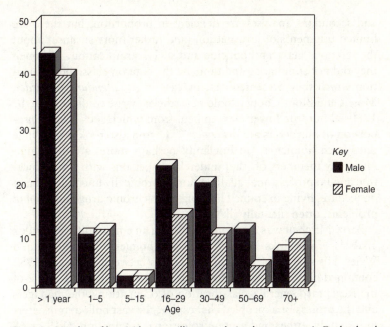

Fig. 1.8 Number of homicides per million population by age group in England and Wales: 1993

The killing of children, like all homicides, is a very rare event, but, when they *are* killed, it will characteristically have been by those with whom they have the closest and most frequent dealings, and by their parents above all. Of the 285 homicide victims under 18 killed from 1989–91, 170 (or 60 per cent) were killed by their parents, 43 (15 per cent) by friends or acquaintances and only 38 (13 per cent) by strangers.[80] The second exposed group is that of young men who are in one another's power. Leyton remarked that: 'Young men can be dangerous fools, too emotionally uncontrolled and physically powerful: two-thirds of all homicides in England are committed by men younger than thirty-five.'[81]

Homicide is almost certainly contingent on class. No statistics are collated and published formally by the State on the racial[82] and class composition of victims and offenders in England and Wales,

[80] *Information Briefing No 5 (1992 revision): Child Abuse Deaths* (National Society for the Prevention of Cruelty to Children, London, 1992).

[81] E. Leyton, *Men of Blood* (n 47 above), 209.

[82] See House of Commons written answer by David Maclean, 17 Dec. 1993.

and secondary analyses are deficient in proportion, but there are limited fragments of information (and rather more surmise) about the relations between homicide and social stratification. Although they did not summarise and tabulate the data on class and occupation which they presented case by case in *A Calendar of Murder*, Morris and Blom-Cooper could nevertheless write confidently in the 1960s about 'the lower class milieu, from which such a large proportion of murderers are drawn...'[83] Leyton also took it that 'nine out of ten homicides [in England], perhaps more, are now committed by members of [the] underclass—persons with little education and no professional qualifications, chronically unemployed and on welfare, living in council housing, with chronic drug and alcohol problems, often mentally ill.'[84]

Barry Mitchell was alone in conducting an empirically- grounded analysis of the links between class and homicide in England and Wales. His sample of 250 homicide cases between 1978 and 1982 contained only four defendants who came from classes 1 and 2 of the Registrar General's classification of occupations, the managers and the professional people. The residue, the vast bulk of murderers in his study, either had a non-professional occupation, (119 or 48 per cent), or were unemployed at the time of the offence (114 or 46 per cent).[85] And evidence from other countries is quite compatible with Mitchell's.[86]

The only major qualification one might introduce is that the figure of homicides would include larger numbers of skilled working class and middle class victims were it to extend to deaths from negligence and corporate manslaughter, such as the Herald of Free Enterprise disaster, although those homicides are notoriously difficult to bring to conviction.[87] The families of those victims were

---

[83] *A Calendar of Murder* (n 42 above), 281.

[84] *Men of Blood* (n 47 above), 10.

[85] *Murder and Penal Policy* (n 23 above), 46.

[86] For the United States, see, for example, R. Dennis, 'The Role of Homicide in Decreasing Life Expectancy', in H. Rose (ed), *Lethal Aspects of Urban Violence* (Lexington Books, Lexington, Mass, 1979), 17; R. Gelles, *The Violent Home* (n 75 above), 120; D. Prothrow-Stith, *Deadly Consequences* (HarperCollins, New York, 1991), 17; M. Wolfgang, 'A Sociological Analysis of Criminal Homicide', in M. Wolfgang (ed); *Studies in Homicide* (n 45 above), 15. For Australia, see K. Polk, *When Men Kill* (Cambridge University Press, Cambridge, 1994), 5.

[87] See, for example, S. Box, *Power, Crime and Mystification* (Tavistock, London, 1983); G. Slapper, *Law and Political Economy: Legal Responses to Deaths at Work*, PhD dissertation, London School of Economics, 1995; C. Wells, *Corporations and*

certainly visible in the politics of survivors, many of them being grouped together in Disaster Action, a federation of separate organizations acting on behalf of the survivors of disasters.

Because people are slain largely by insiders, by their own family, friends, and acquaintances in transparent circumstances, not only are suspects readily detected, but knowing witnesses and informants are very often at hand to name them. It has long been assumed that murder and manslaughter have high reporting and clear-up rates (although there are sceptics on the margins who point to the possibility of a number of homicides remaining secret and undetected). Ease of identification brings it about that some 95 per cent of homicides are recorded as cleared up by the police,[88] and most tend to be cleared up quickly: 70 per cent of murders are solved within two or three days, and a further 10 per cent within a fortnight. The remainder, involving outsiders, solitary victims, or murder by strangers, are much more difficult to solve.[89]

The victimology of homicide

If homicide tends to be found in very particular locations where victims and offenders are tightly pressed and enmeshed together, it is but a step for criminologists to claim that it must be analysed as a facet of social relations in which killers and killed both play roles, only another step to talk about the victim's causal contribution to his or her own death, and from thence to conclude that homicide is a causally and morally ambiguous event. Of victimology's broader discovery of the victim's complicity in crime, Antilla remarked that: 'New scapegoats are available for explaining criminality... Generally, one can say that the earlier stereotypes of "black and white" have been exchanged for "grey versus grey".... [T]he stereotype of the innocent and unsuspecting victim has proved to be false....'[90] Homicide itself is now routinely depicted by the victimologist and criminologist as a grey, victim-precipitated offence.

Criminal Responsibility (Clarendon Press, Oxford, 1993) and C. Wells, 'Cry in the Dark: Corporate Manslaughter and Cultural Meaning', in L. Loveland (ed), *Criminality* (Sweet and Maxwell, London, 1995).

[88] See, for example, *Criminal Statistics England and Wales 1992*, 47.

[89] *Evening Standard*, 3 Jan 1995.

[90] I. Antilla, 'Victimology—A New Territory in Criminology', *Scandinavian Studies in Criminology*, Vol 5 (Martin Robertson, London, 1974), 8.

The idea of victim-precipitated homicide had its effective origins in 1948 in *The Criminal and His Victim*, the work of an early victimologist, Hans von Hentig. In a chapter entitled the 'Victim's Contribution to the Genesis of Crime', and using police data from New York City between 1936 and 1940, von Hentig argued for a 'duet theory of crime'. Homicide is particularly amenable to such a form of analysis, he claimed: 'About 85 per cent of the murder and manslaughter cases [entail]... [a] motive of killing [that] indicates the operation of a partnership. The murderous act is a more or less adequate response to stimuli and irritating agents...'[91] It would follow, said von Hentig, that the victim may often be described as the necessary cause of what befalls him or her: 'there are cases in which they [victim and offender] are reversed and in the long chain of causative forces the victim assumes the role of a determinant.'[92] Overall, he concluded; 'Among common situations... We do not find the evildoer–evil-sufferer group.... There is a definite mutuality of some sort.'[93]

The idea of victim-precipitated homicide fanned out. It entered the work of Porterfield and Talbert in 1954: 'the intensity of interaction between the murderer and his victim may vary from complete non-participation on the part of the victim to almost perfect cooperation in the process of getting killed.... It is amazing to note the large number of would-be murderers who become the victim'.[94] And it passed into Marvin Wolfgang's immensely influential[95] *Patterns in Criminal Homicide*[96] in 1958 (Wolfgang himself reflected that 'von Hentig... provided the most useful theoretical basis for analysis of the victim–offender relationship.'[97]). *Patterns in Criminal Homicide* claimed that a quarter of 588 consecutive cases of criminal homicide in Philadelphia between 1 January 1948 and 31 December 1952 had been precipitated or caused by their victim.

[91]   H. Von Hentig, *The criminal and his victim; studies in the sociobiology of crime* (Archon Books, Hamden, Conn, 1948), 397.

[92]   ibid, 383.

[93]   ibid, 384.

[94]   A. Porterfield and R. Talbert, *Mid-Century Crime in Our Culture* (Leo Potishman Foundation, Fort Worth, 1954), 47–8.

[95]   It was influential, in part, because it was the very first major sociological study of homicide and so set the mould for the rest.

[96]   M. Wolfgang, *Patterns in Criminal Homicide* (University of Pennsylvania Press, Philadelphia, 1958).

[97]   M. Wolfgang, 'Victim-Precipitated Criminal Homicide', *Journal of Criminal Law, Criminology and Police Science*, June 1957, Vol 48, No 1, 1.

Victims might, for example, have struck the opening blow, becoming the 'first aggressor', or behaved provocatively, menacingly or abusively. Who finally became the murderer and who the victim could then hinge merely on which person had been more successful in reaching for a weapon[98] or pulling a trigger.[99]

The idea of victim-precipitation has become an orthodoxy within the victimology of homicide at large. In 1977, for example, Luckenbill drew on Wolfgang to describe criminal homicide as the culmination of an intense and antagonistic interchange between victim and offender, a 'situated transaction',[100] to which both contributed. In 1978, Duncan and Duncan turned to Wolfgang when they maintained that some people virtually sought to commit suicide by provoking others to kill them.[101] In 1987, Silverman and Mukherjee described murder as a social event centred on actors in a 'social relationship that plays a dynamic role in the way that the homicide unfolds'.[102] And again, in 1994, borrowing directly from von Hentig and Wolfgang, Polk defined homicide in Australia as a 'social act' which should be examined within 'the duet frame of crime'.[103]

In England, the idea of victim-precipitation was pursued by Morris and Blom-Cooper in their *Calendar of Murder* in 1964 (although their work was not directly prompted by *Patterns in Criminal Homicide* and did not cite Wolfgang). A number of the victims described in their book, they wrote, 'might well have been capable of killing on their own account, while others so goaded their killers either by provocation in words or deeds, or by incessant nagging that they directly precipitated their own deaths'.[104] But they were to have a later connection with Wolfgang. In 1967, they published a

---

[98] See Wolfgang (n 97 above), 84.

[99] Lawyers certainly hold to that view. In studying the work of a Crown Court centre I was told by a barrister, 'There is a famous opening ... in an affray case and it was the shortest opening that one can think of in an affray: "Members of the jury, an affray is a fight in a public place between a large number of people ... In the dock stand the winners and I'm going to call the losers one by one to tell how they lost".' in *The Social World of an English Crown Court* (Clarendon Press, Oxford, 1993), 72.

[100] D. Luckenbill, 'Criminal Homicide as a Situated Transaction', *Social Problems*, Dec 1977, Vol 25, No 2.

[101] J. Duncan and G. Duncan, 'Murder in the Family', in I. Kutash *et al* (eds), *Violence: Perspectives on Murder and Aggression* (Jossey-Bass, San Francisco, 1978), 179.

[102] R. Silverman and S. Mukherjee, 'Intimate homicide: An analysis of violent social relationships', *Behavioral Sciences and the Law*, 1987, Vol 5, 37.

[103] K. Polk, *When Men Kill* (n 86 above), 3.

[104] *A Calendar of Murder* (n 42 above), 322.

paper on 'The Victim's Contribution' in a collection which he edited, and they there recited the principal contention of the victim-precipitation thesis: 'homicide "out of the blue", in which the victim is struck down without reacting in any way, is exceptionally rare.'[105] One of the very few other English criminologists to write about murder, Neville Avison, also turned to Wolfgang six years later:

By definition, acts of aggression culminating in homicide involve an interaction between participants: homicide is a social relationship. A study of the nature of such interaction, its degree and extent, suggests that the role of the victim is not restricted to precipitation of the crime as set out in the now classic description given by Wolfgang, in which he applies it to cases involving the victim inducing his death *through his own* menacing actions. The victim can contribute in many different ways to the interaction preceding the aggressive behavior, and it may be more meaningful to consider such involvement on a continuum ranging from participation...through varying degrees of provocation, and culminating in active precipitation by the victim.[106]

It is difficult to quarrel with the proposition that crimes are social processes mediated by exchanges between their principals. Victims, offenders, bystanders, and others do shape crime through a running sequence of actions, reactions, and interpretations. The victims and offenders of violence do tend, moreover, to stem from a common social world[107] in which injuries may be freely meted out and received (the Canadian criminologist, Ezzat Fattah, argued that 'offender and victim populations, particularly in violent crime, are homogeneous populations that have similar characteristics. The affinity between the victim and offender populations should not come as a surprise',[108] and David Kennedy argued of youth homicide in Boston 'the profiles of both victims and offenders were remarkably similar...'[109]). In many concrete instances, then, it

---

[105]   T. Morris and L. Blom-Cooper, 'The Victim's Contribution', in M. Wolfgang (ed), *Studies in Homicide* (n 45 above), 70.

[106]   N. Avison, 'Victims of Homicide', in I. Drapkin and E. Viano (eds), *Victimology: A New Focus* (Lexington Books, Lexington, Mass, 1973) 58.

[107]   Wolfgang and Ferracuti would have said that that world bore a 'subculture of violence' which engendered and framed disputes. M. Wolfgang and F. Ferracuti, *The Subculture of Violence* (Tavistock, London, 1967).

[108]   E. Fattah, *Criminology Past, Present, and Future* (Macmillan, London, forthcoming), 247 (MS).

[109]   D. Kennedy, 'Juvenile Gun Violence and Gun Markets in Boston', Research Preview, National Institute of Justice, Washington, DC, Mar 1997, 2.

may indeed be difficult to resolve the precise moral identities and roles of the participants in an exchange that resulted in death. The fog of battle can be very dense on occasion and, even when it does lift, scholars may find it hard to see monsters. The extraordinary can become ordinary when it is stared in the face.[110] The distinguished Norwegian criminologist, Nils Christie, observed:

I have looked for monsters in and out of prisons, among drug drug users, among people sentenced for violence as well as for disgusting sexual behaviour, but it seems possible to understand nearly everything without concepts that push the offenders outside the family of man. Once I was supposed to meet a guaranteed monster...He had killed several people and put the blame on his girl-friend....I went to see him and met a man like most men.[111]

Yet what cannot be heard in the analysis of victim-precipitated homicide are the voices of the victim, the victim of attempted murder, or the 'secondary victim'.[112] Their definitions of the situation have been silenced through death or neglect,[113] and, in their place, we are supplied with analyses of secondary accounts in police files and newspapers and of primary accounts tendered at trial. I have argued elsewhere[114] that those accounts are characteristically motivated. They are constructed and presented for a purpose, being often intended precisely to diminish the defendant's culpability whilst inflating that of the victim, and so blur moral differences. In Lamb's words: 'At the root of all victim-blaming are the perpetrator's own attempts to present the victim as the cause of his violence or abuse....Perpetrators will...claim that their victims are almost directly responsible for their fates, that the little girl wanted to be fondled, that the raped woman was asking for it,

---

[110] See N. Christie, *Fangevoktere i konsentrasjonsleire/Guards in concentration camps* (Pax, Oslo, 1972); and H. Arendt, *Eichmann in Jerusalem* (Faber and Faber, London, 1963).

[111] N. Christie, 'Roots of a Perspective', in S. Holdaway and P. Rock (eds), *The Social Theory of Modern Criminology* (UCL Press, London, forthcoming).

[112] See *Final Report*, Task Force on the Victims of Crime and Violence, American Psychological Association, 1984, 56: 'In spite of the ever increasing number of homicides in this country and the recognition that the death of a close family member is highly stressful...the impact that homicidal violence has on survivors of the victim has been neglected as an area of research.'

[113] After all, under the 'year and a day rule', the victim of murder may still be able to give an account for some.

[114] 'Murderers, Victims and "Survivors": The Social Construction of Deviance', *British Journal of Criminology*, forthcoming.

and that the abused wife provoked her beating with her comments or behavior.'[115]

In law, it should be remembered, there are defendants, witnesses and, until conviction, alleged victims, but there are no secondary victims, indirect victims, or survivors: those are roles which are still being contested on the outer fringes of the criminal justice system. Secondary victims of homicide are not a legal entity, they have no rights of audience, and disputes about their legitimacy are part of the theme of this book.

Where there is murder and manslaughter, where the victim cannot answer back, and the victim's family and friends have not been invited to answer back, what can remain but the impression of causal, phenomenological, and moral greyness which Antilla described?[116] Consider the remarks of an experienced practitioner, not an Englishman, but an Assistant District Attorney in San Francisco, who had prosecuted some thirteen homicides:

The strongest three defences [are] the crime didn't occur, which is hard to argue when you have a cracked skull or a bullet in a brain. The second is the crime happened, someone murdered him, but it wasn't me, and that will be used unless there's sufficient eyewitnesses to show that it was the defendant. Well, the defence can't argue the other two, so the only defence left is 'I have an excuse' and the excuse is 'I thought he was going to kill me'. And what happens in reality is sure . . . you take the cases that I've had, I've had a lot of cases involving public housing projects, and usually there is a dispute, there are words, people are angry, and many of the young and older males in housing projects . . . have violence in their record. I don't know how much. I haven't done a study. I wouldn't even say 50 per cent, but I will say that it is rare that I find in those poor areas of the city where the victim and the victim don't have records . . . . And you should take this into account . . . I do not believe that every single one of those defence witnesses who got up there

---

[115] S. Lamb, *The Trouble with Blaming: Victims, Perpetrators, and Responsibility* (Harvard University Press, Cambridge, Mass, 1996), 78, 79.

[116] It is interesting that when Wolfgang's student, Menachem Amir, transposed the model of victim-precipitation wholesale to the investigation of rape, he was to encounter a group of victims who were not only alive but whose representatives were politically organized and vocal precisely around the issue of violence against women. Amir's and others' analysis was rejected by many feminist criminologists and they themselves were accused roundly of 'victim-blaming'. See M. Amir, *Patterns of Forcible Rape* (University of Chicago Press, Chicago, 1971) and, for his critics, L. Clark and D. Lewis, *Rape: The Price of Coercive Sexuality* (The Women's Press, Toronto, 1977); A. Morris, *Women, Crime and Criminal Justice* (Oxford, 1987); S. Walklate, *Victimology* (London, 1989). The moral would seem to be that some versions of victimology succeed best where the victims cannot reply.

and talked about violence were telling the truth. And so what happens in our adversarial Court system is, I believe, that you have exaggeration of the violent or bad tendencies of the victim by the defence in order to have a defence. That's the system.

It has become all too easy in certain quarters to dismiss homicide as a matter of relatively small importance, the outcome of quarrels between members of an underclass who were long inured to pain, effectively segregated from the wider world and as much sinning as sinned against.[117] How else does one understand Avison's observation that 'it is extremely difficult to find instances of wholly "innocent" and uninvolved victims'?[118]

Perhaps what is partly at issue is the sheer difficulty of conceding that innocent victims may indeed be struck down because such a concession would jolt any sustainable faith in a properly-ordered, just, or decent world. It is simpler by far to maintain that, in some fashion, the victims may actually have deserved what happened to them,[119] that moral balance has not been threatened.

Matters seem otherwise to members of the survivors' organizations. In this book, I shall attempt to reconstruct and explore some part of their response not only to homicide but also to those commanding representations of homicide, giving a different but complementary reading of the phenomena of violent death,[120] and explaining how it was that a special politics came to emerge in the 1980s and 1990s.

---

[117] I have in mind particularly the comments of some jaded prosecutors and defence counsel who represented murderers and victims as the interchangeable members of an unfeeling and morally insensible stage army who passed continually through the criminal courts.

[118] N. Avison, 'Victims of Homicide' (n 106 above), 65.

[119] See M. Lerner, *The Belief in a Just World* (Plenum Press, New York, 1980).

[120] After all, the 'same' phenomena are susceptible of many different structured interpretations. The point in sociology is not necessarily to adjudicate between them, but to understand how they arose, how they are aligned, and how they affect lines of action. It was in this vein that Robert Park argued that 'sociology is not interested in facts, not even in social facts as they are commonly understood . . . Sociology wants to know how people re-act to so-called facts, to what is happening to them.' Quoted in W. Raushenbush, *Robert Park: Biography of a Sociologist* (University of North Carolina Press, Durham, NC, 1979), 112.

2

Bereavement after Homicide

The initial shock and horror is enough to kill.[1]

Introduction

I shall now turn to the impact which violent death has upon those who are left behind. The *Shorter Oxford English Dictionary* defines bereavement as a state of deprivation or destitution, of being robbed, stripped, dispossessed, plundered, widowed, or orphaned, and those are words that convey an imagery of the unwelcome loss which leaves one sad, despoiled, and reduced. Of course, not everyone who is bereaved will mourn, and not all those who mourn will mourn in quite the same way. But, if only for a while, the death of another can leave a social world more empty, a life more purposeless, and a self diminished and more vulnerable.

If homicide has its demography, so does grief. The most sorely afflicted tend to be the poor rather than the rich (because they more frequently lack social and material resources); men rather than women (because they are generally less expressive); the young rather than the old (because they are less accustomed to loss); those who have lost children; those whose loss is sudden and brutal; and those who had entertained an unresolved and ambivalent relation with the person now dead.[2] In short, bereavement appears to be peculiarly acute for those who mourn the unexpected, violent deaths of children and adolescents. The experiences of homicide survivors, and the parents of murdered children in particular, are *sui generis*, and it is the phenomenology of those experiences that I shall now consider.

---

[1] David Howden, speaking in a video recording; *No Chance to Say Goodbye*, Jo Marcus, no place of production, 1996.

[2] Taken from W. Stroebe and M. Stroebe, *Bereavement and Health* (Cambridge University Press, Cambridge, 1987), ch 8.

Bereavement and the Homicide Survivor

What follows in this and the next two chapters is an ideal-type that has been simplified and accentuated expressly for purposes of analysis. It draws largely on my own observation and interviews, and centres chiefly on responses to murder in the family that were displayed by survivors who founded or maintained special organizations for themselves and others like themselves. The particulars of those murders will be described as this book unfolds, but it should be made clear at the outset that two major forms of homicide were not apparent in the survivors' narratives. One was the death from criminal violence of a man (or woman) who had himself been heavily implicated in criminal violence: there were no victims of 'gang' conflicts, for example. The other was the killing of one member of a nuclear family by another, where the survivor mourned the dead but was still sentimentally attached to the killer. The existential world of the survivors' groups could not readily accommodate such moral contradictions, and I shall return to that theme in Chapter 4.

What cannot be said with any authority is what else it was that distinguished the members of the new groups from those who did not join. As I shall show, the groups did not keep useful data about themselves, and *After Homicide* would have been transformed into quite another study had I attempted to track down and compare joiners and non-joiners. It will certainly become evident that joining was often more a matter of contingency than of deliberate choice, of the bereaved having chance meetings at opportune times with others in lay referral networks. And one co-ordinator of SAMM, Ron Rodgers, did conjecture that becoming a member tended to be a last resort for those who were desperate or for whom other voluntary agencies had proved inadequate.

Figure 1.8 made it clear that the victims of homicide are disproportionately young, and it may be presumed that many will have had living parents. The death of a child is, as I shall argue, particularly harrowing, and it is not perhaps surprising that the two pioneering survivors' organizations in England and America were both independently called Parents of Murdered Children. It is for that reason that I have chosen to construct the argument of this chapter principally around the reactions of parents bereaved by the deaths of their children. If I seem repeatedly to refer only to a few individuals, it is because such homicides are not numerous in England and Wales, and the world of activist survivors is smaller still.

The ideal-type is based largely on the first- and second-hand accounts of the survivors themselves, and it distils themes that were to be heard and observed again and again. Although it is a reconstruction, the sheer strength and pervasiveness of those themes make it apparent that there is a firm interpretive logic shared by activist survivors. In major part, it stems from a traumatic confrontation with violent death, but it also flows from the interpretations that come to be shaped and ratified by survivors in their subsequent talk with one another.[3]

Homicide centres on death, and death is irrevocable, final, and irreversible. Unlike other crimes, there is no undoing of death, no possibility of making good the damage that has been inflicted. Ronan Byrne of the San Francisco Court Victim/Witness Program remarked:

Sexual assault victims have the trauma of the sexual assault and...it's pretty much a crime of intimacy, you know. But it is a crime which, when it's over, you're alive. In a homicide, it's sudden, it's complete. There is no fixing it. There is no therapy that can fix it. The person is dead and that's the way it is. What you're left behind with is the mother or father, brothers and sisters, husbands, wives—the whole shebang—who have nothing.

Bereavement after homicide, and particularly after the homicide of children, is especially disturbing.[4] It is sterile to compare disasters and griefs, but it is a mode of bereavement probably quite unlike the 'normal' grieving process.[5] Two professionals who had worked extensively with homicide survivors in New York City claimed that: 'The depth of emotional reactions was overwhelming and cannot be overstated.'[6] Survivors themselves cannot imagine anything more terrible. Ann Virgin, a founding member of Justice

    [3] See T. Walter, *The Revival of Death* (Routledge, London, 1994), 27.
    [4] See C. Murray-Parkes, 'Psychiatric Problems Following Bereavement by Murder or Manslaughter', *British Journal of Psychiatry*, 1993, Vol 162, 49.
    [5] See A Burgess, 'Family Reaction to Homicide', *American Journal of Orthopsychiatry*, Apr 1975, Vol 45, No 3, 391; D. Magee, *What Murder Leaves Behind: The Victim's Family* (Dodd, Mead and Company, New York, 1988), p. xiii; R. Knapp, *Beyond Endurance: When a Child Dies* (Shocken Books, New York, 1986) 86; and L. Videka-Sherman, 'Effects of Participation in a Self-Help for Bereaved Parents', *Prevention in Human Services*, 1982, Vol 1, 69.
    [6] G. Getzel and R. Masters, 'Serving Families who Survive Homicide Victims', *Social Casework*, Mar 1984, Vol 65, No 3, 139. And see A. Amick-McMullan, J. Kilpatrick and L. Veronen,' Family Survivors of Homicide Victims: A Behavioral Analysis', *The Behavior Therapist*, 1989, Vol 12, No 4, 75.

for Victims (a group which I shall discuss below), a woman whose partner, Martin, had been killed in a street attack near a public house, said, 'there is no worse crime. There is no worse thing that anyone can do to hurt you.' Joan Bacon, the mother of Martin, and a fellow founder of Justice for Victims, said, 'the very, very worst thing has happened to us.'[7] Frank Green, one time chairman of SAMM, and a man whose sister had been murdered by her former partner, declared that 'Families and friends of the victim face a level of distress that is unimaginable to those who have never experienced it.'[8] And, in a poem (one of the customary ways of trying to express the inexpressible), the parent of a murdered child reflected that:

> I'm feeling so helpless and low at this time
> Desperately trying to save what is mine
> No one can understand how I feel
> The pain and the horror has become so very real.

Homicide survivors tend to feel they are a group apart, a special minority, quite unlike anyone else.[9] Jill Palm's seventeen-year old son, Robert, had been stabbed in 1986 outside a public house: 'he was sitting on a bench with his girlfriend and a boy he knew came up and whispered to him, and said he wanted to see him "round the corner" and he just took out a knife and stabbed him.' She had been the second co-ordinator of the English group, POMC (Parents of Murdered Children). She reflected, 'you feel so . . . different, and you do get . . . the usual thing—probably people have told you that as well . . . where someone says "oh yes my Mother died, I know how you're feeling . . ." or "I had a still-born child" or something, but it's just not the same . . . because there's so many different feelings with murder, so much anger as well.' And Gill Pennicard, whose sister-in-law's daughter had been killed, POMC's last co-ordinator before it was transformed into SAMM, remarked, "There is no way, however compassionate and kind you are as a person, there is no way you

---

[7] Minutes of meeting held at Home Office, 20 Apr 1994

[8] 'SAMM Talks given by Frank Green, Chair SAMM . . . At Victim Support National Conference July 1995', mimeo, p. 1.

[9] In that feeling, of course, they are affirming not only their distinctiveness but also the extraordinarily harrowing force of their grief. Other groups such as rape victims and war veterans make much the same claims about themselves. Most powerfully, so do holocaust survivors. See A. Hass, *The Aftermath: Living with the Holocaust* (Cambridge University Press, Cambridge, 1995), 40, 86.

can understand or feel the pain that other people feel unless they are in a similar position. You cannot learn that from a book, you cannot learn it from a person, you cannot learn from me how if it was one of your children. You can't envisage it." As I shall argue, that is a potent sense of distinctiveness, and it can unite and part survivors.

The survivors' conception of their peculiar standing tends often to be affirmed in their dealings with outsiders. They consider themselves to be *treated* as importantly different. After all, it is a cliché that death is the last taboo, a matter which one cannot contemplate with ease,[10] and those too closely associated with mortality, the bereaved and the funeral director,[11] mortuary attendant, forensic pathologist, and others, complain of being seen as blemished, unclean and unwelcome.[12]

The contaminating power of association with murder and manslaughter is especially ancient and frightening. It tends to keep those most affected, the families and friends of the victim and the killer, at a distance from everyday life[13] and, if only for a time, it denies them the right to participate fully in its routines. The children of murdered mothers, for instance, tend to be ostracised at school.[14] Jayne Zito, founder of The Zito Trust, whose husband Jon had been killed seemingly at random by a mentally disordered offender on the platform of a London Underground Station, reflected that 'They're just letting us become untouchable people.... When I say "untouchable", it's because murder is an ugly thing. You feel it if you become one of society's leftovers that nobody wants to know about at all.' It is a power that has been likened to a 'highly infectious disease'[15] and to leprosy.[16]

---

[10] Help the Aged, for instance, state in their pamphlet on bereavement that 'In our society, the subject of death is often taboo. We tend not to talk about it, and may even deny it...'

[11] See G. Howarth, *Last Rites* (Baywood, Amityville, NY, 1996).

[12] C. Murray-Parkes, *Bereavement: Studies of Grief in Adult Life* (Tavistock, London, 1972), 8.

[13] See P. Mellor and C. Shilling, 'Modernity, self-identity and the sequestration of death', *Sociology*, 1993, Vol 27.

[14] See D. Black, 'Parents who have killed their partner', in P. Reder and C. Lucey (eds), *Assessment of Parenting* (Routledge, London, 1995), 220; and D. Black and T. Kaplan, 'Father Kills Mother', *British Journal of Psychiatry*, 1988, 153, p. 626.

[15] D. Magee, *What Murder Leaves Behind* (n 5 above), 164.

[16] The term was used by Norman Black, who was to be a member of SAMM; *Woking News and Mail*, 17 Nov 1994.

On occasion, it is almost as if the bereaved are cursed.[17] One woman said simply 'they don't want our bad luck', and Ann Robinson, co-founder of Parents of Murdered Children, talked of an 'atavistic fear that if they have anything to do with you, that some of the evil might contaminate them'. Anticipating a stigmatising response, they may come to avoid others who have not been benighted as they have. Pat Green, co-founder of SAMM Merseyside, said:

[Other bereaved people] do recognise that we're all experiencing the same type of grief, I wouldn't say the same type of pain, but the same type of grief, the anger, the bitterness ... you feel as though you're being institutionalised .... It's strange ... I mean, when I go shopping I just feel as though I'm just labelled. People ... ignore me you know ... ignore me. When I see somebody walking towards me I feel as if they're saying 'there's that woman who's son was murdered', not 'there's Pat' as a person ... I feel as though I've lost my identity.

Some (but not all[18]) bereaved people may become isolated, withdrawing[19] and being thrust into withdrawal by others.[20] After an initial flurry of interest and sympathy, and after the funeral—a supposed turning-point—in particular, supports and contacts begin to melt away.[21] Ron Rodgers of SAMM said, 'everyone's gone, all the family have left, and there's no one else, the funeral's finished ... and suddenly you're sat in this big void.' A long established member of Parents of Murdered Children, later SAMM, recalled that 'you were inundated with friends because they wanted to know all the ins and outs, and then suddenly there isn't any friends any more, and the ones you think are your friends won't talk to you because either they don't know how to or they avoid you ...' And, in almost identical terms, Jill Palm said, 'at first you

[17] See G. Riches and P. Dawson, 'Communities of feeling: the culture of bereaved parents', *Mortality*, 1996, Vol 1, No 2 144. To be sure, these are the survivors' readings of their lot. Those who appreared to avoid survivors might well have done so for other reasons—for fear of embarrassment, for instance. But it is the survivors' readings that are significant for the development of this argument, because it was the survivors' responses that engendered the organizations which are its theme.

[18] See, for instance, the report about the Baldocks, members of The Compassionate Friends who had lost their son through murder, in *Medway News*, 3 Feb 1995.

[19] One woman, for instance, would shop at a distance from her home town in order to avoid meeting people she knew.

[20] See D. Warren, *Helping Networks* (University of Notre Dame Press, Notre Dame, Indiana, 1981), 12.

[21] See 'No death so sad', *Nursing Standard*, Jan 1988, 32.

find that you've got so many friends that you didn't know you had, and really all they want to know is the gory details, and then, sort of, you're left after two weeks and they've satisfied themselves— you're sort of left to cope on your own.' It is as if audiences cannot bear any longer to listen to deeply harrowing narratives,[22] especially when there is constant repetition and no sign of change in the survivor. They may be confused by the scale of the family's grief and their own inability to respond adequately to it.[23] They may not know what to say to each other, and what words to use (words such as 'murder', and the very name of the victim, are often avoided as if they were improper) and conversations will falter.[24] Ann Robinson talked about how 'most people found it very uncomfortable to be with me ... I was aware that people don't know how to treat you, they don't know what to say...'[25] A letter to SAMM observed, 'Everything stopped, I could no longer talk to my friends and family.'

References to that sense of acute isolation have become part of the litany of SAMM: 'Everyone expects you to be "all right", but you feel that you will never be "normal" again. The world goes on much the same as before, while inside you feel alone, isolated and no-one really understands the pain, emptiness and anger which you are suffering.'[26] It is difficult not to begin to define oneself as tainted, isolation and stigma conspiring together to induce feelings of shame despite the absence of any specific fault.[27] And those feelings may be amplified by the responses of others who can come to blame the victim and so distance themselves from him or her. After all, Lerner argued, it is difficult for most of us to accept that such tragedies as homicide can occur in a just world unless the

---

[22] See L. Langer, *Holocaust Testimonies* (Yale University Press, New Haven, 1991), 20.

[23] See A. Robinson, 'The Aftermath of Murder' (The Compassionate Friends, Bristol, 1987), 1.

[24] Glennys Howarth observes that this is 'Very true of many parents whose children have died, [this is] something also to do with the taboo around childhood death.... It was not until 1896 ... that parents could expect their children to outlive them.... [Until then] children were prepared for premature death—a situation so alien today.'

[25] From 'All Things Considered', BBC Radio Wales, 13 Dec 1987.

[26] Leaflet for SAMM Merseyside.

[27] Jack Katz remarks that 'Isolation from community, if sufficiently extreme, will for many people provoke shame without any element of specifiable fault and independent of any relationship with a particular other...', 'Shame and the Self', mimeo, 1995, pp. 9–10.

victim somehow invited and, indeed, deserved his or her fate. Victims and survivors are very easily represented as those who suffer because of their own misdeeds, as people who should indeed be ashamed.[28]

The special features that so signally transform bereavement and the bereaved can best be related by homicide survivors themselves. Consider four different[29] accounts of how parents learned of the deaths of children or relatives. It is worth reproducing them at length because they have an immediacy, poignancy, and descriptive power that no second-hand report could ever convey.

Diane Watson, the daughter of a couple who were to become the founders of Families of Murdered Children, a Strathclyde-based group, had been stabbed by another girl in the playground of the school of which she was a pupil. Her mother recalled:

On the 10th of April 1991 Barbara Glover and two of her friends lay in wait for Diane to come out of her class. While Glover's two friends held her coat and bag, they followed Glover as she pursued Diane, waving a large kitchen knife. Glover cornered Diane against a car, tormented her with the knife, before viciously stabbing Diane, leaving the large kitchen knife in Diane's body. Diane pulled out the knife herself. I did not witness any of this, but those horrendous images are etched forever in my mind. Diane, with the help of some friends, tried to make the short distance home. I was just about to leave to go to work when a very distressed girl came to tell me Diane had been hurt. I looked down the stairs and saw three or four girls half-carrying Diane. I called my husband, Jim, and I ran down to Diane. She was looking straight at me, her eyes full of pain, holding her side, her white tee shirt covered in blood. I remember holding Diane's face, telling her she would be alright. Diane just kept staring at me.[30]

Tessa, the daughter of David and Heather Howden, had been killed at night in her bedroom by an intruder. David Howden was later to be the first chairman of Parents of Murdered Children, and he helped to superintend the transformation of Parents of Murdered Children into SAMM:

Tessa had just been promoted or changed her job—she worked for the *Croydon Advertiser*. It was January 10th that she was murdered, 1986. I

---

[28] See M. Lerner, *The Belief in a Just World* (Plenum Press, New York, 1980), 39–40, 50–51.
[29] These accounts are probably no more or less harrowing than others, although no account could be called 'typical'.
[30] Fax of 15 Sept 1997.

went to bed first and I woke up in the morning and just thought she had overslept and the terrible events unfolded that morning. I went into her room and I could see that she wasn't in bed—it was dark and windy and horrible and wet. I started to go downstairs and had that panic feeling—I think we all have it lots of times and usually nothing comes of it but of course this time it did. I went back upstairs and she was covered over by the side of the bed. I screamed...

Susan, the sister of Frank Green, had been murdered by a former boyfriend. She had been killed and subjected to an 'act of necrophilia. He had taken Su's life, and in death taken away her dignity.' Frank Green was to be the second chairman of SAMM:

Until May 1986 I was part of what would be considered a typical family, mum and dad both worked, I was married with one son and my sister Su had returned to higher education... On Saturday 24th May that changed. I received a phone call from mum. To say that she was distraught was an understatement. Through the sounds of crying that I never want to hear again, she was only able to say over and over 'you've got to come home, something's happened you've got to come home'. At that time, I was a gliding instructor... and tried to explain that I needed to know what had happened so that I could explain to the CO why I needed to go. Through more sobs I heard the words 'Su's dead'. My sister, 29, single mum to Jo, student, full of energy, who I'd looked up to through high school, argued incessantly with through late teens, was dead. I booked off duty, and drove home all the while questioning what? Where? How? I cursed being low on fuel and having to stop for petrol on the way, I was angry that other people at the service station were in front of the queue to pay and that they could be so cruel as to be talking and laughing, as if nothing had happened... I remember thinking that mum had got it wrong, she must mean Nan, after all she was 81 and not too well, but no she'd said 'Su's dead'. Then it dawned on me, the motor bike, that must be it. Su had recently started to use a small motor bike to get around on... At last at home... My wife told me that the police had apparently called early that morning and told mum and dad that Su had been killed in suspicious circumstances... What the hell are suspicious circumstances? My mind was acting like a 486 computer with pentium processor one minute, and an abacus the next...[31]

Ron and Christine Rodgers were co-founders of the Devon branch of SAMM, and Ron Rodgers was later to be the third chairman and then the co-ordinator of SAMM nationally. Their son, Jeffrey, was killed by his girlfriend's former husband:

[31] Transcript of Members Seminar: Victim Support and SAMM—Working together, Victim Support Annual Conference 1995.

... our Jeffrey was going to become engaged to his ex-wife, and he sort of took exception to this and ... he harassed Jeffrey for ... it must be nearly six months, basically stalked him for six months, 'phoned him up, threats ... wherever he went he was standing there ... you know the usual stalking routine ... and then one night he came 'round to the house, my wife answered and he said he wanted to speak to Jeffrey. Christine knew who he was obviously at that time, and ... this was at 11 o'clock at night, and she immediately could tell he'd been drinking, he smelled a little bit of drink but not a lot, and she said 'no', and he then ... became excited—he tried to force an entry, Christine tried to stop him entering. By this time, I'd heard the commotion. I was upstairs and I'd actually gone to bed. Christine was sat down, just chatting with Jeffrey. ... Jeffrey had obviously heard the commotion by this time, he came out to the door, saw who it was, and sort of got him out of the house, and it all then took place on the front doorstep. By that time, I'd managed to put a pair of trousers on and a tee shirt and by the time I got downstairs, basically Jeffrey was lying against the wall. I could tell he wasn't ... there was something desperately wrong with him, but at the same time I saw the chap that did it, just standing there ... and as far as I was concerned then, I just wanted ... him the other side of the gate, keep the gate shut, and if he was the other side of the gate then I've got control of the situation ... and then I could attend to Jeffrey. But, as it was, I felt a thump to the stomach and I thought it was just a thump, so basically by then I got him by the scruff of the collar and I threw him out through the gate, clicked the gate shut. I was then worried about Jeffrey, and as ... as I felt the thump I heard Jeffrey shout to us 'Look out he's got a knife' but it didn't register at the time. Again, I just picked him, by the collar of his jacket, and shoved him out through the gate and kicked the gate shut ... I was then concerned about Jeffrey ... went over to Jeffrey and I could see he was desperately ill. Then it registered he had a knife. Christine was on the doorstep, so I got hold of Jeffrey, pushed Christine into the house again, because then immediately I thought he may come back through the gate ... [I] grabbed hold of Jeffrey, basically carried him into the house, kicked the front door shut and that was it. As far as I was concerned he was out the way then, I forgot all about him. And basically [I] could see Jeffrey was in a desperate condition, his breathing was very shallow, very rapid ... ragged and he was losing colour ... lips were turning blue ... so immediately I thought either a) he's choking or b) there's something ... but there was no real, there wasn't the amount of blood that I expected from a knife attack. He had foam on the lips, I went through all the normal first aid, checked to see what it was, at first I thought it may be a lung wound, tried to find where the wounds were, but I found two wounds in his chest ... that were just wounds, there was no blood. I then turned him ... he was sat on ... sort of sat on the stair, leant him over my shoulder so I could see his back, there was one wound there that showed signs of blood but not that much ... but there was a little bit of froth. So immediately that's when it sprung to mind that he had a lung puncture, yeah ... so covered it with my hand but there was no ... how can I put it? there was no vacuum or pressure there. I don't know if you know it, but if you have a lung wound and you're still trying to breathe, you do get this feeling of difference in air pressure, shall we say, and that's what you're trying to combat. But there was nothing there, there was no real blood, which I found disconcerting, and by this time he was slipping away.... Christine and I were calling to him to ... to stay with us ... and when I came into the house [I] got Christine to 'phone for an ambulance.... [We] got hold of the ambulance and they came round, luckily the police were sitting with the ambulance, so they both came at the same time. That's about when I noticed I had a hole in my stomach but there was no pain. Again, there was no blood, no real blood so, as far as I was concerned, I wasn't worried about that: it was just a matter of seeing to Jeffrey. [I was] still not sure about his lung when I put him down, normal first aid procedure is to put him on the side with the wound so supposedly his good lung would have no extra pressure on it ... But ... he was slipping away all the time, and I couldn't find the blood, so that's when it registered that obviously he's bleeding internally, and he's bleeding pretty heavily by the way ... it only took a few minutes for the ambulance to arrive but you could see it on their face that [he was gone].

What then is distinctive of bereavement after homicide? First, murder and manslaughter tend to be sudden and unexpected, and there can be no state of readiness for them. Colin Murray-Parkes, the psychiatrist, told the 1995 Annual General Meeting of SAMM: 'Traumatic bereavements are always devastating because we are unprepared for them, they are much more damaging in the sense of that feeling of being overwhelmed than bereavements that have been anticipated and prepared for.' Learning about sudden death can be overpowering, abrupt,[32] and unassimilable.[33] One woman observed at a SAMM Meeting, 'it's just like a stroke'. And a father told me: 'The interesting thing is of course that this is one thing you can't prepare people for—nobody thinks they are going to have a child die, nobody does ... somebody who has never been through it—the impact is so great you can't believe what is happening to you.' There can be no anticipatory mourning, no reconciliation and,

[32] Indeed, the family and relatives may well learn of the death first through the mass media. See A. Shearer, *Survivors and the Media*, Broadcasting Standards Council, Research Monographs Series: 2 (John Libbey, London, 1991), 16.

[33] See 'Survivors of Homicide Victims', *Network Information Bulletin*, National Organization for Victim Assistance, Oct 1985, Vol 2, No 3, 1.

very often, no proper leave-taking. David Renhard of The Compassionate Friends said simply, 'our child has gone and we never said good-bye'—his daughter had been killed by a stranger whilst she was walking and taking photographs in the Peak District in Derbyshire.

When the victim is a partner or an adolescent child, moreover, there may well have been a mass of unfinished emotional and practical business which will cloud subsequent recollections, prevent the possibility of a fitting farewell[34] and lead to a continuing sense of the presence of the dead,[35] and that is another matter which I shall discuss below.

If one of the crucial tasks of culture is to mask the risks and dangers lurking in the world around one, to 'edit reality in such a way that it seems manageable',[36] culture itself can fail when confronted by the shocking revelation of a homicide or sudden death. It is as if there had been a terrifying irruption in the fabric of everyday life, and there may be no civilised conventions at hand to reconcile oneself to what has been so suddenly announced, no recipe knowledge, roles,[37] rules, coaches, mentors,[38] or words[39] to capture and objectify its attendant sensations (Brigitte Chaudhry, founder of RoadPeace, said simply 'I had no idea what to do. I had no idea about anything.'). One survivor wrote to SAMM, 'No-one taught me about the way to feel when someone you love has been murdered, no-one could guide me through the range of emotions that I experienced.' Another, whose father had been killed for political reasons by a deranged man in North Africa, wrote, 'there are no right words, there is no script...'[40] And Gill Pennicard said, 'there's not a book'.

After all, murder and manslaughter are so rare that they fall far outside the practical knowledge of almost everyone. Each event is stark, not at all commonplace, less readily assimilated or understood. In Stan Cohen's words, it 'must mean something

[34] See I. Ivison, *Fiona's Story* (Virago, London, 1997), 210.
[35] See R. Blauner, 'Death and Social Structure', *Psychiatry*, 1966, Vol 29, No 4, 381.
[36] K. Erikson, *A New Species of Trouble: Explorations in Disaster, Trauma, and Community* (W.W. Norton and Company, New York, 1994) 152.
[37] See M. Peach and D. Klass, 'Special Issues in the Grief of Parents of Murdered Children', *Death Studies*, 11, 1987, 84.
[38] See C. Murray-Parkes, 'Psychiatric Problems Following Bereavement' (n 4 above), 51.
[39] Herman remarked that 'Traumatic memories lack verbal narrative and context....' J. Herman, *Trauma and Recovery* (Pandora, London, 1994), 38.
[40] G. Stokes, *A Witness for Peace* (The Kates Hill Press, 1994), 114.

more'[41] (and, paradoxically, it may also mean less) in England and Wales than in countries such as Colombia or South Africa where homicide is not uncommon at all.

Where grief is acute, its effects may be compounded by the ineffability of an experience which is diffuse, inarticulate, and bound up with the peculiar inner world of the body and the self. Sociology lacks a proper analytic apparatus for examining such embodied processes, preferring instead to lean on the more convenient model of a calmly-appraising and rational actor.[42] Major bereavement is not calm, appraising, and rational. It is instead at once a physical, emotional, and symbolic process that is built around a bewildering[43] cacophony of intense sensations[44] that suffuses fields of experience.[45] The deeply bereaved can feel bodily pains in the chest and a hollowness in the stomach. They can be restless, numb, shocked, anxious, enervated, breathless, over-sensitive to noise, sleepless, exhausted, nauseated,[46] and unable to concentrate. They may have an impaired memory,[47] palpitations, headaches, panic attacks, and muscular aches. They can have nightmares, hallucinations, and wild imaginings. All those physical sensations map a sensory field of expression which gives a definition, locus, and geography to emotion and thought (the body, said Damasio, is a 'theater for the emotions'.[48]) And physical sensations serve also to excite those very emotions and thoughts, sustaining them in a kind of counterpoint, tears inducing sadness and sadness tears, pain simulating anger and anger pain. So it is that the activities of learning,[49] talking, or writing about emotional events can prompt

---

[41] Letter.

[42] See N. Denzin, 'A Phenomenology of Emotion and Deviance', *Zeitschrift für Soziologie*, July 1980, Vol 9, No 3, 251.

[43] See M. Osterweis *et al*, *Bereavement: Reactions, Consequences, and Care* (National Academy Press, Washington, DC, 1984), 47.

[44] See R. Huntingdon and P. Metcalf, *Celebrations of Death* (Cambridge University Press, Cambridge, 1979), 23.

[45] See N. Denzin, *On Understanding Emotion* (Jossey-Bass, San Francisco, 1984), 94.

[46] See P. Marris, *Loss and Change* (Routledge and Kegan Paul, London, 1986), 25.

[47] See L. Brown *et al*, *Family of Murder Victims Project, Final Report* (Victim Support, London, 1990), 21.

[48] A. Damasio, *Descartes' Error: Emotion, Reason and the Human Brain* (Grosset/Putnam, New York, 1994) 155.

[49] See J. Pennebaker, 'Social Mechanisms of Constraint', in D. Wegner and J. Pennebaker (eds), *Handbook of Mental Control* (Prentice Hall, Englewood Cliffs, New Jersey, 1993), 205.

bodily changes:[50] 'If you hear of an acquaintance's death, your heart may pound, your mouth dry up, your skin blanch, a section of your gut contract, the muscles in your neck and back tense up while those in your face design a mask of sadness.'[51] There is even an emerging lay diagnostics amongst the survivors' groups themselves. Members are becoming increasingly convinced that their own life expectancy has been cut short by the stresses of grief, that men die of heart attacks and women of cancer. One's very body can thereby encapsulate and symbolise the larger disorder without.

A common response to the shock of homicide is rank denial,[52] insensibility,[53] disbelief, and incomprehension.[54] David Renhard observed '*it is the most shattering experience* I have had in my life.... So what happens? 1) Rejection that it has happened 2) Numbness and pain.'[55] And in almost identical words, the parents of a murdered child wrote:

The initial reaction to being told a loved one has been assaulted and is either lying badly injured in hospital or already dead is one of total disbelief. You go cold, numb, what is being said is being heard through a haze.[56]

And that is not all. There is a pervasive structural disorder that reproduces the chaos within. The loss of another, and especially that of a member of the family, forces unwanted and bewildering changes on the social universe of the survivors. Take one illustration: mourning and yearning for one may well lead to a neglect of the others who remain, and to an emotional imbalance, divisiveness, and sense of injustice that create abiding discontents. Take another illustration: the problem of how to answer outsiders who ask how many people there are in a family. If one has lost a son or daughter, what reply should one make? Should one include the

[50] See J. Pennebaker, *Emotion, Disclosure, and Health* (American Psychological Association, Washington, DC, 1995), 5.

[51] A. Damasio, *Descartes' Error: Emotion, Reason and the Human Brain* (n 48 above), 135.

[52] See G. Breakwell, *Coping with Threatened Identities* (Methuen, London, 1986), 81.

[53] See J. Harris Hendricks, D. Black and T. Kaplan, *When father kills mother: Guiding children through trauma and grief* (Routledge, London, 1993), 13.

[54] See C. Murray-Parkes, 'Psychiatric Problems following Bereavement After Homicide', *British Journal of Psychiatry* 993, Vol 162, 50

[55] 'The Death of a child—The Parent's Point of View', speaking notes, no date. Emphasis in original.

[56] V. and B. Chalk, 'What is Murder?', *Parents of Murdered Children Newsletter*, Autumn 1990 (?), 3.

names of the dead or omit them, and what consequences would flow from encompassing or expunging someone in that way? So small a dilemma can leave the survivor perplexed and distressed. After all, we are built symbolically around our significant others, we incorporate them into ourselves, and to lose or deny another is to deny part of oneself.[57]

Saint-Exupéry once said that death is a rearrangement of the world,[58] and so it is with homicide. A system of relationships will have been thrown into disorganization.[59] Family members will have abruptly to change role and status. Pat Green said: 'When they took Phillip's life, they didn't just take him. They took the grandchildren he might have given us, the wife he might have had, Stuart's brother. They've changed a family forever.'[60] The death of a child can become a metaphor for the collapse of the family itself.[61]

Symbolically, then, the bereaved can confront *anomie*, a partial collapse of meaning, in which the familiar representational structures which shaped their lives no longer hold, and where the inner and outer materials of the self are in disarray. The future will appear emptier and much that made sense in the past will seem to be without significant purpose. If our awareness of the past establishes who we are,[62] and if recollections of the past have become infused with confusion and doubt, it may become difficult indeed to sustain a tolerable sense of identity.[63]

Survivors may wonder why they have been singled out for loss and what a death might portend about the moral order. They may protest at the unfairness of some people dying whilst others live on. They may feel guilt that they have survived and the dead have not, or wonder whether they are being punished for some wrong or

---

[57] See A. Hass; *The Aftermath* (n 9 above), 41–2. Rita Edmond-Norris observed that a prime need becomes: 'To develop a new self-identity based on a life without your loved one. Part of your self-identity was based on the relationship you had with the loved one you lost. How you see yourself and how others see you had now changed.' 'Griefwork. . . .', Families and Friends of Murder Victims, Inc, *Newsletter*, Oct 1996, Vol 1, Issue 10, 5.

[58] A. De Saint-Exupéry, *Flight to Arras* (William Heinemann, London, 1942), 16.

[59] See G. Getzel and R. Masters, 'Serving Families who Survive Homicide Victims' (n 6 above), 141.

[60] *Guardian Midweek*, 8 Nov 1994.

[61] See G. Getzel and R. Masters; 'Serving Families who Survive Homicide Victims' (n 6 above), 141.

[62] See F. Davis, *Yearning for Yesterday* (Free Press, New York, 1979), 35.

[63] See G. Breakwell, *Coping with Threatened Identities* (n 52 above), 49.

omission. Mourning may be accompanied by yearning, and by a quest for the dead person who once made the self and its circle complete.[64]

A second distinctive feature of homicide is that it is a death that was never inevitable or 'natural', but intended and purposive or reckless and negligent. It appears arbitrary:[65] someone actually *wanted* the victim to die or was indifferent to the consequences of his actions.[66] Ann Robinson, co-founder of Parents of Murdered Children, said, 'you know it shouldn't have happened and that somebody else is involved. It's dreadful to think that somebody has done that to your child.' Joan Bacon of Justice for Victims said, 'somebody chose to do that to you—it's not an accident— how dare they! It's totally different—it's been chosen by a person to take a person, it's a sacrilege, it's nothing else. It goes to the, what D. H. Lawrence called the kernel, it goes to the very inside. It can't go any further and it obliterates your teaching, your growing up.' And Pat Green said, 'I couldn't believe anyone could take a life . . . I mean, if I'm out in the car with my husband and I see somebody walking down the road and I say to him "can you imagine anyone just coming up and killing that person?," he said "no". But they do. And I can't comprehend that the person that's done this is just living a life. When he's done such a horrendous act and intended to do it.'

Survivors tend overwhelmingly to conceive murder and the murderer as a moral assault, as a manifestation of evil (an observation which I shall amplify at length in Chapter 4), and it is a cardinal property of evil that it lays waste to structure and significance: 'If "good" can be defined as that which encourages the integrity of the whole, then "evil" becomes anything which disturbs or disrupts such completeness.'[67] Society itself will have become more threatening and chaotic, insecure and disorderly, and it will become so in

[64] C. Murray-Parkes, *Bereavement* (n 12 above), 44.

[65] Interestingly, in the case of assaults, victims and offenders will give very different accounts of angry encounters. Victims characteristically represent attacks on them as arbitrary and meaningless, whilst perpetrators depict them as meaningful and comprehensible. See R. Baumeister *et al*, 'Victim and Perpetrator Accounts of Interpersonal Conflict: Autobiographical Narratives about Anger', *Journal of Personality and Social Psychology* (Nov 1990, Vol 59, No 5), 994–1005.

[66] See K. Erikson, *A New Species of Trouble* (n 36 above), 237; J. Harris Hendriks, D. Black and T. Kaplan; *When father kills mother* (n 53 above), 9; C. Murray-Parkes; 'Psychiatric Problems Following Bereavement' (n 54 above), 49.

[67] L. Watson, quoted by J. Updike in 'Elusive Evil', *The New Yorker*, 22 July 1996, 62.

ways that defy ready responses.[68] One member of SAMM said to another at a meeting in November 1995, 'it degenerates into chaos'. And a new SAMM member wrote in his application, 'I am so bitter, my whole life has been turned upsides down. I just can't get out of this mess.'

Having encountered danger in so frightening and abrupt a fashion, survivors find themselves and their circle newly vulnerable[69] and helpless,[70] beset by new risks[71] (and particularly when the killer is still at large or has been released[72]). Fearing that fate will strike again,[73] they may well lock themselves up in their homes, becoming fortress-bound recluses.[74] They may not venture out to use public transport. They may fear strangers[75] and much else, becoming phobic.[76] They may become exceptionally protective of their remaining children. A mother of a murdered child, Daphne Vaughan, wrote: 'A certain fear envelops you. You become paranoid over your surviving children going out and wait anxiously for their return. You become fearful of facing people and to hear someone walking behind you fills you with dread.'[77] It is as if so rude a shock has jolted the survivor into awareness. The bereaved suddenly become in truth, privy to the real, feral nature of the world. Those

[68] Edwin Lemert was one of the few sociologists who attempted to take the matter of evil seriously, and he did so by defining it as a special kind of subjectively-constituted anti-social act that resisted ordinary social controls. See E. Lemert, *The Trouble With Evil: Social Control at the Edge of Morality* (State University of New York Press, Albany, 1997).

[69] See M. Creamer *et al*, 'Posttrauma Reactions Following a Multiple Shooting', in J. Wilson and B. Raphael (eds), *International Handbook of Traumatic Stress Syndromes* (Plenum Press, New York, 1993), 201.

[70] One woman said at a local meeting of SAMM, 'when you write to the Home Office, when you write to Michael Howard [the Home Secretary], all you get is standard letters. They say "it's up to you" but how can we do it when we've just had our children taken from us, when we're so distressed, so distraught, we don't even know what day it is!?'

[71] In that, once more, they share much in common with genocide survivors and other survivors of profound trauma. See A. Burgess and L. Holmstrom, 'Rape Trauma Syndrome', *American Journal of Psychiatry* (Sept 1974, Vol 131, No 9), 984; and A. Hass, *The Aftermath* (n 9 above), 43, 55.

[72] See *Daily Mirror*, 11 Nov 1994; *South Wales Echo*, 14 Nov 1994.

[73] See S. Felman and D. Laub, *Testimony: Crises of Witnessing in Literature, Psychoanalysis, and History* (Routledge, New York, 1992), 67.

[74] See C. Murray-Parkes, 'Psychiatric Problems following Bereavement' (n 54 above), 51.

[75] See R. Kilroy-Silk, 'The Suffering Continues', *Police Review*, 20 May 1988.

[76] See A. Burgess, 'Family Reaction to Homicide' (n 5 above), 395.

[77] D. Vaughan, 'Death by Murder', mimeo, n.d.

who continue to think otherwise are held to be little more than mystified by the deceptively reassuring appearances of things. Justice for Victims, for instance, wrote that: 'Whilst the Law and general society keep the Victim problem at bay—silently swept under the carpet—it can pretend it does not exist—to do otherwise opens up other peoples vulnerability.'[78] A SAMM leaflet recited that: 'Murder makes us aware of how unsafe and vulnerable we really are. When things go badly wrong we can see how easily it can happen. The world around us can now seem much more dangerous and threatening. This can make us frightened...' And Jayne Zito observed that she was continually surprised by the obliviousness of others to the hazards around them: 'You see how people get on with their lives and they don't know what's going on out there.... I think the most frightening thing about Jon's death, and I still feel it when I see people going about their business, is that it could be you at any time.... I go down to... sometimes and there are so many mentally ill people on the platform and I saw one of the station managers confront one of them and I thought "you're a brave man". People don't realise the risk...' The bereaved may well adduce numerous arguments to show that the universe is a very perilous place, and wonder why anyone should pretend otherwise.[79] So it was that the June 1997 newsletter of the Californian group, Citizens Against Homicide, included a panel containing the assertion, laid out in capitals and bold font, 'REMEMBER ALL MURDERERS LIVE NEXT DOOR TO SOMEBODY.'

Isolation, disbelief, numbness,[80] strength of emotion, and incredulity about mundane activities can bring alienation from the self and from a once familiar society. Like holocaust survivors, the bereaved may no longer feel at home in the world.[81] Brigitte Chaudhry of RoadPeace said 'I just think the whole world is mad.

---

[78] Murder Survivor Victim Families: Discrimination and Lack of Human Rights, mimeo, n.d.

[79] See K. Erikson, A New Species of Trouble (n 36 above), 154–5. The tendency is not uniform. For instance, the Suzy Lamplugh Trust, established by parents in the aftermath of the death of a young woman, is at pains to argue that the risks of attack from strangers in public space are very low. See 'Out and About: A Guide to Safe Travel for Disabled People' (The Suzy Lamplugh Trust and Mencap, London, n.d.).

[80] NOVA states that the bereaved feel that they are at a distance even from their own bodies; Survivors of Homicide Victims, 2.

[81] See L. Langer, Holocaust Testimonies (n 22 above), 35. Alienation does seem to be a common feature of bereavement (see G. Riches and P. Dawson (n 17 above)), but its duration and intensity may well vary.

I feel totally alienated against this world. There is no way I can live any normal life again and none of the people that I know...I just think the world is crazy, absolutely mad, and the families are shattered.' It is almost as if such powerful and unfamiliar events must be happening to someone else.[82] Jayne Zito reflected that 'the feeling I was left with that I was just as dead as Jon at the time.... Everything else is going on around you and you're not part of it anymore.' And a Lockerbie survivor said, 'you feel right outside the normal course of events, you are outside the normal world as it stands.' The bereaved are in society but not of it, separated by their sense of distinctiveness, no longer taken up with the dull, everyday preoccupations of those around them. Matters that used to concern them can appear petty and inconsequential. One observed on a *Kilroy* television programme of 3 July 1995 that: 'It affects *everything*. It makes *everything* trivial. If you've got to do anything, one can't be bothered.'

If bereavement is ineffable and idiosyncratic, different mourners may comport themselves in different ways and grow apart.[83] A member of SAMM said: 'I mean I couldn't even look at my husband for three years. I hated him, didn't want him near me, because I couldn't cope with his...I couldn't recognise his pain. It was only me that was in pain. I didn't even want my other son. All I wanted was——.' Issues can grow emotionally-charged. Another member of SAMM said: 'we've split into two now and there are three of our daughters that I don't see and seven grandchildren because we were too close and because our opinions varied so much—"hang them", "don't hang them", and all the things around it.' Each survivor may find the load of grief unbearable, and retreat into a privacy which undermines mutual support. A member of the The Compassionate Friends who had lost a daughter through murder said: 'there is a fallacy that if there is trouble in the family they will stick together but it is just the opposite...My marriage split up afterwards.' And Ann Robinson, one of the two founders of Parents of Murdered Children, recalled after the death of her son that:

my daughter was nine, not quite ten, and it was obvious that she was very deeply shocked and in grief, and I just didn't know how to cope with

[82] See B. and V. Chalk, 'What is Murder' (n 56 above), 13.
[83] C. Murray-Parkes; 'Psychiatric Problems following Bereavement' (n 54 above), 51.

her...I just didn't know what to do. I couldn't cope with my own feelings, let alone her's. My husband's way of dealing with it was to clam up. He just couldn't talk about it. He threw himself back into work, and it really was dreadful, it's so hard to put it into words. I think every awful emotion that you could think of was there—the horror of what had happened, the rage, the feeling of helplessness and inadequacy, frustration...[84]

Survivors claim that they are exceptionally prone to divorce, and they will quote American estimates that between 70 per cent and 90 per cent[85] of marriages collapse in the wake of homicide. (Whether or not such figures are accurate is less material than that they serve further to confirm the survivors' identity as centred on an unremitting trial.)

Matters can become even more unbearably complicated when the victim and the offender both stem from the same nuclear family because relations will then be riddled by divided allegiances, feuds, and moral ambiguities.[86]

'Anger' is the one word which is used repeatedly to describe those emotions, although one might suppose that it is an approximate, and perhaps not wholly adequate, description not only of the mass of turbulent and contradictory experiences which I have listed, but also of a larger feeling which embraces the survivor, the victim, the killer, and others around the self as an expressive unity.[87] David Howden reflected that 'the emotions are just too varied and difficult to isolate or explain, but it is just like an explosion.'[88] And the English sister of a man killed over Lockerbie on Pan Am Flight 103 recalled:

The police were interviewing my sister-in-law and they would not give her his seat number, and they told me that was confidential information...Our response to that was out of all proportion to the piece of information. We went absolutely through the roof, and that's the anger, you see, these things set up the anger in you. It was with anger that people came together. I mean the Lockerbie relatives group was formed in March within a few months and the first few meetings were total chaos because people were taking all their anger out on each other...

[84] From 'All Things Considered', BBC Radio Wales, 13 Dec 1987.
[85] 'What Happens to a Marriage When a Child Dies?', Hope for Bereaved Parents, mimeo, n.d.
[86] See D. Black, 'Parents who have killed their partner' (n 14 above).
[87] See N. Denzin, *On Understanding Emotion* (n 45 above), 69.
[88] David Howden, speaking in a video recording; *No Chance to Say Goodbye* (n 1 above).

'Grief' and 'aggrievement' share the same etymological root,[89] but the intentional, reckless, and chaotic character of homicide can excite a quite extraordinary and unrelenting anger which is directed both at the world at large and at specific others, and at the killer above all.[90] Irene Ivison described how 'I was so angry I sometimes didn't know what to do with myself. I used to take the car out into Derbyshire, drive into some remote area and scream. I would hear this terrible demented screaming like a madwoman or someone possessed and realised that it was me.'[91] On occasion, indeed, it is as if all the emotions once vested in a broken relationship have become transmuted into hate.[92] Hullinger, co-founder of the American organization, Parents of Murdered Children, said: 'Violent death brings anger so intense most people can't stand it.'[93] Any emotion so unremitting and powerful could not but be a major cause of action (despite sociology's reticence about regarding emotions as causes[94]), and its strength and diffuse influence must be remembered as the argument of this book takes shape.

Following Graham Wallas, Karl Weick once asked: 'How can I know what I think until I see what I say?'[95] One might similarly enquire, 'how do I know what I am until I see how I behave?' Anger

[89] Taken from remarks by Colin Murray-Parkes at SAMM meeting, Warwick, 19 Mar 1995.
[90] Anger is one of the sequels to homicide most frequently mentioned at first and second hand. Getzel and Masters, for instance, talk about a 'consuming rage'. ('Serving Families who Survive Homicide Victims' (n 6 above), 139); Burgess describes 'strong feelings of anger and outrage' (Family Reaction to Homicide' (n 5 above), 393); and Rynearson refers to an omnipresent feeling of anger and retributiveness towards the murderer ('Bereavement after Homicide', *American Journal of Psychiatry*, 141, 1984, 1453). Colin Murray-Parkes observed 'Deaths by human agency often cause severe and prolonged suffering because of the way in which anger and guilt complicate the work of grieving and undermine personal security.' Law Commission Consultation Paper N 137: Liability for Psychiatric Illness, Views of Dr Colin Murray-Parkes, July 1995, 6.
[91] I. Ivison, *Fiona's Story* (n 34 above), 270–1.
[92] See L. Von Franz, *Shadow and Evil in Fairytales* (Spring Publications, New York, 1974), 132. Ann West said 29 years after the murder of her daughter, Lesley Ann Downey, 'The power of love is very strong, but so is the power of hate. Both have kept me going over the years. My health and happiness have been destroyed by my frustrated love for Lesley Ann and my loathing for her bestial killers.' A. West, *For the Love of Lesley* (Warner, London, 1993), 9.
[93] Interview in *People Magazine*, 16 Mar 1981, 116.
[94] See T. Scheff, *Bloody Revenge: Emotions, Nationalism, and War* (Westview Press, Boulder, Colorado, 1994), 63.
[95] K. Weick, *Sensemaking in Organizations* (Sage, Thousand Oaks, Calif, 1995), 18.

becomes real in its instantiation. It is best understood as a context-bound practice[96] which has no phenomenological existence outside angry people displaying angry reactions (and responding to themselves and others displaying those reactions) in angry situations.[97] People 'don't just "get" angry, they "do" their anger…'[98] and, being thus performed, anger defines a self and its world. Such anger can be authentic and compelling only if it is lived fully and in its immediacy (*'Emotions only exist in action…'*[99]) If one pauses to stand back and reflect, merely taking an attitude towards one's emotions, one no longer lives in the experience but becomes alienated from it. To be an activist survivor is in large measure to *be* angry, and numbers of the bereaved have come to build their very identities around enacting an abiding rage as a form of validation, as a sign of the righteousness and power of their convictions.[100] Susan Cohen, an American who had lost her only child on Pan Am Flight 103, reflected that: 'Of all the emotions I have felt since Theo's murder, anger is the best. Rage gives me energy. Rage makes me strong.'[101]

One difficulty, of course, is that the manifestations of anger and passion, what Littlewood called 'wave after wave of violently contradictory emotional impulses',[102] tend to be considered unseemly in the West, showing an embarrassing want of self-control and rationality.[103] There appears to be little endorsement of unconfined

---

[96] See N. MacKinnon, *Symbolic Interactionism as Affect Control* (State University of New York Press, Albany, 1994), 124, 128.

[97] See R. Harré, 'An Outline of the Social Constructionist Viewpoint', in R, Harré (ed), *The Social Construction of Emotions* (Basil Blackwell, Oxford, 1986), 4.

[98] J. Katz, 'Pissed Off in L.A.', mimeo, p. 37.

[99] I. Burkitt, 'Social Relationships and Emotions', *Sociology*, Feb 1997, Vol 31, No 1, 53 (emphasis in original).

[100] Joan Bacon of Justice for Victims wrote: 'Parole Boards should either be abolished or must include the victim of the crime or the victims family to make representation if they wish. Only they know the impact of the violence meted out—they took the blows—heard the assailant yell and threaten—only the victim sees the true face of the criminal—from everyone else he has something to gain!! Who has standing to label our anger irrational?!!!!!!!' 'A "Civilised Society"?—1994, The Other Side of Murder', 1994, mimeo, p. 2.

[101] S. Cohen, 'Rage Makes Me Strong', *Time*, 29 July 1996.

[102] J. Littlewood, 'The denial of death and rites of passage in contemporary societies', in D. Clark (ed), *The Sociology of Death* (Basil Blackwell, Oxford, 1993), 73.

[103] See C. Stearns, '"Lord Help Me Walk Humbly": Anger and Sadness in England and America, 1570–1750', in C. Stearns and P. Stearns, *Emotion and Social Change* (Holmes and Meier, New York, 1988).

public expressions of grief,[104] and those who are in the immediate company of the bereaved may not only be discomfited but also wonder awkwardly whether they are themselves to blame for their behaviour.[105]

Those expressions may indeed frighten and embarrass oneself. They have no discipline or dignity. 'Anger, frustration, hate and all the other terrible emotions'[106] can often appear inappropriate, disorientating, and unreasonable,[107] and they frequently lead the bereaved to question their own sanity and normality.[108] Ann Robinson, co-founder of Parents of Murdered Children, wrote that: 'The intensity of feelings can be frightening—the parents may think they are going mad...'[109] One woman asked me part-anxiously, part-ironically, on a march: 'am I going mental? I must be going mental!' Another survivor consulted a stress clinic because 'I wanted to be sure I wasn't going mad.'[110]

Unseemly emotions can be ugly when they are turned inwards in self-blame.[111] And they can be ugly and alienating in others, a mirror of what one is or could well become. Survivors do not always find each other admirable and congenial. To the contrary: others' reactions may be disturbing and unattractive. A father said: 'anger comes out in different ways. You go to some of these meetings and these people are *vicious* with their anger—and I understood why when you listened to their case of what had happened to their child.' And a woman, who had lost her husband through murder, remembered that:

People started to contact me and I started to contact people and I was meeting Parents of Murdered Children and I couldn't feel part

---

[104] See N. Elias, *The History of Manners* (Basil Blackwell, Oxford, 1978), 141; and A. Faulkner, 'Developments in Bereavement Services', in D. Clark (ed) *The Future for Palliative Care* (Open University Press, Milton Keynes, 1993), 71.

[105] See D. Magee, *What Murder Leaves Behind* (n 5 above), 67.

[106] Oral evidence taken from David Howden before the House of Lords Select Committee on Murder and Life Imprisonment, 5 June 1989, HL Paper 20-xxiii (HMSO, London, 1989), 506.

[107] See L. Terr, *Too Scared to Cry* (Harper and Row, New York, 1990), 238.

[108] See J. Harris Hendricks *et al, When father kills mother* (n 53 above), 36.

[109] A. Robinson, 'When a Child is Murdered', The Compassionate Friends Parents of Murdered Children Group, leaflet, n.d.

[110] Jane Cooper, SAMM's first co-ordinator, recalled that 'Am I going mad?' was a 'very common' phrase in conversations with new SAMM contacts.

[111] See G. Getzel and R. Masters, 'Serving Families who Survive Homicide Victims' (n 6 above), 141.

of them at all. They were so angry... It's like men being hurt in war. It's the infection that gets in, and I suppose what I was trying to do at the time [was] keep hold of how much I loved——really in order to get through it and not let the hate take over... They were very, very angry and I couldn't join in with that and I felt quite guilty about it... And I think there's competitive grief that goes on as well. That's quite ugly, and I just couldn't feel a part of it.

The bereaved share a community of pain and sympathy that is quite palpable on occasion. But, as they grapple to understand and define their loss, they sometimes trace corrosive boundaries that set minority against minority. One bereaved mother had worked as a paediatric nurse in intensive care, and she had known parents who had lost their babies, but, she said, 'I felt so empty inside I couldn't feel for those parents, but I *can* feel for families who have lost children like myself... I know it might sound awful... they've never known life... I had eighteen years and they could say to me "I didn't have eighteen years". Yeah... So...?' It is as if the indefinable qualities of grief sometimes obstruct a fellow feeling with others, as if there must be a competitive championing of claims for the depths of one's own grief to be acknowledged, and, most importantly, as if the diffuse anger of grief continually seeks people to accuse and targets to attack in a dialectic of affirmation and repulsion (and those are matters to which I shall return more than once). So it is that the loss of a grandson may be defined as of less consequence than the loss of a son, or that of an adopted child less than that of natural children. Such a ranking, called by Jane Cooper a 'league table of pain', appears to be common enough in self-help groups for the bereaved.

Third, there is the sheer ugliness of violent death. Stabbing, strangulation, and hitting and kicking, the most common methods of killing, can maim the victim and leave behind hideous visual images.[112] A detective inspector remarked that 'most murders are not pretty. Looking at it from a sensible point of view, it's not what we want a loved one to have in their mind.' If it is part of the survivor's quest to cherish a memory of the dead, a quest I shall touch on below, the violence of murder and manslaughter is a gross attack on any tolerable meaning that can be bestowed. Survivors are

[112] ibid, 42.

prone to dreams and fantasies[113] about what might have happened, about the pain, terror, and feelings of helplessness that may have been endured, and about their own powerlessness to intervene.[114] Ann Robinson observed that 'Nightmares are perhaps a safety valve mechanism for our feelings. However, relatives of the victim may suffer from recurring nightmares which may express the victim's agony...'[115] And Pat Green wrote: 'Relatives who had not been present at the scene, torture themselves with vivid images of what the Victims' last moments must have been like.'[116] She was to say later: 'I have terrible thoughts from what Phillip looks like—terrible.' Matters can be worse still when no body has been recovered because the imagination will then be even less fettered.[117]

Contrast homicides with the ideal of a good death. A good death once had a peculiarly vivid iconography:[118] the dying person was supposed to be elderly and 'full of years'; lying in bed, after a noble struggle with pain or after no pain at all, surrounded by a grieving family whom he or she would address with solemnity, making a dignified composition with the past and the present; under solicitous medical and religious supervision; receiving the last sacraments and extreme unction; and making some final affirmation of faith in salvation;[119] before passing away in peace.[120] It was orderly rather than disorderly, 'natural' rather than 'unnatural'.[121] Robertson Davies's Samuel Marchbanks described it perfectly in anticipation:

[113] Quite common are nightmares about depredation and decay centred, for instance, on worms and rats. See, for example, the *Woking News and Mail*, 17 Nov 1994.

[114] Knapp remarks that 'We are seldom able...to conjure up images of children being murdered. It is difficult to comprehend this type of destructive act. In many respects the murder of any human being represents an act that is uniformly condemned by all. The violent and wanton destruction of the human body, particularly when it is a child, is often too gruesome for the mind to grasp...' *Beyond Endurance* (n 5 above), 85.

[115] 'The Effects of Murder on the Family/Relatives', mimeo, n.d.

[116] 'Breaking Negative Cycles', mimeo, n.d.

[117] See J. Littlewood, *Aspects of Grief* (n 102 above), 55–8.

[118] See P. Blauner, 'Death and Social Structure' (n 35 above), 392.

[119] See P. Jalland, *Death in the Victorian Family* (Oxford University Press, Oxford, 1997).

[120] This is based on P. Spierenburg, *The Spectacle of Suffering* (Cambridge University Press, Cambridge, 1984), 45–6.

[121] See M. Bradbury; 'Representations of "Good" and "Bad" Death among Death-workers and the Bereaved', in G. Howarth and P. Jupp (eds), *Contemporary Issues in the Sociology of Death, Dying and Disposal* (Macmillan, London, 1996), 85, 89.

My desire is to die in my own bed, leaning back on a heap of pillows, wearing a becoming dressing-gown and a skull-cap, blessing those of whom I approve, gently rebuking my enemies, giving legacies to faithful servants, and passing out clean handkerchiefs to the weepers; I should also like a small choir to do some really fine unaccompanied singing within earshot.[122]

Homicide is none of these things. It is unattractive, violent, disorganized, unrehearsed, and arbitrary, and it cannot possibly be represented as a 'good death'. It will take the form of a particularly bad death when the victim is a child. After all, childhood epitomises innocence, and the violent death of the young is taken to be a shocking and undeserved assault on the vulnerable and blameless. It is untimely, cutting short what might have been a fruitful life[123] whose possibilities can now only be projected in the imagination[124] (one mother exclaimed: 'Oh God! How unfair to be just robbed of your life like that! Robbed of your future, robbed, just totally robbed...!'). It is in violation of the natural order[125] and the proper succession of the generations, not at all in the fullness of a person's years, and an affront to the expectations that people should reasonably share about the structuring of their lives.[126] One does not expect to outlive one's child (Ann Robinson reflected that: 'It's so much harder to accept because it's such a wrong thing to happen. You have always expected your child to outlive you, and because murder is so obscene, so ugly, it turns your beliefs upside down.'). There is none of the conventional consolations accompanying the good death; one cannot say that a murdered child 'had a good innings', had a 'good end', 'wanted to go', or 'passed away peacefully'.

Fourth, violent, intentional death is linked inextricably with images of powerlessness—the powerlessness of the victim to resist, and the powerlessness of the bereaved to intervene at the time of the killing and to control events thereafter. David Renhard talked of

---

[122] 'My Desire is to Die', *The Table Talk of Samuel Marchbanks* (Clarke, Irwin, Toronto, 1949), 120–1.

[123] See RoadPeace, *Newsletter*, No 2, Spring 1994.

[124] See B. Raphael, *The Anatomy of Bereavement* (Hutchinson, London, 1984), 229.

[125] Or at least what has become the natural order, where, in the West, there has been a radical decline in infant mortality rates and the typical and normative-appropriate death has become that of an old person rather than that of a child. The age at which the death of an infant is mourned appears to have been steadily declining. See T. Walter, *The Revival of Death* (n 3 above), 51.

[126] See C. Murray-Parkes, *Bereavement* (n 12 above), 85.

'the feeling of helplessness of not being there to defend them'. The parent's power to protect the child has been challenged, often by one known to the parents, and there may be a fervent desire for retaliation.[127] 'Being a victim', said the husband of a murdered woman, 'is about having things taken out of your control.'[128] Pat Green wrote of how: 'Parents feel a deep sense of guilt that they had not done more to protect their child...'[129] And a mother said at a meeting of a Parents of Murdered Children chapter in California, 'we spent so much time in control, looking after our children, taking them to hospital. So totally responsible for so many years and then when this horror comes along we can't do anything.'

Having been willed and intentional, homicide could have been otherwise,[130] and the existential reality of the survivor is centrally bound up with pressing questions about how it could have been permitted, whether it could have been prevented,[131] and what it signifies about the workings of the moral and social order.

There are abundant reasons to pore anxiously over the circumstances of the death and wonder quite what would have happened 'if only' the survivor had done more or known more.[132] The survivor may well dream of undoing the past, forestalling the crime, and rescuing the victim.[133] 'Our "if onlys" come...flooding back in force...if only I hadn't agreed that the girls could stay', said one of the parents of Sophie Hook, a small girl murdered after she had been abducted from a tent.[134] Georgina Lee, the mother of a murdered eight year old, 'couldn't forgive myself for not being there...' And a Hungerford police officer whose father had been killed by Michael Ryan in the massacre of August 1987 reflected: 'There's been lots of people who've told me they feel guilty for one thing or

---

[127] See M. Peach and D. Klass, 'Special Issues in the Grief of Parents of Murdered Children' (n 37 above), 82.

[128] *Sunday Times*, 21 July 1996.

[129] 'Breaking Negative Cycles', MS, 1.

[130] Jane Cooper has reminded me that, in rather different manner, the same could be said of suicide, and suicide also poses grave problems for those who remain behind.

[131] See P. Whent, 'Murder in the Family', *Police Review*, 12 Jan 1990, 74.

[132] See, for example, I. Ivison, *Fiona's Story* (n 34 above), 76–7 and A. West, *For the love of Lesley* (n 92 above), 58, in which Lesley Ann Downey's brother repeatedly reproached himself for not having accompanied her to the fairground where she was abducted.

[133] See E. Rynearson, 'Bereavement After Homicide' (n 90 above), 1453.

[134] *The Times*, 20 July 1996.

another. They feel that perhaps they could have done . . . People said to me "If I'd had a shotgun perhaps I could have gone out and shot Michael Ryan". I've met many police officers who did their best but feel guilty for some reason. So many people come out with this feeling guilty.'[135] All those matters will be at the core of the next chapter.

That loss of control, the inability to intervene, amplifies feelings of self-blame and guilt. The leader of the Californian Golden Gate chapter of Parents of Murdered Children said at a meeting of the group, 'We all play the stupid game of "what if?" . . . if, if, if—and you start feeling guilty yourself . . .' It is indeed but a short remove to guilt, the guilt of the survivors that they have lived and that the dead have not, and the guilt and, indeed, self-hatred,[136] about all the things that might have been done better when the dead were alive.[137]

Conclusion

There is a tension between the content and forms of grief. I have observed that, for the most part, major grief tends to be sensed as personal, intense, overpowering, inchoate, and incommunicable.[138] It is a confusing experience for which there are only meagre scripts, an experience which swamps the etiquette of everyday life, and social estrangement can follow. A grieving father of a murdered son recollected the inadequacy of talk in conversations with his wife: 'we found that . . . trying to discuss it and trying to make decisions on our future and what was going to happen, what we were going to do . . . we found almost impossible. Either one of us, or both of us, would break down and we would fall out. We would shout at each other.'

Yet it is also clear that there *are* a few conventions which are used to impose a discursive form upon grief and bring it into the public

---

[135] *Hungerford Ten Years On*, BBC2, 19 Aug 1997.

[136] See R. Knapp, *Beyond Endurance* (n 5 above), 102.

[137] See G. Getzel and R. Masters, 'Serving Families who Survive Homicide Victims' (n 6 above), 143.

[138] Merleau-Ponty would say that one cannot translate such emotions into speech: 'There is . . . an opaqueness to language. Nowhere does it stop and leave a place for pure meaning; it is always limited by only by more language, and meaning appears within it only set in a context of words.' *Signs* (Northwestern University Press, Evanston, 1964), 42.

realm: there are the greater collective ceremonies of the funeral and memorial service with their special language and rites, and there are the lesser vernacular rituals of poems, shrines, pilgrimages, photographs, flowers, and candles whose local expression within the community of the survivors' groups I shall discuss in Chapter 4. Survivors have laboured hard to find ways of making their feelings more objective, visible, external, communal, impressive, and intelligible. Indeed, the very existence of their groups is part proof of those labours.

Perversely, too, the very incoherence and namelessness of the feelings constituting grief can give rise to manifest and recognisable similarities of experience.[139] Littlewood, for instance, wrote about grieving as 'a process which is universally associated with pain, confusion and distress'.[140] I shall show that it is a claim made by members of survivors' groups that they can immediately distinguish the outward signs of those who have suffered as they have done.

Above all, the development of bereavement after homicide is lent form by external processes, and it is those processes and their consequences which I shall consider in the next chapter.

[139] See J. Green and M. Green, *Dealing with Death* (Chapman and Hall, London, 1992), 124.
[140] J. Littlewood, *Aspects of Grief: Bereavement in Adult Life* (Tavistock/Routledge, London, 1992), 40.

3

Bereavement as a Career

Introduction

'Normal' grief has been held by some to have a natural history, a series of linked stages through which the bereaved will pass as they become restored and return to the everyday world, having successfully disengaged from the deceased.[1] The prototypical descriptive scheme, an extrapolation of ideas about traumatic maternal deprivation, was developed around three phases by Bowlby in 1961,[2] but it was later amended to include one other phase that was supposed to unfold at the very beginning. In its latter version, Bowlby proposed that the loss of a close relative will trigger a patterned sequence of responses, starting with a numbness which may be 'interrupted by outbursts of extremely intense distress and/or anger'; leading to 'yearning and searching for the lost figure'; a phase of disorganization and despair and culminating in a phase of reorganization.[3] That language of numbness, yearning, and reoganization may be recognised repeatedly in the schemes that followed.

One of the earlier and most commonly cited models, a model that came to influence Bowlby's own revisions to his first scheme, was developed in Colin Murray-Parkes's study of widowhood. It envisaged a succession of 'clinical pictures', beginning with numbness, and moving through pining, searching, and depression to eventual recovery.[4]

---

[1] See P. Silverman and D. Klass, 'Introduction: What's the Problem?' in D. Klass, P. Silverman and S. Nickman, *Continuing Bonds: new understandings of grief* (Taylor and Francis, London, 1997), 4.

[2] Bowlby was certainly not the first to map the natural history of grief. Earlier still, for example, was E. Lindemann, 'Symptomatology and Management of Acute Grief', *American Journal of Psychiatry*, 1944, Vol 101, 141–8.

[3] J. Bowlby, *Attachment and Loss, Volume III, Loss: Sadness and Depression* (Penguin Books, Harmondsworth, 1981), 85.

[4] C. Murray-Parkes, *Bereavement; Studies of Grief in Adult Life* (Tavistock, London, 1972), 7.

Influential too in depicting grieving as an orderly process was Elizabeth Kübler-Ross, although she wrote less about survivors than about the dying as they tried to cope with their own impending end. Kübler-Ross's subjects would advance from stages centred on shock and denial, rage and anger, and bargaining with God to a final acceptance of their impending demise.[5] Her's may have been principally a depiction of the dying, but it has also been adapted to capture the responses of the bereaved themselves.

Such models have become existential guides for the bereaved and diagnostic templates for those who minister to them professionally.[6] Perhaps their chief role has been to impose a semblance of intellectual order on disorder, allowing bereavement to be better described and managed.[7] But they have also acquired a prescriptive and inspirational aspect,[8] not only describing what appears to be the case, but being championed as a therapeutic guide to be followed lest the bereaved remain unhealed. It is as if those who do not graduate through all the steps must be aberrant.[9] David Renhard of The Compassionate Friends reflected that, 'if you're not careful you can start talking about stages of development, which is alright in theory—it gives you a framework you can judge things against, I suppose. But if somebody isn't going through those stages in the same order or the same speed, they begin to think there's something wrong with them, which doesn't follow.' Colin Murray-Parkes was himself circumspect about the scope and utility of such schemes: 'I don't find the stages of grief very useful,' he said to me in 1995, 'they are a model which has some value but which can easily be misused.'

It should be noted that the precept that there can be a finish to grief is a subject of some ambivalence amongst homicide survivors. It is resisted by many, but not all, active members of the new

---

[5] E. Kübler-Ross, *Living with Death and Dying* (Collier Books, New York, 1981), 42.

[6] See, for example, A. Faulkner, 'Developments in Bereavement Services', in D. Clark (ed), *The Future for Palliative Care* (Open University Press, Milton Keynes, 1993); and J. Worden, *Grief Counselling and Grief Therapy* (Routledge, London, 1992).

[7] See J. Gubrium, 'Structuring and destructuring the course of illness', *Sociology of Health and Illness*, Mar 1987, Vol 9, No 1.

[8] See T. Walter, *The Revival of Death* (Routledge, London, 1994), 71.

[9] Silverman and Klass observed that: 'In this view, maintaining an ongoing attachment to the deceased was considered symptomatic of pathology. Indeed, pathology was defined in terms of sustaining a relationship to the dead.' 'What's the Problem?' (n 1 above), 5.

organizations. Those who are loath to accept the idea of a finish would claim that support groups are not chiefly devoted to easing people through crisis but to supporting them in what is held to be a permanently bereft state. To suggest otherwise, to impose an alien developmental programme that proposes that one should 'move on' or 'get over it', is very often taken not only to belittle the scale of their grief and invalidate their very special identity as deep mourners,[10] but also to betray the dead for whom they grieve.[11] Hass would say that the need to retain a memory prevents closure.[12]

There can be marked resentments when acquaintances appear to expect survivors to change, recover and resume their 'normal' lives. A man who had lost his daughter said at a local meeting of SAMM: 'They're embarrassed. They don't know what to say. Some are alright—close friends are—but even they think we should have pulled ourselves together after six months or so.' Colin Caffell, one time member of SAMM, wrote of how 'the pain actually got worse as the state of shock began to wear off. This was further exacerbated by the fact that certain well-meaning but insensitive people, who thought there was some kind of time limit on grief, told me that I ought to be getting over it now and that I should pull myself together.'[13] Diana Lamplugh, co-founder of the Lamplugh Trust, whose daughter Suzy, working for a firm of estate agents, had been murdered by a stranger who had initiated a bogus house viewing, said at a memorial service for the victims of homicide held on 9 December 1995, 'it's been a very long journey and it's a

---

[10] The American National Organization of Parents of Murdered Children, the largest in that country, stated that 'Grief has been described as: "an emotion that heals itself: or "the process that allows us to let go of that which was and be ready for that which is to come..." But for those of us who have experienced the death of someone we love by murder, the trauma experienced lasts a lifetime.' Leaflet for 'The Courage to Grieve: A Weekend of Hope and Healing', n.d., POMC, Cincinnati, Ohio.

[11] Of course, those who *do* fall away are no longer active and cannot be heard.

[12] A. Hass, *The Aftermath: Living with the Holocaust* (Cambridge University Press, Cambridge, 1995), 46. Jane Cooper, the first co-ordinator of SAMM, found it a comfort to herself and others to quote one of Dietrich Bonhoeffer's letters from prison that concluded: 'the dearer and richer our memories, the more difficult the separation. But gratitude converts the pangs of memory into a tranquil joy. The beauties of the past are not endured as a thorn in the flesh, but as a gift precious for its own sake. We must not wallow in our memories or surrender to them, just as we don't gaze all the time at a valuable present, but get it out from time to time, and for the rest hide it away as a treasure we know is there all the time. Treated in this way, the past can give us lasting joy and inspiration.'

[13] *In Search of the Rainbow's End* (Coronet Books, London, 1994), 161.

journey without a chance of cure.' There are special resentments that people will continually scrutinise survivors for signs of recovery: 'you think, "well, I better not put that lipstick on tomorrow because they'll think I'm over it"...You know...you're being judged by other people.' And the leader of the Golden Gate chapter of the American Parents of Murdered Children told the members of her group, 'there is in America this rush toward happy endings. When they ask you how you are, don't say "I'm fine". You're not.'

On the other hand, it is easy enough to slip into a language of stages, 'milestones', and movement for want of any alternative, even if there is no full-blown commitment to all its implications. And some homicide survivors have endorsed their own and others' developmental models.[14] For example, the American organization, Parents of Murdered Children, furnished its own description of a four-stage mourning process,[15] beginning with shock and numbness, proceeding to searching and yearning, then to disorientation, and terminating in re-organization;[16] and its lesser, sister organization, the Californian group, Justice for Murder Victims, adopted a ten stage model that evolved from shock through emotion, depression and isolation, physical symptoms, panic, guilt, anger and resentment, and resistance to hope and the 'affirmation of reality.'[17] In England, the Home Office's own *Information for Families of Homicide Victims*, prepared with the collaboration of Victim Support, SAMM, and Justice for Victims, also talked expressly of stages of recovery.[18] Rather differently, Bereaved Families of Ontario

[14] For example, Colin Caffell, once an energetic member of SAMM, became impressed by the ideas of Elizabeth Kübler-Ross, trained under her, and attempted to disseminate her methods himself. See his *In Search of the Rainbow's End* (n 13 above), 22, 186. Similarly Greg Stokes, again of SAMM, cites Colin Murray-Parkes and Elizabeth Kübler-Ross with approval: G. Stokes, *A Witness for Peace* (The Kates Hill Press, 1994), 149.

[15] The American POMC's parent organization, the American group, Compassionate Friends, have devised their own language of stages, beginning with 'newly bereaved', and then passing through 'into their grief', 'well along in their grief', and cuminating uncertainly in 'resolved as much as it will be'. See D. Klass, 'The Deceased Child in the Psychic and Social Worlds of Bereaved Parents During the Resolution of Grief', in D. Klass *et al, Continuing Bonds* (n 1 above).

[16] Source, 'People who Care', Victims of Violence, Ontario, Canada, nd.

[17] 'Grieving: The Ten Stages of Grief', Justice for Murder Victims, San Francisco, Calif, nd.

[18] 'Coping when someone close has been killed', (Home Office, London, 1995), 4. I shall discuss the history of the working party that compiled the information pack below.

offers a series of twelve-week programmes which are intended to steer the bereaved through a succession of critical issues, from the dying and death of a child through guilt and anger and spirituality to 'saying "goodbye" (group termination).'[19]

The matter of progression is of consequence because it goes to the very heart of what a survivor *is*, whether his or her status is liminal, in motion towards a return to the commonplace world, or forever doomed to apartness and grief.

Bereavement after homicide certainly does undergo movement of a sort. People change, if only because they have change forced upon them. They are unlikely to remain shocked and disbelieving forever; their depression and isolation may come to an end; they may lose their jobs; their partners may die or leave; they may divorce and re-marry; and their remaining children will grow up and leave. Even if those changes do not conform to a strict model of recovery, they will undoubtedly amount to a rough process of becoming.

Bereavement and the criminal justice system

But what is more important still is the special, orderly, institutionally-imposed change that most homicide survivors will experience. If a definition of a career is that it is 'a series of related and definable stages or phases of a given sphere of activity that a person goes through on the way to a more or less definite end-point...'[20] or 'a sequence of steps, of changes in the individual's behavior and perspectives,'[21] it is the fifth distinctive feature of bereavement after homicide that it acquires a clear, career-like organization from without. Ann Robinson reflected that 'when it's a murder...it is prolonged and protracted by outside influences.'[22]

Careers after traumatic bereavement have a dual aspect. There is not only the natural history of the psycho-social career of the relatives and friends of the victim but also the career imposed by the passage of the fixed stages of the criminal justice system. The two intersect, the psycho-social developing as survivors are

[19] See S. Fleming and L. Balmer, 'Social Support for Survivors', in L. DeSpelder and A. Strickland (eds) *The Path Ahead* (Mayfield, Mountain View, Calif, 1995).
[20] J. Roth, *Timetables* (Bobbs-Merrill, Indianapolis, 1963), p. xviii.
[21] H. Becker, 'Kinds of Deviance', in *Outsiders* (Free Press, New York, 1963), 23.
[22] 'All Things Considered', BBC Radio Wales, 13 Dec 1987.

propelled through a series of transitions that are tightly harnessed to institutional processes in and about the criminal justice system.[23]

A problematic death will pass through several sets of hands before it comes before the courts as a criminal homicide, and each stage will prepare an attendant experience for the family and friends of the deceased, transform grief into public property, and lay the foundation of an enforced career. A survivor said at a meeting of SAMM Merseyside: 'we're victimised first by the crime and then victimised again and again and again afterwards.' And Ann Robinson wrote:

When a child is murdered, the stages of mourning are complicated and often prolonged by intrusions into the parent's grief. The news media, Police, the seemingly endless questions, legal problems, the traumas of the trial . . . all combine to intensify and protract grief. A murder is an ongoing event . . . [24]

Let me consider some illustrative examples of those stages,[25] relying heavily on statistics for one pivotal year, 1986. I have hit upon that year because it was at that time that the politics and practices of responses to homicide began to change, and their history can be better told by moving back to the state of affairs as it was near the beginning. In 1986, Victim Support was coming to move towards a greater involvement with violent crime, and with homicide in particular. Sponsored by Victim Support, the Crown Court Witness Service was about to be founded (I shall discuss that service briefly in Chapter 6). It was about that time, too, that a number of the principals in the history of Parents of Murdered Children and SAMM were beginning to be thrust into political and practical activity centred on the survivor. Thus, the second co-ordinator of Parents of Murdered Children, Jill Palm; the first Chairman of SAMM, David Howden; and Frank Green, the second Chairman

---

[23] See American Psychological Association Task Force on the Victims of Crime and Violence; *Final Report*, 57; A. Amick-McMullan *et al*, 'Family Survivors of Homicide Victims: A Behavioral Analysis', *The Behavior Therapist*, 1989, Vol 12, No 4, 75.

[24] 'When a Child is Murdered', Parents of Murdered Children Group, The Compassionate Friends, Bristol, mimeo, n.d.

[25] I wish merely to convey an impression of the structuring of the career rather than supply a comprehensive list and description of every stage, because an understanding of that structure is a prerequisite for grasping the organizational dynamics of survivors' groups. It is for that reason that I shall not touch on the funeral, and inmates' applications for home leave, release, and parole, for instance.

of SAMM, all lost relatives through homicide in that year. A number of the accounts of critical survivors thus refer to events that unfolded in and around the mid-1980s.

The police

Encounters with the police mark the first stage of that structured career, and they are compounded out of quite diverse and contradictory experiences. They may, for example, entail shock at the revelation of sudden death; a disturbing confrontation with moral ambiguity at a time of existential insecurity; an abrupt loss of control over domestic space and intimate relations; and, eventually, and in almost every instance, the extension of trust and gratitude.

Called to a suspicious death, the immediate task of the police is to freeze the scene and assume absolute control so that there can be no physical interference from anyone. Families are often dismayed by the fact that the victim may have to be left unattended and in a distressing condition for quite some time, perhaps ten hours or more, depending on the time of day and the availability of forensic experts. The victim has ceased to be a person who can be cared for and has become instead an exhibit that must be wrapped, insulated, and sequestered because, as a Detective Inspector remarked, 'an awful lot of evidence can [otherwise] be lost. There can be no access to the room or the body (and we don't know whether the family member is a suspect or not) lest forensic evidence is negated.' Pam Dix of Disaster Action commented, 'I now do a lot of work with the police, and of course at this point, that sense of the preservation of the scene of a potential crime is so important to them that it overrides other needs.'

The victim himself or herself will eventually be removed to be kept in a semi-frozen condition until the post-mortem examination, and it will be frozen thereafter, being thawed from time to time as people are permitted to view it.

Circumstances will differ between homicide and homicide, but there is always a reasonable expectation at the outset that, where there is a family, it will be one of its members who will have been responsible for the killing of a child or a woman.[26] Moreover, the

---

[26] See The *Sunday Times*, 21 July 1996, and A. West, *For the Love of Lesley* (Warner, London, 1993), 46, 51.

police methodology of case construction[27] would not implausibly have it that the making of fervid protestations of innocence are no guide to the truth—that is precisely the kind of behaviour which a guilty person would be expected to deploy.[28] The very father, sister, or partner who makes an impassioned, tearful appeal at a press conference for information which could lead to the arrest of a killer may turn out to be that self-same killer himself or herself.[29] Whatever may be said at first, however energetically denials are made, there is a strong presumption that a close relative must have been complicit in the death.[30] The police are trained professionally to be suspicious of the outsider and the outsider's utterances. Their's, after all, is a jaundiced occupation which keeps civilians at bay.[31] I was told by a detective that he had at all times to keep his 'distance and perspective' because he 'needed a clear head about who might be the offender'.

It is a consequence that, just at the time that a family is trying to assimilate the unassimilable, they may find themselves under suspicion, stripped of control, kept at a distance, and subject to repeated, intense, and often aggressive interrogation. A father later cleared of involvement in the murder of his family said; 'The police tell you straight away that in family-type murders 90 per cent of times it's another family member that's done it. So instantly I was a prime suspect which added very much to the pressures on me.'[32] The co-founder of the Californian group, Citizens Against Homicide, remarked:

As it turns out, over 95 per cent of the perpetrators are family members or family friends, but that concept is so foreign to an individual like [the other

---

[27] See M. McConville et al, The Case for the Prosecution (Routledge, London, 1991).

[28] Indeed, it may well be the member of the family who makes the most impassioned plea for information about a killer who is the one later arrested for murder. See, for instance, the report of the arrest of the wife and daughter of Richard Watson: The Times, 18 July 1997.

[29] At the end of Sept 1997, one television documentary made the claim that there were at least four cases pending where the family member who had made the appeal at a press conference was awaiting trial for murder (Cry Murder, Channel 5 Television, 28 Sept 1997).

[30] A police officer observed 'I've had many cases where it's been a family affair and they've never said a word or concocted a story between them.'

[31] See R. Reiner, The Politics of the Police (Wheatsheaf, Hemel Hempstead, 1992).

[32] The Times, 11 Jan 1997.

co-founder] or myself, that anyone could even conceive of the fact that we were capable of committing homicide, so you have that first barrier goes up, after the detectives talk to you for a while.... Finally, the penetration through all the grief and the anguish and the emotion, you look at this man and you say 'are you suggesting that maybe I've had something to do with this!?' And so there's an inbred hostility. Instead of working closely with this man, you're indignant, you're hurt, you're angry. I kicked a detective out of my house. I told him to leave....I said 'get out. I'm not talking to you anymore'. I mean the thought! The fact that he could even think I could have killed this lady!

Although they might be avid for information that could explain what has befallen them, the family may be told very little at first for fear that they are themselves implicated.[33] They may be segregated so that what each reveals and is told under questioning cannot contaminate the testimony of the others. They will be permitted no contact with the victim or the crime scene for fear that evidence will be spoilt. A police officer said, 'no one who is possibly a suspect will be allowed near the body. Many people will want to touch the body, particularly if it's a child. They'll want to touch the body, pick it up, cuddle it, but that we won't permit.'

At a point of extraordinary vulnerability, moreover, the family may discover discreditable or puzzling things about each other and the victim that will compromise their ability to understand and make moral judgements.[34] A police officer remarked, 'we're going to have to ask a lot of intimate questions. We often deal with individuals and find they're leading a double life, so we really have to go into it. We have to dig and dig and dig. And they learn things they've never realised about their family.' After all, a significant proportion of homicides (and particularly those committed in public) take place in and about groups bearing Wolfgang and Ferracuti's subculture of violence, groups where the moral boundaries between victim and offender, good and evil, are often hazy. So it was that many of the more activist survivors, the survivors who were the more energetically engaged in the new politics of victims, had had to contend with disquieting moral ambiguities at the very time they were confronting the calamitous news about their loss, and the

[33] See oral evidence given by Helen Reeves to the House of Lords Select Committe on Murder and Life Imprisonment, 5 June 1989.

[34] The most discreditable and shocking news, of course, is precisely that a close relative is the killer. See Colin Caffell's remarks on his discovery that his step-brother had killed his wife and children. *Daily Telegraph*, 14 Sept 1995.

extraordinary existential difficulties which they faced may have driven them to extraordinary compensating feats of organization. Pat Green, a woman active in SAMM, discovered that her son had been killed at a rendezvous where he had hoped to buy drugs: 'I didn't know my son was taking cannabis—and I feel guilty because I didn't realise.'[35] In identical fashion, Valerie Richards, the founder of the Californian group Families and Friends of Murder Victims, lost her son who was murdered when he was 'set up and robbed' in a bogus drugs buy. Irene Ivison, another person active in SAMM and Victim's Voice, learned that Fiona, her adolescent daughter, had been killed by a client in her very first days as a streetwalker.[36] She was reported to have said: 'I strongly resent Fiona being called a call girl, vice girl or a hooker. She was a child victim of exploitation as far as I am concerned.'[37] And yet another woman wrote to SAMM to tell of her distress when she learned that her son had been killed whilst engaged in burglary. A review of the preliminary findings of Victim Support's Families of Murder Victims Research Project observed that: 'The police role in direct support [is] often complicated by their need to closely question the family.'[38] At the very time when matters should be at their least equivocal, then, they can suddenly attain a moral complexity which is difficult to master.

The initial stage of police suspicion is likely to be short-lived, culminating in an arrest inside or outside the family. Remember that most homicides are not only cleared up, but cleared up very rapidly in England and Wales. If an outsider has been apprehended (and it *will* almost invariably be an outsider where activist survivors are to be found) police mistrust of the family will probably dissipate quite quickly.

Following a recommendation of Victim Support's *Families of Murder Victims Project* report of 1990, it has become conventional to appoint a family liaison officer to maintain contact every week or so for perhaps a year (trials tend to be listed in the Crown Court on or about the first anniversary of the homicide). The family may then find themselves becoming, in effect, the confidants of the police,[39]

---

[35] See *Liverpool Echo*, 24 Aug 1994.

[36] See I. Ivison, *Fiona's Story: A Tragedy of Our Times* (Virago, London, 1997), 3.

[37] *Sunday Times*, 29 Dec 1996.

[38] Note of Jan 1989.

[39] Irene Ivison wrote that one of the officers who broke the news of her daughter's murder became a 'family friend'. See I. Ivison, *Fiona's Story* (n 36 above), 217.

offered news about information as it emerges, being told if no new information is to be had, and being steered through a number of the stages that succeed murder, viewing the victim, the inquest and *post mortem*, funeral, and press conference. Murder is one of the most pressing and demanding of crimes for the police, and it is the subject of intense media interest. There can be no greater distress displayed than that of those who are left behind; police and survivors are likely to meet often and at length, and their relations can become close indeed. They are, after all, effectively allied together in what may seem to be a stark moral conflict and in the execution of what is the most 'real' of 'real' police work.[40] What started in detachment can then evolve into intimacy, particularly when there is a death of a child, a death that is likely to outflank professional cynicism, and the officer will become a mentor who steers the family through some of the hazards ahead. One such officer, attached to the family of Richard Everitt, who was murdererd in Somers Town in 1995, was reported to have said: 'I defy any family liaison officer to say they haven't felt emotional at some point.... You have to be a human being.'[41] (That intimacy may well seem too close to some senior officers. Peter Whent, formerly Detective Chief Superintendent in the Essex Police, who was to become closely involved with the development of formal responses to the aftermath of homicide, said: 'I have the view which is alien to most other senior investigating officers, of putting in a victim support worker within 24 hours. Now, that is alien because they don't want to do that. There's a number of dangers if you don't do that. You end up with there being too much of a bond between the family and a police officer, and one difficulty in that is when I want to extract the police officer... The family want him to stay because they've got a bond.')

All but a few survivors spoke with praise of the police officers in their case. Their hunger for information, their alienation, disorientation, loss of control, and helplessness, induced such a need—and the need was answered in such a way—that the police came to be awarded a special standing.[42] The police, as Jane Cooper has

[40] See M. Punch, *Policing the Inner City* (Macmillan, London, 1979), 114.

[41] In R. Cowen, 'The man who helped a couple cope with murder', *Hampstead and Highgate Express*, 26 Sept 1997.

[42] To be sure, close links between the police and survivors were not always to be found. One obvious deviation was that of the relations between the police and the survivors of people who had died in custody. See M. Ryan, *Inquest* (UCL Press, London, forthcoming).

reminded me, represent order in a disordered world. Even the activist Justice for Victims had no complaints about the police. At a meeting with Victim Support, they were quite emphatic that: 'We have absolutely NO criticism of the police, they do a wonderful job under adverse conditions.'[43] The word survivors used repeatedly was 'exceptional'. Typical was a Suffolk couple who reported that 'the police have been exceptionally good to us, and they kept us informed at all times'. After all, homicides and sudden deaths[44] are extraordinary events for the police too, and they elicited an extraordinary response. Officers were even reported sometimes to have attended trials or funerals when they were off-duty and not formally obliged to do so. Take the Glasgow police who had been assigned to the Watsons, founders of Families of Murdered Children. They were said to have been 'excellent': 'even after the trial [we thought] "that's it, it's over and done with". But he was different. He used to come up and send flowers up. He was great. . . . In our case, they were excellent.'

Victim Support

Victim Support, formerly the National Association of Victims Support Schemes, is the prime voluntary organization for victims in England and Wales[45] and it is inevitable that it came to play a major part in the evolution of homicide survivors' groups. I shall explore the history of the somewhat tangled and variable political relations between survivors, survivors' groups, and Victim Support in its own separate chapter, Chapter 6, and in other chapters thereafter, but the part played by Victim Support volunteers in the career of the individual survivor does warrant preliminary attention here.

Victim Support volunteers are held symbolically to represent the community in a society whose indifference to the victim can increase alienation and hurt. Their main function is to listen to the victim and so alleviate distress and personify compassion, but they

---

[43] Minutes of meeting held at Victim Support, 16 May 1994. Capital letters in original.

[44] Margaret Mitchell estimated that, on average, police officers could be expected to be exposed to sudden deaths only once or twice a year. 'Police Coping with Death', in G. Howarth and P. Jupp (eds), *Contemporary Issues in the Sociology of Death, Dying and Disposal* (Macmillan, London, 1996), 139.

[45] I traced its history and work in detail in *Helping Victims of Crime: The Home Office and the Rise of Victim Support in England and Wales* (Clarendon Press, Oxford, 1990).

also undertake practical work by arranging repairs to homes in the aftermath of burglary or malicious damage, mobilising wider professional help, assisting in the submission of insurance and compensation claims, and explaining what might still lie ahead. They seek chiefly to ease victims out of the victim role instead of confirming them in it, and the model encounter is 'short-term crisis intervention' rather than a sustained relationship which might freeze the victims' identity and create dependency.

Referrals of victims, long an issue in the work of Victim Support, stem almost entirely from the police, and one of the main preoccupations of its National Office has been to secure 'credibility' with the police. 'Automatic referrals' were at last won in the mid-1980s, the police no longer pre-selecting which names would be transmitted to schemes, and the character of the victims seen by volunteers began to change. What had begun with the brief and avowedly non-professional support of burglary, theft, and robbery victims then moved increasingly towards the quasi-professional and prolonged support of the direct and indirect victims of racial harassment, rape, domestic violence, and homicide (those last three groups being composed of people who were referred only with their express consent).[46] Victim Support observed in its annual report for 1987–8 that 'many more victims of violence are now being referred to Victim Support.... And it is all the more essential for us to acquire greater understanding of their needs and how best to meet them.'[47] By 1991, Victim Support began to assess the workload of its schemes by 'recording the length of contact with victims, as well as the number of cases referred'.

257,083 victims had been supported by some 7,000 victim support volunteers in 1986. The volunteers themselves were attached to 305 schemes across the country, each scheme being administered by a local co-ordinator and management committee, and the whole being subject to politic[48] control by the eleven permanent staff of the National Office in London.[49]

[46] Anne Viney said: 'Throughout the organisation's history, local volunteers and staff in daily touch with victims of crime have wanted to go into new areas because victims have come to them wanting help.'

[47] *Victim Support Annual Report 1987/88* (Victim Support, London, 1988), 10.

[48] 'Politic' because Victim Support has always had to tread a diplomatic path between a rigorous enforcement of standards and promotion of 'credibility' with formal organizations in the criminal justice system, on the one hand, and, on the other, a deference to numerous schemes' strong sentiments of local independence.

[49] Constitutionally, Anne Viney has reminded me, the precise position is that the members of Victim Support elect the Council, who appoint the national staff through

26,857, or 10 per cent, of those referrals, were the primary or secondary victims of violent and sexual crimes, and it was a proportion that was increasing rapidly, in part, because the new system of 'automatic referral' had begun to feed all crimes unfiltered to the schemes. In 1984/5, only 50 murders had been referred, in 1985/6 the number was 76, and, in 1986/7, it was 152, or 23 per cent of the total notified to the police. Murder was becoming newly problematic in the work of the schemes, and a Working Party on Families of Murder Victims had been convened in that year to consider the needs of '"secondary" victims of homicide... much of the time available has been spent in pooling information from people drawn from a number of groups and agencies.'[50] The history and consequences of that Working Party will be traced in Chapter 6.

Victim support volunteers are supposed to make contact with victims within hours of the referral of a serious crime, and they come to represent an early and significant face of the public response to homicide. Appearing at a time of high confusion and emotion, it is perhaps inevitable that they should sometimes attract a correspondingly emotional response. Pat Green of SAMM Merseyside observed: 'they've got to be a very, very strong person to deal with families like us, because of the abuse we can give them.' It is inevitable too that some survivors might not always remember with the greatest clarity who visited them and what it was they did at first. After all, the consequences of trauma include confusion and a sense of dislocation. An article in an undated edition of the Stockport *Express Advertiser* reported a bereaved mother, Diane Allman, whose husband had been shot and killed by a 'madman': 'The first few weeks are a daze. Apparently I spoke to someone from Victim Support the next day and I still don't remember doing it....' And volunteers themselves averred that it was sometimes as if they were invisible, not knowing whether they should leave or remain, and, if they did elect to leave, whether they should return. The co-ordinator of a Crown Court Witness Service scheme recalled of a particularly anguished family of survivors, a family which later became prominent in the politics of homicide, that the volunteer 'was constantly

the Director, Helen Reeves. The Council agree the Code of Practice on behalf of the members. Staff are responsible for monitoring. Technically, this makes staff to some extent responsible for monitoring their own employers.

[50] *Seventh Annual Report 1986/7* (National Association of Victims Support Schemes, London, 1987), 34.

saying to me "I've tried and I talk but they treat me as though I'm hardly there". They were, for whatever reasons, and I wouldn't know, so hooked on the anger that anything else is not really relevant.' So it was that angry allegations and counter-allegations have very occasionally been traded in public about what precisely victim support volunteers did or did not do for particular homicide survivors in the immediate aftermath of sudden death. At stake is the survivors' keen sense of the kind of treatment they deserve, on the one hand, a sense that may underwrite claims that it is only professional counsellors or survivors who can properly tend survivors; and the reputation, competence and public credibility of Victim Support, on the other.

In Chapter 6, I shall describe how, in an early pilot project conducted in Essex under the auspices of the Families of Murder Victims Working Party in 1986–7, thirty homicide referrals were made to victim support schemes, and volunteers acted as intermediaries with the police, mortuary officials, coroners, funeral directors, and others, providing 'bridges between the families and the outside world'.[51] Support for the most part lasted a year, and the families themselves were reported to 'have been very appreciative of the volunteers' willingness and ability to provide help'.[52] Diane Allman of Stockport had herself continued:

Victim Support helped. They spoke to the children, kept them in another room while the police were here. Throughout all of this you're in limbo and just go along with your emotions. . . . Victim Support will always respond. I think they show experience of dealing with people in distressed states.

One inevitable effect at the beginning stemmed from the small numbers of homicides in England and Wales. Even after the provision of special training, victim support volunteers could not expect to have seen many survivors, and survivors would detect their inexperience. Ruth Fuller, a survivor who worked as a volunteer in the SAMM office, recalled that 'my victim support lady, I was her first murder case—she knocked on my door. . . She said "hello, my name's Erica, I'm from Victim Support. I don't quite know what I'm going to do. It's my first murder". And I said, "okay, it's mine too. Come in.". . . I was given so much by Victim Support, and some

---

[51] Families of Murder Victims Project; *Final Report* (Victim Support, London, 1990), 30.
[52] ibid, 32.

people say they hate them, but I was very lucky.' But Ron Rodgers of SAMM said of the volunteer who visited him, "I feel sorry for the poor lady but she didn't know where to start and it was quite apparent... the way, the initial contact and all the rest of it was wrong, shall we say... And we weren't discourteous to the lady, but we spent all our time sidelining and backing her off.'

In the main, Victim Support was said to have acquitted itself very well in supporting homicide survivors, but the aftermath of homicide is fraught and some have expressed strong resentments about victim support, flowing, it may be presumed, as much from their diffuse rage as from particular discontents with volunteers. I shall explore the activist survivors' conception of the moral world in fine detail in the next chapter, and I shall argue there that a fundamental organizing principle is supplied by a sense of balance: the balance between the resources devoted to the offender and those devoted to the victim and the victim's family, and the balance between the seriousness of the offence of homicide and the gravity of the formal response extended to it by the criminal justice system.

It was that idea of balance that led occasional angry survivors to claim what they identified as the allocation of an unpaid and 'amateur' volunteer to a secondary victim of homicide showed a want of gravity and proportion.[53] In effect, it was argued, it equated the sufferings of the survivor with those of the mere burglary victim, and the perceived slight could rankle. More, it was argued that the distinctiveness of bereavement after homicide creates an existential gulf between survivors and the mundane world. Those who are not themselves bereft by murder and manslaughter can neither understand nor aid those who are. Sandra Sullivan of Justice for Victims, whose daughter Katie had been killed by a mentally disordered offender, informed a Home Office minister and his officials, 'we told you we are an enigma—we are totally separate from any other crime—Victim Support is dealing with everything like Marks and Spencers [a chain of department stores], they sell everything—but we are not that type of crime—we are totally different, that's why there's nothing for us because they don't know.'[54]

---

[53] Of course, Victim Support would reply that their volunteers are anything but amateur, that they receive specialist training for homicide. But the angrier survivors do protest that they deserve something more that would register the scale of their loss. At bottom, the issue is almost certainly not pragmatic but symbolic.

[54] Report of Meeting held at Home Office, 20 Apr 1994.

Married to other strains in the survivors' world-view, the out-come has been a propensity for some of the survivors who joined the new organizations, but certainly not all, to carp at Victim Support and the victim support volunteer. Indeed, if a number of those who join the new organizations are people who failed to find adequate solace and support in their own immediate networks or the wider society, it may be presumed that they will have something of a disposition to find the volunteer wanting. There is an imbalance in those exchanges. Victim Support's strictures about the confident-iality of the victim–volunteer relationship make it very difficult to formulate a riposte, and the stories that enter the public domain may consequently be unqualified, allowed to circulate freely within the new groups.

A few of the new organizations actually seemed to be built around their dialectical opposition to Victim Support and the ser-vices it supplies in what Alvin Gouldner once called a 'conflictual validation' of identity. For example, David Hines, whose daughter Marie had been killed in June 1992, and who founded the small North of England Victim Association, was reported to have said that 'victims of crime are not being adequately cared for, either by counselling or by compensation. I know this from my own bitter experience, and I have set up the association to try and help vic-tims.... There is a vast amount of public money being spent but very little seems to go to those who need help. Crime victims may get a visit from a woolly-minded social worker [that is, a victim support volunteer] who is wet behind the ears and hasn't enough experience of life to help people with real problems.'[55] (To be sure, there was a much more positive article about Victim Support in a later issue of the *Shields Gazette*).

The inquest

There were 581,203 deaths from all causes in England and Wales in 1986. A police officer, doctor, or Registrar of Deaths confronting a sudden or unexpected death must report it to the Coroner,[56] who

[55] *Shields Gazette*, 23 July 1993.
[56] The Coroner is an an independent judicial officer with medical or legal training who is not formally part of the criminal justice system, and is independent of local and national government. The coroner's court is the one court in England and Wales that works on the inquisitorial model.

will order an inquest if its cause appears to be unknown, violent, or unnatural,[57] and 181,300 of these deaths were reported in that year. Where the Coroner is unable to ascertain the cause, or if the cause appears to be abnormal, an order may be given for the dead person's removal for independent post-mortem examination by an authorised pathologist. 142,900 post-mortem examinations were actually carried out (or 79 per cent of the deaths reported), 22,200 inquests were conducted, and 21,500 verdicts were returned.[58]

Where someone has been charged with an offence in relation to the death, the defence will also be allowed to commission an independent autopsy, and, where there is more than one defendant, each may separately order an autopsy. The defence have, in consequence, obtained what one Coroner described as an 'almost absolute right or veto of release of the body' and long delays can ensue.

The duty of the Coroner is to establish the identity of the deceased, and when, where, and how the death occurred. It is not to assign responsibility for the death—that is the task of the criminal courts. Neither is the Coroner formally part of the criminal justice system, although families may imagine otherwise, looking to the inquest to explain what happened and to allot blame.[59] The inquest is inquisitorial rather than accusatorial, and it is devoid of indictments, prosecution, defence, and all the other trappings of the adversarial system.

Where a death might be due to criminal homicide, the Coroner must send the papers to the Director of Public Prosecutions. There will be an inquest hearing where no one is eventually charged (and 135 verdicts of unlawful and one of lawful homicide were returned in 1986[60]). But, where a person has already been charged, the inquest will be formally adjourned, usually never to be resumed,

[57] In addition, deaths untreated by doctors; occurring during a medical operation; as a result of industrial injury or disease, violence, or neglect; or in prison or police custody must be reported to a Coroner.

[58] Most of the figures cited in this passage are taken from *Statistics of Deaths Reported to Coroners: England and Wales 1986* (Home Office, London, 1987).

[59] Parts of this section are based on G. Howarth, 'Death on the road: The role of the English coroner's court in the social construction of an accident', in M. Mitchell (ed), *The Aftermath of Road Accidents* (Routledge, London, 1997).

[60] To be sure, some of those verdicts would refer to deaths occurring in 1985 and some 1986 deaths would go to inquest in 1987. According to advice given by the responsible Home Office statistician, the discrepancy between the figures for homicides emanating from inquests and the police may be explained by the fact that the inquest will be adjourned indefinitely where there are to be criminal proceedings.

with a formal recording of the death by the Coroner for the death certificate, on the principle that no two tribunals should consider the same evidence for a death. 780 inquests were thus adjourned without resumption in 1986.

From the time of death, the deceased is legally the property of the Crown and its representative, the Coroner. For evidential and forensic reasons, there has to be a well-documented continuity of control, the body of the victim progressing directly from police supervision by ambulance or undertaker to the mortuary for autopsy, to cosmetic preparation[61] for formal identification by a person, usually a close male relative,[62] through a window in a special room where only the victim's face is made visible.

Others can later view the dead person for purposes of leave-taking, but as Glennys Howarth remarked, they are often advised to do so when the dead person is with the undertakers, 'as he will have "tidied-up" the body and applied "cosmetology"'. Initially, viewing can take place only at the discretion of the Coroner,[63] and they cannot then touch the dead person.[64] Indeed, survivors may well be advised not to see the dead person at all (for example because of the scale of disfigurement)—and they are easily enough deterred in their vulnerable state[65] (although those who do visit the mortuary

[61] Of course, there are limits to what can be done. A woman running a Victim Support course training volunteers in the support of homicide survivors, observed of facial scars arising from post-mortem examination that 'they do stitch them up but it's huge stitches like Frankenstein time.'

[62] Men, rather than women, are generally asked to view, tending to sustain the disbelief and redoubling the grief of women. See Family of Murder Victims Project; *Final Report*, 12.

[63] The families of the victims of PanAm flight 103 were not allowed to see the bodies, for instance. They reported that: 'The decision not to use visual identification . . . does not take into account the fears given to relatives by the fact that, as far as they could understand, visual identification was not physically possible; in addition, the undertakers took it upon themselves to advise against viewing the bodies. Again, this advice was dispensed as a policy, without any consideration of the different individual states of the bodies and the remains, or the essential element of choice that should be given to the bereaved, whatever the condition of the dead.' *Lockerbie Disaster: The Truth Must be Known*, Status report from UK Families Flight 103, Nov 1991, no place, 16. One survivor recalled, 'I decided I wanted to see my brother's body at the crematorium, whereby the undertaker said to me 'it's against crematorium regulations'. So I said 'alright then. The body's gone forever and that's the end of the matter'. And a few years later, I discovered that he was lying. He was doing that because he was protecting me.'

[64] Ann Robinson talked of her sadness that she had not kissed her son before his burial. See 'Murder in London', *Time Out*, 14–21 Jan 1987, 1.

[65] See C. Murray-Parkes, 'Psychiatric Problems following Bereavement', *British Journal of Psychiatry*, 1993, vol 162, 50.

invariably declare afterwards that they had no regrets). There may then be a tendency for fears to be excited about the dead person's condition.[66] Ann Robinson observed that 'Imagination is often worse than reality; seeing the body can be the first step towards acceptance . . .'[67] And the relative of a road crash victim wrote:

The interminable journey to the hospital mortuary. By then all trace of reality has vanished. You are in an emotional whirlpool, a bad dream, then trance and your senses are failing. You feel as if you're walking through a dark tunnel . . . What I want to stress is that the relative NEEDS to be allowed to do what he or she feels necessary. The moment when your worst fears are confirmed, that's when the grieving process should be allowed to begin . . . You need to be able to say 'goodbye' to your loved one, especially while they still appear as they always did. You will never get this chance again. What does it matter if you become disturbed or even hysterical—you've every right to be. If you are not allowed to do what you personally need to do, it may be the start of painful worries and doubts, things not done, words unsaid, nightmares and fears.[68]

Such an extended loss of ownership and control over the dead person constitutes one of the most potent symbolic assaults suffered by families in the wake of murder and manslaughter. After all, the dead person is almost all that physically remains of the victim (being quite literally 'the remains'); in ambiguous fashion, it still *is* the victim himself or herself; and what is done to it can stand for the regard which is paid to the victim and the seriousness with which his or her death is taken.[69] Even official talk about 'the body' can anger survivors:[70] a member of Justice for Victims remembered when her daughter had been so described by a policeman: 'I hit him. I said she has a name!' And Pat Green said, 'they talked about the way in

---

[66] See C. Murray-Parkes, 'Psychiatric Problems following Bereavement' (n 65 above), 12.

[67] A. Robinson; 'The Aftermath of Murder' (The Compassionate Friends, Bristol, 1987), 1.

[68] J. Lawrence, 'The Role of the Police at the Mortuary', *RoadPeace Newsletter*, Spring 1994, No 2, 5. Emphasis in original.

[69] Ann West recalls the search for her daughter: 'There was something obscene about the rubbish container being searched for Lesley's body. It defiled her in some way . . . Lesley was being treated as something that could be cast away, abandoned as useless, discarded.' A West, *For the Love of Lesley* (n 26 above), 50–51.

[70] See an article describing how Ann Virgin of Justice for Victims resented her partner being called 'the body'. The *Guardian*, 28 Dec 1995. It was for that reason that I have studiously used the words 'victim' or 'dead person' instead of 'body'.

which our children are regarded as the deceased; their bodies properties of the State. To us, they're our children. They have names!'

That loss of control can become a token of a wider loss of
influence over the deceased. It signifies that one can no longer care
properly for the victim, and not being allowed even to touch the him
or her will chafe.[71] It interferes with the capacity to arrange a
funeral, delaying matters perhaps for months[72] (the most frequent
lapse between death and funeral cited by survivors was 4–5
months). If the funeral is a caesura in time that emphatically
marks the physical departure of the victim,[73] its delay can prolong
the uneasy liminal state in which the victim is at once here and not-
here.[74] Joan Bacon of Justice for Victims said, 'what was a real
insight . . . was that the defence barristers or solicitors were holding
on to Martin. They took him away. He didn't belong to us any more
at that time. They insisted on a longer time and a longer time and it
was four and a half months before the funeral was held and to me
that is absolutely obscene.' Pat Green said of her son that: 'From the
moment Philip was killed, he ceased to belong to us. He became a
body of evidence; the property of the state. He had to be kept in a
mortuary for eight weeks and there were three post mortems carried
out on him. We had to spend Christmas, New Year and our eldest
son's 21st birthday with Philip lying in a morgue.'[75] To some
survivors, a London Coroner observed, 'I'm the devil incarnate.'

The law does not mention the secondary victims of homicide and
they have no rights at the inquest. They must be informed about an
inquest if they ask specifically to be told. It is to be expected that a
close relative or friend will be so informed because they will be
required legally to make a formal identification of the deceased. The
Coroner himself has complete 'discretion over which witnesses to
call and what evidence to call . . .'[76] In the main, and as a matter of
courtesy, a member of the family will be invited to speak about the

---

[71] See 'What Price Justice?', *Sunday Telegraph*, 25 Sept 1994.

[72] See the report on the Baldock family in the *Medway Times*, 3 Feb 1995.

[73] See C. Murray-Parkes, *Bereavement* (n 4 above), 65. David Renhard claimed
that recovery begins at the funeral ('The death of a child—the parent's point of view',
speaking notes).

[74] Yet, even so, in their alienated state, the funeral may seem to survivors to be a
distant event occurring to others. See B. and V. Chalk, 'What is murder?', *Parents of
Murdered Children Newsletter*, Autumn 1990, 4.

[75] *Liverpool Echo*, 24 Aug 1994.

[76] G. Peart, 'Death of a Child and the Legal System', mimeo, 1995, 4.

character of the dead, but, said one Coroner, 'you have to do it indirectly through the framework of the law as it exists. It has to get raised in the framework of the law.' That is, what is said must be relevant to the purpose at hand:[77] 'Bereaved parents quite naturally think that . . . purpose . . . is to answer their questions regarding their child's death. Regrettably, this is not so. The inquest is there purely to ascertain how the child died.'[78]

The trial

In England and Wales in 1986, 660 offences were initially recorded by the police as homicide. Of these, 94 were subsequently deemed not to be homicide, leaving 566 offences. No one was charged in 21 cases; 5 of the suspects died; and 46 committed suicide. Of the remaining 494 cases, there were 5 instances of proceedings being discontinued or not initiated; 27 suspects were acquitted at trial; 3 were found to be insane; 205 were decided at court to be guilty of murder; 82 of Section 2 manslaughter; 171 of 'other manslaughter'; and 1 of infanticide.[79] There were thus rather fewer than 10 trials for homicide every week, scattered amongst the competent Crown Court centres in England and Wales.

Survivors may have to wait for a year or more for a trial, and the trial will be expected by many to accomplish a diversity of tasks. It will be supposed to act as an instrument of justice and vindication; restore moral balance; provide a catharsis, symbolically acknowledging the magnitude of the harm that had been done; serve as a means of satisfying the vast appetite for information which drives survivors in their quest for understanding and control (Jill Palm said 'you know everything about your children's lives and you need to know everything about their deaths before you can accept it'); and provide one more, very late opportunity to appear on behalf of the dead, to speak for those who can no longer speak

---

[77] Specifically, 'An inquest is an enquiry which is held to establish the facts. The purpose of the inquest is to ascertain the identity of the deceased, when, where and how the death occurred, and to establish the particulars which have to be registered by the Registrar of Deaths. The inquest does not attempt to allocate responsibility for the death, as a trial would do.' 'The Work of the Coroner' (Home Office, London, 1984).

[78] G. Peart, 'Death of a Child and the Legal System', *Compassionate Friends Newsletter*, Summer 1995.

[79] Based on written answer to Parliamentary Question, 6 Dec 1994.

for themselves.[80] One mother said 'I need to be there, to represent my son and to try to share his last hours.'[81] I shall return in the next chapter to the importance which survivors attach to testifying on behalf of the dead.

Matters were otherwise in practice. The families of homicide victims have no legal or moral standing in the court unless they appear as witnesses. They are members of the public, with no right to be heard, and, in the mid-1980s, they were entitled to no expenses, and to no special space of their own in the courthouse or the courtroom[82] (the allocation of physical space has an exceptional meaning in that it defines who is an insider and who an outsider in the court's affairs[83]). They were almost never directly consulted about possible changes of charge or plea from murder to manslaughter,[84] a symbolically-laden decision because the word 'murder' has powerful resonances which 'manslaughter' lacks, and because plea-bargaining suggests that the fate of the victim has been haggled for reasons of expediency that belittle the crime and neglect the interests of the family. A member of PETAL (People Experiencing Trauma and Loss), a Scottish group, complained that: 'The system of plea bargaining is a nightmare as the prosecution and defence go into a little room together and work out an outcome you have no say in.'[85] Prosecution barristers would rarely speak to survivors (after all, counsel represented the Crown, not the victim, and certainly not the victim's family). There would be no Crown

[80] The bereaved are silenced in England and Wales. It is otherwise in parts of North America. Ronan Byrne of the San Francisco Court Victim/Witness Program observed that: 'I think it's cathartic and it's therapeutic for them to able to say, you know, "this is what it cost me. I had my wife or I had my child. I don't now. And when my child was alive, this is what this beautiful, wonderful person was, and I'm not going to have that anymore."'

[81] Quoted by Ann Robinson in 'The Aftermath of Murder' (n 67 above), 2.

[82] Although, after 1990, the Lord Chancellor did direct that members of the victim's family could sit in the well of the court at the judge's discretion.

[83] See P. Rock, *The Social World of an English Crown Court: Witness and Professionals in the Cross Court Centre at Wood Green* (Clarendon Press, Oxford, 1993), ch 6.

[84] At best, the police might be invited to consult the family but that would not always be feasible on the day of the trial itself, when so many changes of plea occur. Prosecuting authorities are nervous about appearing too partisan, of aligning themselves too closely to the victim and the victim's supporters (see my *Social World of an English Crown Court* (n 83 above), chs 4 and 5). A Chief Crown Prosecutor told me in connection with this book that 'we're very sympathetic to to the interests of victims and witnesses . . . but we tend to draw back from being too closely involved.'

[85] L. Tiernan, 'PETAL', *Motherwell People*, 7 July 1995.

Court witness service to support them until 1989 when the first
seven pilot projects were established.[86] Indeed, if they were to play
an active part and appear as witnesses, they would be excluded from
attending the bulk of the proceedings altogether for fear that their
own and others' evidence would be contaminated. Because defence
lawyers can have trepidations about the impact which the sight of
visibly distraught or angry relatives might have upon the jury,[87] they
may name relatives as witnesses, and so exclude them from the
proceedings and the public gallery, even though they may never
ultimately be called.[88]

It often became evident that the trial did not revolve around
the victim or the victim's family at all. Jill Palm recalled that
'Robert wasn't there. It was as though he was forgotten. The
whole thing was geared up for somebody else and Robert was
just an incidental.' The trial was not conducted in the name of the
victim but that of the defendant, as if the victim had been an-
athematised. Prosecutions were not brought in the victim's name
but in the name of the Crown: 'The Crown Prosecution service as an
independent prosecuting authority does not act on behalf of victims
or their families.'[89] Joan Bacon recalled: 'I said to the policeman
'where is Martin Bacon's trial?', and he said 'there's no Bacon here'.
And I said, 'his mother has been every day, the family has been every
day. I know I'm right'. And he said, 'it's not his trial, it's the person
that did it'.'

The one person who can never testify or make claims and
counter-claims about events and people is the victim and, in
phrasing their allegations, it is always possible for the defence to
define the victim in a way that most effectively services their case.
They are obliged, after all, to take instructions and convey the
defendant's account of what happened, and those accounts are
not only self-serving, but framed in the offender's own distinct

---

[86] For a general introduction to the history of the origins of the witness service,
and the particular history of one pilot project, see my *The Social World of an English
Crown Court* (n 83 above).

[87] See, for example, the report of the trial of Tracie Andrews, *The Times*, 17 July
1997.

[88] For a report of such a strategem being employed in a trial in the United
States, see J. Berendt, *Midnight in the Garden of Good and Evil* (Random House,
New York, 1994), 213. More generally, see NOVA, *Survivors of Homicide Victims*
(NOVA, Washington, Oct 1985), 3.

[89] Letter from official of Casework Standards Division, Crown Prosecution Service, to Brigitte Chaudhry of RoadPeace, 6 Dec 1993.

rhetoric of causality and purpose.[90] Unable to answer back, the victim can readily be depicted as morally grey or provocative, as one who had struck the first blow, a person against whom the killer was obliged to defend himself—in short, as one who had effectively brought about his or her own demise. In the making of mitigation pleas, above all, there is a constant blurring of causal and moral boundaries for pragmatic ends. So it was that Robert Palm and Diane Watson were represented as school bullies and Tessa Howden, daughter of David and Heather Howden, was said to have 'lived a double existence, having secret assignations with her murderer.'[91] I shall return to Diane Watson below.

If victims cannot be heard, survivors themselves certainly could not act on their behalf to correct what they may fervently believe to be a gross defamation of their public character.[92] What galls survivors is that no one is there to speak for the dead. Jayne Zito told the Home Office minister, David Maclean, 'victims should have a voice to represent the people who have died.'[93]

Slurs linger and obstruct subsequent attempts to reconstruct the past, and that, as I shall argue in the next chapter, is a significant problem indeed. A letter from a bereaved wife to SAMM recited how: 'We were treated like the criminals ourselves at the Old Bailey...My son of thirteen years was laughed and sneered at by the accused whilst entering the court....Every day I live with the fact my husband is dead, a good, kind, loving, not a violent man, as they portrayed him in court....' Ruth Fuller, too, said, 'he said my son provoked him, but Trevor wouldn't provoke anyone. He was a gentle soul...The whole thing still upsets me now, that is the worst—to talk about the hearing.'

Thrust, as many of them were, into the public spaces of the courthouse; obliged to queue with voyeurs, the tourist, the casual spectator, the press, and the defendant's 'supporters'

---

[90] Interestingly, in the case of assaults, victims and offenders will give very different accounts of angry encounters. Victims characteristically represent attacks on them as arbitrary and meaningless, whilst perpetrators depict them as meaningful and comprehensible. See R. Baumeister *et al*, 'Victim and Perpetrator Accounts of Interpersonal Conflict: Autobiographical Narratives about Anger', *Journal of Personality and Social Psychology*, Nov 1990, Vol 59, No 5, 994–1005.

[91] In E. Dunn, 'In Sorrow', *Telegraph Magazine*, n.d.

[92] See 'Murder in London' *Time Out*, 14–21 Jan 1987.

[93] Report of Meeting held at Home Office, 20 Apr 1994.

and family; seated indiscriminately with those selfsame voyeurs,[94] strangers, and supporters; listening to the casual comments of others in the public gallery; unable to demonstrate their emotions without reproofs and possible ejection from the court; unable to ask questions; unable to speak; starved of information when the trial is abandoned or not contested;[95] survivors were kept at a distance from the deliberations of the tribunal that affected them most closely. Ann Virgin of Justice for Victims observed at a meeting with Victim Support: 'We are not allowed to grieve, not allowed to cry or show any emotion but still have to listen to idle, stupid comments made by tourists in the public gallery. It is inhumane and completely unnatural to expect us to act like robots with no emotions.'[96]

Some survivors appeared to have been better treated than others. Much comfort could be had from a kindly victim support volunteer or police officer who accompanied them to court (one couple remembered that 'the police were very good—they took us to the courtroom prior to the trial; showed us the layout of the room...We'd got police with us the whole time just as support, and they were the same police that were with us from the word "go"'); or from a compassionate word (David Renhard recalled that the judge presiding over the trial of his daughter's murderer had called her an 'angel' in his summing-up, and that 'had helped a lot').

But other survivors lamented the scale of their physical and symbolic marginality.[97] Jill Palm said simply: 'I was excluded from the word "go".' And Kate Wilkinson, writing of the experiences of members of Justice for Victims, observed that: 'The proceedings seemed to conspire to make them invisible.'[98] Such survivors were, in the words of Victim Support's and Parents of Murdered Children's evidence to the Committee on the Penalty for Homicide, 'isolated, unacknowledged and uninformed.'

[94] See L. Johnston, 'Justice for Victims', *The Big Issue*, 20 Nov 1993.
[95] See P. Whent, 'Murder: The Police Investigation (2)', *Police Review*, 12 Jan 1990.
[96] Record of a Meeting held at Victim Support, 16 May 1994.
[97] See G. Getzel and R. Masters, 'Serving Families who Survive Homicide Victims', *Social Casework*, Mar 1984, Vol 65, No 3, 140; and 'Victim: Murder in the Family', *Sunday Times*, 21 July 1996.
[98] K. Wilkinson; 'No Entry: How the justice system shuts out victims' families', *agenda*, Dec 1994, 8.

It was as if the survivors had been forcibly evicted from their own tragedy, denied a part in the events that dwelt so publicly and centrally on their grief. Pat Green said that 'having spoken to the other members of the [SAMM] group, they all feel the same . . . It's like the barristers, you know: 'these trials and things have nothing to do with you'.'

The mass media

Shadowing the survivors was the Greek chorus of the mass media. They worked on the career in numerous ways, clamouring for responses and emphasizing benchmarks and anniversaries[99] at every turn; transforming private lives into public news; making the subjective visible and external; amplifying and articulating structure through their running narrative; translating and interpreting events; and continually conferring meaning. So vital were the mass media to this history, such was their effect on the shaping of the new organizations, that I shall return to them in another chapter. What I shall discuss here is the particular part they played in the career of the survivor.

The public salience of crime, violence, and death is proportionate to its extraordinary features, to its dramatic immediacy, sensationalism, sexual content, moral urgency, and 'human interest'.[100] It is hardly remarkable that murder and manslaughter should long have been a central preoccupation of the mass media. If only for a while, and particularly at the beginning, when a homicide has just been announced,[101] survivors can well be the subject of quite extraordinary attention. Jill Palm recalls the press 'banging on the door and shouting through the letter box'. Colin Caffell said that 'the

---

[99] And they did so even when survivors did not formally mark those anniversaries themselves, giving structure to events in ways which the survivors might not have desired. In the week beginning 18 Aug 1997, for instance, the press in Britain made much of the fact that the inhabitants of Hungerford did not propose to commemorate the tenth anniversary of the killing of 16 people and the wounding of 15 others by Michael Ryan.

[100] See T. Walter *et al*, 'Death in the News', *Sociology*, Nov 1995, Vol 29, No 4, 583; and J. Ditton and J. Duffy, 'Bias in the Newspaper Reporting of Crime News', *British Journal of Criminology*, Apr 1983, Vol 23, No 2.

[101] Indeed, the press may be the very agency which first announces the death. See A. Burgess, 'Family reaction to Homicide', *American Journal of Orthopsychiatry*, Apr 1975, Vol 45, No 3, 394.

doorbell never stopped ringing'.[102] The word most commonly employed to describe that onslaught was a 'siege'.[103] Reporters might lie in wait for hours, badger and lie to gain admission to homes, and steal objects such as photographs when they did enter. Survivors found that their sense of besetting chaos had been compounded by the unruliness of reporters and photographers.[104] David Renhard remembered that:

I couldn't believe it. They came inside my house and camped outside immediately after. A chap rang up from the local radio station wanting to know what I thought about hanging. You've just had your daughter murdered and he wants to know what you think about hanging! You become public property in a way you've never realised. You're not prepared for it at all . . . you're vulnerable because emotionally you're all twisted up anyway. I didn't realise how the press worked—you were literally hounded all the time.

Survivors can be distressed at seeing their emotions broadcast (and reporters are professionally attracted to displays of emotion).[105] They will be distressed at their loss of control over public representations of the crime, the victim, and themselves. They will have become objectified. At a memorial service, Diana Lamplugh said of her daughter, 'she became no longer our own. She was owned by the papers. We couldn't protect her and ourselves.'[106] They will be distressed at inaccuracies in reporting, inaccuracies which not only betoken a negligence in the public response to their plight, and deform public representations, but also advertise the scale of their own powerlessness to correct what is said so publicly.[107] They will be distressed at the moral ambiguities injected into what should not be ambiguous at all.

[102] See C. Caffell, *In Search of the Rainbow's End* (n 13 above), 80.

[103] See A. West, *For the love of Lesley* (n 26 above), 124.

[104] See *Families of Murder Victims Project Final Report*, 26.

[105] See A. Shearer, *Survivors and the Media* (Broadcasting Standards Council, London, 1991), 5.

[106] The Lamplughs had been particularly upset by an author who had been commissioned to write a biography of their daughter and who alleged that their daughter was promiscuous, lonely, and 'foul-mouthed'. See *the Guardian*, 15 Oct 1988.

[107] See, for example, 'Complaint from the [*sic*] Sir Michael Marshall, MP, on behalf of Mr and Mrs Squires—Adjudication' (The Broadcasting Complaints Commission, London, 1995). The complaint related to the dramatised re-enactment of the murder of Penny McAllister by her husband's mistress. The adjudication found that 'there was no public interest justification for showing the film. . . . [It] upheld

One very transparent instance of what survivors regard as the oppressive power of the press was the reporting of a Scottish murder that had taken place on 10 April 1991.[108] The September 1992 issue of the magazine *Marie Claire* published an article about British children serving life sentences, and it was written in criticism of what its author, Meg Henderson, took to be an insupportable anomaly in Scottish legislation. Children in other parts of the United Kingdom must be sentenced for a specified length of time, but it is otherwise in Scotland where they may be committed to custody 'without limit of time'.

The principals of the *Marie Claire* story were Barbara Glover ('Jean') and Diane Watson ('Donna'), the daughter of the couple who were later to become founders of Families of Murder Victims in Scotland, and it had been based solely on the victim-blaming allegations made by Glover after her conviction and in interview with Henderson in a secure unit.[109] The features editor of *Marie Claire* nevertheless told the Watsons' solicitor that the report 'was in fact based on what was stated in court. We are quite happy to put your clients' point of view, but in view of the case before the court, it is not for us to appear to accept that your clients' version was more accurate . . . The manner in which your clients' daughter was alleged to have behaved towards Barbara Glover, formed the back bone of the defence—and we were perfectly entitled to repeat this.' The family's solicitor remonstrated that: 'The general tenor of the circumstances as given in the article is that our client's daughter *deliberately instigated a course of conduct towards the other girl with the intention of provoking and humiliating her*. This is certainly not correct' (emphasis in original), but the editor remained adamant.

The Watsons recall that the author of the article had given 'false and inaccurate information to the readers of the magazine . . . [and] we . . . had to get the transcript of the trial before the Editor of the

complaints that it unwarrantably infringed the privacy of Duncan MacAllister and his family, and that of Penny MacAllister's parents. Both families had repeatedly pleaded with Carlton Television not to go ahead with the film they had commissioned about the tragedy.' The victim's parents said that the film had been 'totally degrading' to the memory of their daughter (*Sunday Times*, 29 Oct 1995).

[108] The incident was to be reproduced in dramatised form by the BBC in its *Crime Limited* series, focusing on the ordeal experienced by different survivors, that was broadcast on 30 Aug 1994.

[109] After prolonged discussions with Mr and Mrs Watson, I agreed not to reprint *verbatim* the story which had appeared in that issue of *Marie Claire*. Despite a

Marie Claire Magazine... would print any kind of an apology for the deep pain and anguish they had caused us as a family.' And that transcript does reveal that Glover's allegations and Henderson's ensuing article were indeed without substance. Not only had no witness confirmed Barbara Glover's description of Diane Watson's actions but she herself was found guilty of two separate attacks on Diane Watson—the murder of 10 April as well as a separate assault on the previous day.

After a long and extremely vigorous campaign targeted directly at Glenda Bailey, the editor, the magazine did eventually publicly concede in its April 1993 issue that 'we explained the position of Diane Watson's killer... by repeating allegations made by [her] defence counsel at her trial. This could have been misleading, as we omitted to publish what the prosecution said about Diane's character. We should also have put Diane's side of the story...'

The Watsons themselves had felt 'rage, rage' at the article. They concluded that 'in this country you can say what you want about the dead and there's no law to protect us'. They are convinced that their only other child, Alan, killed himself as a direct consequence of what *Marie Claire* had published. His suicide note said 'I just want to be with Diane'. When I asked her what had given her the energy to pursue *Marie Claire* so vigorously into publishing a retraction, Margaret Watson answered with a single word: 'hate'.

Yet media reporting can also reinforce the survivors' sentiments by endorsing their sense that something awful has happened, legitimating their feelings of outrage and giving stature to their loss. Public reports give the dead a continuing presence. Pat Green said: 'To me, speaking about my son on television is a memorial—I don't want him forgotten.' And, for that very reason, survivors may be perturbed if they are *ignored* by the mass media, because that would signal the lack of public importance that has been attached to their tragedy. David Howden, former Chairman of SAMM, gave an account of how 'a woman arrived on my doorstep in a desperate state. Her son had been murdered in the same area recently. When Tessa was killed it was all over the media for days. Tessa was a young woman.

number of amendments to the text of this chapter, the Watsons still felt that the re-appearance of the false allegations made against their daughter would have caused them enormous distress, and, on balance, I decided that I should defer to their wishes. Their continued loathing of the story was so profound that it powerfully underscores my argument about the impact which the press can have upon families.

Nothing much was happening in the news at the time. But a young bloke being killed is not the same sort of story. The boy's mother said: 'Why was my son only worth two lines in the local paper?'

Survivors are not entirely without resource. The police may steer them through some of their encounters with the mass media. They will, for instance, almost always discuss the drafting of press releases with the family before they are made public. They will deliberate about the prudence of arranging a press conference with the survivor ('is it going to further my case and is it going to mess up that person?' asked a detective inspector). If a press conference is to take place, they will strike compacts with the mass media, offering them the opportunity to question the family then, and only then, if they will leave them alone thereafter. They will ask the family to supply the press with their most attractive photograph of the victim, to make it less likely that other, quite different pictures will be published against the family's wishes, to protect them from being pestered for pictures in the future, to prevent photographs being purloined by the press, and to retain a favourable image of the dead. They may orchestrate press conferences given by a survivor, trying to ensure that the person who appears will be 'sensible' (and certainly not a suspect) and coaching him or her in what may be said ('there may be aspects of the murder which we may wish to withhold. We will then brief the family member, and hope to God they'll stick to that brief'). Press conferences may be restricted in size, confined, perhaps, to a single television company, one or two national newspapers, and one or two local newspapers ('it will mean that the family are not treated to a bear pit conference').

The bereaved themselves may enter into their own tacit or explicit contracts with the press. After all, the investigation and prosecution of murder cases may extend over time and family or friends can threaten to withdraw from further dealings if the mass media (and the local media in particular) do not conduct themselves in what is taken to be a proper manner. Of course, for survivors to do so will require an uncommon composure, command and experience, but, as a prime source of news, they do have a limited capacity to negotiate conditions. One Suffolk man said of the local press: 'we tended to have a good relationship with them, and there were things that they agreed. I made sure my position was quite clear right from the start. I said if they start mis-printing [statements], photographing the children, anything like that, I said, contact would be completely stopped.' John

Baldock of The Compassionate Friends observed: 'They were really very good. In the early days after [my son] was killed, it was only really the local papers that came and then I have had a certain amount of experience in dealing with them . . . and while everything was going on, I brought them in to here and just sat in here and talked to them quietly.' And Ruth Fuller of SAMM recalled, 'I 'phoned up our local newspaper, it's a very good local newspaper, and I said 'now, I'll tell you' because I needed them to know, and [they reported things fairly].' She had used the press quite deliberately as a conduit to convey her own version of what had happened: 'I wasn't necessarily courting publicity. I just needed everyone to know the real story.'

Time and the career

The orderly succession of processes in and about the criminal justice system encouraged survivors to talk about stages and movement, even though, as I shall show, those stages and that movement tended not to appear linear but cyclical, events seeming to repeat themselves and leading nowhere. I have suggested that bereavement after homicide is marked by alienation from the problems of everyday life, a besetting preoccupation with the death and its aftermath, and an abiding anger, and that is a combination which contrives to turn survivors away from mundane ways of reckoning and measuring.

Conventional timetables, in particular, no longer seemed to apply to them. What Schutz and Luckmann would call their flow of experience of inner duration became divorced from 'world time',[110] the very pace and phasing of their personal time having changed.[111] It was difficult to conceive of their lives moving forwards. The anguished memory offering no hope for the future, no purpose, and no goal.[112] Indeed, it is a property of anger that it locks a person into the time of injury,[113] emotionally fixing him or her on powerful images and sensations that obscure the present and freeze time, space, and being into a 'single slice of experience'.[114] So

[110] A Schutz and T. Luckmann, *The Structures of the Life-World* (Heinemann, London, 1974), 58.
[111] See J. Littlewood, *Aspects of Grief: Bereavement in Adult Life* (Tavistock/Routledge, London, 1992), 45.
[112] See L. Langer, *Holocaust Testimonies* (Yale University Press, New Haven, 1991), 79.
[113] See A. Hass, *The Aftermath* (n 12 above), 174.
[114] N. Denzin, *On Understanding Emotion* (Jossey-Bass, San Francisco, 1984), 77.

it was that, in one sense, time seemed to stand still,[115] heading nowhere, robbed of the incident and structure that could displace the one besetting tragedy of violent death[116] (William Faulkner once said 'The past isn't dead. It isn't even past.'). But, paradoxically, it seems, time could also race past, devoid of the detail and changefulness that would give it complexity, duration and direction. Ann West talked of how she lived 'from one featureless day to the next.' 'For me,' she said, '25 years ago is like yesterday.'[117]

In place of conventional methods of time-keeping, homicide survivors worked with new measures that borrowed largely from the events of the death, the stages set by the criminal justice system and the personal calendar of the family. They would refer repeatedly to the anniversary of the date of the homicide itself, each anniversary being set aside as special, as a time for retreat or escape,[118] understood by fellow survivors as a trying period when people were exempt from normal demands. It would loom large as a test of self-discipline in the face of difficult emotions (one mother wrote to the co-ordinator of SAMM: 'I coped rather better with the anniversary of——'s death than I thought I would', and another mother, bereaved by the massacre at Dunblane, was reported to have said, 'it's difficult for us to see anything ahead. There have been many comments made about what you should be doing, about find the way ahead, and so on, but it's difficult for other people to understand. I feel myself becoming more and more worried about the anniversary and everything it symbolises as the time approaches.'[119] Two other mothers of children killed at Dunblane called the first anniversary a

---

[115] Coline Covington, in a paper on narrative ('No Story, No Analysis?') quotes Emily Dickinson on this theme:

> 'Pain—has an Element of Blank—
> It cannot recollect
> When it begun—or if there were
> A time when it was not—
>
> It has no Future—but itself'

E. Dickinson, *The Complete Poems* (Belknap Press, Cambridge, Mass, 1951).

[116] See J. Nuttin, *Future Time Perspective and Motivation* (Leuven University Press, Leuven, 1985), 13.

[117] A. West, *For the Love of Lesley* (n 26 above), 58, 59.

[118] David Howden, for example, was reported to have said that, on the anniversary of his daughter's death: 'We went away to Hastings for that weekend to escape. We would not have wanted to wake up here on that anniversary morning.' The *Advertiser*, 5 Feb 1988.

[119] 'Dunblane Remembered', *The Times*, 24 Feb 1997.

'hurdle' to be surmounted.) Trials could become especially fraught because they tended to coincide with the date of the killing,[120] and they could establish a simultaneous double anniversary.

Anniversaries also formed part of a system of calculating the years, and magical multiples of years, since the victim was killed (a mother said at a meeting 'we're putting our own minds to the 10th anniversary of——'s death.'). They measured grief and defined the self as a survivor (it has become conventional for one survivor to introduce himself or herself to another by saying, 'it's now eight (or nine or ten years) since my child died').

Birthdays, wedding anniversaries, Christmas,[121] New Year's Eve, the start of the school year, and, in North America, Thanksgiving and Halloween, were times made poignant and trying[122] by associations with the absent victim.[123] Jill Palm remarked of her son's killer, who had pleaded guilty to a reduced charge of manslaughter, 'I mean, this guy is walking around. It's as if Robert never existed. . . . I bumped into him. It was Robert's 19th birthday and John and I were coming out of the cemetery and there he was, crossing the road. He had those earphones on. I chased him. I was thinking, 'It's my son's birthday, and you're sauntering across the road!'

The time marked out by the natural history of many homicide survivors was not therefore apprehended as linear. Rather it tended to be cyclical, recapitulating old experiences again and again without evident progression,[124] a repetitive series of anniversaries made significant by the facts of death. Pat Green said: 'It's like a wheel on a bike that keeps turning. . . . You're just thinking, "oh well, it's going to be Christmas, it's going to be his anniversary, it's going to be his birthday."' And it was a consequence that many survivors experienced a form of temporal suspension that estranged them yet further from mundane society. In the next chapter, I shall consider the kind of moral world they entered in its stead.

---

[120] See *Families of Murder Victims Project: Final Report*, 20.

[121] David Howden wrote: 'We of P.O.M.C. know that at times such as Christmas it is a time of sadness . . . I know from my own experience that the Chistmas bells have a hollow ring.' POMC *Newsletter*, Dec 1990.

[122] One woman said on the *Kilroy* TV programme of 9 Dec 1994: 'It's now just day to day. There's nothing to look forward to . . . It's coming up to Christmas again and it's harder to keep things together.'

[123] See the *Observer*, 21 Nov 1993.

[124] Michael Young argued that 'the cyclical keeps things the same by reproducing the past and the linear makes things different by introducing novelty.' M. Young, *The Metronomic Society* (Thames and Hudson, London, 1988), 4.

4

The Moral Economy of the Homicide Survivor

> Where is a height without depth, and how can there be light that throws no shadow? There is no good that is not opposed by evil.[1]

Introduction

This will be the last of the three chapters mapping the phenomenology of bereavement after homicide. It will continue to develop a strong ideal-type, building on what has gone before, and exploring the roots and workings of an identity and moral vision which not only infuse the logic-in-use of survivor organizations, but also, paradoxically, fold back on the experience of bereavement to give it shape and causality.

I should repeat that what follows is an ideal-type, an accentuation of traits for purposes of analysis and demonstration, and not every activist and group can or will comply with it in every particular. There is a spectrum, and it is inviting always to go to the ends of the band for the clearest and most forthright expressions of a worldview. But it should not be forgotten that I encountered many people who did not inhabit the Manichaean universe which I am about to portray, or who did not do so at every point.[2]

---

[1] C. Jung, *Psychological Reflections* (Routledge and Kegan Paul, London, 1971), 235.

[2] One obvious example of such an exception was Jayne Zito, founder of The Zito Trust that memorialised her husband of three months standing. Jayne Zito has been described as a 'passionate campaigner for reform of mental healthcare' ('Making a killing', *Sunday Times*, 26 Feb 1995). She described herself as having been made 'extremely angry' at the evidence that had emerged at trial on the mental health of Christopher Clunis, her husband's murderer. She campaigned for a public inquiry, had got 'on a bandwagon [to] scream and shout and things like that—we did sort of

Trauma and chaos

I have shown how the disclosure of violent death in the family can lead to a sense of shock and bewilderment, to distortions in the structure of time and the self, and to feelings of alienation, disbelief, obsessiveness, fear, anger, and panic. Kai Erikson conveyed the process well when he described how: 'Something alien breaks in on you, smashing through whatever barriers your mind has set up as a line of defense. It invades you, takes you over, becomes a dominating feature of your interior landscape, and in the process threatens to drain you and leave you empty.'[3] It is in precisely that fashion that responses to homicide can shatter the world, leaving it more chaotic, senseless, and dangerous.[4] After the trial, especially, the survivor will find himself or herself in a limbo in which nothing much makes sense. One of the phrases most frequently used by

the media circuit, my mum and I.' Not only did she succeed in obtaining an inquiry and an important report (North East and South East Thames Regional Health Authorities, *The Report of the Inquiry into the Care and Treatment of Christopher Clunis* (HMSO, London 1994)), but she founded a trust devoted to the fostering of proper community care, the closure of 'old-style psychiatric hospitals' ('The Zito Trust: Background Information', n.d.) and the provision of victim support. She came in time to be recognised as an authority on the mentally-disordered offender. Yet Jayne Zito and her colleagues did not profess fiercely monochromatic views of the world of crime and criminal justice. She was to be praised by the report of the Clunis Inquiry as a 'most impressive witness. She was quiet, restrained, yet at the same time forceful' (*Report, op cit*, 5.) Of herself, she was to say: 'I've learned that I've got to teach them [officials and others in and about the criminal justice system] that I'm not just pursuing a personal crusade . . . . they've learned that I won't shout at them.' Part of that discipline presumably stemmed from biography. Jayne Zito's mother had been a social worker in child protection and she herself had been an art therapist and a mental health service practitioner: 'my professional background was in mental health, so I had worked as a deputy manager in social services . . . managing teams and organizing services for clients who were very young when they had their first psychotic experience and we were offering a very . . . intensive therapeutic environment for them when they were first discharged from hospital.' She had then moved on to further social work training and a probation placement 'and I was visiting prisoners who had committed murder in prison . . .' It was perhaps a consequence of her early grounding in the work and ideology of the criminal justice practitioner, and of her close professional acquaintance with offenders, that she sought to avoid making simple moral judgements and becoming embittered by what she called a 'destructive pattern of grief.' And there were many others, not unlike her in judgement, to be found in the major offices of SAMM, The Compassionate Friends, and elsewhere. They were the pragmatists, those whom I shall call the young Turks, who were to eschew bitterness and turned towards constructive action.

[3] K. Erikson, *A New Species of Trouble: Explorations in Disaster, Trauma, and Community* (W.W. Norton and Co, New York, 1994), 228.

[4] See G. Getzel and R. Masters, 'Serving Families who Survive Homicide Victims', *Social Casework*, Mar 1984, Vol 65, No 3, 141.

survivors is 'my life has been turned upside down'. A member of Justice for Victims cried out triumphantly at a committee meeting that she had solved the riddle of criminal justice: 'it's wrong to be right, and right to be wrong!!'

Some large part of that upheaval has been captured by the clinical term 'post-traumatic stress disorder',[5] a term which has been liberally applied to the aftermath of homicide by professionals,[6] journalists,[7] and survivors themselves.[8] Traumatic disorder as a psychological and psychiatric metaphor had its origins in John Erichsen's 1866 diagnosis of 'railway spine' (later to be called 'Erichsen's disease'), a state associated with the injuries that could be inflicted by crashes on the new railways.[9] The chief symptom of railway spine was a pain that did not seem to stem from any discernible physical injury. It was as if the physical consequences of psychological damage could be as great as those flowing from any somatic cause. The mind had its wounds too.

What came in time to be known as post-traumatic stress disorder pointed to the profound disorganization which could be experienced by people who had witnessed or faced a frightening personal threat that could be neither fought nor fled. Incapacitated and defenceless, they were unable to cope with what had happened,

---

[5] Perhaps it should be noted that 'post- traumatic disorder' is a diagnosis whose authority and generous use have been questioned. See, for example, A. Young, *The Harmony of Illusions: Inventing post-traumatic stress disorder* (Princeton University Press, Princeton, NJ, 1996).

[6] See A. Amick-McMullan *et al*, 'Family Survivors of Homicide Victims: A Behavioral Analysis', *The Behavior Therapist*, 1989, Vol 12, No 4, 23; D. Black *et al*, 'Children Who Witness Parental Killing', in C. Thompson and P. Cowen (eds), *Violence: Basic and clinical science* (Butterworth Heinemann, London, 1993), 215; C. Murray-Parkes; 'Psychiatric Problems Following Bereavement', *British Journal of Psychiatry*, 1993, Vol 162, 51; and E. Rynearson; 'Bereavement after Homicide', *American Journal of Psychiatry*, 141, 1984, 1452.

[7] See 'No help in times of trauma', The *Independent on Sunday*, 4 Dec 1994.

[8] For example, Derek Rogers of Justice for Victims, describes the effects of homicide as 'life long post traumatic stress' in his preamble to 'For the Attention of the Home Affairs Select Committee for Inclusion into the Inquiry on Mandatory Life Sentences', Justice for Victims, Feb 1995. PTSD was regarded as a major constituent of the survivor's condition and identity, and there was unhappiness in some quarters about attempts to discredit it. Ron Rodgers, who became chairman and then co-ordinator of SAMM after 1996, said 'there appears to be the start of a reaction against PTSD DIAGNOSED IN "SECONDARY VICTIMS". As you may guess it is a concern to the group. I will be keeping an eye on developments....' *SAMM Newsletter No 39*, Jan 1997.

[9] See I. Hacking, *Rewriting the Soul* (Princeton University Press, Princeton, NJ, 1995), 185.

and the sequelae were shock, denial, incredulity, disorder, humiliation, anxiety, hysteria, and all the other attributes which I have listed. Presented with situations redolent of the original threat, they may, in the language of survivor groups, become 're-traumatised' and 're-victimised', as if they were living again some of the experiences which had so disturbed them. Even small slights can acquire large proportions to excite strong emotions.

The idea of post-traumatic stress disorder was to be elaborated in various guises by Janet,[10] Freud,[11] Brown,[12] and others; it became linked to people's responses to a succession of appalling experiences—to combat in war[13] (where it was first identified as 'shell shock'[14]); the Holocaust; genocide; incest; disasters; homicide; road crashes;[15] and rape;[16] and it was finally classified as a discrete mental disorder by the American Psychiatric Association in 1980.[17]

I would not want to apply the clinical portrait of post-traumatic stress disorder wholesale in this book. There are elements which do not seem to fit the adult homicide survivor (the idea of repressed memory appears to have no useful place, for example). But I do wish to emphasize the portrait's theme of the collapse of meaning that can follow a harrowing event. The matter was raised in Chapter 2 where I remarked that the recipe knowledge of everyday life does not seem to enable people to deal with the facts of homicide. NOVA, the American National Organization for Victim Assistance, claimed that: 'It is clear that learning of a loved one's murder is intense, sudden, and virtually impossible to understand.'[18] Instead of possessing a plausible structure, the world is reduced to virtual futility, becoming anomic and disorganized, a place without apparent

---

[10] P. Janet, 'Les actes inconscients et le dédoublement de la personalité', *Revues Philosophiques*, 1886, Vol 22, No 2.

[11] S. Freud, *Psychopathology of Everyday Life* (T. Fisher Unwin, London, 1914).

[12] See W. Brown, 'The Treatment of Cases of Shell Shock in an Advanced Neurological Centre', *Lancet*, 17 Aug 1918.

[13] See A. Glass, 'Psychotherapy in the combat zone', *American Journal of Psychiatry*, 1954, 110.

[14] See R. Leys, 'Traumatic Cures: Shell Shock, Janet, and the Question of Memory', *Critical Inquiry*, Summer 1994, 623.

[15] See *Impact of Road Death and Injury* (European Federation of Road Traffic Victims, Geneva, 1996).

[16] See A. Burgess and L. Holmstrom, 'Rape Trauma Syndrome', *American Journal of Psychiatry*, Sep 1974.

[17] *Diagnostic and Statistical Manual of Mental Disorders, Third Edition* (American Psychiatric Association, Washington, DC, 1980).

[18] NOVA, 'Survivors of Homicide Victims', 1.

sense. A member of SAMM was reported to have said: 'Nobody tells you anything.... You're floundering in a sea of despair.'[19] And, in the wake of the death of his mother, a child wrote: 'I cry every night hoping that I will wake up and it will all be a bad dream and now its over, but it won't and it never will. Why me? Why anyone? I don't understand...'[20]

The symbolic systems that once gave people a sense of control, orientation, significance, and connection will have been over-whelmed,[21] the devices used to protect them against meaningless-ness destroyed. It is then, in de Ruggiero's dramatic language, that, 'On the threshold of being we encounter the gaping abyss of noth-ingness.'[22] That is a shocking prospect.[23]

What is principally at issue here is an apparent collapse of *moral* meaning, attended by a deep sense of injustice and unfairness, that can leave the survivor quite distraught. After all, as Lerner argued, the

'belief in a just world' is ... one of the ways, if not *the* way, that people come to terms with—make sense out of—find meaning in their experiences. We do not believe that things just happen in our world; there is a pattern to events which conveys not only a sense of orderliness or predictability, but also the compelling experience of appropriateness expressed in the typically implicit judgement, 'Yes, that is the way it should be'.[24]

A description of a meeting of a Canadian support group declared that: 'There are many parents who want only revenge, who are bitter beyond Job's bitterness, who have tasted an experience which has snapped their belief in everything strong, good and

---

[19] Quoted in 'Sharing the pain', *Victim Support*, Winter 1994, No 56, 11.

[20] Manuscript in SAMM files.

[21] See J. Herman, *Trauma and Recovery* (Pandora, London, 1994), 33.

[22] G. De Ruggiero, *Existentialism* (Secker and Warburg, London, 1946), 31.

[23] Berger observed that 'Society is the guardian of order and meaning not only objectively in its institutional structures, but subjectively as well, in its structuring of individual consciousness. It is for this reason that radical separation from the social world or anomy, constitutes such a powerful threat to the individual.... He becomes anomic in the sense of becoming worldless. The socially established nomos may thus be understood, perhaps in its most important aspect, as a shield against terror. The ultimate danger of ... separation is the danger of meaninglessness. This danger is the nightmare *par excellence*, in which the individual is submerged in a world of disorder, senselessness and madness. Reality and identity are malignantly transformed into meaningless figures of horror.' P. Berger, *The Social Reality of Religion* (Penguin, Harmondsworth, 1973), 30, 31, 32.

[24] M. Lerner, *The Belief in a Just World* (Plenum Press, New York, 1980), p. vii.

decent.'[25] And a parent protested at a meeting of a chapter of Parents of Murdered Children in America: 'You all start questioning some of your values. Is there a God? Isn't there a God? Why me?'

If one of the achievements of religion in the West has been to moralise the universe,[26] it can be the work of violent death to threaten to undo that achievement and make the universe appear cold, unsafe, and indifferent. Good is not rewarded. Neither is evil punished.[27] One bereaved mother wrote to SAMM in commentary on a draft of a leaflet: 'Suddenly the world has become a very unsafe place—The unthinkable has happened in your family—You may feel that there is more evil about than good.' Survivors wondered why that could be so. How was it that the wicked could be allowed to prey unchecked on the innocent?[28] Sandra Sullivan mused: 'You start to question the whole morality of a good person's life. Should I have brought up my kids to help other people, and always to do right? I should have said, go out and steal a car, murder somebody— then you'll be treated with respect, and kept safe by the system.'[29] Derek Rogers told a meeting at the Home Office: 'I have done nothing wrong . . . . we are victimised victims!!'[30]

Disturbances in the moral universe evoked such turmoil that they incited many to embark on a compelling search for pattern and meaning. Survivors had somehow to claw back order, forge new identities, and tell new stories,[31] so that they could regain their moral bearings. It was difficult to concede that immoral and tragic events could be without design and purpose.[32] Catastrophes must have had a human agency.[33] Someone must have been responsible for what had happened.[34] To argue otherwise, to deny that death

[25] 'Victims of Violence: People who Care', Newmarket, Ont, n.d.

[26] See E. Pagels, *The Origin of Satan* (Vintage Books, New York, 1995), p. xvi.

[27] See A. Hass; *The Aftermath: Living with the Holocaust* (Cambridge University Press, Cambridge, 1995), 5, 13.

[28] See M. Peach and D. Klass, 'Special Issues in the Grief of Parents of Murdered Children', *Death Studies*, 11, 1987, 84.

[29] In 'The Valerie Grove Interview', *The Times*, 23 Sept 1994.

[30] Minutes of Meeting held at Home Office, 18 Oct 1993.

[31] See T. Walter, *The Revival of Death* (Routledge, London, 1994), 5.

[32] See I. Glick *et al*, *The First Year of Bereavement* (Wiley-Interscience, New York, 1974), 42–3.

[33] See T. Drabeck and E. Quarantelli, 'Scapegoats, Villains, and Disasters', in J. Short (ed), *Modern Criminals* (Aldine Press, Chicago, 1970), 161.

[34] Mary Douglas made the larger point that: 'The theme, well known to anthropologists, is that at all places at all times the universe is moralized and politicized. Disasters . . . are generally turned to political account: someone already unpopular is

has meaning and pattern, and that violent and undeserved death has special meaning, would have been to teeter too close to a lawlessness in which human endeavour had become stripped of importance. For some, it was as if they were being tested by God.[35] For others, it was tempting to blame oneself[36] or other members of the family for not exercising proper care and foresight. Others would blame the criminal justice system for not protecting the victim, or for paroling prisoners, or for awarding them home leave; and they would criticise the staff of special hospitals for discharging mentally-disordered offenders into the 'community' without taking adequate precautions.

Out of that consuming drive for structure came an equally consuming appetite for information about the circumstances of the homicide,[37] and, indeed, about homicide, victims, and survivors in general. It was as if matters would become clear if only more were known. Survivors would compile voluminous dossiers of correspondence, materials from groups for the bereaved, scientific articles and newspaper cuttings about their own and others' cases, dossiers that assisted them reflexively to constitute themselves as experts on their own condition. In exceptional cases—where, for instance, there had been no prosecution—survivors might even mount their own independent and lengthy investigations into the circumstances of the death.[38] They might undertake research. One, a member of the Stoke branch of SAMM, prepared a report, based on ten interviews and secondary sources, on 'Homicide: What the Official Statistics Don't Tell You!' as part of the requirements for entry to an LL B degree. The report concluded, *inter alia*, that survivors believed that the impact of homicide is little understood; there is a 'lack of justice, in out of only nine cases only seven resulted in a conviction for the offender;' 'Five of the individuals had a bad experience at the Court Hearing where they felt they were given little consideration'; and

going to be blamed for it.' *Risk and Blame: Essays in Cultural Theory* (Routledge and Kegan Paul, London, 1994), 5.

[35] See E. Wiesel, *Night* (Bantam Books, New York, 1982), 42.

[36] See S. Lamb, *The Trouble with Blaming: Victims, Perpetrators, and Responsibility* (Harvard University Press, Cambridge, Mass, 1996), 30.

[37] See P. Dix, 'Disastrous way to treat grief', *Guardian*, 17 May 1995.

[38] See, for instance, the interview by Bill Frost of the father of Caroline Dickinson, a girl who had been murdered on a school trip to France (*The Times*, 30 June 1997); and the article on John Ward, who was reported to have visited Kenya 70 times and spent over £500,000 on investigating the death of his daughter, Julie (The *Sunday Times*, 20 July 1997).

'No one expected the problems that they had run in to as a result of the complications of the crime. Many expected a natural right to justice and found out the hard way that does not always happen.'

In their passion for comprehension,[39] they were at one with the survivors of other crises.[40] An accumulation of information might enable them to master events and reduce some of their horrors. Again and again, they said that they needed to learn every detail of the homicide to make sense of the unintelligible: had the victims suffered, what had been done to them, where had they been taken, why and how they had been picked out for death? Flo Halliday, co-founder of a local branch of Parents of Murdered Children in the Midlands, and later to be a SAMM local contact, said of the parents she had met; 'They yearn to go through every angle of their loss to try to make sense of it.'[41] A newly-bereaved father told a meeting of the Golden Gate chapter of the American Parents of Murdered Children, 'the biggest problem is finding out what happened that evening. The biggest problem is all those unanswered questions.' And Jayne Zito, who was to campaign effectively for a public inquiry into her husband's death, said, 'we felt very much abandoned and the need to know just grew and grew after the trial. The need to know why this could have happened, or how it could have happened, and realising that it needn't have happened, just took over...'

If information was not forthcoming, the imagination would invariably supply materials in its place (Ann Robinson described it as 'like a big monster waiting for me at the top of the stairs and I used to lay in bed and go over all the permutations, because it wasn't a quick death.'[42]). The son of a man murdered in Suffolk, later to become a member of the SAMM executive committee, observed, 'I felt for the rest of my life it would be something that would always be in the back of my mind, so I think I just needed to

---

[39] See *Disaster Action Newsletter*, Spring 1992, No 1, 1, where it is claimed that too many families feel deserted and isolated, lacking information.

[40] For a discussion of the reactions of those who survived old, collapsed political regimes, see S. Cohen, 'State Crimes of Previous Regimes: Knowledge, Accountability, and the Policing of the Past', *Law and Social Inquiry*, Winter 1995, Vol 20, No 1, 18. For a discussion of what she called the 'obsessive reviewing of the events that led up to the death', see J. Littlewood, *Aspects of Grief: Bereavement in Adult Life* (Tavistock/Routledge, London, 1992), 46.

[41] 'Femail', *Evening Mail*, 4 Oct 1994.

[42] From 'All Things Considered', BBC Radio Wales, 13 Dec 1987.

be clearer in my mind, however gruesome, or whatever happened, I just wanted to know... It does help, to put a picture to it, otherwise you fabricate so much.' And a parent said to a national meeting of SAMM in March 1995:

One of the problems is that you are often not told exactly, the information isn't available to you, because of confidentiality or the rules of justice. So, your imagination runs completely riot. My daughter died of head injuries, but she was also strangled, and I was told that she was knocked out first, but I'm not sure that that's what happened. The murderer has pleaded guilty and he has got life but there was no trial as such, so I am still unsure. So I still have my imagination. I still have to wonder how exactly she did die. I asked if I could have access to the statement of the man who killed her, and was told no. So this is one of the problems.

Ann Robinson, co-founder of the English Parents of Murdered Children, whose son had been murdered in Germany without an inquest, said in like fashion:

I would have liked to have had the opportunity because it was many years before I actually found out, and I'm still not sure that I know all the facts, exactly what happened. You may or may not be able to understand this but I, personally, and I know most of the parents do, have a great need to know. The police, the military police, tried to protect me from the full horror of what happened and I know they did that for the right motives, but it was in fact the wrong thing.... It wasn't in fact until I wrote and said 'I beg you to tell me', and I gave them the facts that I knew... It was some years after-wards when I found out, for example, that the mutilations occurred after death. Now I didn't know that, and for many years I thought that he had been tortured.... I know the overall thing. But it was just one thing less that could have helped if I had been told.

Survivors thereby sought information, a restoration of control, and an end to the marginality which magnified their feelings of power-lessness and kept them apart from important sources of understand-ing. They frequently surmised that someone somewhere must know the truth, and they suspected that cabals were at work if they could not reach it (one woman, who had lost a child in the Marchioness disaster, told a meeting that: 'we don't want to campaign but corruption and secrecy make it necessary for us to fight.'). They would engage in vigorous campaigns, marching, petitioning, and writing letters to police and probation officers, prison governors and parole boards, civil servants, ministers and Members of Parliament, about the progress of criminal investigations, inquests, trials and appeals, about sentences and the tariff, and about home leave and parole procedures.

Survivors would be especially wracked where no arrest had been made (June Patient, the other co-founder of Parents of Murdered Children, said that, 'for us, it is unfinished. It is still torture not knowing who killed our daughter, why they killed her; we just do not know.'[43]). They would be wracked where there had been an acquittal (one woman wrote to SAMM: 'this has driven both I and my brothers to new depths of grief.... I want to know the truth and I will not be silenced until I know the full facts of my mums death.'). They wanted to attend the trial where a defence *was* mounted (one woman said: 'I wanted to know everything, every knife wound. I suppose I wanted to go as near to death's door as I could with Peter.'[44]). They wanted transcripts of inquests and trials[45] (Derek Rogers of Justice for Victims said at a meeting with Home Office officials: 'The trial meant more to me than to anyone else in the courtroom...I want to know everything that was said. I have a right to know.' And his colleague, Sandra Sullivan, followed by demanding: 'How dare you even ask why we want it—we have to know everything surrounding our children.'[46]).

The principles of moral reconstruction

There may have been a quest to rebuild order,[47] but, for many activists, any order that was restored could never recapitulate their older, more comfortable and complex styles of thought and belief. Their sense of things had been defined in extraordinary ways by extraordinary events,[48] and nothing could ever be quite the same again. In common with other survivors,[49] they looked upon their

[43] Oral evidence to the House of Lords Select Committee on Murder and Life Imprisonment, *op. cit.*, p. 507.

[44] In 'The bitterness of two women who live with murder...', *Woman*, 24 Oct 1987.

[45] That issue of the right of the homicide survivor to receive those transcripts has recently been championed by Victim Support.

[46] Minutes of Meeting held at Home Office, 18 Oct 1993.

[47] See J. Rowland, *Rape: The Ultimate Violation* (Pluto Press, London, 1985), 337.

[48] See K. Weick, *Sensemaking in Organizations* (Sage, Thousand Oaks, Calif, 1995), 1.

[49] See L. Langer, *Holocaust Testimonies* (Yale University Press, New Haven, 1991), 49; L. Shamgar-Handelman, *Israeli War Widows* (Bergin and Garvey, South Hadley, Mass, 1986), 17;

experience of crisis as a partial death of the self,[50] as a process akin to passing through a chemical furnace to emerge transmuted, former identities having been dissolved, old assumptions and definitions no longer seeming to hold. Diana Lamplugh talked about how: 'friends kept wanting us to be the same. We have been so changed. We have been through that catalyst, and that fire, and we won't ever be the same. We've changed.' Over and over again, survivors would remark that 'everything changed'. Indeed, it was thought, the murderer had not only succeeded in extinguishing the victim but threatened their own extinction as well.[51] One woman wrote to SAMM, 'I cannot allow my daughter's murderer to kill me.'

Welling up out of chaos, that process of transformation could appear at times to be quite primordial and primitive. Stark experiences lead to stark interpretations. In their fervour and sense of urgency, in their anger and bewilderment, most survivors could have had no patience with anything but a simple and certain morality, and they turned to unambiguous schemes that would subdue doubt, establish firm boundaries between order and disorder, expel confusion, and point to directions for action.

It was as if on occasion survivors were recapitulating the plot of some very ancient myth,[52] moral disorder turning to order, flux to structure, in a manner reminiscent of Paul Ricoeur's 'drama of creation' where evil and chaos were converted into coherence;[53] of *Genesis* and the dividing of the light from the darkness; or of Hesiod's *Theogony* in which the Abyss was severed into night and day. And it was a process powerfully fuelled by the abiding anger which I have already described.

Anger may be conceived as an activity simultaneously of self-assertion and of accusation.[54] It is intentional, establishing not

---

[50] Colin Caffell, for instance, remembered that, on being told that his wife and children had been killed, 'A huge part of me died that lunch-time—was burnt away to nothing—vaporised.' *In Search of the Rainbow's End* (Coronet Books, London, 1994), 28.

[51] See the article on Ann Virgin of Justice for Victims in The *Guardian*, 28 Dec 1995.

[52] One is reminded of Robertson Davies's preoccupation with the interplay between myth and everyday life. 'Myth,' said Judith Grant, Davies's biographer, 'is the unchanging wax, our individual lives are the infinite variations; the basic patterns are relatively few, recurring again and again as the basic plots of literature and life...' J. Grant, *Robertson Davies: Man of Myth* (Penguin Books, Toronto, Ont, 1994), 591.

[53] See P. Ricoeur, *The Symbolism of Evil* (Beacon Press, 1967), 172, 177.

[54] See C. Warner, 'Anger and Similar Delusions', in R. Harré (ed), *The Social Construction of Emotions* (Basil Blackwell, Oxford, 1986), 140, 152.

only the angry subject but also the object against which the anger is directed. It energetically tears ambiguities apart to create the dualisms of subject and object, this and not-this, us and not-us. Jack Katz reflected that 'There is something very deep here about how self-definition in times of profound crisis finds its way through constructing an extreme opposition to the "not me".'[55]

The new dualisms of the bereaved were continually to be reinforced and celebrated in the narrative structures of activist groups,[56] and they were to be echoed by typifications outside the groups. They were to be refracted by the adversarial language of the press (the world of crime reporting is replete with heroes and villains, with the innocent and the wicked in antagonistic relation[57]). Sanders and Lyon reflected that: 'Homicides typically receive maximum media attention, especially if the circumstances of the offense are dramatic and involve victims who are "innocent"...'[58] They were to be refracted by the speech of the trial.[59] McConville and his colleagues argued:

The complexities...are usually not apparent...because police and prosecutors structure their accounts of cases to fit into legal categories. These categories are simple, often dichotomous (guilty/not guilty; sane/insane; intentional/not intentional; reckless/not reckless; voluntary/involuntary) and deny the ambiguities and uncertainties of the world of experience.[60]

So it was that moral chaos gave way to the most elemental of all schemes, the either/or of the binary opposition, the twinned

---

[55] Private communication.

[56] See J. Lofland, *Protest: Studies of Collective Behavior and Social Movements* (Transaction, New Brunswick, New Jersey, 1985), 214; and M. Pendergast, *Victims of Memory* (Upper Access, Hinesburg, Vt, 1996) 488. Ironically, binary oppositions are not only to be found in survivor groups, but in activist groups at large, including those campaigning against the death penalty. See D. von Drehle, *Among the Lowest of the Dead: Inside Death Row* (Fawcett Crest, New York, 1995), 128.

[57] Sharon Lamb contends that 'Reading a newspaper story...we search for representatives of two extremes, perpetrator and victim, two archetypes who will represent for us evil and innocence, a hero and an antihero for our modern-day sagas of woe.' *The Trouble with Blaming* (n 36 above), 5.

[58] C. Sanders and E. Lyon, 'Repetitive Retribution: Media Images and the Cultural Construction of Criminal Justice', in J. Ferrell and C. Sanders (eds), *Cultural Criminology* (Northeastern University Press, Boston, 1995), 34. Note the iconicisation of the idea of an innocent victim which was touched upon in Chapter 1.

[59] See foreword by H. Kennedy to J. Nadel, *Sara Thornton: The Story of a Woman who Killed* (Victor Gollancz, London), p. ix.

[60] M. McConville *et al*, *The Case for the Prosecution* (Routledge, London, 1991), 12.

polarities of us and them. Just as fairy tales, the simplest and most moral forms of story-telling, dispel chaos and ambiguity by 'bring [ing] some order into [a disorganized] world view by dividing everything into opposites...without intermediate stages of degree and intensity, things are either all light or all darkness',[61] so with the new vision of the survivor. As the history central to this book develops, there will be a repeated visiting of the ideas that flowed from that dissolution of ambiguities into fundamental polarities.

Various closely-aligned metaphors have been devised to catch the workings of that bifurcating process. There is the dialectics of the schoolmen which insisted that everything is defined by its negation. There is semiotics which treats language as a methodical means of differentiating signs from one another.[62] There is deconstructionism which purports to explore the dominant polarities of Western thought.[63] There is the fourth metaphor, already flagged, of the structuralists, who, borrowing from Lévi-Strauss, talked about binary oppositions, the 'connotation[s]—positive or negative'[64] of structural terms:

The structuralists begin with the premise that the human mind universally orders the flux of experience into binary oppositions: male/female, sacred/ profane, pure/impure, in/out, kind/other, and, most of all, nature/culture. People make sense of the world through these binary oppositions and make use of the sense data of the world—plants, animals, colors, human bodies, weather, geography—to arrive at cognitive order.[65]

The survivor tends to live in a new world scoured by multiple oppositions between innocence and guilt, goodness and evil, insiders and outsiders, the feeling and the unfeeling, the interested and the uninterested, particularism and universalism. At its very core is the key opposition between the victim or the survivor on the

---

[61] B. Bettelheim, 'Bring Order into Chaos', in *The Uses of Enchantment: The Meaning and Importance of Fairy Tales* (Penguin Books, Harmondsworth, 1978), 74.

[62] See M. Merleau-Ponty, *The Prose of the World* (Heinemann, London, 1974), 31.

[63] See J. Derrida, *Points: Interviews 1974–1994* (Stanford University Press, 1995). In particular, there is Shildrick's interesting work on the relations between the monstrous and the natural. See M. Shildrick, 'Posthumanism and the Monstrous Body', *Body and Society*, Mar 1996, Vol 2, No 1, 2.

[64] C. Lévi-Strauss, *Structural Anthropology* (Allen Lane, The Penguin Press, 1968), 142.

[65] C. Mukerji and M. Schudson, 'Introduction: Rethinking Popular Culture', in C. Mukerji and M. Schudson (eds), *Rethinking Popular Culture* (University of California Press, Berkeley, Calif, 1991), 19.

one hand, and the murderer on the other (but, importantly, as I shall show in other chapters, weaker oppositions can also be traced between a whole host of other pairs, and particularly between survivors-like-us and survivors-not-like-us).

Victims and murderers are set against one another in constant juxtaposition. Survivors observed that the victim and the survivor had no choice, but that the killer could choose; the victim is dead, but the killer lives; the victim has no future, but the killer does have a future; the victim has no rights, but the killer does; there are numerous charities and organizations devoted to the offender, but almost none to the victim and the survivor; offenders are protected whilst victims are not; and the offender may serve a life sentence but so does the survivor in his or her life-long grief.

Each of those twinned oppositions constitutes the other in a dialectic of antagonism, each takes its very being from the other. Without an offender, indeed, there would be no victim, and without a victim, no offender. Frank Green, the second chairman of SAMM, once said, 'if there is an offender, there is an offence, *ergo* there is a victim. There is an inextricable link which cannot and should not be dismissed.'[66] That interdependence is something quite fundamental to the working of moral language. Jack Douglas wrote:

... when we observe and analyze the moral communications in our every-day lives we find that the social meanings of either deviance (immorality) or respectability (morality) can be adequately understood only if reference, whether implicit or explicit, is made to the other, its opposite. As some Christian theologians have argued ... without evil there would be no good, without Satan no God.[67]

What is entailed is more than a simple dialectic of fission. There is also an explosive symbolic process which hurls typifications in opposite directions. It is helpful to turn to other kinds of metaphor to grasp its dynamics, although it is not necessary to accept them in every particular to appreciate their bearing on the peculiarities of intense grief after violent death. If they work only as a form of literary device, that may be enough to advance understanding a little further.

---

[66] Transcript of 'Victims' Rights Presentations', Victim Support Annual Conference, 1995.

[67] J. Douglas, introduction to *Deviance and Respectability* (Basic Books, New York, 1970), 3.

One reservoir of metaphors is psychoanalysis and its talk about a 'splitting' of the self into the good and the bad, the bad being projected outwards to attach itself to some external object, the good remaining to be vested in the self and those close to it.[68] And very closely allied is analytical psychology's depiction of splitting as a dualistic projection of oneself into the self and its 'shadow', the shadow being not only an inverse representation of one's own self, one's 'dark brother'[69] who is everything that we find painful and regrettable, everything we are not, everything we would not wish to be,[70] but also a collective phenomenon objectified in the shape of devils,[71] deviants, or witches.[72]

Jung said that the shadow is 'the inferior and less commendable part of a person' that discloses itself especially clearly when one 'is seized by a strong emotion' or an 'uncontrolled emotional manifestation'.[73] The most graphic illustrations of the self and its shadow are to be found in fiction, in the *personae* of Jekyll and Hyde, and in Dorian Gray and his portrait,[74] but the criminal can also embody our shadow: he 'becomes a popular figure because he unburdens in no small degree the consciences of his fellow men, for now they know once more where evil is to be found.'[75] It is impossible not to recognise affinities between that portrait and the tragic ties uniting the victim/survivor and murderer.

There are literary and mythological sources of metaphor. People have long toyed in their imagination with the dualities of those who are joined but apart,[76] by the good and the bad

[68] See B. Bettelheim, *The Informed Heart* (Paladin, London, 1970), 203.

[69] See J. Jacobi, *The Psychology of C.J. Jung* (Kegan Paul, Trench, Trubner and Co, London, 1942), 102.

[70] Colin Caffell certainly wrote about how he came to recognise monsters, the dark murderous part of himself, allowing him to understand the mind of the killer. See *In Search of the Rainbow's End* (n 50 above), 311.

[71] Pagels, for instance, wrote in her account of Satan that: 'I invite you to consider Satan as a reflection of how we perceive ourselves and those we call "others". Satan has, after all, made a kind of profession out of being the "other"; and so Satan defines negatively what we think of as human.' *The Origin of Satan* (n 26 above), p. xviii.

[72] See F. Fordham, *An Introduction to Jung's Psychology* (Penguin Books, Harmondsworth, 1959), 50.

[73] C. Jung, *The Integration of the Personality* (Kegan Paul, Trench, Trubner and Co, London, 1940), 20.

[74] See H. Philp, *Jung and the Problem of Evil* (Rockliff, London, 1976), 92.

[75] C. Jung, *The Integration of the Personality* (n 73 above), 70.

[76] Thus, in Greek myth, Pallas and Athene, Kore and Demeters were both separate beings and aspects of the one being. See R. Calasso, *The Marriage of Cadmus and Harmony* (Vintage, London, 1994), 314.

twin,[77] the self and its double, each mirroring and threatening the other: 'One self does what the other self can't. One self is meek whilst the other is fierce. One self stays whilst the other runs away. These are meanings which can be discovered as we patrol the secret passages of the literature of duality, and they can also be discovered in folklore.'[78]

Throughout all these metaphors there are resonances of much larger antagonisms between the linked parts of a single entity, between the secular and the sacred, the world of Satan and the world of God, in short, of the theodicy of the Catharist, the Paulician and the Manichaean who saw all life as a struggle between contending moral forces. Survivors themselves talked from time to time as if they too were caught up in a global conflict between good and evil.[79] Consider the remarks made by a woman at a special session devoted to SAMM at the 1995 annual general meeting of Victim Support:

[My] sister [was] murdered 15 years ago...I am a Christian and I have worked with the church...and I fortunately had a vicar who was of the same sort of ideas, the same training that I was brought up with—there is wrong, there is evil and there is good and there isn't anything in between, certainly not anything like murder—because my husband said 'don't go near the vicar, he's going to upset you more, he's going to talk about forgiveness', and he didn't do that, he actually called him the devil.

If moral entities in the survivor's cosmology engender their own antitheses, if entities are coupled together in symbiosis, what mediates their relations is a form of analogical reasoning that furnishes the fundamental logic of the survivors' world. Sir James Frazer would have called it 'contagious magic', the 'notion that things which have once been conjoined must remain ever afterwards, even when quite dissevered from each other, in such a sympathetic

---

[77] L. Fiedler wrote of joined twins that 'the confusion of self and other, substance and shadow, ego and other, is...terrifyingly confounded.' *Freaks: Myths and Images of the Secret Self* (Simon and Schuster, New York, 1978), 84.

[78] K. Miller, *Doubles: Studies in Literary History* (Oxford University Press, Oxford, 1985), 416.

[79] And others in the survivor's world may also allude to the tangibility of evil. For example, Alfred Kirby, a Detective Superintendent who had investigated the murder of James Bulger in Liverpool, recalled of one of the two young killers, there was 'one boy in particular, where you could actually feel that evilness and you could say, "yeah, that boy's done that, I believe that", because there was an actual aura, a presence...' In *Roots of Evil*, Channel 4 Television, 28 Sept 1997.

relation that whatever is done to the one must similarly affect the other'.[80] There is a simple algebra which stipulates that changes in one entity will effect equal and comparable changes in the other. So it is that the treatment of the offender will be interpreted as a form of vicarious treatment of the victim and the survivor. The treatment of the victim will vicariously affect the offender. David Renhard, a member of The Compassionate Friends, reflected:

I think [there] was a general feeling that the victims were completely ignored. It's always the criminal. I do get infuriated when I read that some action has been taken to improve the lot of prisoners. I don't mean prisoners should be treated like animals, I'm not getting at that at all, but so much effort seems to come from some voluntary quarters about the prisons and prisoners, but you hear very little about the people who have suffered, and you'll be amazed at the number of people who suffer from murder...

In their meetings with officials, and in their own internal delibera-tions, survivors would lay out their reasoning as a series of moral equations (the complaint most often made being that offenders get 'everything' and the victim 'nothing'). An obvious example, repeated again and again, was that a 'life sentence should be given for a life', that the gravest offence warrants the gravest sentence. David Howden, then Chairman of POMC, told the House of Lords Select Committee on Murder and Life Imprisonment, that his mem-bers 'all take it is an insult that a sentence should be 15 years. Any one of us, and I am sure any one of you, would give up 15 years of your liberty for the life of your child. It is rather an insult to regard 15 years as life.'[81] CADD, the Campaign Against Drinking and Driving, argued that 'it must never be forgotten that taking an innocent life is the ultimate sin. There can be no restitution and close relatives will live the horror for their lifetime. It is important therefore that any sentence imposed on those responsible for caus-ing such suffering should reflect the seriousness of the crime com-mitted.'[82] Ann West hoped that Myra Hindley would die as cruelly and slowly as Lesley Ann Downey had done.[83]

---

[80] Sir James Frazer, *The Golden Bough: A Study in Magic and Religion* (Macmil-lan, London, 1959), 37. The notion is not, of course, wholly disingenuous. Particles and anti-particles do react alike at a distance, for instance.

[81] Oral evidence given to the select committee on 5 June 1989. *Minutes of Evidence*, Select Committee on Murder and Life Imprisonment, 507.

[82] Submission to the Committee on the Penalty for Homicide, May 1993.

[83] A. West, *For the Love of Lesley* (Warner, London, 1993), 9.

There is a host of lesser equations as well. If offenders have a professional organization servicing them in the guise of NACRO, so should survivors.[84] If offenders have 'rights' and 'privileges', so should survivors[85] (a police constable whose daughter had been murdered reflected that: 'People are demanding some basic rights. The scum that carry out these acts of murder automatically have rights.'[86]). If a dead victim can no longer have holidays and family celebrations, neither should his or her killer ('we again face a meaningless Christmas without our only daughter... because of——'s action', wrote the father of a murdered woman to the governor of a prison in protest at the proposal that her murderer might be given home leave). If offenders are given copious advice and support, so should survivors (a woman wrote to SAMM: 'These men [who had killed her husband] were arrested and had the best of everything, doctors and solicitors. Every wish was granted. Whilst me and my children struggled on. We were offered nothing!' And a woman said at a local meeting of SAMM: 'If a man or a woman commits a crime, there's the probation service, social service. The offender doesn't have to go looking for help. How come victims had to go and ask?... The probation service recognises the offender. Why can't the same service recognise the victim?!'). If prisoners know their date of release, so should survivors. If offenders have a Home Office, victims and survivors should have a Ministry for Victims. If prisoners have an ombudsman, so should victims. If there was a criminal justice system, there should be a victim justice system. Money spent on offenders should be matched by spending on victims and survivors.[87] A standard question posed in SAMM's leaflets is: 'we are all aware of organizations who offer help to offenders, ex-offenders and their families. How many organizations can you think of who offer help to the families of murder victims?' It is a question that has entered the stock rhetoric of survivors' organizations.[88] The

[84] The word 'amateur' was used by Joan Bacon to describe the support given to survivors at a meeting at the Home Office, 18 Oct 1993.
[85] See S. Scheingold et al, 'Sexual Violence, Victim Advocacy, and Republican Criminology', Law and Society Review, 1994, Vol 28, No 4, 736.
[86] C. Casey, 'A Life Sentence', Police Review, 14 Oct 1994, 26.
[87] See the report of the launch of the North of England Victims Association in Shields Gazette, 23 July 1993.
[88] See, for example, the use of identical wording in a report of the launch of Yorkshire Victims of Road Crime, Spen and Calder News, 11 Nov 1993, and SAMM Newsletter Autumn 1995, 9.

underlying logic-in-use of the opening words of a leaflet drafted by Justice for Victims in March 1993 should now be transparent:

RIGHTS FOR THE WRONGED
...
This loud appeal[89] is on behalf of VICTIMS, demanding recognition, rights and justice.

1. Rights to meetings with CPS/Barrister—as defendant has.[90]

2. Rights to free expert legal advice (not Citizens Advice Bureau!) help and assistance—as defendant has.

3. Right to character witnesses—as defendants family has....

Feeling pained, ignored, and helpless, many activist survivors held that what would add symbolic weight to their portion of the moral equation was 'recognition', 'dignity', and 'respect'.[91] Joan Bacon told a Home Office minister at a meeting in April 1994, 'you could start by swinging the pendulum back, start by balancing the scales, give the victim the respect they deserve...' Seven months before, Pat Green had told another meeting at the Home Office,[92] 'we don't want money. We want recognition.' Survivors wanted variously to be consulted about procedures and outcomes; a place and a right to speak at the inquest and the trial; representation at meetings of parole boards and tribunals of inquiry;[93] and membership of

---

[89] It was a 'loud appeal' because, the Victims of Crime Pressure Group (as Justice for Victims then called itself) announced in its press release, 'only criminals make loud appeals—we must correct this imbalance.'

[90] Under the Victim's Charter of 1996, and for the first time, there was an obligation laid on the CPS to communicate to families through the police any such changes of plea.

[91] For example, in Maryland in Nov 1994, a coalition of victims' advocates pressed for a constitutional amendment which would lay down, *inter alia*, that: 'A victim of crime shall be treated by agents of the state with dignity, respect, and sensitivity during all phases of the criminal justice process.' 'Balance the Scales of Justice for Victims of Crime', Maryland Coalition for a Constitutional Amendment, Maryland, 1994.

[92] It is evident that officials and ministers heard the language of the survivors, because the second edition of the Victim's Charter, issued by the Home Office in 1996, opened with a foreword by the then Home Secretary, Michael Howard, which acknowledged that yearning for respect: 'In 1990 we published the Victim's Charter... Since then we have listened to what victims say they want and we have learnt from their experiences... They want to be treated with respect when they attend court as witnesses.... We are striving to make sure that... the criminal justice system treats them with respect.' *The Victim's Charter* (Home Office, London, 1996).

[93] See P. Rock, 'The Inquiry and Victims' Families', in J. Peay (ed), *Inquiries after Homicide* (Duckworth, London, 1996).

bodies deliberating about policy; an acknowledgement, in short, that they were also substantial parties to the conflict that had resulted in the victim's death and its subsequent management by the State.[94]

The reconstruction of memory

In the activist survivors' dialectic, victim and offender, good and bad, us and them, so centrally opposed in core symbolism, were to be driven by anger, revulsion, and distress to ever greater distances from one another. One pole would come to embody all that was admirable, the other all that was deplorable, the dead and those who mourned them being idealised and the offender demonised.[95] A member of Justice for Victims complained at a meeting with the Parole Board in August 1994 that 'the life of the murderer is seen as paramount compared with the life of the victim which was so special, beautiful and important.' It was for that reason that many survivors would have liked the right to give victim impact statements to act as symbolic counters to the pleas in mitigation made before sentencing.[96] Ann Virgin of Justice for Victims said, 'we should be allowed to say...Katie, Lynne, Martin were nice people. They were honest, hard-working people...'

The third feature of the logic-in-use of the survivor, then, is that effort will be expended on enforcing symbolic separations[97] and reconstructing memories and typifications.[98] Ann Robinson talked of how: 'that was all I had left, my memories. I wanted to talk about him and even now I'm pathetically grateful when anybody mentions his name...'[99] And an article on 'griefwork' in an American group's newsletter put it that it was imperative: 'To convert your relationship with the person who died from one of co-presence to memory.

---

[94] See N. Christie, 'Conflicts as Property', *British Journal of Criminology*, 1977, Vol 17, No 1.

[95] See B. Raphael, *The Anatomy of Bereavement* (Hutchinson, London, 1984), 94.

[96] Victim impact statements have been put to various uses in different jurisdictions. What many homicide survivors seemed chiefly to seek was the catharsis of announcing to the world what had been lost rather than an immediate and tangible influence over sentencing decisions.

[97] See D. Black and T. Kaplan, 'Father Kills Mother', *British Journal of Psychiatry*, 1988, vol 153, 628.

[98] See G. Rochlin, *Griefs and Discontents* (Churchill, London, 1965), 211.

[99] 'All Things Considered', BBC Radio Wales, 13 Dec 1987.

The relationship you have with the person you have lost is now about memories.[100]

If relationships have become tied to memories, the survivor will have to strive to rid memory of its terrors, visual scars, symbolic assaults, and moral ambiguities. After all, images of homicide are hedged about with ugliness. Diana Lamplugh said: 'you do have to regain the memory and you have to work very hard to do it.' Howarth observed more generally that: 'People talk about the dead.....[T]hey construct a new understanding...a new biography. In a broader sense the deceased may be brought to mind by poignant memories of significant moments or significant places, by pieces of music, particular scents...'[101] What may well emerge is what Fred Davis would have called a *nostalgic* memory, a memory that softens, edits, and compliments, rather than raw, uncensored recollections of pain and mutilation. It is a property of nostalgia that it is relatively conservative and free of blemish, that it supplies sentiments which reduce anguish.[102] It was surely something of a nostalgic memory that prevailed when one member of SAMM said of his son, 'the memories of——, we found no problem with that, because they were always happy memories and it was fun to talk about him that way...He was a son, a friend, a colleague...'

The deceased are eulogised by the living,[103] and their eulogies will be framed by culturally-embedded prototypes of the untarnished dead, the good family,[104] and the 'ideal victim'. The 'ideal victim', Christie argued, possesses 'a sort of public status of the same type and level of abstraction as that for example of a 'hero' or a 'traitor'...[Ideal victims] can be exemplified by...the little old lady on the way home in the middle of the day after having cared for her sick sister. If she is hit on the head by a big man who thereafter grabs her

---

[100] R. Edmonds-Norris; 'Griefwork....', *Families and Friends of Murder Victims Newsletter*, Oct 1996, No 1, 5. (emphasis in original)

[101] G. Howarth, '"Breaking down the walls of heartache": dismantling the boundaries between life and death', unpublished paper, June 1997, 6.

[102] See F. Davis, *Yearning for Yesterday* (Free Press, New York, 1979).

[103] In the case of the idealisation of dead children by members of an American chapter of The Compassionate Friends, see D. Klass, 'The Deceased Child in the Psychic and Social Worlds of Bereaved Parents During the Resolution of Grief', in D. Klass *et al, Continuing Bonds: new understandings of grief* (Taylor and Francis, London, 1997), 205.

[104] Cohen writes more widely about narratives of the idealised family which are embedded in popular talk and recollection. See P. Cohen, *Rethinking the Youth Question* (Macmillan, London, 1997), 222.

bag and uses the money for liquor or drugs—in that case, we come, in my country, close to the ideal victim.'[105]

The words characteristically used by survivors to fix victims in memory were 'good', 'special', 'beautiful', 'shining', 'important', 'loving', and 'innocent'. One mother talked of her daughter as 'a bright, shining girl with an infectious laugh...' Another said: 'you want to talk about your child, the one you've lost, you want them to understand how good this child was and they didn't deserve to die in that way...' A survivor wrote to Victim Support: 'my husband was only 45 years old, he worked all his life from leaving school...He was an excellent dad husband and grandad. I love him very much....he lived for job & family and only wanted to give love. Instead that was taken away from us all...'

Amongst survivors there has arisen a potent iconography and ritual to sustain that work of memory and memorialisation. Partly as an individual response, partly as a collective practice, they have developed methods to represent grief, reconstitute memory, and celebrate the dead. The most conspicuous form of memorialisation is the founding of organizations bearing the victim's name, but there is also a mass of lesser forms which may be found throughout Britain and North America.

First, there is the preservation of things as they were, a deliberate freezing of the past (often aided by anger which is itself attached to the past[106]) so that it should not lose its immediacy, so that nothing should be allowed to intervene between the death and the memory, and change is halted. A father would read a nightly story to his son killed a year before at Dunblane.[107] Derek Rogers of Justice for Victims refused to sell, move, or tax his dead daughter's motor car that remained parked in a public street.[108] Children's bedrooms would remain untouched, possessions laid out as they had been before the death, as if their occupants were expected shortly to return.

The home can be transformed into a sacred place, domestic spaces in the bedroom or elsewhere being transformed into shrines,

---

[105] N. Christie, 'The Ideal Victim', in E. Fattah (ed), *From Crime Policy to Victim Policy* (Macmillan, London, 1986), 18–19.
[106] See N. Denzin, *On Understanding Emotion* (Jossey-Bass, San Francisco, 1984), 222, 229.
[107] See *The Times*, 5 Mar 1997.
[108] See *Sunday Telegraph*, 25 Sept 1994.

decked out with toys, photographs, and trophies (and in north America with college and school pennants), to become the objects of small household rituals centred on the lighting of candles, the placing of flowers, and the nightly kissing of photographs. One survivor had had a small service in his house as a 'cleansing thing', to rid the place of its evil associations.

Other lesser shrines have grown up more or less spontaneously as part of a folk tradition in the West: the placing of flowers at the scenes of traffic crashes and murders; the heaping-up of toys, and especially teddy bears, at Dunblane and other places where children have been killed; and the placing of football scarves on the gates and fences of stadiums where disasters have occurred. In Pittsford, New York, four-year old Kali Poulton, missing for two years and eventually found murdered, had been the subject of a massive search organized by her mother. A raised flower bed, dedicated to her on the first anniversary of her abduction, was to become a place of pilgrimage for the many people who had become concerned about her kidnapping: 'Eerily, necessarily, the garden began to grow as the visitors left flowers, balloons and stuffed animals. They left hundreds of candles, so many that neighbors' children became their full-time caretakers.'[109]

Third, there are the collective and individual rituals of annual pilgrimages to the murder scene,[110] memorial services in chapels,[111] churches and cathedrals, rituals that are marked by the reading of poems, the scattering of flowers, the lighting of candles, and the reciting and commemoration of names at the altar or some other special place.[112] On 6 March 1997, for instance, the tenth anniversary of the Zeebrugge ferry disaster, prayers were said, hymns were sung, and flowers were cast on the sea at the place where the ship *The Herald of Free Enterprise* had capsized with the loss of 190 people.

---

[109] The *New York Times*, 7 Aug 1996.

[110] For a description of the annual pilgrimage to Lockerbie of the families of victims of PanAm flight 103, see the *New York Times*, 19 Aug 1996. There were individual pilgrimages as well. More than one survivor would return to the place of death every year.

[111] One such service was held, for example, at the chapel of Manchester Airport on the tenth anniversary of the disaster there. *Disaster Action Newsletter*, Autumn 1995, No 3, 2.

[112] See *Road Peace Newsletter*, No 4, Spring/Summer 1994, 10.

Fourth, there is the creation of special monumental artifacts such as quilts,[113] murals,[114] 'murder walls' inscribed with the names of the dead,[115] books of remembrance, and memorial photograph albums (the newsletter of the South East Region local group of SAMM remarked that: 'It is not a morbid thing, but a feeling of warmth that they are at peace together'[116]). Like memorial services and pilgrimages, they represent obvious borrowings from other rituals for the dead, from the requiem mass, war memorials, and the AIDS quilts, and they mark an attempt to impart a familiar, solemn, objective, and communal form to emotional performance, to transpose the orthodox, silent language of grief to settings as yet unorthodox.

Fifth, there is the space reserved in groups' newsletters for reflections, maxims, obituaries, poems, and eulogies, one of the very first being the 'memory corner' established in *The Compassionate Friends Newsletter* in Spring 1982. A large proportion of almost any group's newsletter will be taken up with a special form of refined writing appropriate to deep emotion. Take the Winter 1994 issue of the *SAMM Newsletter*. It contained two poems, one on the inside cover:

THE NEW YEAR

The New Year comes
When all the world is ready
For changes, resolutions
For us, to whom
This stroke of midnight means
A missing child remembered,
For us, the New Year comes

[113] See *RoadPeace Newsletter*, No 2, Spring 1994, 12.

[114] For example, a mural for murder victims was organized by Parents of Murdered Children in Tucson, Arizona, in October 1996. It was dedicated to Diana Vicari and other local victims whose remains had not been recovered or whose killers had not been found or convicted. 'As family members walked to the wall to add a loved one's name, a song played in the background: 'Don't be afraid....I'll be watching you from above.... Just think of me, and I'll be there'. Vicari was killed and dismembered four years ago this month. Her arms were found Oct 24 in a trash bin in the alley. 'We don't have a body (to bury)', said Debbie Vicari, Diana's sister. 'This is our grave site. This is all we have'. Debbie said she and Diana's friends have come to the alley every year since Diana's death to write messages on the wall.' *Tucson Citizen*, 25 Oct 1996.

[115] See *1995 Annual Report*, National Organization of Parents of Murdered Children, Inc, Cincinnati, Ohio, 1996.

[116] SAMM South East Region Newsletter, undated.

More like another darkness.
But let us not forget
That this may be the year
When love and hope and courage
Find each other somewhere
In the darkness
To lift their voices and speak:
Let there be light.

The Winter 1995 issue of the twenty-page *SAMM Newsletter* contained five poems, and I shall reproduce the last two virtually at random. The first recited:

A thousand words won't bring
back my Son
I know, because I've tried
Even with a million tears
I know, because I've cried
I want my son to be here to love
Instead he is with God
I only hope you give him Love
The way his Mum would.

And the second:

In one sense there is no death.

The life of a soul on earth last beyond his departure.

You will always feel that life touching yours,

that voice speaking to you,

that spirit looking out of other eyes,
talking to you in the familiar things
he touched, worked with, loved as familiar things

He lives on in your life
and in the lives of all others
That knew him.

What seems to be the most frequently reproduced poem of all, seen in newsletters throughout Canada, Britain, and the United States, is Henry Scott Holland's[117] 'Death is Nothing at All', and its beginning and end read:

---

[117] Holland (1847–1914) was to become Regius Professor of Divinity at the University of Oxford.

Death is nothing at all
I have only slipped away into the next room.

I am I, and you are you,
Whatever we were to each other,
that we still are.

Call me by my old familiar name,
speak to me in the easy way
which you always used....

I am waiting for you,
for an interval,
somewhere very near,
just around the corner.

All is well.

Many find solace in such writing, and survivors may well be encouraged to write memorial poems or stories themselves.[118] A woman from Stoke-on-Trent wrote to the SAMM newsletter: 'Believe it or not the wonderful poem on the front cover [of the recent newsletter] brought about an amazing turning point in the healing process since my sisters Murder.'[119] Another woman sent a poem to SAMM saying, 'my son was murdered in 1993 and its hard to find any words of comfort but I came across the verse opposite...' And a third woman wrote to 'express [her] disappointment in the recent SAMM newsletter. Previous news have been enjoyable to read, and have offered comfort. From the SAMM newsletter, I like to see more poems...'

The survivors' memorialising speech and the newsletters' poetry work with a conventional, high language of the emotions, a medium for expressing the inexpressible, objectifying and translating recollection, giving meaning to that which comes perilously close to being meaningless, restoring dignity to thought and speech, and ennobling memory and redeeming it from ugliness. They draw on recognised eloquence to elevate the mind. They are, in short, part of a project to re-moralise the universe, an attempt to alleviate pain and suffering by 'seeking coherence in meaning through belief.'[120]

---

[118] Such a recommendation is made, for example, in the *Families and Friends of Murder Victims Newsletter*, Nov 1996, 5.
[119] *SAMM Newsletter*, Autumn 1995, 14.
[120] D. Handelman, review of R. Firth, *Religion: A Humanist Interpretation*, in *The Times Higher*, Education Supplement, 7 Mar 1997.

They lean heavily on a loose religiosity—more close, perhaps, to spiritualism than to the teachings of the established church—which beatifies the dead and points to their continuing presence, confirms the steadfastness of the mourner, anticipates the possibility of some final reunion of the dead and the living, and foretells the victory of good over evil. So it was that a joint Justice for Victims and Victim's Voice Memorial Service held at the church of St Martin-in-the-Fields on 9 December 1995 celebrated the theme of 'love and peace and the triumph of light over darkness'. The service was opened by the Rev John Pridmore who said: 'we meet as those who must remember. We meet in grief... We also meet in hope. If we had surrendered to despair we would not be here today. We reach out in mutual support and love... We hope that love and life, not hate and death, will win...' And it ended with the placing of forty-two lighted candles, one for each victim mourned by the congregation, the candles symbolising 'three things: 1) undying love; 2) light is stronger than darkness and 3) not to give way to darkness but to go on living in the light of all that is true and good.'

A number of survivors lived in a world of feelings and symbols that was rather remote from the dull realm of everyday rationality. It was not unusual to see works on spiritualism, reincarnation, and the Eastern religions in their homes (The Compassionate Friends' twenty-six page lending library list in circulation in the mid-1990s contained three pages of titles on 'religion and philosophy' and two on 'Life After Death, Spiritualism'.). Theirs was often a new existence full of signs and portents in which the dead were all about them in visible[121] and invisible form (and in their alertness to the otherworldly, they were not very different from other groups of the bereaved[122]). It was as if the dead formed their own world that was also part of the larger community of SAMM.

It was also as if members could not bear forever to exclude their dead children from their lives.[123] A mother said 'I'm with —— [her

---

[121] See, for instance, the description of the visions seen by the parents of the children who were killed in the Dunblane massacre of 1996, in P. Samson and A. Crow, *Dunblane: Our Year of Tears* (Mainstream Publishing, Edinburgh, 1997), 134.

[122] See J. Littlewood, 'The denial of death and rites of passage in contemporary societies', in D. Clark (ed), *The Sociology of Death* (Basil Blackwell, Oxford, 1995), 81; P. Marris, *Loss and Change* Routledge and Kegan Paul, London), 25; C. Murray-Parkes, *Bereavement*: Studies of Grief in Adult Life (Tavistock, London, 1972), 44; and T. Walter, *The Revival of Death* (n 31 above), 82.

[123] See T. Walter, 'A new model of grief: bereavement and biography', *Mortality*, Mar 1996, Vol 1, No 1, 10.

son], I'm with —— all the time anyway, and ——s with me.' And another activist remarked: 'I feel that my son's helping me—it may sound a bit strange to you—but you know, I feel very spiritual at times.' An American survivor was reported to be certain that her son had returned as a house fly.[124] Ann West was amazed by the 'two huge white dogs' who walked calmly through the house after the funeral of Lesley Ann Downey: 'To this day [we] can[not] fathom what those dogs came for or what, if anything, they signified.'[125] Irene Ivison described a 'beautiful golden light' which she had seen when her father died and when her daughter was murdered.[126] And Colin Caffell was struck by the opening of two wall-flowers on the day of his twins' funeral; by a robin which he was certain had acted as an emissary of the dead; by hearing his childrens' voices; and by a conviction that a sculpture he made would embody their spirits.[127]

Survivors may then maintain that they represent not only themselves as the secondary victims of crime but also the mute, dead, and sometimes watchful primary victims as well; and their accounts were turned inward and outward, not only towards and for the victim, but also towards the world.[128] Whether the dead were still in attendance or not, survivors were their voice and their champion; the custodian of their reputations and interests; the ones who spoke for 'those who saw the Gorgon',[129] the true witnesses who had known the truth but could not now speak for themselves; and some large part of their authority was conceived to flow from the quasi-religious mandate which that conferred.[130] They had a strong moral purpose in testifying: believing, as other survivors believed, that 'to bear witness is to take responsibility for truth'.[131] Attending

---

[124] D. Magee, *What Murder Leaves Behind: The Victim's Family* (Dodd, Mead and Company, New York, 1988), 46.

[125] *For the Love of Lesley* (n 83 above), 95.

[126] I. Ivison, *Fiona's Story: A Tragedy of Our Times* (Virago, London, 1997), 23–4.

[127] See *In Search of the Rainbow's End* (n 50 above), 82, 103, 109, 213–4, 231, 249.

[128] See I. Hacking, *Rewriting the Soul* (n 9 above), 211.

[129] P. Levi, *The Drowned and the Saved* (Michael Joseph, London, 1988), 64.

[130] In this, the survivors of homicide were again not alone. Holocaust survivors also took it that they spoke on behalf of the dead. See T. Des Pres, *The Survivor: An Anatomy of Life in the Death Camps* (Oxford University, Press, Oxford, 1976), 37. See also the interview with Simon Wiesenthal in *The Times*, 12 Apr 1996: 'I feel guilty that I survived . . . I recognise that I should be the mouth of them, they are forever silent.'

[131] S. Felman, 'The Return of the Voice', in S. Felman and D. Laub, *Testimony: Crises of Witnessing in Literature, Psychoanalysis and History* (Routledge, New York, 1992), 204.

a trial, said a bereaved father, 'was the last thing you can do for them, isn't it?' Stan Cohen would set that purpose within the larger Enlightenment project, in an 'old-fashioned faith in the power of knowledge',[132] which would lead to change through testimony.

Jayne Zito told a meeting held at the Home Office that: 'My husband has been murdered. I haven't any children. I would like to ask on behalf of everyone that we should have a mandatory right to make representations on behalf of the victims who have died...'[133] She later told me that 'it's a way of fighting for Jon and it still is. It's like he had no chance.... It's about making his presence known somewhere.'

Boundaries and taboos

It may then be understood how very urgent was the need to keep memories unsullied, how deeply felt were slurs and calumnies which threatened the public face of the victim, and how imperative it was that the survivor should simultaneously defend that face from symbolic attack and ensure that warring representations were kept far distant from one another. Joan Bacon of Justice for Victims inveighed against the sense of contamination she felt:

I just felt that we have led good honest lives and I just couldn't wash this filth and scum away.... These people are the dregs of society, they're not normal, they're not the people that we've always mixed with and worked with and socialised with and been with, they're the absolute dregs of society, they're just nobodies, nothing, there's just nothing decent about them at all, and I just felt that their indecency had washed into my family, and I just couldn't wash it away.... I think what about my grandchildren and I look at their little faces, open and honest, and I feel that this filth has just crossed over into our lives and it has no right to... You've always thought that there's good and evil and goodness must come out on top but the way things are now, it doesn't.

Survivors could be offended by discourtesies, hurts, and slurs, sometimes, no doubt, offered quite inadvertently by those with whom they had dealings. They resented being identified as suspects by the police. They resented the casual and unceremonious manner in

---

[132] S. Cohen, *Denial and Acknowledgement: The Impact of Information about Human Rights Violations* (Centre for Human Rights, Hebrew University of Jerusalem, Jerusalem, 1995), 12.
[133] Report of Meeting held at Home Office, 20 Apr 1994.

which they were sometimes given death certificates.[134] They resented not being able to hug the victim after death. They resented the return of property still marked by blood stains or labelled 'contaminated health risk'.[135] They resented the victim being called 'the body' at inquest and trial. They resented attacks on the victim's character delivered at trial and by the press. They resented inaccuracies in the spelling and detail of names and events ('Victims should not become printing errors'[136] said Greg Stokes of SAMM, whose father had been murdered in North Africa). They resented larger distortions in reporting (recall the distress of the Watsons at the story published in *Marie Claire*). They resented anodyne attempts at comfort, at being asked how they felt, or whether they 'had got over it yet'. The parents of a murdered child would resent being told that 'you can always have another one' or that 'you always have the other children'. The children of a murdered parent would resent being told that the loss of an older victim was of less account. RoadPeace, the organization representing the victims and secondary victims of traffic crashes, resented the word 'accident'.[137] Survivors resented the slighting of the gravity of murder and murders in the reporting of the mass media.[138] David Renhard of The Compassionate Friends, the father of a murdered girl, recollected:

[134] See *Families of Murder Victims Project: Final Report*, 16.
[135] Ibid, 17.
[136] *A Witness for Peace* (The Kates Hill Press, 1994), 144.
[137] See *RoadPeace Newsletter*, Autumn 1994, No 3, 11. That recommendation was also made by other bodies. For example, the Independent Working Party convened by Victim Support also urged on p 39 of its report, *Support for the families of road death victims*, published in 1994 that the word 'accident' should be replaced by words such as 'crash, incident, fatality or road death.' The working party contained representatives of such organizations as CRUSE, ACPO, RoadPeace and CADD. In an unpublished paper, 'Changing a Media Production Process: From Aggressive to Injury Sensitive Traffic Crash Stories', Sandra Ball-Rokeach and others argue that the very word 'accident' is conducive to aggression because it is a 'subtle form of depersonalization . . . that implies forces beyond anyone's control, whereas crash implies that incidents can be prevented' (8–9).
[138] Perhaps the kind of material they would have resented was the heavily jocular article written by Theodore Dalrymple on English murder. One paragraph, little different from the rest, could serve as illustration: 'Most of the murderers of my acquaintance . . . commit their crimes as a 'one off' as they so touchingly put it. Their murders bear more resemblance to the burgundy of Thurber's cartoon—naive and domestic, with just a hint of amusing presumption—than to the planned, cold-blooded and advantageous acts of murder mysteries, or to the serial killings of sexual psychopaths. The average murder, I am afraid, is singularly lacking in literary possibilities. I miss a good poisoning. . . .', 'Murder Most Anglo-Saxon', *Sunday Times*, 1

I got very cross one day four or five years ago. I had read an article in the *Independent* about murder and I was so incensed—I had actually been interviewed by the *Independent* a year or two previously—and I wrote a letter because this woman had tried to say that murder was very ordinary—it was just a family murder—she was talking about a student that murdered another student—it's a very ordinary murder, just one of these events that happen—and I was livid. I wrote a letter in reply and they put it in as the lead letter the next day which I was rather pleased about.

The article that had so upset him described the murder of a student, Rachel McLean, by her former boyfriend as a prosaic thing, of no real interest—precisely the kind of typification that is so prevalent amongst criminologists and expert commentators—and it had begun: 'It was a humdrum murder of an ordinary girl, and that is its real interest. The events that preceded it were ordinary.... In killing her, John Tanner, rejected as a future friend, achieved a murderer's version of cosy intimacy he wanted: 'a domestic', the most banal kind of murder. Domestic killings are so normal that most do not receive more than a few paragraphs of press coverage....'[139]

Renhard's reply, published in the *Independent* of 10 December 1991, deserves reporting at length because it conveys so well many of the themes of this book:

I was most disturbed on reading Sandra Barwick's article . . . It showed that the writer knows nothing of the effects of murder. . . . No murder is ever ordinary or humdrum, it is horrific and overwhelming, whatever form it takes. The effect it has on the immediate families and the wider circle of friends is devastating, difficult to describe and can be understood only when experienced first hand. It shocks, numbs and turns your whole life upside down. It is nearly nine years since my 21-year old daughter was murdered by a total stranger. The events of that time were brought back vividly by the trial of John Tanner. I still grieve, feel depressed at times, and occasionally reduced to tears. I still have to come to terms with a gap in my life that cannot be filled. I still think of what might have been had my daughter lived.

Oct 1995. Consider too part of Marcel Berlin's equally flippant review of Douglas Wynn's *The Crime Writer's Handbook*: 'A properly wielded axe scores nine for effectiveness but, not surprisingly, a high eight for detectability—the same as using the venom of a poisonous snake which, however, is more difficult to get hold of than an axe. Defenestration is terrific on non-detectability, but finding a suitable window can be a problem. Decisions, decisions.' *The Directory, The Times*, 26 July 1997.

[139] S. Barwick; 'Young love and ordinary murder', The *Independent*, 7 Dec 1991.

Modern society treats murder as entertainment, both in the world of the novel and the film, and also the closely reported real-life drama of a murder trial. The real tragedy, as shown by the devastation caused to the lives of loved ones left behind, does not make good reading and is therefore seldom explored. It certainly does not help the rehabilitation of the victim's family when one reads articles such as the one you published which explains murder away in trivial terms . . .

Survivors resented the more general transformation of homicide into entertainment for others.[140] After all, it is the paradigmatic crime in crime fiction and films, the crime that quite overshadows all others.[141] So it was that, in November 1993, under the acroynm MINE (Murder Is Not Entertainment), the American National Organization of the Parents of Murdered Children began to campaign against the commercial exploitation of homicide in games, television, drama, and fiction, protesting in the words of Elie Wiesel, the holocaust survivor, that: 'There may be times when we are powerless to prevent injustice, but there must never be a time when we fail to protest.' A leaflet issued by Parents of Murdered Children continued:

Murdertainment' continues to re-victimize those who have already been affected by the murder of a loved one, ignores the aftermath of murder, and sets a poor example for the nation's youth. . . . It is tragic that children can purchase knives that scream and ooze blood, murder video games, murder comic books and murder trading cards. But why not? After all, adults 'play' murder by participating in murder mystery dinner theaters and weekends.

The Table of Voices

It may also be understood how difficult it was for families and organizations to contain moral ambiguities. In July 1989, for instance, The Compassionate Friends, a self-help organization for bereaved parents (and the subject of the next chapter), was

[140] A routine example was offered at Toronto's Royal York Hotel in the summer of 1997 by the Murder Mystery! Dinner Theatre which invited people to 'Come and Join the Fun! Participate in the solving of a hilarious Whodunit! . . . Encourage team building while reducing stress through laughter!'

[141] See R. Reiner, 'Media Made Criminality', in M. Maguire *et al* (eds), *The Oxford Handbook of Criminology* (second edition, Clarendon Press, Oxford, 1997), 206.

approached by the National Society for the Prevention of Cruelty to Children with the request that NSPCC 'clients' should be allowed to join its groups. It declined, arguing, in the words of one of its officers, 'that the "NSPCC parents", so to speak, could become the focus for mis-directed and/or inappropriate anger... it was a question of protecting the NSPCC parents...' So too with murders committed within the family,[142] because a small intimate group would then be obliged to house the victim and the offender in close and conflicting relation.[143] The leader of a local group reflected:

there's one family whose son murdered her other son, now she wants to come to the meetings, I mean, I don't know how you go about this because there are people in that group who are going to be cursing the murderers, and there the mother's sat there, whose son has been murdered by her own son, she's trying to grieve for her son who she's lost and visiting her son in prison.... I haven't dealt with her, my other colleague's dealing with her, because she's had liaison with her. I've never spoken to her. [My colleague] doesn't believe she should come to the group.... She doesn't believe she

---

[142] Or, indeed, other small moral communities. The Mayor of Hungerford, Ron Tarry, reflected that the murder of 16 residents of that town in August 1987 was particularly poignant for him because: 'I knew many of them... that made it all the worse and [w]hat made it all the worse was that it was one of the townsmen who perpetrated these terrible acts' (Hungerford Ten Years On, BBC2, 19 Aug 1997).

[143] See E. Rynearson, 'Bereavement After Homicide' (n 6 above), 1454. Colin Murray-Parkes, a psychiatrist with a long history of working with the bereaved, recalled: 'One woman I met, she was from Sri Lanka and her daughter was killed by her husband's younger brother who came to stay in this country with them. It's a complicated story with the charge of murder being reduced to manslaughter—but her rage against this man was so great she wouldn't even allow her husband to speak to any other member of his family because she damned the lot of them... That's half the problem [in any self-help group] because your family is split down the middle, you have identity problems—to actually say I come from a family of murderers in a group where murderers are baddies.' In addition, there may well be profound identity problems for those individuals whose own loyalties can be torn in two. Consider a letter published in *The Toronto Star* of 3 Aug 1997: 'The death of my youngest brother at the hands of my older brother was my initiation into survivorship. With family tragedy, there is no black and white, good or bad, but an area of greyness that one risks forever being lost in it. There was no one for me to hate and no one to whom I could say, 'Yes, you are evil and I curse you'." Interestingly, for those rejected by survivors' groups, the chief defining link may become transformed into the relation to the *offender* rather than to the victim. There is a parallel self-help group, Aftermath, founded in 1988, which defines itself as serving 'the other victims of crime', the families of the 'serious offender'. Rather more than a third of its members are related to people convicted of homicide, and Stephen Will, its chairman, believed that many of them were in a position of considerable moral ambivalence.

should come to the group because she feels that if she comes to the group people are not going to come back again.

In effect, as Coline Covington has reminded me, there was the abiding problem that any memory of the offence and the victim required survivors to remain symbolically in contact with the offender—after all, the offender was an ineradicable component of knowledge of the homicidal act—and any such contact could not but be a continuing source of revictimisation. If there could never be a cleansing that would retain only the ideal and the good, remote from evil, there was nevertheless a ceaseless struggle to separate and purify memories.

That struggle was directed particularly at the pollution which can emanate from an excessive symbolic proximity between murderers and those whom they have murdered. One powerful instance was supplied by the anathematisation of a murderer from the published recollections of those who had been affected by the Dunblane massacre. Sixteen five-year old children and their teacher had been killed at a school in Scotland in March 1996. The book which commemorated the massacre made copious mention of the names of those who had been murdered but it did not identify the murderer by name at all, referring only to 'the devil, in the guise of a sick, twisted man . . . [whose] name is not worthy of appearing in print alongside those men, women and children who were affected by his wanton destruction.'[144] Another instance was provided by an activist survivor who, objecting to some of the content of an earlier draft of this book, instructed me to 'remove [my daughter's] words about respect because although she most certainly did say what you have written, I do not feel your book is the right place for her words to be printed.'

It is evident that the moral economy of the homicide survivor can take intense iconographic form, becoming a matter of the phenomenology, morality, and politics of representations of death and victimisation. It was given poignant expression in the furore deliberately excited by the decision taken by the Royal Academy of Art to stage an exhibition of art, entitled *Sensation*, in September 1997. The exhibition contained a number a pieces expressly designed to shock. The most prominent, and most fervidly debated, was a portrait of Myra Hindley, the notorious child murderer, based

---

[144] P. Samson and A. Crow, *Dunblane: Our Year of Tears* (n 121 above), 15, 21.

on a police photograph, and composed, in *pointilliste* fashion, of a child's handprints. The exhibition was mounted despite re-monstrations from the mothers of Hindley's victims (the Royal Academy maintained that there 'is no such thing as real art which is immoral'[145]). It was picketed by members of MAMAA (Mothers Against Murder and Aggression) and others. And the picture of Hindley itself was attacked with ink and eggs by two separate protestors on the first day of the exhibition itself. Amongst the pickets was Winnie Johnson, the mother of one of Hindley's victims, and she was reported to have said of the attacks that they were 'brilliant and they should do it every day. I'm thrilled to bits it's happened...' She had declared earlier: 'It is criminal and it is disgusting. She [Hindley] is not a person. She is a monster.'[146]

As vivid a demonstration was offered by an exhibition of installa-tion art held by Richard Kamler at the San Francisco Art Institute in the Autumn of 1996. Kamler, an artist and activist, had long been involved in public debates about prisons, having been artist-in-residence at San Quentin Prison in 1980:

When I went into this art, the emphasis had been almost exclusively on institutions and prisons and the horrors of all that. There was nothing more I could say about it and I was getting tired of it. For some reason, I was beginning to think there was an equation here of the keeper and the kept, and there was a third component here, which was the victim, and unless I really dealt with that, and with their very, very legitimate needs for restitu-tion and remorse and, maybe, somewhere down the road, reconciliation, but I don't know about that...looking at those two things, and the media looked at those two things, they manipulate that and they drive the frenzy of prison building and more punishment.... So I thought I ought to look at the victims. So I went to these meetings [of survivor groups], all these meet-ings...for six months, a year, and I'm beginning to realise that the victims feel extremely frustrated, they have no voice whatsoever, and it's true.

The outcome was to be Kamler's 'The Table of Voices' which charted an alternative to 'our notions of correcting and punishing, housing people in prisons, denying them, in many cases, basic human rights and services.'[147] It consisted of a long table, set

---

[145] *The Times*, 18 Sept 1997.
[146] *The Times*, 19 Sept 1997.
[147] R. Kamler, 'The Table of Voices' (San Francisco Art Institute, San Francisco, 1996), 6.

down, as it were, in the basement of a cellblock,[148] bisected by a
sheet of safety glass, resembling a prison's visiting room. Seats were
arrayed on either side of the table, and, before them, telephones:
'Pick up the phone on one side of the table and hear the voice of a
parent of a murdered child telling her story. Pick up the phone on
the other side and hear the voice of the perpetrator telling his story.
These voices seek a common ground, a context for communication
and healing to occur. Surrounding the table is art created by guards,
inmates and the victims.'[149] Kamler had done what others in penal
reform had done before him.[150] He had sought in restorative justice
a solution to the polarisation and alienation of relations embedded
in the criminal justice system, a bringing-together of those who had
been sundered by conflict.

One recorded voice was that of Valerie Richards, founder and
executive director of the Californian survivors' group, Families and
Friends of Murder Victims. She recounted on tape how the police
had called upon her in August 1991:

'You have a son named Daniel?' And I said 'Yes, is there something wrong?'
And they said 'Yes'. I remember reaching out and touching his lapel and I
said, 'Please tell me is he OK and he said, "No, he is not". Then I screamed
for my husband and I looked back up at the detective and said "Did he
suffer?" and he said, "He was shot twice in the head". And that was the start
of the nightmare.'[151]

When they saw what had been done in their name, many of the
survivors' 'voices' declared their revulsion, particularly at the moral
equivalence traced between the offender and the parent of a murdered child, on the one hand, and at the physical proximity of the
victims' artifacts to those of the killers, on the other. It is impossible
not to hear in their dissent a protest about symbolic defilement and
the violation of deep taboos. The 'voices' declarations were to
become so emphatic that a public meeting was called at the San
Francisco Art Institute on 26 September 1996.

---

[148] It was planned that the exhibit would move from San Francisco to Alcatraz in
October 1996.
[149] Ibid, 10.
[150] I narrate a little of the history of restitutive justice in *Helping Victims of Crime:
The Home Office and the Rise of Victim Support in England and Wales* (Clarendon
Press, Oxford, 1990), ch. 7.
[151] *The Table of Voices* (n 147 above), 11.

The meeting was to be opened by Richard Kamler who asserted that 'the table came about as an attempt to give voice to communities and groups who had no voice . . . to give a voice to the victims.' It was then introduced by a chairwoman who likened it to 'a community conversation, a live version of the table, around a number of people who came to tell us their feelings.' Present on a panel were, *inter alia*, the mother of a murderer, an ex-offender who was working in a rehabilitation project in East Palo Alto (called the 'murder capital of America', like so many other towns in the United States, by those who lived in the neighbouring Palo Alto proper), and Valerie Richards. Instead of delivering a history of herself and answering a battery of prepared questions about violence and its remedies, as she was supposed to do, Valerie Richards made a statement:

As many of you know, the reason I'm sitting here is that in 1991 my only son was murdered. But before I go into that story, I need to make an announcement . . . Once I came here and saw this display, I had some problems with it which I addressed with Richard. We were on the 'phone for quite a while and we came to a few agreements. After that, I was contacted by the family of Dean Lewis. Now, Dean Lewis was the 16-year old who was murdered by Greg ——, and after I talked with Mrs Lewis at length, and her daughter at length, I asked myself 'how much, what am I willing to spend, in order to get my voice out there? *Where is my line?*' And I have to say that the display of my son's things and my voice in *this exhibit as it stands now is unacceptable and reprehensible to me* and to victims that are here with me. *I feel, it is my opinion, that the line of decency has been crossed.* Now you may ask why. The reason is because Greg —— is being featured in this display. To create a shrine-like setting to a man who beat a 16-year old with a framing hammer, striking him 26 times . . . ! After the murder of Dean Lewis, and because these things are on display, the victims that I'm involved with feel that this is not acceptable. When the Lewis family found out about this display they were retraumatised and revictimised all over again. Most of you cannot imagine the excruciating pain associated with revictimisation . . . but I understand what my fellow victims are saying to me. Featuring murderers who have served their time, who have been released, and now lead productive lives, is one thing. We understand that. But featuring an incarcerated murderer and thereby retraumatising the victim is another. . . . *We are all requesting the immediate removal of all things belonging to Greg —— from this exhibition. If our request is not met, we shall ask for the immediate removal of our things in the next few days.*[152]

---

[152] My transcription, emphasis added.

In her talk about lines of decency, in her insistence that the close juxtaposition of an imprisoned murderer's possessions with those of a victim was deeply offensive, Valerie Richards was affirming the profound power of adjacent representations and artifacts to corrupt one another. The murderer's possessions were subsequently removed when the Table moved to Alcatraz. Valerie Richards was later to say to me, there was 'an insult . . . and we wanted the things separate so he did separate them, but he didn't remove that display. . . . It was terrible. . . . It hit me right in the face that's complete lack of respect for the victim . . . I was very insulted and I just kept thinking of my son.'

The special moral standing of the bereaved

I would argue that out of the alchemy of grief there may emerge (particularly in its strongest and most activist form) a very special conception of the survivor as a self transformed.[153] Survivors would talk and write to SAMM about 'the day that changed our lives forever' and about the ending of 'our normal life'.

So conceived, the survivor was one who had been set apart by extraordinary grief, scourged by suffering, fired by anger, and tried by adversity. He or she would have crossed an existential divide to attain unparalleled experiential knowledge,[154] a unique and ir-reproachable moral authority to speak for and about the living and the dead, and a mission to act. Jane Cooper, then co-ordinator of SAMM, told a Northern Ireland Victim Support Workshop on Victims of Violent Crime in January 1995; 'We may not be "professionals" but we are the only ones who know what murder is really like', and that phrase, and others like it, were to be heard again and again. It is impossible not to see in that conception a form of 'creative mythology' which gives pattern and purpose to the survivor's new life. Campbell, who writes about creative mythologies,

---

[153] See, too, L. Langer, *Holocaust Testimonies* (Yale University Press, New Haven, 1991), 49.

[154] See, for instance, D. Magee, *What Murder Leaves Behind* (n 124 above), p. xvi. A leaflet from the American Stephanie Roper Foundation, 'A message for Victims of Crime', contained a poem, 'To One in Sorrow' by Grace Crowell, whose first two stanzas read:

'Let me come in where you are weeping, friend
And let me take your hand.

I, who have known a sorrow such as you, can understand . . .'

endows them with three chief functions: to reconcile the waking mind to the mystery of the universe, to offer an interpretive image and to enforce a moral order.[155] Some such work may be discerned in the new tales that are being told about the survivor.

The survivor's repeated theme was that 'people who haven't been through it don't understand'.[156] In 1980, the American Jermaine L. Jefferson Memorial Fund issued a pamphlet, 'Is there anything I can do to help: Suggestions for the Friends and Relatives of the Grieving Survivor'. Item 10 read: 'Do not attempt to tell the bereaved how he or she feels. You can **ask** (without probing), but you cannot **know**, except as you are told' (emphasis in the original). SAMM's own leaflet described the working of the group: 'By understanding (as a self help organisation perhaps we are the only people who can understand)...by experience, we are well qualified to help!'

The paradox of reflexivity

In all this, there was evidently something rather curious about the shaping of motives and memories. In talking about many matters with seasoned campaigners,[157] I seemed rarely to encounter naive first recollections but stories that had been told and heard many times before. In his own anthropology of death, Barley observed that:

Our own urge to see life in narrative terms is clear in the creation of heroes whose lives must fit into an acceptable narrative form with alternative endings to please different factions. . . . Death does not just exist. In order to have coherence and to find its place, it has to be integrated into a wider scheme of things.[158]

The utterances and sentiments which I have reproduced could not have been naive, unrehearsed, or solitary. To the contrary, they tended to be the result of prior deliberation and discussion. Much had already been published or aired in collective settings; much had

---

[155] J. Campbell, *Creative Mythology* (Penguin, New York, 1968).

[156] That particular version of the phrase was employed by David Hines of NEVA in an article in *The Big Issue*, 5 Oct 1993.

[157] 'Many' rather than all, because I was fortunate enough to get to know some survivors quite well over time, and we were to discuss organizational and other issues touching on the new groups which were not part of their familiar discourse about homicide and bereavement.

[158] N. Barley, *Dancing on the Grave: Encounters with Death* (Abacus, London, 1997), 73, 151.

already been read, heard and distributed amongst an audience of fellow-survivors;[159] and sentiments had thereby come to give and be given a communal character. How else could it be? Violent or premeditated death so defied reasonable canons of story-telling that much repetitive work had to be done to give it intelligibility. The principals in this history had written books about themselves, appeared in court and been examined and cross-examined, they had been interviewed on radio and television, been the subject of copious newspaper stories, and become experts and campaigners who told politicians, officials, and practitioners about the reality of the aftermath of murder and manslaughter. Some, indeed, would brandish the longer newspaper articles about themselves as trophies. Their lives and feelings had necessarily been given a structured, external, and public form. As the last chairman of POMC and the future first chairman of SAMM, it was said, David Howden had 'become accustomed to re-examining the events of that January night and morning after, when he found his daughter and the harrowing sequence of the following years.'[160]

The holocaust survivor, Primo Levi, who had written and talked at length about his memories of Auschwitz, reflected that it is 'true that a memory evoked too often, and expressed in the form of a story, tends to become fixed in a stereotype, in a form tested by experience, crystallised, perfected, adorned, which installs itself in the place of the raw memory and grows at its expense.'[161] In common with other survivors who had come to lead public lives, homicide survivors experienced an inevitable loss of innocence, another form of alienation.

No longer do people simply 'tell' their...stories to reveal the 'truth' of their...lives: instead, they turn themselves into socially organised biographical objects. They construct—even invent, though that may be too crass a term—tales of the intimate self...Are their stories really to be seen

---

[159] For instance, copies of American materials from the Stephanie Roper Foundation and the Jermaine L. Jefferson Memorial Fund were sent to me by Ann Virgin of Justice for Victims.

[160] E. Dunn, 'In Sorrow and in Anger', *Telegraph Magazine* (issued by Victim Support London without date or other particulars as part of its homicide training pack for victim support volunteers). Howden had not only been subject to copious stories in newspapers and on television, but had also spoken about his bereavement to victim support volunteers, CPS officials, police officers, and others. He appeared in a training video for counsellors and others: 'No Chance to Say Goodbye: Traumatic Bereavement and its Management', Jo Marcus Productions, no place, no date.

[161] P. Levi, *The Drowned and the Saved* (n 129 above), 11–12.

as the simple unfolding of some inner truth? Or are their very stories something they are brought to say in a particular way through a particular time and place? And if so, where do they get their 'stories' from?[162]

It was in this sense that the survivors' stories had tended on occasion to become prepared, virtually public scripts for surviving, for describing surviving, and for helping other survivors to under-stand surviving, and they flowed back into experience, ordered memory, and guided future action: the narrator and narrative being at once subject and object, actor and process acted upon. Antze and Lambek observed that: 'Memories are produced out of experience and, in turn, reshape it...there is a dialectical relation-ship between experience and narrative, between the narrating self and the narrated self.'[163] And more graphically still, Plummer observes of other survivors' narratives, 'there is a complex process of...lives entering stories, only to find the stories creating the lives.'[164]

Survivors' memories and identities were historically-situated, collective accomplishments, an outgrowth of what Ian Hacking called the process of 'making up people'. Survivors have not always existed as a social type. They have been *constructed*, and con-structed recently, and my own analysis has reported some of the themes that now run through a received way of talking about a new role. The emotionally chaotic and formless had been given form, aided in part by the interpretations which others had conferred, by a process which is still quite opaque to sociology.[165]

What, in each case, was first-hand and what second-hand in that talk, what was learned through immediate, lived experience, and what through the mediated reports of others, was not a matter which I could readily determine after the event and at a time when the survivors had already established an identity and *habitus* for themselves. Perhaps many survivors themselves could not do so either. Perhaps it did not matter. After all, as Hobbes once remarked, 'Imagination and Memory are but one thing.' Hearing

---

[162] K. Plummer, *Telling Sexual Stories* (Routledge, London, 1995), 35.
[163] P. Antze and M. Lambek (eds), *Tense Past: Cultural Essays in Trauma and Memory* (Routledge, New York, 1996), pp. xii, xviii.
[164] K. Plummer, *Telling Sexual Stories* (n 162 above), 107.
[165] Denzin once remarked that we have still to learn 'how...emotionality [is] taught and how...the feelings of self [are] interiorized and made part of those biographical structures we call persons'. N. Denzin, 'Emotion as Lived Experience', *Symbolic Interaction*, 1985, Vol 8, No 2, 234–5.

and telling survivors' stories certainly made it difficult to distinguish between surviving and ideas about surviving. It made it difficult for a survivor not to recognise himself or herself in story and be influenced by that recognition and that representation:[166] after all, narratives are reflexive projects.[167] What *was* clear is that survivors thought and remembered the facts of bereavement in marked, consequential ways, partly, but not wholly, through a logic-in-use that was to hand, and it is a sociological axiom that 'if men define situations as real, they are real in their consequences'.[168]

Having read an early draft of what I had written about that paradox, one of the prime movers of the new organizations, Ann Robinson, confessed to her uneasiness about the argument. As one of the founders of Parents of Murdered Children, she was a woman who had appeared often on radio and television, and she had herself written and talked publicly about her own and others' grief. It was the case, she conceded, that people 'will pick up jargon and learn better phrases', 'you do work out a speech, if you like', and 'feelings were refined', but, beyond that, the brute facts of traumatic bereavement *did* remain, and they remained very similar throughout the long succession of histories that were related to her as the co-ordinator of POMC by survivors who had not had time to be schooled in narrative structure: 'as with any trauma, the stories were identical.'

It was as if the *content* of traumatic experience was embedded, personal, and concrete, lacking rehearsal, and emerging as an immediate reaction to unassimilable knowledge. Further, it was as if that unassimilable knowledge of violent death generated very much the same responses (and that is certainly the way in which I have tried to relate the matter in the early chapters of this book). But the *forms* through which those responses could be expressed acquired communal character over time. Experience was shaped socially, and in being shaped, it became objectified and estranged, but it was none the less 'authentic' for all that.

[166] That is a point which I have borrowed from Charles Stafford's ethnography of the very different world of childhood in Taiwan: *The Roads of Chinese Childhood* (Cambridge University Press, Cambridge, 1995), 17.

[167] See A. Giddens, *The Consequences of Modernity* (Stanford University Press, Stanford, 1990).

[168] W.I. Thomas, *The Child in America* (Alfred Knopf, New York, 1932), 572.

Conclusion: the imperative to organize

It is in turn not difficult to understand how exceptional survivors may take it that they are impelled by moral and political obligation to act as the champion not only of others who are similarly beset but also of the dead whom they mourn. They may say that they wish to act so that others will not suffer as they have done. They may seek justice or a full disclosure of what may have happened (the Lockerbie survivors were particularly incensed at the public mystery still surrounding the bombing of PanAm Flight 103[169]). They may wish to restore political balance to those who have been bereft of power.[170] They may wish to counter the guilt or humiliation felt at not having been able to do more to protect the victim.[171] They may wish to restore moral balance to the universe, converting the consequences of an evil act to good and so partially neutralising it,[172] and that is a most important preoccupation (SAMM called it the 'way in which members . . . - try to put their own dreadful experiences to some positive use'[173]). Diana Lamplugh said: 'we all have the power of those we have lost, that love is power, and with that power we may do some good.' A man said of his mother's murder at a SAMM conference in November 1995: 'I've had a lot of regret. I didn't have information. You're not in a state to deal with legal questions. The rationality comes in 2–5 years down the road. So it's great to help people, to be creative rather than destructive. That's really good, because there's so much anger.' Again, at a meeting of Victim's Voice, one member said to another 'maybe some good came out of the bad', and she met with accord, 'that's why we're all here, to let good come out of bad.'

Survivors may wish to memorialise the dead so that, through their actions, the victim will be remembered and remain a force in the

[169] Pam Dix of UK Families Flight 103 wrote that: 'Our two main aims are to provide mutual emotional support and friendship, and to press for an independent inquiry into the disaster and aviation security in general. Initially much of the anger, frustration and hurt that we felt was channelled inwards, and towards each other. As far as possible we have turned that hurt into a driving force for change in airline and airport security systems, and to seek the truth surrounding the events that led to the bombing of Flight 103.' *Disaster Action Newsletter*, Spring 1992, No 1, 3.

[170] See A. Burgess, 'Family Reaction to Homicide', *American Journal of Orthopsychiatry*, Apr 1975, Vol 45, No 3, 393; M. Peach and D. Klass; 'Special Issues in the Grief of Parents of Murdered Children', *Death Studies*, 11, 1987, 86.

[171] See T. Des Pres, *The Survivor* (n 130 above), 40.

[172] See C. Murray-Parkes, 'Psychiatric Problems Following Bereavement' (n 6 above), 52.

[173] 'Information Sheet', SAMM, n.d, 2.

world.[174] So many of the new organizations bear the names of the dead: the Suzy Lamplugh Trust; The Zito Trust; the Manwaring Trust; the Gemma and Oliver Graham Memorial Foundation; and others. Laws in America have even come to be known by the names of the victims who inspired them. There is 'Megan's Law', arising from the murder of a young girl by a paedophile neighbour, which requires the publicisation of the names of sex offenders living in a community. The 'three strikes and you're out' law in California was indissolubly linked with the social and political response to the murder of Polly Klaas in 1993.[175]

Ann Robinson told a conference of the European Forum for Victim Services held at Stockholm in June 1990: 'For me, the most poignant moment was when Bjorn, the chairman, dedicated that part of the conference to the memory of my murdered son, Andrew—I couldn't hold back my tears of gratitude and pride. Pride in my beautiful son's life and gratitude that his life and death had been acknowledged and given meaning.' She was later to observe to me: 'that was wonderful because I've always said that if something positive has come out of something which is so evil, and I look at my son's photograph, and I think, yes, I'm sure somebody would have got this group [POMC, later SAMM] going, and it would have gone on, but the fact remains that it was Andrew's death and Tracy's death, June's [Patient] daughter…'

At times, it is almost as if survivors were so consumed by a restless, turbulent energy, compounded out of anger and sorrow, that they had to secure a release through vigorous action (Ann Elvin, the mother of a man killed in the workplace, founder of the Relatives Support Group for Justice, said: 'It is said that to feel anger and bitterness is soul destroying but that is an old wives tale, because my soul feels perfectly all right. I have never felt stronger in my life. My hate has given me strength.'[176]).

One can discern recurrent images of a hydraulic model of the emotions so subject to internal pressure that it must find a discharge

---

[174] Pat Green of SAMM Merseyside said: 'I want to keep Philip's memory alive. I don't want these people to think they're going to forget him. They'll never forget him because they'll always hear me, and I feel it's very important to me…'

[175] See R. Surette, 'News From Nowhere, Policy to Follow: Media and the Social Construction of "Three Strikes and You're Out"', in D. Schichor and D. Sechrest (eds), *Three Strikes and You're Out* (Sage, Thousand Oaks, Calif, 1996), 179.

[176] A. Elvin, *The Invisible Crime: The true story of a mother's fight against the government's cover-up of workplace manslaughter* (Ann Elvin, London, 1995), 105.

(Diana Lamplugh of the Suzy Lamplugh Trust said: 'that energy has absolutely nowhere to go because you have no rights, you can't go and find your child, so the energy had to go somewhere'). And Colin Murray-Parkes, the psychiatrist advising POMC and then the SAMM/Victim Support Steering Committee, told SAMM at its meeting in March 1995:

Traumatic bereavement inevitably causes an enormous amount of rage, and one can't just turn that off, one shouldn't turn that off. I think anger is not in itself either good or bad. It can have good or bad consequences according to how it's expressed, and if we can find a focus, if we can find something which we can do with it, if we can turn it into something creative rather than just hitting out wildly at the people around us . . . then it can become a force for good. I know that one cannot undo what has been done, by punishing someone we can't, for instance, bring back a dead person. Having said that, maybe there is something that you can do which will put something else in balance.

He then proceeded to talk about how SAMM activists had become involved in campaigns about the criminal justice system and how, in Northern Ireland, bereaved mothers had been running the peace movement rather than 'going out and making more bombs to kill people'.

I would contend that many activist survivors see organizing as a personal and a collective project which will take them out into the world not only to rebuild the self but also to restore moral proportion and sense to a society gone seriously awry. David Howden, first chairman of SAMM, declared that he wanted to do 'something worthwhile' about his daughter's death. Irene Ivison of SAMM and Victim's Voice told the 1996 Annual General Meeting of SAMM that 'you've got to contain your anger. If I didn't do this, I'd be isolated and lonely.' A man said of his campaigning wife, 'after we've been to a meeting and talked and perhaps shouted, we go home and feel absolutely drained. . . . If she didn't have this to do she'd be finished.' And Derek Rogers of Justice for Victims said 'it also helps me to cope . . . it's the only thing that gives me a purpose.' Survivors seek to reverse the destructive power of violent death by transforming chaos into purposeful and benign action. In the rest of this book I shall explore the early history of the groups that were to emerge out of that demiurge to act and organize.

5

Beginnings: From The Compassionate Friends to Parents of Murdered Children

Introduction

The organizations whose history is to be traced in this book may be described as 'self-help' groups, although they are more besides. There is no authoritative definition of 'self-help', but the Self-Help Centre of the National Council of Voluntary Organisations[1] did provide a description in its 'training pack' for new groups, and that training pack was eventually to become in the possession of SAMM. If definitions are reflexively self-validating, that of the NCVO must be regarded as a good enough guide to some part of what Jane Cooper, the first co-ordinator of SAMM, and her colleagues learned to regard as 'self-help'.[2] A self-help group, wrote Judy Wilson in the NCVO pack, will be organized around a common problem or condition, its members 'join[ing] to meet their own needs', and taking responsibility for themselves and for the joint management of the group.[3]

---

[1] The NCVO was established in 1919 'as the representative body for the voluntary sector in England' and claims a membership of some 600 national organisations.

[2] She was eventually to tell Victim Support that '...individuals always talk of feelings of isolation, and of no one being able to understand their distress, their own "personal hell". This is where self- help or mutual support comes in...some reduction in personal isolation can be helped by talking to someone who has experienced a similar tragedy, and someone who has found some inner strength to survive that tragedy. It is so important to recognise that feelings and behaviours are normal; that they are not weird, strange or losing their minds. It is normal to feel weak, helpless, powerless, confused and out of control. People need to be helped not to feel negative about this...'; talk to N. Ireland Victim Support Victims of Violent Crime Workshop, 20–22 Jan 1995.

[3] J. Wilson, *Self-Help Groups: Getting started—keeping going* (Longmans, London, n.d.), 5.

It is conventional for writings[4] on self-help to refer back to the intellectual and political inspiration of Samuel Smiles and Prince Kropotkin, but I heard no homicide survivor talking about *Self-Help*[5] or *Mutual Aid*.[6] To the contrary, whatever influence they may once have exerted has been lost in what Husserl would have called the groups' *Stiftung*, their unexcavated foundational knowledge. Neither did survivors allude to therapeutic communities, therapeutic groups, or the resurgence of self-help as a political and existential movement that emerged some thirty years ago as part of what Horowitz labelled the 'politics of experience'[7] and Habermas 'legitimation crisis'.[8]

Groups of people in the late 1960s and early 1970s, representing themselves as socially and epistemologically oppressed, came to spurn the authority of experts to define and manage their condition, and asserted their own existentially-based competence in its place. The professional, they said, did *not* know best.[9] Established knowledge was largely spurious and tyrannical, part of a wider hegemonic control that alienated people from their 'species being'. Rather than the expert teaching the laity about their condition, it was the laity who should become the instructor.[10] Who could possibly be wiser than the person actually undergoing a debated experience? So it was, just at that pivotal time—in 1969—that Haug and Sussman could write of 'the revolt of the client' as a ubiquitous political event:

---

[4] See, for example, A. Katz and E. Bender, *The Strength in Us: Self-Help Groups in the Modern World* (New Viewpoints, New York, 1976), 8, and J. Vincent, *Constraints on the Stability and Longevity of Self Help Groups in the Field of Health Care* (Centre for Research in Social Policy, University of Loughborough, 1986), 17–18.

[5] S. Smiles, *Self-Help: With Illustrations of Character, Conduct and Perseverance* (centenary edition, John Murray, London, 1958). Its opening paragraph began: 'Help from without is often enfeebling, but help from within invariably invigorates. Whatever is done for men or classes, to a certain extent takes away the stimulus and necessity of doing for themselves; and where men are subjected to over-government, the inevitable tendency is to render them comparatively helpless.'

[6] P. Kropotkin, *Mutual Aid* (Allen Lane, Harmondsworth, 1972, first published in 1902). Kropotkin, a prominent anarchist, had argued that mutual aid, not Darwinian competition, was the basic law of human evolution, and that the future should lie in small communities based on voluntary co-operation.

[7] I. Horowitz, 'The Politics of Drugs', *Social Policy*, July–Aug 1972.

[8] J. Habermas, *Legitimation Crisis* (Heinemann, London, 1976).

[9] See S. Cohen, 'It's All Right For You to Talk', in R. Bailey and M. Brake (eds), *Radical Social Work* (Edward Arnold, London, 1975).

[10] See G. Tracy and Z. Gussow, 'Self-Help Health Groups: A Grass-Roots Response to a Need for Services', *The Journal of Applied Behavioral Science*, Summer 1976, Vol 12, 390.

The situation...is that professional knowledge, service, autonomy, and organizational authority is being challenged at various levels of society and among widely diverse groups. Students...deny the expertise and good will of their educators, while they demand an end to administration and faculty power to meddle in their private lives. Poverty group members arguing that they know more about their community needs, problems, and solutions than the professional social workers and are more concerned, have organized for a voice in welfare benefits and their distribution. Cutting across social class lines, the blacks confront professors, teachers, and social workers with their demands for more adequate services, while hospital patients organize to hold professional control over their lives in bounds.[11]

Those with discontents and problems in the late 1960s and early 1970s turned inwards towards themselves and others thought to be like themselves for more satisfying classifications, interpretations, and solutions. Almost every human condition became the focus of its own attendant group:[12] women turned to women in 'speak-outs' on rape; blacks to blacks; Vietnam veterans to Vietnam veterans; homosexuals to homosexuals; paedophiles to paedophiles; ex-patients to ex-patients; students to students; ex-alcoholics to ex-alcoholics; gamblers to gamblers; narcotics users to narcotics users; and congregants to congregants. They traded practical knowledge so that Sorbonne students emulated the Berliet workers, prisoners radical students, psychiatric patients unionised workers, and people on drug recovery programmes former alcoholics. Often hostile to large bureaucratic organizations,[13] emphasizing the superior experiential understanding of their own members, furnishing a countering community of the like-minded (indeed frequently acting as a form of surrogate community[14]), recognising problems dismissed or misinterpreted by others, advocating local initiative and self-improvement, they had widespread political and ideological appeal. Any practice rooted in Fanon, Freud, Kropotkin, Marx, Maxwell Jones, and Smiles could not have failed to have had a catholic allure.[15]

[11] M. Haug and M. Sussman, 'Professional Autonomy and the Revolt of the Client', *Social Problems*, Fall 1969, Vol 17, No 2, 157.

[12] See A. Gartner and F. Riessman (eds), *The Self-Help Revolution* (Human Sciences Press, New York, 1984), 18.

[13] See A. Katz and E. Bender, *The Strength in Us* (n 4 above), 11.

[14] See M. Lieberman *et al*, *Self-Help Groups for Coping with Crisis* (Jossey-Bass, San Francisco, 1979), 182.

[15] In 1986, Sir Keith Joseph, for instance, wrote a sympathetic preface to a Penguin re-issue of *Self-Help*.

The principle of mutual help was to be put to correspondingly prolific use. A self-help group could disseminate information about problems, research, writings, and services to members. It could counter and neutralise stigmatising typifications; endorse its members' sense that the wider world was unjust or callous; normalise responses to abnormal experience, and so persuade members that they were neither pathological nor ill; help the isolated and frightened by offering collective support against threat;[16] and re-establish trust where trust had been fractured. It could elevate the afflicted by defining them as survivors or combatants rather than as victims; translate tragedy into action; capitalise on strengths and so furnish assertive models of behaviour; and tailor words to challenge the language of handicap, disability, and disempowerment.[17] It could establish an appropriate emotional field and setting for the expression of pain and anger, and supply an understanding and patient audience for those who wished to talk when people in everyday life did not understand and had tired of listening.

The groups tended to be little democracies, their organization characteristically anarchistic and hierarchically flat (although, paradoxically, they could also revolve around an inspirational founder or founders who were given exceptional authority[18] and a small minority of activists who 'do all the work'[19]). After all, they had been established as part of a counter-politics which denied the presumptive right of others to prescribe and judge. Equal suffering bestowed equal authority, and insensitivities about the rights of others could always be represented as an extension of the oppressiveness of the external world which could be translated in the group's local idiom into accusations of racism, sexism, exploitation, reaction, or revictimisation.

Networks of support were supplied by telephone communication, newsletters, weekly or monthly meetings, and, perhaps, annual national or regional conferences. A superstructure of writings,

---

[16] See G. Breakwell, *Coping with Threatened Identities* (Methuen, London, 1986), 130.

[17] See M. Oliver, 'Speaking Out: Disabled People and State Welfare', in G. Dalley (ed), *Disability and Social Policy* (Social Policies Institute, London, 1991).

[18] Such structural contradiction is not uncommon. For its working in groups of young people, see S. Blackman, *Youth: Positions and Oppositions* (Avebury, Aldershot, 1995), 26.

[19] See A. Richardson, 'English Self-Help', in D. Pancoast *et al* (eds), *Rediscovering Self-Help* (Sage, Beverly Hills, Calif, 1983), 206.

artifacts, and rituals was created.[20] The groups mushroomed. They became a political and social movement,[21] and their growth and influence came to be described as explosive and revolutionary. By 1976, Katz and Bender estimated that there were some 500,000 self-help groups in the United States.[22] So too, it would appear, in England, although no one actually counted their numbers.[23]

Self-help groups became something of a conventional way of responding to a mass of different social problems, a common template for action, which could be employed again and again. Perhaps therefore it was not so very remarkable that, in 1968, at just the time when self-help was coming into its own, Simon Stephens, assistant chaplain at the Coventry and Warwickshire Hospital, seeking to help two sets of parents mourning lost children, discovered the virtues of mutual aid. No existing lay or professional groups possessed the competence or will to help those bereaved by the loss of a child. Death was a taboo about which people did not speak and for which they did not prepare. Ministering separately to the families of two dying boys, it was reported, Stephens 'saw how much more help two sets of bereaved parents were to be to each other than were the "professionals" around them.'[24] He remarked himself that: 'Immediately a warm friendship developed, which, based as it was on a mutual understanding of the sorrow and heartbreak which had accompanied their own personal tragedies, was of tremendous therapeutic value to both families.'[25] It was a most illuminating encounter, one that might well be likened to an epiphany, and it was similar in form and effect to other dramatic encounters, and to the near-contemporary 'speak-outs' of the women's movement[26] and the gay liberation movement[27] in particular. People who had been set apart against an alien world were

[20] See M. Osterweis *et al*, *Bereavement* (National Academy Press, Washington, DC, 1984), 242.

[21] See K. Back and R. Taylor, 'Self-Help Groups: Tool or Symbol?', *The Journal of Applied Behavioral Science*, Summer 1976, Vol 12, 295.

[22] A. Katz and E. Bender, *The Strength in Us* (n 4 above), 36.

[23] See A. Richardson, 'English Self-Help' (n 19 above), 203.

[24] Undated, untitled leaflet by The Compassionate Friends.

[25] S. Stephens, *Death Comes Home* (Mowbrays, London, 1972), 75.

[26] For a description of the inception of one of the first women's refuges, see E. Pizzey, *Scream Quietly or the Neighbours Will Hear* (Penguin, Harmondsworth, 1974), and of Women Against Violence Against Women see *Daily Telegraph*, 1 Sept 1980.

[27] See, for example, *Gay Liberation* (Red Butterfly, New York, 1970).

brought together to find a common understanding and a new identity. I would argue that it was to be the first of three such critical turning-points, part of a recurrent dialectical process which, fractal-like, ran through the history of groups for homicide survivors.

The Compassionate Friends

The notion of sharing grief through mutual aid was to be generalised into a new voluntary organization, The Compassionate Friends (known colloquially by its initials as TCF), that was founded formally in January 1969 at a meeting of six members held in Coventry.[28] 'Oh yes, that group of bereaved parents…knew just how "the others" felt and they were determined to help them',[29] said Simon Stephens. Within a year TCF had become a national organization intended for any parents and relatives who had been bereaved by the death of a child. It took its name from the good Samaritan and its organizational structure from the stock pattern of the self-help group.[30] It was divided up into local groups clustered by county, and administered by a national committee, consisting of a chairman, secretary, treasurer, and co-ordinator, that was based in Bristol and staffed by a full-time office administrator.[31] It served, said one of those first two sets of parents, as 'a memorial to our beloved children'.

TCF does not advertise itself. Neither does it campaign politically, having become registered as a charity in 1972. It protects its members from prurient interest, refusing to give journalists their telephone numbers without their express consent. It eschews public prominence where there is a risk of what it regards as the 'trivialisation' of tragedy. In April 1991, for example, Jillian Tallon, its then national secretary, wrote to a colleague about her reluctance to support the participation of TCF members in a television studio debate on the film *The Silence of the Lambs*: '[I have] a strong feeling of unease, of "cheap entertainment", of titillation masquerading as something else. The media glorify every kind of crime—

[28] See H. Davidson, 'Development of a Bereaved Parents Group', in M. Lieberman *et al, Self-Help Groups for Coping with Crisis* (n 14 above), 81.
[29] S. Stephens, *Death Comes Home* (n 25 above), 77.
[30] Although there were to be other influences as well, amongst them the Samaritans proper and Elizabeth Kübler-Ross.
[31] 'Introducing The Compassionate Friends' (The Compassionate Friends, Bristol, 1994).

and then wonder why crime is increasing?! It's sheer lunacy.' She was later to write to the show's producer: 'I am sure you will understand that, from our (that is bereaved parents) point of view, murder cannot simply be a news item. For any parent to consider that their child could be abducted, terrified, assaulted and then killed is horrifying.... Before we ask any parent to put themselves through that, we have to ask "What is it for? What will all that relived agony achieve? For whom?" And that in the context of a "magazine programme".'

TCF has worked discreetly, avoiding direct publicity, and recruiting its members at second hand and through the professionals who deal with death. Jillian Tallon reflected that 'our aim in making TCF known is not to aim it at the general public because people don't want to know. If they have got children of their own, the last thing they want to think about is the death of their own child. So we have tried to make ourselves widely known to groups of professionals that we see are involved...' Because it has no great public prominence, recruitment has tended in practice to be organized by the vagaries of professional and lay referral networks, by people learning about TCF through chance acquaintance or after receiving overtures by others.

There were no membership fees and no formal lists of members[32] (Jillian Tallon remarked: 'we reckon that we've all paid the highest price to join a club that we never wanted to join'[33]) and membership has been estimated on a rough calculation of the readership of its newsletters. By the mid-1990s, a different, and more precise calculation, based on the causes of death of children contained in the TCF database, showed that there were just over 5000 deaths mourned by its members nationwide.[34] Presumably the association's full 'membership' of bereaved parents and relatives would have formed an appreciably larger number.

[32] See L. Videka-Sherman, 'Effects of Participation in a Self-Help Group for Bereaved Parents: Compassionate Friends', *Prevention in Human Services*, 1982, Vol 1, 72.

[33] That phrase 'we're the one charity no one wants to join' became fixed in the language of TCF (see, for instance, the article on the Baldocks, Kent county co-ordinators for TCF, in *Medway News*, 3 Feb 1995) and then in the groups that were sired by TCF. It is now a stock description used by SAMM members.

[34] It is not easy to establish what proportion of that 5023 had died from homicide. 144 deaths were classified as 'murder', but none was described as manslaughter or infanticide, and there were fatalities from car crashes and 129 deaths from reckless driving listed separately.

The initial aims of TCF were to 'offer friendship and under-standing to any person, irrespective of colour and creed, who finds himself or herself heartbroken by the death of a child.'[35] 'Having suffered similar tragedies themselves, [members] play a crucial role in befriending the newly bereaved.... families need outlets for the relief of pent-up anxieties and of feelings of guilt, anger and hopelessness. Hence, it is vital for them to feel able to talk freely to an understanding and compassionate friend.'[36] The cardinal themes of TCF were *listening* ('Great relief comes as the parents find the listener wants to hear about the child...'); *sharing* ('The new[ly] bereaved are often frightened by the magni-tude of their own feelings, some of which are completely alien to them.... [Sharing] giv[es] the bereaved the sense that they are not alone and unique in their suffering'); *consolation*—the provision of comfort and the 'consolation that in time—after the pain and turm-oil—life will come to have some meaning once more'; *belonging*— TCF are open to any bereaved parents irrespective of the age of the child; and *activity*, participation in meetings, coffee mornings, and 'get-togethers of various kinds.'

The special competence of TCF inhered in the experiential know-ledge of its members: a TCF member at a meeting of SAMM Merseyside observed to murmurs of agreement, 'I was a bereave-ment counsellor, but until you've lost a child yourself, you know *nothing*!' Bereaved parents would be introduced to one another and, said David Renhard, former national chairman of TCF:

The first question they almost always ask is 'what happened to you?' They don't want to know what happened to you. All they wanted to know is that you know what you're talking about. You've got the ex-perience they're going through. That's all it's about. So we never set up as counsellors or experts or psychiatrists or people like that. We're just people who have suffered like they have.... [We] just let people talk basically and also let them listen if they needed to and, in a meeting, if somebody came in and was in an awful state, you let them cry, let them do what they liked.

That structure, language, and culture were to become, in turn, a prototype for the organizations for homicide survivors which were to grow out of The Compassionate Friends.

[35] S. Stephens, *Death Comes Home* (n 25 above), 77.
[36] 'No death so sad' (The Compassionate Friends, Bristol, n.d.).

In the mid-1990s, there were more than 5,000 members in 138 local groups. By the standards of English self-help organizations, TCF was well-established, and its membership was numerically large and geographically widespread. It was to act as one of the very few self-help groups of its kind for some fifteen years, representing virtually the sole forum in which those bereaved by homicide could meet, and it was inevitable that many of the people who came to play a role in this history moved in its circles at one stage. Because it was a practice to link those who had had similar experiences together for better understanding and support—homicide survivor to homicide survivor, those mourning a cot death to those mourning a cot death—those early relations were to coagulate into a series of smaller, enduring networks centred specifically on homicide, just as other networks and groups came to form around their own specific griefs. Brigitte Chaudhry, founder of RoadPeace, had attended TCF meetings.[37] So had Pat Green, co-founder of SAMM Merseyside; Gill Pennicard, later to be co-ordinator of POMC; the Watsons, founder of Families of Murder Victims; and Graeme Peart, later to be director of Victim's Voice. So, most importantly, had June Patient and Ann Robinson.

June Patient, Ann Robinson and the founding of Parents of Murdered Children

I have referred to June Patient and Ann Robinson in earlier passages of this book. They were to come together within TCF to form Parents of Murdered Children, and Parents of Murdered Children, in its turn, begat SAMM. Let me describe how those very first developments took place.

June Patient and her husband lost their daughter, Tracy, in New Zealand in 1976:

We went there to live and in January 1976 she went to a friend's house which was not that far away, and a friend walked her to the corner which would have been about 10 minutes from home, but she never got home. She was taken. I don't know by whom. She was nearly 14. They were never caught, the people who killed Tracy. . . . We brought her back to England to bury her. We visit the grave still now, regularly. Some people say 'why do you still visit the grave?' I think because I still don't know why she was killed. The police don't know why. There was no motive to it whatsoever. I came back here and then my sister rang up. My sister lived in Bow and I lived in

[37] *RoadPeace Newsletter*, Spring 1994, No 2, 2.

South Woodford at the time, and she said there's a group started for bereaved parents called Compassionate Friends, would I like to go? I said we would [and] John and I went to the meeting.

June and John Patient were to join The Compassionate Friends and become central figures in the organization, particularly in Essex—two of the very few members at that time and in that place who had been bereaved by homicide.

Two years later, Ann Robinson and her husband Peter also lost their child, Andrew, in Germany:

I read an article in a magazine and it mentioned Compassionate Friends and the feelings that the lady was expressing in the article mirrored my own. I felt so terribly alone with my feelings, although I had sympathetic friends. Obviously, you felt that really nobody could understand and I just felt the desperate need to get in touch with the person who wrote this article. Fortunately, there was actually an address for Compassionate Friends so I wrote . . . from Germany. They linked me with June because the policy is to link people who have lost children in similar ways, and in fact at that time I think June was the only active member of Compassionate Friends who had lost a child through murder. . . . I corresponded with June initially, and when we came back to England, I met her and it was just incredible. . . . Immediately June and I met, even before that, with the letters, there was this terrific empathy and relief at meeting somebody else who had been through the same sort of thing and could really understand how you felt. June and her husband and myself and my husband became very close friends, but it wasn't until some time later that I realised I was actually helping June, because I always felt that I was leaning on June, she was helping me. And then one day, she turned round to somebody and 'Ann has helped me so much, I don't know how I would have managed without Ann'. It was at that point I realised it was very much a two way [process].

June Patient, for her part, also acknowledged that special rapport:

We found that we had this thing between us because there was nothing (apart from Colin Murray-Parkes) there is nothing in this country to help people like us. I talked—I used to go to the meetings in Compassionate Friends and there were various . . . some children had died under operations, some in car accidents, some cancer in hospital—and I can remember going to one meeting—this may sound wrong to some people, this lady said that she was with her daughter when she died, and she was holding her hand in hospital, and I almost envied her because Tracy died alone and in terror. I wished that I was in her position. I wished Tracy had died in hospital that I could have been with her. She had the nurses in the hospital whereas Tracy and other victims like her, they just—I don't care what the doctors say, they say some of them don't suffer, nobody knows, do they? She was strangled and the police doctor said that whoever did it knew what they were doing, they did it in a torniquet so that she didn't suffer, but who knows? . . . they said it could have been a matter of seconds, but the thing is, she knew she was going to die and this is the thing. After 19 years I think of her last moments. I don't think she was killed when she was walking along. I like to think she was, I like to think she was taken by surprise from somebody behind, but, deep down, I don't think so, because she was found quite a way away. I think she was taken in a car and then it happened but nobody can prove it. I don't know, the police don't know what happened. . . . a lot of people, I suppose, wouldn't agree with me, but I felt different. I really felt different until I met Anne Robinson. I knew what she was going through and she knew what I was going through, and this is what happens when somebody does lose a child. I can read the paper and think 'my God, what that woman is going through. I know what she is going through'. It is different.

It is useful to report those recollections at such length because they describe the central dialectic of fusion and fission that has structured the evolution of homicide survivors' organizations. Consider what had been said. Both June Patient and Ann Robinson declared that they had felt aberrant, lonely, and little understood, even by their intimate friends and family. Ann Robinson reflected that: 'you feel so terribly alone, you feel so isolated, apart from the group. In normal circumstances, and in one's normal circle of friends, you are highly unlikely to meet somebody else or know somebody else . . . who has had somebody murdered.' Both had been profoundly alienated until they met, and their meeting was described almost as a second epiphany. There was a shock of recognition and a pleasure in mutual understanding that led to an immediate empathetic union. That was the fusion. But it was a fusion quite emphatically defined by the two women's shared sense of what they were *not*, of what they did *not* share with others, even if those others had also lost children in tragic circumstances. The two stood somewhat apart from parents bereaved through illness, suicide, or other misfortune.[38] And that was the fission.[39]

---

[38] In a radio interview, Ann Robinson was to say 'I did feel slightly apart . . . because of the way Andrew died, that's how I felt.' 'All Things Considered', BBC Radio Wales, 13 Dec 1987.

[39] It is interesting that Road Peace, another survivors' group, was, in identical fashion, to have had its origins within the matrix of TCF. Brigitte Chaudhry, mourning the death of her son, killed in a road crash, had attended a number of meetings of

Both women sensed they were significantly and irrevocably different from other members of TCF. Ann Robinson was later to write in an untitled paper: 'we ... realised that [although] the actual loss and grief was as devastating for all bereaved parents, no matter HOW their child died, the sheer horror of what our children suffered and the fact that another human being had brutally ended their lives, somehow set us apart.' Fusion and fission were facets of a single process—manifestations of the binary oppositions described in the previous chapter—that was to reverberate throughout all the subsequent history of groups of homicide survivors.

What had happened in TCF in England in the early 1980s was not idiosyncratic. Rather, it exemplified a pattern repeated across the world. Fusion, fission, and separation were spurred on by dynamic forces that were lodged deep in the social response to the appalling experience of bereavement itself. Consider, for example, an identical sequence narrated by one of the co-founders of Citizens Against Homicide, a northern Californian survivors' group:

I went to Compassionate Friends right after my daughter was murdered. Her father and I both went and we only went for one meeting, and later I chatted with other people to explain to them my feelings as to why I really couldn't stay and become part of their organization, and that was because I had just gone through a murder and I could not relate to people that were discussing a child who died from leukemia, a child that died in a horseback riding accident, or things of this nature, because they had all the answers. They knew everything that they needed to know, and in my case murder is so totally different from all of these other deaths, and they are not remotely related.... I would have so much preferred that she'd died riding a horse ... as opposed to being brutally murdered by another human being that just act out violently on her. So, I just couldn't comprehend, did not fit into the group at all.

The two women came to form the centre of a web of homicide referrals within TCF (Ann Robinson said: 'Over the next two or

---

TCF, and had then become part of a small group also centred on road crash victims which was disbanded: 'I got in touch with the national secretary [of TCF] and I thought I could include something in the newsletter... So I printed the letters and they went with the newsletter, and that's how I got another batch of letters back from Compassionate Friends, and when I had 150, I knew that something must be done.... [They] were all saying the same thing—innocent death being treated as if it were nothing, and as if the children were cattle fodder, no lessons learned... The people that came to us from Compassionate Friends... say that "we don't fit in with people that have lost their child through cot death or cancer..."'

three years we had parents of other children put in touch with us. Some of them could not relate to the other bereaved parents...'[40]). Ann Robinson herself began writing and being interviewed by journalists about the special problems and reactions of those bereaved by violent death, acting, in effect, as a new source for interpreting, representing, and normalising extraordinary experience. She would reassure survivors that their responses were not pathological despite their higher levels of bitterness and anger, heightened guilt, 'feelings of powerlessness and meaninglessness', 'sense of being abnormal freakish', and 'difficulty in being able to reach a resolution of grief when the murder remains unsolved'.[41]

First June Patient and then, in 1984, Ann Robinson became Essex County Secretaries of TCF. By September of that year, a critical mass of homicide survivors seemed to have formed within the area, and, with the encouragement of the TCF national committee, it was decided to hold a meeting solely for them. Ann Robinson recalled that 'there were about a dozen parents and the empathy there—it was almost tangible, and the relief, because we all felt that we could actually talk about even the gruesome details, because, even amongst other parents, you get "was he sexually assaulted?" and "what happened?" and you felt it wasn't for sympathy... But you felt that with the other parents, that you could actually share that, and sharing is therapeutic.'

Having determined that it had 'identif[ied] a very specific need to meet others who had experienced the same form of isolation and grief,'[42] the group continued to meet at six-weekly intervals in the two women's houses. It adopted the title of Parents of Murdered Children,[43] and remained under the aegis of TCF: 'which was good,' said Ann Robinson, 'because we had the support of them, we got referrals from them, we had all their excellent leaflets to use, their library... I couldn't believe how quickly it grew, it just escalated. Most of the referrals at that stage were coming from

---

[40] 'No death so sad', *Nursing Mirror*, Jan 1988, 32.

[41] A. Robinson, 'Some Facts about Murder and Views on its Prevention', n.d.

[42] A. Robinson, 'The Special Needs of Families of Murdered Children', MS, 9 Apr 1987.

[43] Just as, for identical reasons, other organizations had formed within TCF. One was SOS, or Shadow of Suicide, for those whose children had killed themselves. Another was SIBS, for the siblings of those who had died. Ann Robinson said of POMC that it was a 'memorial to our dead children' (report about European forum for victim services, 1990, MS).

Compassionate Friends.' But referrals also trickled in from the police,[44] Victim Support,[45] doctors and nurses, and principally and adventitiously 'by word of mouth'.[46] Ann Robinson and June Patient themselves wrote to parents when they learned about the violent death of a child, they advertised the new group in the TCF newsletter, and, quite by design, they and others became increasingly prominent in the mass media ('If any of you are approached by your local papers, if you can please try to mention the Group . . . we need victims to be aware of our existence—and this is an uphill task'[47] urged the group's newsletter.).

Recruitment procedures were somewhat *ad hoc* initially. Many of the early referrals were clearly contingent on the chance workings of networks of information and support. Thus Joan Bacon, later of Justice for Victims, learned of TCF because she had been referred by a friend of a relative whose son had died as a dental patient. Jill Palm, later to be co-ordinator of POMC, learned of TCF because her friend's neighbour's niece had been killed. Pat Green had received a leaflet from a woman whose two children had been killed in Crete. The Watsons of Families of Murdered Children were told of the group by a police woman. After a time, however, a measure of deliberate searching and self-selection must have played a part. Some members of the Group came to be especially vigilant in contacting those who might be in need of support. For example, Sandra Sullivan, later of Justice for Victims, was to be mentioned repeatedly as one who would approach bereaved people who had been named in the press. So it was that Ron Rodgers, subsequently to be chairman and co-ordinator of SAMM, learned of POMC through her.

Parents bereaved by homicide began to be sifted through TCF, moving towards the new group (June Patient recalled: 'when people came into Compassionate Friends . . . that had had a child murdered, they'd come to our meetings. . . . We felt different from the

---

[44] An undated POMC newsletter reported that leaflets were ready for distribution to hospitals, citizens advice bureaux, social services, victim support schemes, doctors' surgeries, and public libraries.

[45] Members of Parents of Murdered Children would speak at Victim Support conferences, establishing an early connection which was to have important consequences. The Autumn 1990 POMC newsletter, for instance, contains a page-long report by Ruth Fuller on her attendance with Jill Palm, the group's co-ordinator, at the Victim Support national conference in July of that year.

[46] The phrase is David Howden's in his evidence to the Select Committee on Murder and Life Imprisonment, 5 June 1989.

[47] POMC Newsletter, Dec 1990, 3.

others.'). When Ann Robinson, as the first co-ordinator, received a referral, she would send TCF leaflets and arrange for three or four existing members simultaneously to befriend the family, at first by telephone and then by personal visit where possible: the choice of supporter being guided by criteria of availability, geographical propinquity, and the similarity of the circumstances of the death.[48] To be sure, some families were sifted out. Although it was ostensibly open to all, Parents of Murdered Children could not readily manage the moral ambiguities of members who had split loyalties. One co-ordinator remembered 'one instance where a fellow had murdered his child, and the mum did come to the group but she was still visiting the dad in prison . . . . That created a lot of problems.' And an observer from TCF reflected that: 'the meetings I have been to they have actually said sometimes that they cannot tolerate what they call domestic murders by someone in the family. . . . It's not black and white. With what you call a domestic murder there are shades of grey.' Ann Robinson herself recalled: 'I could handle [domestic murder] personally, but some of the members couldn't, and it wasn't a success, I must say . . . which was very sad. . . . Practically all of [the murders] at the beginning were [committed by] strangers, then it was more people who knew—friends, maybe another relative . . . ' Those entering the new group were thus prone to self-selection, and that reinforcement of traits was particularly marked at first.

The cumulative result was that the new cadet group's relations did solidify spatially and socially,[49] and its numbers swelled, from 10 in 1984, to 60 in 1987, 200 in 1988 and 290 in 1990. 'It just got bigger. We couldn't believe how it was growing', said June Patient.

Once again, there had been a powerful sense of fusion, of the experientially alienated meeting one another and no longer feeling quite so alienated. And once again fission was to be the other face of fusion. Parents of Murdered Children had constituted itself as a separate entity within TCF in 1984 to signify the distinctiveness

---

[48] TCF had insisted that parents should have been bereaved for at least two years before they were ready to support others, but there were too many demands and too few members to apply that policy to the POMC group. Support was sometimes offered by those who were themselves still very bruised by grief.

[49] Vincent notes that that unevenness of coverage is the way of self-help groups. See her *Constraints on the Stability and Longevity of Self help Groups in the Field of Health Care* (n 4 above), 4.

of the experience through which its members had passed: 'The group was set up by June Patient and Ann Robinson who felt that, as good as Compassionate Friends were at helping bereaved parents, they could not fully understand the totally devastating effects that follow murder and the special needs of the parents, family and friends.'[50] Ann Robinson said; 'You feel very, very isolated. Really nobody can understand unless they've been through it.... The feelings are so intense.'[51] The Parents of Murdered Children Group was a group that defined itself as quite apart, unlike any other, and it wished symbolically to reinforce the discreteness of its identity (June Patient said: 'we wanted this to be just for parents of murdered children.').

To be sure, the actual magnitude and substance of those alleged differences could never be properly ascertained. How could one ever pretend to penetrate the inner recesses of one's own and another's griefs,[52] ineffable as they are, and make such a comparison? No doubt the differences that were claimed conveyed as much about the fervour with which the group desired an outward semblance of control, shape, and demarcation for its anguish as about any perceptible gulf, but they were thought to be real enough, they offered signifiers for moral character, and they did separate many parents of homicide victims from the rest. And that was to be a symbolic process that would be recapitulated more than once in the history of survivors' groups.

It is interesting that The Compassionate Friends organization in America, formed in Florida in 1971, had also undergone just such a fissiparous evolution, having given birth to an organization also calling itself Parents of Murdered Children in Ohio in 1978.[53] Deborah Spungen of American POMC anticipated word for word the reasons given for fission in England:

[50] 'Information Sheet', POMC, n.d.

[51] 'Good Morning Britain', TVAM, undated videotape in Ann Robinson's possession.

[52] George Herbert Mead reflected, for example, that: 'the "I" does not get into the limelight; we talk to ourselves, but do not see ourselves.... I cannot turn around quick enough to catch myself.' *Mind, Self and Society* (University of Chicago Press, Chicago, 1934), 174–5.

[53] See 'Parents of Slain Children', *Newsweek*, 12 Apr 1982. The propensity to split is not universal. For example, Bereaved Families of Ontario, a Canadian counterpart to TCF that was founded in 1978 under the auspices of Toronto's Hospital for Sick Children, did not undergo fission. In 1997, it retained members who had lost children through stillbirth, suicide, homicide, cot death, and many other causes.

there is a difference in the death of a child who dies violently as opposed to other means. This does not mean to mitigate the pain on the other side. I don't think that one can put a number on pain, but it is just different and has to be treated differently. The parents who have come to us at Parents of Murdered Children (POMC) from Compassionate Friends feel they have been helped a great deal more by being in our group. I think that being in POMC is helpful because there is no one else that really understands what has happened. You'll also find that you will be in a room full of experts, not just experts on grieving, but experts on the criminal justice system and other things that have to be handled. This is not the same as for parents whose children have died in another way. The bottom line, I was told by someone in Compassionate Friends in the United States, was that my child had died, but I still do not agree about that.[54]

There had been the most tenuous and fleeting of contacts between the two sister organizations in Britain and America,[55] but Ann Robinson and June Patient disclaimed any major connection or borrowing between them. Even the title, Parents of Murdered Children, was not devised as a deliberate echo of its American counterpart. It 'just seemed appropriate . . . We couldn't think of a more appropriate name', said Ann Robinson.

The English POMC would work as other self-help groups had done before them. It described itself as 'offering understanding (perhaps we are the only people who can understand), support, sympathy, being an ear to listen and a shoulder to lean on, and by being a safety-net at times of severe emotional crisis.' It would normalise the extraordinary, reassuring members that they were not aberrant in their behaviour (Ann Robinson remarked: 'you get all sorts of feelings expressed and quite often you think you're going mad, you think it isn't normal to feel like this, but what's normal? It's a relief when you can share those feelings and there is somebody else as well—'yes, that's how I am'. For example, a lot of the parents feel that their children are watching them and that they can't resume sexual relations . . . That's something that is quite personal to talk about.'). POMC was to be a 'cross' between the Samaritans and Citizens Advice Bureaux. It would memorialise its members' dead

---

[54] Letter to David Renhard, 5 June 1985.
[55] Nancy Munch, executive director of POMC in America, did recall that Charlotte Hullinger, its co-founder, had visited England to give advice, but June Patient's own recollection of that visit had been that 'somebody came over from the States and she rang me at my house and said she would have liked to have met me but she said she couldn't . . .'

children.[56] It would represent something 'positive' that could grow out of pain and grief. It would end isolation, offer friendship,[57] and symbolise the solidarity and communality of the bereaved. And it would present the survivor's stance to the outer world ('more people', the POMC committee was to argue, 'should be encouraged...to become involved with T.V. Programmes or chat shows as new faces are needed.'[58]).

POMC was organised as TCF (and many other voluntary groups) had been organised before it, equipped with a membership defined only by subscription to a newsletter, and a national committee formed of a chairman or woman, a secretary, treasurer, and co-ordinator elected annually. There was to be a quarterly newsletter following the pattern of TCF. It was the co-ordinator's task to staff the telephone, field enquiries and receive requests for support, offering consolation, allocating members to support one another, and supporting the supporters when they were in distress ('my supporters would come back to me with all their problems and say "what do I do now?"' said Jill Palm, one co-ordinator).

POMC as a catalytic organization

Something unusual evidently occurred within the crucible of POMC meetings. There was a pronounced intensity and communality of feeling (Joan Bacon said: 'I can't begin to describe the grief in that room.'[59]), and it opened up a gap between POMC and TCF. For many members of POMC, the group offered a sanctuary in which they no longer needed to feel abashed about the depth of their emotions ('I've got to show some hate and that...That's not what those people [members of TCF] are there for, and I felt guilty.... They just sit and look at you and say "well!" and look dumbfounded.'). Observers from TCF were indeed a little dumbfounded on occasion. One woman said 'there is an almost tangible sense of grief and of loss at a POMC meeting. It's far more so. You could almost see simmering going on. They are extremely tense

[56] Ann Robinson told the European Forum for Victim Services held in Stockholm in June 1990, 'an underlying agenda has been a need to create a memorial to all our beloved dead children'.

[57] A. Robinson, 'The Existing Role of Parents of Murdered Children Group, Compassionate Friends', undated.

[58] Minutes of the meeting of 11 Mar 1990.

[59] 'Victims and Survivors', *agenda*, Dec 1994, 8.

meetings... I think the meetings were meant to be very supportive but I'm not always sure they turned out that way. Sometimes venting your anger continually feeds it rather than diminishes it.' Similarly, David Renhard, chairman of TCF between 1987 and 1989, remembered: 'when I went to their meetings, there was, no doubt about it, a lot of anger because of what had happened. I notice that was one of the differences. . . . I'm one of those people who doesn't get angry. I find it very difficult to get angry. . . . So, in a sense, it was very difficult to understand some of the anger.' But there was no unanimity amongst members of POMC themselves. Some felt uncomfortable in the presence of so much raw and unconfined emotion and they turned away, further sifting the membership. An early member later confessed: 'I think [participating in POMC was] a bit scary... There was a shade of a problem, and it was again back down to anger, so I opted out for a couple of years... You can't agree with everybody. When a person has got this deep-seated anger which eats away at you, it isn't doing you any good, and there's going to be problems.'

POMC meetings opened up the self to others to engender inter-subjectivity, the state where 'I' became 'we',[60] where the other became *thou* rather than *you, Du* rather than *Sie*.[61] Jill Palm remarked that 'you do tend to lose yourself in it, and you're sort of swamped in other people's grief.' Intersubjectivity created a strong collaboratively-sustained emotional landscape against which one's own reactions could be pitched and understood,[62] a sense of common plight and common purpose, and a mechanical solidarity that was reinforced by collective rituals such as shared pre-Christmas lunches, and fund-raising activities at car boot sales, jumble sales, and fêtes. Some would even say that the reliving of trauma in groups and therapy is really a reproduction of emotional experience in the present, that the strength of feeling manifest in a group like POMC was almost as much created anew as revisited.[63]

---

[60] See K. Weick, *Sensemaking in Organizations* (Sage, Thousand Oaks, Calif, 1995), 71.

[61] See M. Buber, 'Elements of the Interhuman', *The Knowledge of Man* (London, 1965), 80–1.

[62] See N. Denzin, *On Understanding Emotion* (Jossey-Bass, San Francisco, 1984), 150.

[63] See R. Leys, 'Traumatic Cures: Shell Shock, Janet, and the Question of Memory', *Critical Inquiry*, Summer, 1994, 635, 636.

A strong, autonomous social world was in the making, and it was a world that was becoming assertive. Seen from within, the POMC group could often appear reassuring, structured, and secure. Seen from without, it could appear somewhat enclosed and forbidding. One core member was later to say: 'when I joined it was a very—oh, be very careful here—comforting. I seemed to fit in. But I think in retrospect it was very cliquey. It was . . . because we were all really in this area, it tended to be a very closed shop.'

POMC evidently harboured a remarkable intensity of feeling at its core. From the first, it was to take much of its character and energy from a central cluster of driven and passionate people, its membership being socially and geographically concentrated about a 'small but dedicated group'[64] attached to Ann Robinson and June Patient in East London and Essex[65] (although there were satellite groups forming elsewhere, in Stoke-on-Trent, Scotland, and the Midlands, and a 'help-line' had been established in Bristol, for example). The largest meetings were always held in or around London (Jill Palm, the second co-ordinator, living in Waltham Abbey, observed that 'it was all meetings down this end really, and round East London . . .'). Those living outside the South East of England frequently came with difficulty: after all, it was no easy matter for the bereaved to travel far, poor and worried about the prospect of venturing out in public, as they often were. Lacking the money to stay in hotels, they might have had to be boarded at other members' homes overnight.[66] When people did succeed in coming far, the matter was noted. For instance, it was reported with some fanfare (and no doubt without full seriousness) that the 1990 pre-Christmas lunch had been attended by 'two new members, WHO HAD COME ALL THE WAY FROM PLYMOUTH and had arranged a weekend in London to coincide with the meeting.'[67]

[64] POMC Information Sheet, undated.

[65] The Autumn 1987 TCF newsletter contained a report by Ann Robinson as co-ordinator of the Parents of Murdered Children Group. She observed: 'there are now about one hundred sets of parents linked together throughout Britain. Hopefully, it will soon be geographically viable for some of these parents to meet together on a regular basis in their own areas. The London/Essex meetings are always very well attended . . .' Yet, over three years later, the first three POMC meetings of 1991 were to be held in Enfield, Upminster, and Enfield.

[66] POMC Newsletter, Nov 1989.

[67] POMC Newsletter, Dec 1990. Emphasis in original.

The iron law of oligarchy came into effect,[68] an internal division appearing between an activist minority at the geographical and organizational core of POMC and the wider membership elsewhere. Thus only twenty-one people attended the second annual general meeting in March 1990, less than 10 per cent of the whole membership, and the chairman was obliged to observe that 'since the Group gave support to parents nationally, then the next A.G.M. ought to be held somewhere other than London.... it is only fair that we attempt to cater for members who do not live in London and the Home Counties, who are at present those most inclined to attend.'[69]

It was that hard-working minority which was to animate POMC and give it its special identity, culture, and presence: 'As with all organisations most of the work is undertaken by just a few. The same few attend all the events, write the letters and make the phone calls.'[70] Membership of the Group's organizing committee was to remain static over time, its 1990–1991 composition being identical to that of the previous year, for instance, there being no other candidates.[71] One of the co-ordinators was later to remark that 'there was certain few people that had been in the group from the word "go". They had their own views on everything, and... it's been very, very difficult to expand the group and have different views...'

The unintended outcome was a marked parochialism in POMC, an identification of many of its members with the original Essex and East London-based network. It followed, in the eyes of some centrally-placed critics within POMC and SAMM, that there was an occasional tendency to confuse the universalistic aims of the organization with the particularistic aims of specific friendship groups within the network; for support work to be confused with the sustenance of friendships; and for personal loyalties to be confused with organizational obligations. It is difficult to avoid

[68] See R. Michels, *Political Parties* (New York, 1949).

[69] The December 1990 POMC newsletter gave notice of the next annual general meeting and observed: 'it is necessary for you to start thinking about who you would like to represent you on the committee next year—new faces would be particularly welcome.'

[70] David Howden, reporting on the annual Chigwell police fête in POMC Newsletter, Autumn 1990 (?), 1.

[71] It seems to be a marked trait of self-help groups for the bereaved that the longest-standing members become leaders. See T. Walter, *The Revival of Death* (Routledge, London, 1994), 130.

the appearance of such things in small voluntary institutions based on strong mutual sympathies where official roles and relations can never be conducted impersonally. How is one to distinguish between the reasonable but delineated requirements of a formal position and the unstinting service expected of the dedicated member? Factions and counter-factions, accusation and counter-accusation, could proliferate to scar the internal social relationships of POMC and complicate the orderly succession of its office-holders. One co-ordinator remembered: 'I went out with the hump. I went out with a big bang. I was getting a lot of aggravation.'

Members would meet every six to eight weeks at first, and then monthly, in small groups of ten or so,[72] and they would talk. The text of a draft notice advertising the group stated: 'Here we can talk and weep and no one feels uncomfortable because we have a common bond—victims of violent crime.' Newcomers, said June Patient, would tend to be 'quiet at first, and then they'd hear other people talk, and they'd want to join in'.

Narratives produced in talk are the primary method of organizing experience, and it was through narrative that survivors distanced themselves a little to respond to their own and others' grief, to understand their lives, and justify their actions.[73] Members would speak and listen: comparing histories; discussing their children— how they had died and how the families had been treated thereafter; commiserating with each another; passing one another photographs of the dead; and so constructing accounts about the unspeakable, narratives becoming testimonies that could give shape to experience.[74] Their talk was repetitive, and it was repetitive, it may be supposed, because the content of experience resisted simple mastery.[75] Recall that, following the argument I ventured in the preface of this book, talk and the things it describes are not and can never be

---

[72] For a brief description and photograph of a POMC meeting in Enfield in 1986, see 'Forgotten Victims of Murder', *The Times*, 20 Oct 1986.

[73] See L. Richardson, 'Narrative and Sociology', in J. Van Maanen, *Representation in Ethnography* (Sage, Thousand Oaks, California, 1995), 200 *et seq.*

[74] See J. Herman; *Trauma and Recovery* (Pandora, London, 1994), 177, 181.

[75] In a discussion of narrative and the traumatised patient, Piers observed that: 'Often patients who are describing past traumatic experiences appear to be addressing themselves... That is, they appear to be addressing issues embedded in ongoing workings of their minds, issues that are not fully articulated in consciousness... some patients speak of past traumatic experiences carefully and systematically, as if they are building a case, in an effort to prove to themselves the validity and legitimacy of

the same. The one forever eludes the other. It was a consequence that, because much traumatic experience is intensely painful, embedded, embodied, and ineffable,[76] because it can stop time,[77] those repetitive narratives could also become self-referential and concrete,[78] apparent soliloquies[79] that led members sometimes to talk past one another[80] as they recited their very particular grievances. Jill Palm reflected that 'you would hear the same things over and and over again, and you would touch on the same problems...But because you'd heard them, you could cope, or you knew really how to cope with them.' In a number of cases, however, the same injustices would be aired again and again in what were virtual monologues, and occasionally, it seems, no one was really listening.[81]

Stories are rule-governed. Not every narrative could be regarded as equally well-constructed, plausible, or compelling by members of the group,[82] and especially telling phrases would be used repeatedly to become part of a common linguistic stock.[83] So it was that narratives would sometimes take on stereotyped form as they incorporated the approved sentiments of Parents of Murdered

their own experience.' C. Piers, 'Contemporary Trauma Theory and its Relation to Character', paper delivered to 'Trauma and Memory: An International Research Conference', University of New Hampshire, July 1996, 8, 9.

[76] See I. Glick et al, The First Year of Bereavement (Wiley-Interscience, New York, 1974), 126.

[77] See A. Giddens, 'Living in a Post-Traditional Society', in U. Beck, A. Giddens and S. Lash, Reflexive Modernisation (Polity Press, Cambridge, 1994), 67, 70.

[78] See C. Sykes, A Nation of Victims (St Martin's Press, New York, 1992), 22.

[79] See n 75 above.

[80] See L. Langer, Holocaust Testimonies (Yale University Press, New Haven, 1991), pp. x–xi.

[81] Part of this description flows from inferences based on my own observation of successor groups to POMC and of groups in North America.

[82] See P. Ewick and S. Silbey, 'Subversive Stories and Hegemonic Tales: Toward a Sociology of Narrative', Law and Society Review, 1995, Vol 29, No 2, 207.

[83] Pat Green, for example, wrote in Guardian Midweek of 8 Nov 1994 that: 'We now belong to a tragic minority. We have now become involved in a system we had never known, plunged into a deep dark chasm of evil violence and horror...' Those words were to be very nearly repeated by her in an article in the Daily Post of 26 Jan 1995. She had also written in Guardian Midweek that: 'To be a victim of a criminal is a nightmare; to be a victim of the criminal justice system is a travesty.' Her fellow-member of Justice for Victims, Sandra Sullivan, had remarked in 'A "Civilised Society"?', 'To be a victim at the hands of the criminal is an unforgettable nightmare, to become a victim at the hands of the criminal justice system is an unforgivable travesty.' And there are many other similar examples of phrases becoming joint property.

Children.[84] Set words and phrases emerged which appeared most efficiently to give form to feeling, particular constructions were endorsed by other members of the group, and memories became, in effect, shared, part of a project of what Plummer called community-building.[85] Just as the group became reflexively shaped in narrative, so were the selves of its members, who, in Ofshe's words, 're-create[d] themselves in the mold of the survivor, their beliefs forming the basis of a new identity and world view'.[86]

Entering the group when they were particularly lonely, pained, and vulnerable, many survivors were charged by what they had seen and experienced in POMC meetings, and they emerged transformed. Sometimes their identity and world-view were validated, sometimes re-cast altogether, and a few went on to become activists who would shape the future of POMC, SAMM, and adjacent groups. For example, Pat Green, later to found SAMM Merseyside, recalled how she had gone twice to London from Warrington to POMC meetings, 'and that's where I met Sandra and Joan and Derek and Ann [later to be the core members of Justice for Victims] and you know, I just looked at them, and I thought "there's other people in this!" Because I had never met anybody who was experiencing the same grief as I was experiencing.' And Margaret Watson, who was later to found Families of Murder Victims in Strathclyde, said of her first POMC meeting: 'it was very emotional because that's the first time I'd met someone in the same position as myself. The tears were very emotional.'

David Howden, eventually to become the last chairman of POMC and the first chairman of the new SAMM, remembered:

The first time Heather [his wife] and I attended a POMC meeting, it was at Ann Robinson's Southend home. The fear of again facing the unknown held us back on many occasions, but we eventually made the decision. We were received with kindness, love and understanding, and left with a feeling of well being and support.[87]

And Frank Green, later to be the second chairman of SAMM, was affected in much the same way. He recalled at a special session on SAMM held at a Victim Support conference in July 1995:

[84] See J. Gubrium, *Speaking of Life* (Aldine de Gruyter, New York, 1993), 178.
[85] K. Plummer, *Telling Sexual Stories* (Routledge, London, 1995), 43.
[86] R. Ofshe and E. Watters, *Making Monsters* (University of California Press, Berkeley, 1994), 16.
[87] Speech at launch of SAMM, 30 Sept 1994.

It becomes apparent that it's socially unacceptable to talk about what's happened.... So we shelve our feelings, even come to believe when we are told you should be over it by now. In the next breath you take a strong cup of tea and carry on. The months slide into years and life as they say goes on—but for us life includes fresh flowers on Sue's grave, quiet tears and every Christmas advert seems to be for Harveys Bristol Cream.[88] Last year dad was reading a newspaper and it carried a story about a family whose grandson had been murdered by his father. It talked about a group, Parents of Murdered Children, who met locally. Dad made contact and arranged to attend that weekend. I must admit I was somewhat sceptical—after all no one else had helped us or even bothered to help.... Dad told me that the group was made up of people who shared our experience and so I went to see what he was getting into. The shelves collapsed—the pain, anger, frustration, abandonment, loneliness—the support was instantaneous, not just for a week or a month or a year but as long as we need it. More than that we see a way that we can give something back. I have found the meaning of the word 'sharing' and of course we don't always see eye to eye but I know the place where we are amongst friends—I can shout if I want to, I can curse the system when I want to and I can cry when I need to and no one judges me. They understand. I owe so much.

Fission

The dialectic of fusion and fission unleashed by the meeting of Ann Robinson and June Patient continued to unfold. There was not only a growing affirmation and strengthening of the group's inner conviction that POMC was special and apart,[89] but also an external validation of that conviction by other organizations that have always had an exceptional interest in homicide and its victims. 'If it was just for a bit of gory details to sell a newspaper or a magazine, no way, we wouldn't touch it with a barge pole,' Ann Robinson said, 'but if it was a serious programme, a serious discussion, yes, because... We wanted the group to become known so that people would know we were there and obviously... to educate the public.' The press, television, and radio pursued Ann Robinson and her colleagues. She appeared, *inter alia*, on *Choices*, *Kilroy*, *TVAM* and *Good Morning Britain* (where, in the aftermath of the reporting of the murder of a child, she was given the introduction: 'One person

---

[88] Harvey was the surname of Susan Green's murderer.
[89] See P. Clarke, *Twenty-Five Compassionate Years* (The Compassionate Friends, Bristol, 1994), 45.

who knows how these people feel is Ann Robinson. She has helped organize a group, POMC, which now has about 40 members.'). Most importantly, perhaps, she was to co-operate with Julian Aston, himself a member of TCF and a television producer/director in the making of a Thames Television series on the deaths of children, *Brief Lives*. In the fourth programme, 'Life Sentence', which focused on murder and was shown on 25 June 1987, Ann Robinson and members of the new Parents of Murdered Children group loomed large, and thirty people subsequently joined POMC.[90] The small book that accompanied the series stated that: 'This film examines how the parents of murdered children may also become victims of the crime. For the families involved, feelings of grief and anger are compounded by the intrusion of the media and the inevitable police investigation that follows . . . .' Also critical was to be the invitation issued to Victim Support and POMC in 1989 by the House of Lords Select Committee on Murder and Life Imprisonment to tender evidence about the impact of homicide on the families of victims. POMC had evidently become recognised as an authority by an august body.[91] David Howden, the chairman of POMC, who had given evidence, said: 'The fact was that for the first time that anybody can remember people in authority were asking us how we felt and what we thought and not just doing things on our behalf without considering us—and I think that was a turning point.' Jane Cooper recalled that it 'had [an] immense impact on the Committee'. And Jillian Tallon considered that it marked both POMC's growing separateness and its increasing sense of its own efficacy:[92]

They were heard, they were taken seriously, somebody really wanted to hear and to some extent act upon what they had heard. The rest of us could supply sympathy and those kinds of things but you couldn't actually do anything. The House of Lords Committee was influential and could do something and they had chosen to listen to those people, and I think that was very authenticating in some ways . . . I think it gave them confidence and perhaps some kind of stability. Perhaps they had been going this way and that way before, and weren't too sure of their direction, and maybe that helped to crystallise it for them.

[90] Report on POMC Group, TCF Newsletter, Autumn 1987.

[91] In the minutes of the 1990 annual general meeting of POMC, the chairman was to 'stress the influence the Group had had on the House of Lords Select Committee . . .'

[92] In practice, the only recommendation to be implemented was POMC's request for seats in the well of the court.

Such matters count in the formation of any new organization, and particularly an organization composed of those who complain of exclusion and marginality. The gravity of an association, its symbolic presence, most commonly called 'credibility' in the world of the criminal justice system, depends on the responses of others. The endorsement of others is an endorsement of the self and its significant others, a ratification of who one is and what one says, and who it is, amongst the living and the dead, whom one claims to represent. To define oneself is to define the world.[93]

A number of the POMC group strived to make it autonomous, to distance themselves from the discreet style of TCF and become more prominent as an organization. After all, many of those recruited after 1984 had joined the group directly without passing through TCF, and their allegiance was to POMC, not to TCF, their style of thought set by POMC, not by TCF.

To the TCF, it seemed as if POMC was veering towards militancy. Jillian Tallon, the national secretary of TCF, observed: 'they wanted to become a campaigning organization and the way TCF is set up it cannot be a campaigning organization.' And John Baldock, then POMC representative on the TCF National Committee, observed: 'POMC ... is probably not so concerned with emotional support. They are more into campaigning for better rights and justice (which is fine).'

To insiders, however, campaigning had always seemed to be a relatively minor strain. It had never been the prime intention of Ann Robinson and June Patient that POMC should become an activist group (Ann Robinson remarked that 'my—and June as well—our main theme right the way through ... is to give that emotional support and understanding to other relatives'). When, in 1987, for instance, Ann Robinson had listed the needs of families who had been bereaved by homicide, she made no mention of rights to be secured through political or legal action. Rather, her stress was on families needing to meet others who had 'experienced the same form of isolation and grief'; to give one another emotional support and 'informed practical help'; and to cope with the additional traumas inflicted by the police investigation, press intrusiveness, and the trial.[94] POMC and

---

[93] See K. Weick, *Sensemaking in Organizations* (n 60 above), 20.
[94] 'The Special Needs of Families of Murdered Children', Jan 1987.

its successor, SAMM, was a self-help group, its members sustaining and comforting one another.

There was no simple consensus. Gill Pennicard, a central figure in the small world of POMC, its last co-ordinator, and a woman who was locally regarded as something of an activist, also took it that POMC had always been a support organization: 'June and Ann needed support themselves, and they knew of other people who needed support, so that's how it went . . . . I don't think the momentum [for campaigning] was there.' But she and other, more activist, members of POMC would have preferred it to have been otherwise. The lack of activism in POMC was not to be explained by its members' wishes or convictions, they believed, but by their want of resolution. In Gill Pennicard's judgement, matters were not to be rectified until a small group with dual membership in POMC[95] (and later SAMM) and Justice for Victims (a group which I shall discuss below) came forward to embody the proper determination: 'I think there are certain people now [in June 1995] that are more stronger in themselves and able . . . . The thing is really and truly, I think that, if it was a question about [putting] this to people, I'm sure that the majority of people would be with the thoughts of Justice for Victims, but a lot of people don't have the resources, they don't have the time or the resources or even the strength to do these things.'

It was evident not only that POMC was regarded predominantly as a self-help organization by its members, but that it was also becoming visited by the very first portents of assertiveness. In effect, the organization had been stirred by an awakening of the radical potential of the politics of experience that had given birth to the mutual aid movement only twenty years before.

Secession

By the beginning of 1988, POMC had elected to become semi-detached, a 'branch' or 'specialised group' within TCF, with its own bank account, chairman, and treasurer. But, Ann Robinson was to report to the TCF, 'This was not with any intention of breaking-away from TCF, but simply to acquire some autonomy over

[95] POMC was a formal registered charity which held annual general meetings, elections to committee posts, and the like. It had membership records of a kind, on index cards. Justice for Victims, as I shall explain in Chapter 7, was a much more loosely-organized association without a formal membership.

funds raised by PoMC group members, and to consolidate the group.'[96] Within just another year, however, POMC reported that it was investigating the advantages of becoming fully independent, having drafted a constitution, and seeking recognition by the Charity Commissioners. Its then chairman, David Howden, reflected: 'We would suggest there is a great deal of difference between murder and any other type of death. We feel that a life taken by another human being creates much more anger, frustration [and] hate ... Although the loss is the same, the emotions are somewhat different.'[97] A leaflet of the new POMC would later announce that 'Like all healthy off-spring we grew and wanted to do our own thing, concentrating on the special needs of those bereaved as a result of murder or man-slaughter and, like all good parents, we trust that The Compassion-ate Friends will always be there to offer advice and support.'

The proposal to leave TCF altogether was attended by some discord. Ann Robinson herself was reluctant to effect a break, voting against it in committee ('June and I had very close links with Compassionate Friends. It all started with Compassionate Friends.' 'That was when the wrangling started', she was to observe much later.). There were others who had sentimental or organiza-tional attachments to TCF which they were unwilling to re-linquish.[98] John Baldock, a member of POMC and a TCF county organizer was one: 'I felt when I became more involved with Com-passionate Friends that it is important not to have separation. It is important to keep the links there.' There was apprehensiveness that, whilst TCF was a national body, POMC itself was little more than a local group based principally in and around London ('but, having said that, a lot of the members, especially the London area, won, and they were the ones that were on the committee. They hadn't had a lot to do with with Compassionate Friends.').

There was dissension about the very claim to distinctiveness of those bereaved by homicide. TCF is a catholic organization which

[96] Ann Robinson's report. Minutes of the 64th meeting of the National Committee of The Compassionate Friends, 30 Jan 1988.

[97] Evidence taken from Victim Support and POMC before the House of Lords Select Committee on Murder and Life Imprisonment, 5 June 1989, 506.

[98] Confusingly, a POMC group was still listed as part of TCF four years after POMC proper attained independence. See 'Introducing The Compassionate Friends', The Compassionate Friends, Bristol, 1994. The national secretary of TCH recalled that 'we had some who were members outside POMC, some who were members inside POMC, and some who were members of both.'

maintained, in the words of Jillian Tallon, the national secretary at the time, that: 'there are a lot of very common features for everybody who has lost a child of whatever age and in whatever circumstances, and we in Compassionate Friends recognise that parents of murdered children... have huge additional burdens to bear but it's not totally true that there's no relationship between the different ways in which death comes about.' Some members of the TCF national committee were also concerned about the eschewing of taboos about public visibility and about the self-importance that it might engender ('if you're not careful you can get carried away by giving interviews to people and going on television and radio, and you suddenly start being important when you're not really, if you know what I mean...'). There was dissension about what was conceived to be the 'hijacking' of the POMC name, which was claimed as TCF property.[99]

There was dissension about money. TCF was not financially strong, and there was resentment that the more conspicuous POMC had raised money[100] which it was not prepared to share with its parent organization (a 10 per cent levy having been paid by subordinate groups in the past). Just at the time that the POMC began to detach itself, the national committee of TCF tried to impose greater discipline on the control and distribution of funds in its different branches and groups, and between those branches and the national office (Jillian Tallon recalled that, 'because of the charity position, we needed to know where the money was and we wanted to have the use of it. It would still remain the groups' own money, but it would go into the general melting pot... POMC had been vigorously fund-raising... and they had quite a substantial sum of money in their account.... It wasn't a vast sum, it was something like £600, and in retrospect the whole thing seems so silly. There were two tetchy sort of men on both sides and POMC got the idea that we were actually after their money...'). And Ann Robinson stated: 'to me [the 10 per cent] was good value because we were getting a lot out of Compassionate Friends. At that stage, we were still getting postage, telephones, all their leaflets, the name... But quite a few members didn't see that. They thought we'd worked hard to raise this money. Why should we give it to

[99] Rather later, TCF was to express satisfaction when POMC changed its name to SAMM, allowing them to retain their 'ownership' of POMC.

[100] In January 1990, for instance, its funds amounted to just under £7,000.

Compassionate Friends? And also I suppose they didn't feel any kindred spirit...to Compassionate Friends.'

POMC was given charitable status and *de facto* independence[101] on 30 September 1990 (and it was during the discussions about that transition that the name SAM, Support After Murder, was first aired to distinguish it from small groups of POMC members who might wish to remain within TCF[102]). The newly independent organization was to be based administratively at the home of its first co-ordinator, Jill Palm.[103]

Conclusion

Out of The Compassionate Friends there had appeared a special support group for the parents of murdered children, a group that was to be distinctive because of the strength of its individual and collective griefs and its sense of itself as a body apart. Little by little, the Parents of Murdered Children group was to sever itself from its parent to become quite autonomous in 1990. It was marked always by the vigour and intimacy of a core circle who had enlisted early and were spatially and socially concentrated. They had within them the potential for a new radicalism that was just beginning to stir as POMC acquired its independence.

Yet POMC was also manifestly constricted. Its geographical base was small, compressed in one area and hardly justifying the group's pretensions to be a national organization (although there were undoubtedly 'contact people' to be found elsewhere—in Bristol, for example). The intensity of POMC's relations was evident in its internal cleavages. And, having quit TCF, it had neither money nor strong institutional sponsorship. Patronage is indispensable in the suspicious, adversarial, and loosely-coupled world of the criminal justice system.[104] So too with money. Even minor expenditure on postage and duplicating for the newsletters was proving onerous at

---

[101] But TCF and POMC did remain structurally allied. Ann Robinson urged members of POMC at its first AGM that 'a close association with Compassionate Friends could only be beneficial to the Group.' And David Howden, the chairman, remarked that 'it was not the Group's intention when charity status was achieved to turn our backs on Compassionate Friends.'

[102] Minutes of Meeting of Committee of POMC, 14 Jan 1990.

[103] Minutes of Meeting of Committee of POMC, 11 Mar 1990.

[104] I pursued that theme at length in my history of Victim Support. See *Helping Victims of Crime* (Clarendon Press, Oxford, 1990), ch 1.

the end of 1989 and it was announced that fewer editions would have to be published.[105] 'Whatever we do costs money', the December 1990 POMC newsletter reported plaintively.

David Howden, the last chairman of POMC, was to devote a considerable portion of his time to raising funds, writing pleading letters to businesses and selling *bric-à-brac* at jumble sales (admission ten pence). He and his colleagues were successful in securing small sums: Mott Macdonald contributed £500, Shell UK £100, Granada Television £50 and Snowcem £15, but the effort expended had been considerable (Howden had had to send 1,500 begging letters in 1989). One bazaar in that year was reported to have raised £207.06—mostly, it appeared, as a result of the Group's members loyally buying from one another's stalls. A pre-Christmas lunch in 1990 raised £190, including £130 from raffles and £30 from the sale of cards. Parents of murdered children were to discover what Victim Support had discovered before them: people and organizations in England and Wales (and elsewhere[106]) do not donate money freely to victims of crime. It is as if the pariah identity of the victim wards them off. At the beginning of 1990, POMC's assets amounted to £6,993—not entirely negligible, but insufficient to support paid staff (although the need for a paid co-ordinator was flagged at the group's second annual general meeting in March 1990), pay many expenses, rent accommodation, or take a new organization very far forward.

---

[105] POMC newsletter, Nov 1989.

[106] For example, under the headline 'Too many victims' groups', the Nova Scotia *Sunday Daily News* of 5 Nov 1995 reported the financial collapse of a Canadian victims' group.

6

Victim Support and Parents of Murdered Children

Introduction

I have already introduced Victim Support briefly in Chapter 3 and at length in an earlier book which traced its origins and early history, *Helping Victims of Crime*. Victim Support had been conceived by NACRO in the early 1970s, acquired flesh in a pioneering support scheme in Bristol in 1974, expanded to become consolidated into a national association in 1979, and achieved permanence and scale through significant funding acquired from the Home Office in 1986.[1] By the late 1980s, Victim Support had become the prime voluntary organization serving victims in England and Wales. After much patient and difficult diplomacy in the corridors of the criminal justice system, it had secured the trust of the system's powers, the probation and police services, the judiciary and magistracy, and the Crown Prosecution Service. Above all, and most importantly, it had earned the trust of policy officials and politicians working in the Home Office which funded it.

Victim Support had become the authoritative mouthpiece of the victim and an appreciable 'Service Delivery' organization, itself a new, albeit minor power in the criminal justice system, and it was taken by the mass media, politicians, and officials to be established, sound, informed, and reasonably non-partisan. Its reports are published with a very wide circulation and are supported by professional press campaigns. Duncan Campbell of The *Guardian* reflected: 'I think for a long time Victim Support was the only [organization] that any one had ever heard of and was the one

---

[1] Significant Government funding had started in 1986, when it was determined by the Home Office that Victim Support would receive £9,000,000 over the three years 1987–90. Thereafter, annual funding increased. In 1991/2 it amounted to £5,700,000 and in 1992/3 to £7,300,000.

that people went to.... I would get Victim Support... they're the most solid and you can kind of rely on them to give a fairly steady comment.' And Terry Kirby of the *Independent* said in identical manner: 'Victim Support is a big national organization—lots of credibility. One wouldn't necessarily be disparaging, one wouldn't be disparaging about the single issue groups, but being a single issue group, I suppose they are entirely subjective about what they say, therefore you will have to always bear that in mind.'

Like The Compassionate Friends, Victim Support was a registered charity, and it took the proscription on overt political campaigning seriously, although it would also maintain always that it did campaign in its own fashion. It was an 'insider'[2] or 'acceptable'[3] pressure group. Anne Viney, its Assistant Director in the mid-1990s, observed that: 'what we try to do is to carry on campaigning on victims issues in a way that we hope is helpful...' 'Helpful' campaigning would consist of working by example, experimenting, commissioning research, writing letters, reports and papers, and conveying views in meetings. It would tend towards what Yates called 'silent politics'.[4] It would *not* consist of visible lobbying, marching, petitioning, or the staging of spectacular events intended publicly to confront or disconcert judges, officials, politicians, and others.

As a tried and known Home Office *protegé*, engaging in consultations with administrators and their colleagues in other Departments of State, and with senior officers in the agencies, Victim Support represented victims for all practical purposes in policy-making circles. It participated in bodies such as the Crime Prevention Agency Board and the Interdepartmental Steering Group on Victims.[5] It

[2] W. Grant, 'Insider groups, outsider groups, and interest group strategies in Britain', Department of Politics Working Paper No 19, University of Warwick, Coventry, 1978.

[3] R. Benewick, 'Politics without ideology: the perimeters of pluralism', in R. Benewick *et al* (eds), *Knowledge and Belief in Politics: The Problem of Ideology* (George Allen and Unwin, London, 1973).

[4] D. Yates, *Bureaucratic Democracy* (Harvard University Press, Cambridge, Mass, 1982), 87. See also S. Beer, 'The future of British politics', *Political Quarterly*, Jan–Mar 1955, Vol 26, No 1.

[5] In June 1993, for instance, Victim Support and POMC (with which it had then formed a connection) were the only victims' organizations formally invited to tender evidence to the Prison Reform Trust's Committee on the Penalty for Homicide. In 1995, the Home Office submission to a Justice committee on 'The Role of the Victim in the Criminal Justice Process' referred, under the heading 'Support for victims', only to Victim Support and Victim Support's Witness Service (to be sure, those were the

was heeded. A Home Office official who was directly responsible for the broad area of victims policy in the mid-1990s reflected: 'They have a powerful voice. We have tended to operate through Victim Support [in] dealing with the smaller groups. . . . There's no real sort of competitors for this spot anywhere. There's just a few groups that are specialised in some areas, and even they want very much to be allied with Victim Support.' And that was a position of authority and influence eyed enviously by the more impatient members of those specialised new groups who complained of revictimisation through political exclusion and marginalisation, and of the usurpation of the direct existential knowledge of the victim by what appeared to them to be the bureaucratic expertise of a large, impersonal corporation (although Victim Support is itself a federation of 'community' groups, a 'grass-roots' organization whose 12,000 volunteers saw victims every day). For the newly-founded Justice for Victims, a particularly telling moment occurred when, in late 1993, at a meeting with the director of Victim Support and her staff, the rhetorical question was put by Sandra Sullivan: 'Have you ever been a victim, experienced what a victim does? Have you ever spent a day in a victim's home after their child has been murdered?'[6]

Victim Support overshadowed every other remotely comparable organization (although, strictly speaking, there *was* none to compare with it). It was, in effect, a monopoly supplier of services which claimed to reach 98 per cent of the population of England and Wales. It was even supplying services in areas of crime claimed as the specialist preserve of survivors. In the late 1980s and early 1990s, when the events of this chapter began to unfold, Victim Support's 7,500 volunteers in 370 schemes received some 800,000 referrals annually, including 300 homicides, just under half the reported cases. No new organization touching victims could have avoided entering into relations with Victim Support. Neither could any

only components of support for which the Home Office has responsibility through its funding, but the identification is significant).

[6] Record of meeting between Victim Support and Victims of Crime Pressure Group (Justice for Victims), 8 Dec 1993. The reply had been: 'No, nobody I have personally known has been murdered but I have met a very large number of families who are victims and some parents whose children have been murdered too.' Of course, given the volume of crime in England and Wales, many victim support workers and volunteers will have been victims themselves. Jane Cooper observed that 'that was often a trigger to join. Some VS members [are] also victims of homicide. I can think of 5 straight away.'

organization avoid taking a position towards Victim Support. Indeed, at the beginning, almost all the founders of the new survivors' organizations had themselves been supported by its volunteers, and some by its national staff, including its director, Helen Reeves, herself.

By the mid-1980s, Victim Support was busy with a proliferation of new ventures, including reviews of its work with rape and sexual offences, racial harassment, and burglary. It was preoccupied, above all, with the overarching problem of funding—the organization was at risk of collapsing for want of money, and the Home Office of the time was reluctant to fund—and, in its ministers' judgement, thereby bureaucratise and corrupt—what Leon Brittan, the then Home Secretary, defined as effort given freely and spontaneously by volunteers.

But Victim Support was also vigilant in scrutinising new developments falling within its orbit. Its staff took its position as an authority and responsible power seriously, and they needed to know precisely what was happening around it. A great deal did seem to be happening. There was for the first time a discernible massing of small, often obscure groups and Victim Support did not always know quite what to make of them. So it was that, in 1986, just when the new survivors' groups began to emerge, Victim Support opened a file on 'Other "Victim" Organizations'[7] and encouraged its member schemes to supply intelligence (one of the many press-cuttings that followed was accompanied by a note from a scheme co-ordinator observing that it 'illustrates the phenomenon that you wanted to monitor.'). The file was to swell as organization after organization was logged. Seven years later, in August 1993, for instance, information about a new body was despatched to Victim Support in London with the written comment, 'yet another one!'. A great flood of groups appeared in late 1994 especially. Helen Reeves remarked: 'Things seem more complicated, particularly since last autumn. There seem to be an awful lot of groups around.'

The file was necessary. After all, Victim Support often found itself being questioned at first and second hand about the new groups.[8] It

[7] Its first list contained only 14 bodies, starting with Age Concern and ending with the Women's Royal Voluntary Service. Some entries were effectively an acknowledgement that the group was *terra incognita* ('Much is not known about this Organisation; believe it is essentially a local telephone counselling service.'). POMC was listed.

[8] In 1994, for example, a victim support scheme asked Victim Support about a new organization called the Child Bereavement Trust.

was sometimes asked to endorse their aims, join with them in fund-raising campaigns, co-operate with them in joint ventures, and attend meetings which they organized or attended.[9] Moreover, demands were being put for the right to share the sites of power held by Victim Support, the working parties, conferences, and committees, including the Interdepartmental Steering Group that co-ordinated the work of the Lord Chancellor's Department and the Home Office. It was as if some of the new groups were moving to Victim Support as angry moths to a flame.

Take one quite ordinary incident, one of many. A Hebburn publican, Millie Blenkinsop, launched a campaign in 1994[10] 'to call upon the Government to change the legislation and bring back the birch *or other deterrents* for persistent offenders and those who commit the most sickening crimes in our country. PROTECT OUR OLD AND OURSELVES. We, the public, the people of England, will no longer tolerate such lenient punishment served on these criminals!' (emphases in the original). She faxed Victim Support to ask whether she could be allowed to share Victim Support's stand at the forthcoming Labour Party conference and 'to collect signatures for my petition'. In this and other instances, Victim Support was obliged to take a stance and make a reply, and, in so doing, it had to learn something about the history, character, and intentions of the new groups. It was reasonably well placed to do so. Not only did it employ a press-cutting service but it could also turn to its own widespread network of schemes and contacts in the criminal justice system. In the event, Millie Blenkinsop was to be told that Victim Support 'was very interested to read about your campaign and impressed with the work you are putting into it. We . . . share your concerns about levels of crime in this country. . . . Victim Support does not, however, take a position on the sentencing and treatment of offenders. We would not therefore be able to support a campaign such as yours.' And that was to be a defining principle. Relations could be entertained with groups about which something was known, indeed, they were welcomed, but there could be only the

---

[9] In September 1994, for instance, Victim Support was invited to the launch of RESPOND and a conference on 'From Denial to Justice'. Founded in 1991, Respond was intended to 'highlight the need for people with learning difficulties who have been sexually abused to have access to adequate legal and therapeutic provision following their experience of trauma.'

[10] See, for example, the editorial in the *Shields Gazette*, 17 Sept 1994.

most perfunctory contact with unknown or overtly political organizations. Helen Reeves declared

There is a very clear distinction between the organizations that are providing a service and the ones who are campaigning, and it's a very important distinction for us. We ought to be supporting any organization that is trying to provide a service, but we don't have to work with anybody who is campaigning—or we can work with them sometimes, when they happen to agree with what we want.

It will be remembered that Victim Support had sometimes been attacked by the new groups for its supposed insensitivity or lack of competence in supporting individual victims and survivors. Amongst the most distressed, the logic of the binary oppositions tended occasionally to depict the association as part of the distant, alienating 'system' which so oppressed the bereaved. Recall the public accusations, publicly endorsed by the local press, which had been levelled by David Hines: his North of England Victims' Association had been founded, in part, in direct dialectical confrontation with Victim Support.[11] Consider, too, the written onslaught mounted by Victim of Crime, a little-known group based in Dover, Kent, which opened by asking, in the words of an anonymous victim of violent crime: 'Why has Victim Support ignored the plight and needs of victims? Why is its voice so silent?', and which proceeded to argue: 'If only it was Victim Support. While the government operate a scorched earth policy towards victims, and the justice system crucifies, the one "charity" sits back meekly and criminals dream. Some 40 charities represent and fulfil the needs of criminals, the first is Victim Support.' Victim Support was again obliged to give a reply, a media officer telling Victim of Crime's founder: 'I must admit before I spoke to you I was very surprised and somewhat disturbed by your references to Victim Support... We are fighting very hard for the same cause as you, and I didn't feel it was fair or helpful to denounce our organisation in the way that you did.'

Victim Support was handicapped because its Code of Practice explicitly provided confidentiality for the victims and survivors it supported, and, said Anne Viney, 'This means, if we disagree about matters of fact, we do not always feel in a position to put Victim

[11] See various articles and editorials in the *Shields Gazette* in July 1993, and particularly on 8, 13 and 14 July.

Support's side of the story, despite the damage which might be done to the morale of volunteers or to the confidence of new users of our service.' The ensuing problem was that specific criticisms could be countered only by assertions of general principle.

It was always possible that, however grave or insubstantial specific accusations and counter-accusations might prove to be, they would count in the world of policy-making. They might well be relayed by the press, and reported to Members of Parliament and senior police officers. They might inform parliamentary debates[12] and influence political outcomes, and Victim Support could not fail to attend to its public face and preserve what it called its credibility, lest its reputation be damaged.

It was certainly no light matter that Victim Support was criticised by Justice for Victims in a private meeting with David Maclean, the Home Office minister, and his advisers in April 1994. He was to be told that Victim Support 'are alright if your materials have been stolen, but not good enough if you have your loved ones murdered', and that: 'You must not only talk to people who think they know— you must talk to people who really know!'[13] The two forms of knowledge in the victim's world were there paraded before a powerful politician in open competition, and Victim Support was somewhat embattled. Helen Peggs, its press officer, said:

During the late 1980s and early 1990s Victim Support published a series of reports on the treatment of crime victims. These included reports on racial harassment, families of murder victims, child victims, and victims of domestic violence. All of these reports contained wide-ranging and hard-hitting recommendations, and we worked hard to get maximum publicity for them. We were often very successful.... At the time, I saw Victim Support

---

[12] So it was that Victim Support noted the substance of a debate in the House of Commons on 23 November 1993 in which the Labour Member for Walthamstow, the member representing the Bacons and Ann Virgin, the core of Justice for Victims, Neil Gerrard, stated that: 'The gaps that exist in procedures for dealing with the families of murder victims have been brought home to me by what happened to a family in my constituency. I have talked to those people, who feel completely abandoned by the criminal justice system.... There is a problem for families of victims in cases like that. They are not direct victims of the crime or the material witnesses—they are not directly involved—but certainly in the case of relatives of homicide victims there are great gaps in the support given to them...' Members of Justice for Victims and Victim Support had disagreed quite vehemently about the extent and depth of the support which had been furnished by victim support volunteers.

[13] Minutes of meeting held at Home Office, 20 Apr 1994.

as a small, but vocal organisation which was fast developing innovative services for victims and witnesses . . . We had adopted a campaigning vocabulary and the Victim Support Annual Report for 1993 devotes two pages to 'Victim Support's Campaign for victims' rights. We were also working very hard to raise our profile generally, as we were still relatively unknown. Then, in 1994, I first became aware, via the media, of *Justice for Victims* and of the other victim organisations. It appeared from comments which were being made in the media that not only had these people heard of us, but that we were regarded by them not as a small, vocal, campaigning victims' charity, but as an established agency within the criminal justice system and therefore fair target for criticism. I found the difference between their perception of the organisation, and my perception of our identity, very startling. We were, I think, all hurt by the criticisms which were being made by these individuals.[14]

Just as Victim Support had begun its life in the 1970s as a suspect, ill-defined, and marginal petitioner seeking the patronage and financial aid of the better established and well-defended powers of the criminal justice system, so, twenty years later, it had begun to attract its own retinue of petitioners who also sought to further their ends by winning the sponsorship and organizational resources which it was assumed to command. Thus, in 1987, it was to receive a proposal from CADD, the Campaign Against Drunk Drivers, for a closer connection in which Victim Support would receive referrals of victims and the families of victims of serious 'auto-crime'. Officers of Victim Support were at first nervous that its member schemes might not only find it difficult to undertake 'non-crime' work but also discover themselves being 'swamped', but road deaths did slowly and inexorably become part of the work of victim support volunteers.[15]

Just as Victim Support had attracted suspicion in the beginning, so it was itself to be guarded in its assessment of the motives, intentions and demands of a number of the newcomers.[16] After all, the criminal justice system is aimed quite particularly at the

[14] Letter to author, 9 Sept 1997.

[15] In November 1988, Jane Cooper, then attached to Victim Support, but later to become SAMM's first co-ordinator, wrote an internal memorandum remarking that 'a future priority of VS is serious crime and road deaths warrant serious consideration within this category'.

[16] It was not, for instance, well-disposed to demands for longer sentences or for 'victim impact statements' which could offset the offender's mitigation plea before sentencing. Helen Reeves, the Director of Victim Support, asked: 'should offenders be more liable to detention pending trial and to severe penalties if their victims have

detection and management of rule-breaking. Rule evasion, deceitfulness, conflict, and control are its central preoccupations, and it is a consequence that extraordinary importance is attached to safeguarding knowledge and managing access to people and processes. Matters are often not what they seem, mistrust is rampant, and insiders will regard the unfamiliar, untested, and non-professional outsider with particular wariness. Officials of Victim Support sensed that it was at some risk of finding itself compromised, entangled or over-extended by the as-yet-unknown, unproven, and angry survivors' organizations that seemed to be surfacing all about it. But it was nevertheless moving fast into precisely the areas which those organizations claimed as their own, giving 'longer term support' to the victims and secondary victims of 'serious', sensitive, and politically contentious crime. Table 6.1 illustrates the rapid and substantial increase in the referrals of such victims.

Table 6.1   Referrals to Victim Support: 1991–93[17]

	1991–2	1992–3
Bereavement—homicide or road death	1,274	1,554
Rape	2,303	2,601
Domestic violence	11,652	12,837
Racially motivated crime	1,832	2,306

Sometimes that involvement was actively encouraged by the new organizations. In 1987, for instance, the Suzy Lamplugh Trust sought to engage Victim Support more extensively in supporting the families of missing persons. Sometimes involvement was resisted. But it grew. By 1993, Victim Support was quite specifically advertising itself as a body that dealt with burglary, assault, rape, and murder.[18]

The one major form of service which Victim Support did not and could not readily offer was self-help for the traumatised, although, by the mid-1980s, that was an area in which it was beginning to

punitive attitudes?'; 'Double indignity', The *Guardian*, 8 Mar 1995. Also see her 'Victims', *The Criminal Bar Association Newsletter*, Sept 1994.

[17] Source: *Annual Report 1993* (Victim Support, London, 1993), 5.

[18] By 1993–4, it had received 640 homicide referrals, of whom 92 per cent were contacted.

form an active interest, another gap in the map which it might paint red. It was seemingly inevitable that Parents of Murdered Children and Victim Support would come to have dealings with one another.

POMC and Victim Support

POMC and Victim Support met in the mid-1980s as their administrators searched around them for partners who could supply deficits in their own organizations. On the one hand, Ann Robinson, then co-ordinator of the newly-founded and loosely-attached POMC, attempting to develop the competence, reach, and working relations of her group, cast around her for what she imagined would prove to be the expert assistance of established agencies:[19]

Because of the shock, anger and the time lapse before the trial, skilled bereavement/family counselling is often needed, but is rarely available. Nobody from the 'caring agencies' automatically offers support to families, and consequently they feel let down by a society that mostly leaves them to cope alone. As co-founder and co-ordinator of the group, I contacted several agencies, looking for help. But the answer was usually a stunned silence followed by 'So sorry, but we're not really qualified to help...' Meanwhile, Helen Reeves, the director of the N.A.V.S.S. (the National Association of Victim Support Schemes) was aware that more work was necessary to aid families of murder victims. Some local Victim Support Schemes were already being supportive, but others felt too daunted to become involved. Helen and I met to discuss the problems that members of the group were experiencing...[20]

She was to add later: 'I don't know how far I would have got if it hadn't been for Victim Support. I think the actual support group would have been well established, but as far as all the other bits are concerned, I don't know how far I would have got without them. Initially, Helen had the know-how, the resources...'

On the other hand, Helen Reeves and Victim Support were conscious of the growth in the numbers of homicide referrals[21] and of

---

[19] See 'The aftermath of murder', *Victim Support Newsletter*, Apr 1988.

[20] A. Robinson, 'The Special Needs of Families of Murdered Children', undated MS.

[21] There were some 50 homicide referrals a year in 1985 and Victim Support commented in its annual report for 1984/5: 'While many members believe that Victims Support* is not equipped to deal with such problems, figures show that many Schemes have already offered support to families of murder victims. There are many questions to be asked...' (* The title of the organization changed more than once over the years).

the marked trepidation voiced by some victim support groups about supporting bereaved families.[22] Confronting the bereavement of others could be harrowing and disconcerting for the volunteer too. It would be no bad thing to enlist survivors and draw on their immediate knowledge of trauma to learn more about their problems and needs. Neither would it be unhelpful to demonstrate that they had not been neglected by Victim Support[23] and that the association had attempted energetically to understand their plight. Their's was, after all, *terra incognita*, and Victim Support was unsure of its role. Helen Reeves said:

There were two things—one was that some schemes were getting murders anyway and we recognised they were a different sort of work because they had to be long term and the grief didn't go away and that we couldn't do everything that people needed because it was the distress in the middle of the night, it was that sort of problem that we were dealing with. The other problem was that those schemes that weren't accepting the murders were worried about what was happening to people in their area—so . . . we tried to make contact with the groups that we thought dealt with murder and we had some initial bilateral meetings, one of which was—we wrote to all the people who we thought represented families of murder victims, one of which was POMC which was very young and still part of Compassionate Friends. Another one was——. We wrote and asked for meetings. —— never replied and POMC did eventually agree to meet us and we had a meeting. It was myself and another member of staff, with Ann Robinson who is one of the founder members. She told us that——had been in contact with her and said that she had no intentions of meeting us because she regarded us as not having anything to say, as not having any authority in the field, for example. But Ann wanted to meet us to find out what we were about. It was a very tentative meeting. We were sitting in the large meeting

---

[22]   Ann Viney commented later: 'My experience is that, when new areas of work develop, enthusiasm and reservations may appear in parts at all levels of the organisation. For example, many volunteers will be so driven by their own desire to help people that they will not be willing to wait for training programmes to be devised. In some cases the Co-ordinators who support them, or the local Trustees, who are responsible for their activities, may be more cautious, as indeed the National Association is . . .'

[23]   Helen Peggs, the Press Officer of Victim Support, observed: 'it came along at an opportune moment I think. . . . I think it was very useful timing. I think we would probably have done it anyway. We've not done [it] purely to silence the critics . . . We were approached by POMC . . . at about the same time we started getting public criticism from families of murder victims. . . . It could be a way of working with people rather than appearing to be in some kind of competition with them. There was definitely a feeling of competition around . . . with Justice for Victims suddenly appearing.'

room on opposite sides of the table and Ann was very cautious about what
we wanted, and it began to emerge that she herself and other members of
her group had met with so many professionals who had assumed that they
knew everything, and she cited priests and psychiatrists and psychologists
and social workers, all of whom tended to say that they knew how they
must feel but they had got to get a grip on themselves, or but they've got to
find a way to forgive, and these sorts of messages coming across from
professionals. And so they tended to be very cautious and they've already
got into the idea that they were the only experts. I then pointed out that
from our point of view, our concern was that we did not feel like experts,
that we actually felt very inadequate—and a lot of our members felt that we
would never deal with murder because we're only volunteers and we
wouldn't know what to do and the problem would be much too great for
us to handle. It was in that dialogue that we began to see some accommodation. She told me that they thought they were very good at supporting each
other but that they really needed help in dealing with the criminal justice
process—they didn't have a voice, they didn't know the police, they didn't
know the courts and the compensation system and so on—they had no
money—they meet in each others' homes and pay their own telephone bills
and pay their own fares to go to meetings and, as has continued to be the
case, most of the work was falling on one or two very active people and,
inevitably, it is not necessarily the best helpers who are available, so that
was becoming a problem. I said that we actually were quite good at the
things that they were not good at, in other words we had our contacts, we
had members from the establishment, we knew quite a lot about the courts
and criminal justice and compensation as well. We agreed—it was a very
long meeting—it must have been about three hours that we were talking—
very emotional at times as well, but we agreed that we ought to go on
talking, and it was shortly after that that we set up a very small working
party with a member of the national council who was a member of Cruse
and a representative of Chief Constables and Ann herself and a couple of
members [including an experienced victim support volunteer].[24]

The Families of Murder Victims Project

The first act of that small working party was to contact some thirty
'helping agencies' to discover what was actually offered to those
bereaved by homicide, and it ascertained that almost nothing was
offered. The police were reported to balk at intimacy because of the

[24] The actual membership was Helen Reeves (later replaced by Peter Dalrymple,
then Assistant Director of Victim Support), Ann Robinson, Commander Wally Bore-
ham of the Metropolitan Police, and Doris Sullivan of Islington Victims Support
Scheme.

possible culpability of the family, and other agencies claimed generally not to be qualified, that a very special expertise was required which they could not supply. Helen Reeves surmised that 'a great taboo about violent death caused by another person' led organizations to shy away from the bereaved.

POMC and Victim Support resolved to remedy one another's weaknesses: POMC turned to Victim Support because of its possession of resources, connections, and inside knowledge of the criminal justice system; and Victim Support to POMC because of its own uncertainties about how to proceed in the troubling area of grief after violent crime.[25] POMC was the largest group to embody the survivor's existential knowledge of the aftermath of homicide, and 'they were prepared to work with us [and] there weren't a lot [of such organizations] in the field.'

It is the way of Victim Support to work slowly, politically and cautiously in any new area, advertising its adherence to the forms of a rationally-controlled organization;[26] establishing and evaluating experimental projects;[27] incorporating representatives of the criminal justice agencies on its working parties to enlist their co-operation and allay their suspicions; promulgating guidelines and preparing manuals and programmes of training (by contrast, Ann Robinson remarked simply: 'we didn't have any of that [in POMC]'). The association displays an almost ostentatious regard for the doubts and anxieties of others. It is no small thing for a minor body such as Victim Support to move in on territories guarded by bodies more powerful than itself, and there is always some inevitable trepidation about charges of *lèse-majesté*. Victim Support's Crown Court Witness Service, for example, could well have foundered at first had judges or defence counsel complained that its volunteers were coaching witnesses or contaminating evidence. So too with what was to become the murder project. The working party was intended not only to ascertain what support bereaved families required but also to ensure that any support

---

[25] Ann Robinson herself recalled: 'When I contacted her she said to me "I've known for a long time that there is a need there, but I don't really know how to go about it. It's such a vast thing to get hold of."

[26] See J. Meyer and B. Rowan, 'Institutionalized Organizations: Formal Structure as Myth and Ceremony', *American Journal of Sociology*, Sept 1977, Vol 83, No 2.

[27] Helen Reeves was to tell Justice for Victims in 1993: 'we decided to do some research [on murder victims] partly because that is the way you get people like the Home Office to notice what is going on.'

which was eventually offered would be so purposeful, well-administered, and well-informed that it would not compound the difficulties of families and volunteers. The organization of support should be calculated to attract the co-operation of other relevant groups and agencies, a cardinal object being to ensure that the police would place enough trust in Victim Support to refer all homicide cases—and that would demand diplomacy.

An enlarged and rather differently composed working party began its task in 1986 by establishing a pilot support project in Essex, the home territory of June Patient, Ann Robinson, and much of POMC, and a county with a police force known both to Victim Support and, professionally and as a referral agency, to many of the bereaved members of POMC. Volunteers from the six victim support schemes in the county were trained by members of Parents of Murdered Children and others. Ann Robinson recalled: 'what I wanted to do, one of my aims, was to educate people in how, given confidence if you like, on how to handle [homicide]. And we did that. It was all part of the training.' Helen Reeves vividly remembered the impact of that education: 'We had a very, very powerful message from Ann Robinson herself who said "I know that you will think that you are not qualified, that you don't really want to get involved with something as horrible as this, but all I can say to you is that we didn't want to get involved either, but we didn't get any choice". I remember that, so it was a very powerful message, and I think a powerful message to our volunteers...'

The Essex Police did agree to refer all homicide cases to the support schemes and the pilot project[28] (a policy that remained in place thereafter[29]) and some thirty referrals were received during 1986–7, the first year of the project's life. It was determined sub-

[28] What follows is based in large part on Families of Murder Victims Project, *Final Report* (Victim Support, London, 1990).

[29] Peter Whent, the Victim Support Scheme Liaison Officer for Essex Police, appointed in 1988, announced that in future 'all referred cases are passed direct to the V.S.S. Divisional Co-ordinator by the Detective Inspector in the case and probably within 24 hours...'; 'Victim Support Scheme—Murder/Manslaughter', MS, 4 Oct 1988. Also see his 'The Burden We Must Share', *Police Review*, 31 May 1991. Whent was to say: 'from that moment onwards we developed this system then, where we said that every murder or homicide case we would automatically refer it to Victim Support for murder/manslaughter support whether the victim wants it or not. That was the big change and it was a big scene of change because I believe this: if you ask any person at the moment of the most trauma and stress in their life, "do you want victim support?", they'll almost invariably say "no".'

sequently that the pilot project had been successful: 'volunteer visitors were able to offer worthwhile help to families and give some public recognition of their needs.'[30] The co-ordinator of one of the participating Essex schemes reflected:

Every volunteer at some time asks 'Am I needed? Will I be welcome? Will I be able to cope?' When visiting families of murder victims the answer to all three is 'yes'. The Essex experience confirms that families do welcome a volunteer—it is public recognition of their tragedy.[31]

The working party then proceeded to enlarge, embellish, and extend that experience in January 1988 to a two-year demonstration project in Essex, Merseyside, Sheffield, and a large tract of South London, funded by the Home Office, evaluated by Lyn Brown of Liverpool University and others, advised by Ann Robinson as a POMC representative, and co-ordinated by Jane Cooper as 'project development worker'. Cooper had formerly been the co-ordinator of Camden Victim Support and later an employee of Victim Support: and at Camden Victim Support she had herself supported a homicide survivor who encouraged her to apply for the co-ordinator's post. Jane Cooper remembers that her sympathies were engaged from the first. She met David Howden, the chairman of POMC, at an introductory session in London: 'it was the first time [he'd] spoken and I'll never forget that day...I was sort of high, and so very moved.' She was to play a significant part in the history of POMC and SAMM thereafter.

The project's formal aims were to improve Victim Support's work with homicide referrals by ascertaining the needs of families of murder victims, identifying the skills which volunteers require to meet those needs, preparing a training programme for those volunteers, 'consider[ing] initiating self-help groups for families of murder victims', and working closely with POMC and its network.

I have already made use of a number of the principal findings of that project in the first three chapters of this book. It was claimed that murder and manslaughter were distressing and confusing, leading to a strong demand for clear, reiterated information and compassionate understanding. Families might well need practical help, first in dealing with a home that had been sealed as a crime scene, and subsequently with cleaning or replacing possessions that had

---

[30] Families of Murder Victims Project, *Final Report* (n 28 above), 2.
[31] M. Warren in 'Essex Experience', *Victims Support*, Apr 1988, 2.

been damaged or used for forensic purposes. They were often overly controlled in the selection of who should identify and view the dead person, and women were frequently excluded altogether from the procedure. There were defects in the organization of the Coroner's Court, families being dismissed as uninterested in the inquest and not being informed about when the hearing would take place. Families suffered from isolation, disorientation, and multiple problems flowing from uncertain employment, the travails of inquest and court proceedings, and the timing and notification of the killer's release at the end of sentence.

The volunteers supporting the families worked as intermediaries with the professions and agencies which controlled the aftermath of homicide: the police, undertakers, mortuary officials, coroners, doctors, DSS, and others. They sat and listened to the families in their grief (although it was reported that it could be difficult to 'retain sufficient distance' and avoid being overwhelmed). They provided the highest level of support in the beginning when there were daily visits. Meetings then tapered off to fortnightly or three-weekly intervals, although they fluctuated with the lulls and crises of the moral career of the bereaved, being especially intense during anniversaries and the trial. The volunteers' support had been welcomed by the bereaved families, the report concluded, and Victim Support should further extend its work with the families of homicide victims.

One outcome was the impact on the police force in Essex and elsewhere. Not only was there to emerge a local Essex policy of automatic referrals of homicide cases to Victim Support, but Peter Whent, the Essex Detective Superintendent liaising with the project, later with the British Transport Police, came to reflect and write publicly about the police management of the families of homicide victims.[32] He came to the view that families were entitled to detailed information about the homicide and the investigation, to inspect the victim as he or she lay in the mortuary and much else:

because I went down and spoke to all the families, and I picked out some of their cases (with their consent), I was making notes and asking like you're

---

[32] Those articles included 'Murder in the Family', *Police Review*, 12 Jan 1990; 'The Burden We Must Share', *Police Review*, 31 May 1991; and 'What Friends are For', *Police Review*, 18 Dec 1992, as well as mimeographed advice to investigating officers with such titles as 'Victim Support Scheme—Murder/Manslaughter' and 'Notes on the Manner of Dealing with the Surviving Members of a Family in a Murder Investigation'.

doing now, written up some articles to actually try and change the culture of some of the forces nationally, saying, you know, 'do you realise what you've actually done to the family?' This is not the murder, the murder's great, but look what's happened. These are the things that *weren't* addressed.... The big things really are ... the needs of the family. It's a cultural change in the police service that when there is a death in the family that the family themselves have a right to know what's happened and have a right to know the responses made by the offender...What you really need is an honesty and an openness with the family.

Another outcome was the preparation of a dedicated, standardised training programme for volunteers, consisting of an introduction and six sessions focused on 'murder: the crime and the law', the police investigation, the role of the coroner, the court process, bereavement, and the effects of murder.[33] In all cases, volunteers would be addressed by experts from within and about the criminal justice system: by a Coroner, detective, crown prosecutor, a member of the staff of a Crown Court Centre or the Crown Court Witness Service, experienced volunteers, and a bereaved parent or relative of the victim. There were 'role plays' in which they would take the role of the bereaved, being asked to imagine (in the case of one session organized by Victim Support London) how they would respond to the aftermath of a murder of a woman. They were introduced to the stages of grief mapped by Colin Murray-Parkes and Elizabeth Kübler-Ross. They would be taken to a mortuary and would undergo the process of viewing 'a body'. They were encouraged to introduce themselves, their anxieties and feelings, their hopes, griefs, and fears, to one another. They would be warned about the intensity of emotion and the anger which they would encounter as they supported the bereaved (an organizer said: 'we say this will happen, they will swear, and shout and scream, they will do this and that, but it's not directed at you personally and the volunteers know that...'). They were given copies of statistical digests of homicide and newspaper articles on the bereaved, including ones written by Ann Robinson and David Howden.

David Howden talked to the training session of twenty-one London volunteers which I attended in March 1995. One of those present remarked: 'I think this was the first time it hit me that he was still suffering to such a great degree, whereas I'm used to seeing

[33] *Supporting families of murder victims* (Victim Support, London, 1991).

victims of crime and going home safe in the knowledge that in a month, a year, five years, they will have got over it fairly fully. And these people don't get over it. They just assimilate it into part of their personality.' Howden himself said: 'if we talk to the volunteers and help in their training, make them aware, just talk to them, tell them what we need . . . the experiences we've gone through, they're going to be better equipped to deal with the people they get referred to them . . .'

The theme at all times was that volunteers remained volunteers, amateurs not experts, and their peculiar strength resided in the fact that they were not bereavement counsellors, but what victim support volunteers had always been, representatives of a community, not markedly different from other members of a community, symbolising the community's compassion. The volunteers I observed being trained in March 1995 asserted that homicide work was but an application of earlier, familiar forms of work with rape and other victims, the structure of training and the role being little different (one volunteer said: 'it's purely a continuation and extension of what we're trained to do anyway . . .'). The course organizer herself declared: 'we are not bereavement counsellors. We're not trained like bereavement counsellors are. People call us counsellors but we're not. Volunteers are people who are happy to give up their time, but they're not trained to counsel.' Volunteers were there to help with the completion of forms and claims, the organization of repairs to property, the representation of the victim to other agencies, advice about practical matters and the criminal justice system, and to put survivors in touch with other organizations such as TCF and POMC (Jane Cooper commented: 'so close links with Ann R[obinson] amd Jill P[alm] and referrals to each other'). Above all, they were there to listen (another volunteer said of a man she had supported: 'apart from the practical side, I think initially he needed somebody to talk to. I got the impression that . . . there becomes a difficulty after a while with saying the same thing over and over again to the same person [his wife].' And yet another volunteer said: 'it was enormous value to them—they needed someone outside their family in order to talk things over.' By the end of 1993, 831 volunteers had been trained to support homicide survivors in England and Wales, and 626 homicide referrals had been received in that one year, 125 more than in the year before.

A diversion: the Crown Court Witness Service

Parenthetically, another volunteer project with a slightly different history had come to fruition at very much the same time, further binding POMC and Victim Support together. I have given its earlier history elsewhere[34] but the project does merit a diversion because it flows directly into the theme of this book.

Victim Support's success in attracting automatic referrals from the police, and the attendant growth in its involvement with serious crime, had brought about a prolongation and intensification of the support offered to a small proportion of victims. I have already observed that in 1991, for the very first time, Victim Support had begun to measure the workload of its schemes by recording the length of contact with victims as well as the numbers of victims supported. In that year, 212 schemes reported that over 12,000 cases were still 'active' a month after referral; of those, over 9,000 were active after three months; and, of those, just under 6,000 were still live after six months.

Victims were being supported at greater length, sometimes even to trial, and it was becoming apparent to Victim Support that they experienced the process of attending the courthouse and testifying there as quite alienating, frightening, and disturbing. Victim Support proceeded in familiar fashion, convening a working party in 1986, and mounting, in 1989, seven victim–witness demonstration projects in Crown Court centres across the country.

Volunteers were trained to give aid and comfort to victims and prosecution witnesses, and to the families and friends of victims and prosecution witnesses, in court. Declared a success, and funded by the Home Office, what became known as the Crown Court Witness Service was extended little by little and cautiously into every Crown Court centre, and it reached the most august court of all, the Central Criminal Court at the Old Bailey in May 1993, the court most heavily engaged in the prosecution of serious crimes and homicides. The Old Bailey is a large, eighteen court centre, which takes cases not only from the Greater London area but also from other places when the strength of local feeling makes it advisable to do so. Let me turn to the witness service at that Court to illustrate how Victim Support took yet another route to supporting homicide survivors.

---

[34] *The Social World of an English Crown Court: Witness and Professional in the Crown Court Centre at Wood Green* (Clarendon Press, Oxford, 1993).

The Witness Service at the Central Criminal Court became operational in November 1993. Working in tandem with other victim support schemes outside the courthouse, it had a well-defined and restricted role, in part to avoid accusations of interference in the trial process, in part because contacts could be sustained only for very limited lengths of time:[35] 'you're not there primarily to deal with the bereavement, grieving aspect.... We're there just to try to ease people through the system', said Michael Naish, the scheme's co-ordinator. The service offers information on court procedure and layout, encourages witnesses to become acquainted with the appearance of the courthouse and courtroom in advance or on the day of trial, supplies emotional support and practical information, and refers witnesses to other schemes and projects after the trial. Like its sister witness services at other Crown Court centres, it does not offer legal advice, discuss evidence, or tender victim impact statements.[36]

Homicide trials were more demanding than trials for other offences. Between its opening in November 1993 and April 1995, the witness service at the Old Bailey had provided support in 761 trials, of which 109, or 14 per cent, were for homicide. In all 2,676 people had been supported, of whom 610, or 23 per cent, were involved in homicide cases. The trials also entailed larger numbers of people in apparent need of assistance: an average of 5.6 people had been supported by the service during each homicide trial (the maximum being 32), more than the three and a half people supported in other forms of trial.[37] Of those 610, 225 were described by the service as the 'family and close friends' of the victim. Forty had attended to testify, the others to observe.

By April 1995, the Old Bailey was serviced by a team of twenty-five volunteers who worked in rota. They had been trained in much the same fashion as the supporters of the secondary victims of homicide. When assisting the families of homicide victims, Naish said, there was an emphasis on 'all that's gone before the family actually get to the court... it's to try to get a bit of an understanding

---

[35] The average number of days in which support was given to the family and close friends of victims in homicide trials between the end of 1993 and April 1995 was $3\frac{1}{4}$ days, the maximum being 14 days.

[36] Based on 'The Witness Service at the Central Criminal Court', undated MS.

[37] I am most grateful to Michael Naish, co-ordinator of the Old Bailey's Witness Service, for preparing these figures for me.

about all the anguish they've gone through. [We make use of a] video and...the police talking about what they do and...comments from the family about what it feels like to be excluded from your house for two days or not to see the body for three months...' It was POMC, later SAMM, that again supplied the immediate existental knowledge of bereavement.

Interestingly, POMC and SAMM had referred none of those individuals to the witness service. But what should also be marked is that Victim Support had established yet another set of relations with the families of homicide victims, and it had again employed the services of the survivors of POMC and SAMM in the training of its volunteers.

The securing of relations

A third outcome of the Families of Murder Victims Project was the new importance which survivors received as they were consulted by a significant agency about their needs and aspirations. Lyn Brown, one of the principal researchers, remarked:

One of the things that we picked up [was] the pleasure with which we were greeted. We're not the spotty-faced young people which people have in their minds as researchers, people they felt they couldn't make any connection with. We did feel that it was very important not only to victim support workers but to families because they wanted to be taken seriously...

And a fourth outcome was the consolidation of relations between a number of key members of POMC and Victim Support as they collaborated in establishing and implementing the witness service and the pilot and development projects. I have already discussed how members of POMC, later SAMM, assisted in the training of victim support and witness service volunteers. But there was more. Members of the two organizations regularly attended and spoke at one another's conferences. Jill Palm and Ruth Fuller of the POMC committee presented the Murder Victims Project Report to the 1990 Victim Support Conference, for instance. Ruth Fuller was later to inform her fellow members of POMC that they had been 'looked after superbly by Jane Cooper and Peter Dalrymple....It was a lovely experience.' The report itself was 'tremendous', she said, 'probably the cleverest and most sensible report I have ever read' and 'the response [from members of Victim Support] was embarrassingly overwhelming.'[38]

Those key members of POMC, in effect, joined with members of Victim Support to become part of a specialised homicide group. Together, they tendered evidence to the House of Lords Select Committee on Murder, Manslaughter and Life Imprisonment in June 1989, and they jointly attended the European Forum for Victim Services in Stockholm a year later. Their relations were amiable. Ann Robinson, part of the delegation to Stockholm, was to write later: 'I was rather nervous of being given the responsibility of helping to convey such important issues [focused on the needs of the families of murder victims]. But, as always when among victim supporters, their warmth and sincerity reached out and gave me reassurance—I also chose to remain seated between Jane [Cooper of Victim Support, the murder project's development officer] and Peter [Dalrymple, also of Victim Support] while speaking which made me feel very safe!'[39] She was to tell me long afterwards: 'this is another nice thing that has evolved. You have made a lot of nice friends.'

For her part, Helen Reeves was to tell the House of Lords Select Committee on Murder and Life Imprisonment on 5 June 1989: 'I do not think we are at a stage of knowing precisely what our role is ... but I think we are fairly sure we do have a role in the criminal justice process.... We have also identified the importance of self-help groups such as Parents of Murdered Children, because it is very important that families have an opportunity to support one another and share their experiences. We ourselves learn a great deal from them.'[40]

Victim Support, POMC and self-help

A final outcome was the Families of Murder Victims Project's unsuccessful attempts to promote mutual aid for the bereaved. The development of self-help by an established bureaucratic organization entailed something of a structural contradiction and it foundered. Self-help was an area of activity not yet cultivated but frequently contemplated by Victim Support. Interest seemed first to have been whetted in 1987 by an approach from the Suzy

[38] In *POMC Newsletter*, Autumn 1990 (?), 2.
[39] A. Robinson, 'The European Forum for Victim Services...', undated MS.
[40] *Minutes of Evidence*, 498.

Lamplugh Trust and a gay group about the prospect of fostering mutual aid for the male victims of sexual assault. It had been decided at the time that there were more pressing demands on the association's funds, but the interest did not disappear.

The promise of self-help was aired again the next year by Peter Dalrymple, then Assistant Director of Victim Support, who argued that the needs of certain victims and secondary victims were so acute that they could 'often outstrip the resources of member Schemes.... [I]t was suggested that such needs might be met through self-help groups, especially in the bereavement field.'[41] He suggested that Jane Cooper should be asked to attend a seminar run by the National Self-Help Support Centre of NCVO in June 1988 to examine the appropriateness of self-help to the work of Victim Support.[42] Helen Reeves's own response was sympathetic: 'In the very early stages, the [working party] did consider self help and considered that it was important in cases like murder when the problems are likely to persist for some years. It was also felt the group should have professional guidance to identify special problems and see the group did not go in the wrong direction. That was part of the basic model, and why Ann Robinson was involved.'

Yet Victim Support's attempts to establish such groups aborted. Just as the first prototypical 'walk-in' victims agency—founded in Kingswood, Gloucestershire, in November 1973 by a group called the National Victims Association—had installed a counsellor who waited in vain for victims to refer themselves for support,[43] so Victim Support's own would-be self-help groups in Essex and Sheffield relied fruitlessly on the bereaved to stir themselves into coming forward. 'The difficulty [was] in obtaining commitment from members',[44] reported Ann Robinson. The organizational implications were transparent. A mutual aid movement that celebrated autonomy, spontaneity, self-improvement, experiential knowledge, and

---

[41] Memorandum to Helen Reeves, 9 June 1988.

[42] Jane Cooper did attend and she returned armed with questions about how groups should liaise with outsiders, how they should establish 'credibility', and how they could contend with problems of national co-ordination and the twin difficulties of the 'founder syndrome' and the 'fossil syndrome', where members 'stay in groups too long'. J. Cooper, Memorandum: National Self-Help Organisations Conference, 27 June 1988.

[43] See my *Helping Victims of Crime* (Clarendon Press, Oxford, 1990), 124 *et seq.*

[44] A. Robinson in *Parents of Murdered Children Newsletter*, Dec 1990.

the free collaboration of sufferers sat uncomfortably with bureaucratic direction.[45] Victim Support noted:

Attempts to establish new groups through introductions by Victim Support have not so far been successful, although this is partly due to lack of resources...It can also be argued that self-help, by its very nature, is more likely to be successful if it is initiated and sustained by individuals who have themselves suffered as a result of personal tragedy.[46]

And Helen Reeves herself reflected:

The original research proposal included an attempt to develop self-help, to see whether Victim Support could be an agent for developing self-help. I didn't see it as being run by Victim Support. It was far more a question of getting it organized. Even in Essex, in the very early stages, I think the very first meeting we had with victim support volunteers—they went through their records and they wrote to every family where there had been a violent bereavement over the last couple of years. And I don't think anybody came. They all sat back and waited to see if these people would turn up, and they didn't. It's a dynamic that we still don't really know about.... What we concluded out of our rather meagre attempts was that Victim Support could not run self-help. Self-help really was self-help.... By its very nature, an outside organization cannot start self-help. In our work plan [in 1991] was a determination to find other ways of encouraging self-help. We didn't really know how we were going to do it...

Proposals

Consider the position of the two organizations in the early 1990s. Since 1991, Victim Support had been 'committed to improving the access of self-help support for victims of violent crime',[47] but its own efforts to engender self-help groups had failed because of the familiar organizational dilemma that bureaucracy cannot easily conceive and retain the spontaneous group. Helen Reeves said 'we [couldn't] set up the self-help but we [could] actually support a body that is self-help and help it to expand, which actually [met] all our purposes...'

Some central members of just such a spontaneous group, POMC, recently having become loose-coupled to TCF and obliged to fend

---

[45] See H. Becker, *German Youth Bond or Free?* (Kegan Paul, Trench, Trubner and Co, London, 1946).

[46] 'Self-Help Groups—Discussion Paper and Proposal', June 1993.

[47] 'Parents of Murdered Children 3 Year Project Proposal', Victim Support, undated.

for itself, were seeking a connection with a mentor organization. POMC suffered from the 'liability of newness',[48] that besetting problem in the early stages of any voluntary organization's history when a reputation has yet to be won, political insiders are wary, and funding is difficult to secure. It was growing in size, claiming some 300 members in 1993, and a number were becoming unhappy about a misleading name which appeared symbolically to exclude those who were not parents—the friends, children, grandparents, uncles, aunts, sisters, and brothers of victims, as well as those mourning victims who were not children at all. Although no such exclusions were enforced in practice, the name had begun to jar. Gill Pennicard, the last co-ordinator of POMC, said: 'when it was POMC, it was very singling out, let's say. Mind you, nobody was ever turned away if they said it was "my father that was murdered" or "it was my sister or aunt", nobody, I never said "go away". I would have welcomed anybody who wished it.'

POMC was administratively underdeveloped for an organization with ambition. It had no permanent staff and no permanent funding. Its members paid no fees and it raised money haphazardly from small *ad hoc* donations, raffles, fêtes, and bazaars. It had little adequate management and a database based only on file-cards,[49] and it could not easily match family to family for support,[50] being obliged sometimes to mismatch families or, more frequently, to resort to a small pool of tried survivors. It could not even supervise the progress of the connections that had been made between families and individuals. Although purporting to be a national association, it had foregone TCF's wide web of groups and relations, and was largely concentrated in and around the east of London, centred, some members thought, on a small activitist group who lacked the routine organizational competence of the staff of larger associations. After all, members enlisted because

[48] See J. Singh *et al*, 'Organizational Legitimacy and the Liability of Newness', *Administrative Science Quarterly*, June 1986, Vol 31. For the idea's application to the case of self-help groups, see G. Tracy and Z. Gussow, 'Self-Help Health Groups', *Journal of Applied Behavioral Science*, Summer 1976, Vol 12, 390.

[49] Ann Robinson recalled that the database had contained the name and address of the family and a code for the way in which the victim had been killed; the names of the agencies and people with whom the family had had contact; and the information they had been sent. POMC had been donated a computer, but: 'I didn't have time and I wasn't computer-literate', and the information remained on card.

[50] 'Because', recalled Ann Robinson simply, 'they weren't there.'

they were bereaved, not because they displayed capacities for management. One POMC committee member of the time reflected that:

We really got to the stage where we felt we were going over the top of this mountain and then things happen and you seem to slide down back again and it looked as if it was going nowhere. If people wanted to do things their way, there's always this lack of co-operation, and unless you have an idea how to deal with meetings and how to deal with issues, which a lot of us don't have, and a lot of us never will [have], because not everybody is born to be on a committee or be sensible. But, because there are too many people that get on to committees, instantly want to be on a committee, it doesn't go forward . . . and there are problems.

POMC reported in 1993: 'Victim Support is one of the few bodies who do understand—and have been of great assistance to POMC. The two organisations seem to work well together and are presently looking at ways of co-operating more closely.'[51] In fact, David Howden and Arthur Linsley, the chairman and treasurer of POMC, had approached Helen Reeves at the very beginning of 1993 about the possibility of entering into some form of coalition based on practical collaboration and financial aid. POMC was near insolvent. Its balance sheet showed that at the end of 1993 it had overspent its income of £9,990 by £172.[52] June Patient said: 'it had to happen because we couldn't have carried on. We would have run out of money definitely within the next year or 18 months.'

Victim Support tended to act as the Home Office's trusted broker in many matters in the voluntary sector affecting victims, and POMC had been steered towards it. David Howden said: 'we needed some more money and everybody suggested that perhaps the Home Office should provide something or we should apply to the government for a grant, which the treasurer did and he was referred to Victim Support—any money that they would give or anything they would channel would be channelled through Victim Support and they wouldn't deal with us direct. So the pair of us

[51] POMC Information Sheet, 1993.

[52] The exact financial position of POMC at the time was the subject of some contention subsequently. At my meeting with some of the more activist members of POMC/SAMM/Justice for Victims in August 1997 to discuss the first draft of this book, John Patient was adamant that POMC had been solvent when it metamorphosed into SAMM. The problem had not been an absolute lack of funds, he said, but the modesty of POMC's funds which prevented the organization from evolving in satisfactory fashion. One vital development that POMC could not then afford, for instance, was the employment of a paid co-ordinator.

came along here to Victim Support and had a chat and we were very well received and we put forward a few proposals, we reported back to our committee and things just grew from there really.' Helen Reeves recalled, 'they were struggling because they were getting too big and they didn't have the administrative knowledge or resources, and they needed help. In fact, it all came together perfectly. It was a genuine point in history, when they needed something and we needed something. In fact, after I had met them that afternoon, I think I knocked out the proposal that evening for a joint project and it went through their council and our council almost immediately.'

There were further meetings in February 1993 that culminated in a unanimous decision at the March 1993 POMC Annual General Meeting to make a formal overture to Victim Support. What was envisaged was a semi-detached partnership which would permit the two organizations not only to retain their independence but also work in tandem on a three year project.

It was thought that Victim Support might assist POMC by providing some form of affiliated or associate membership; guidance on a code of practice; advice on the selection and training of members who could offer support to the newly bereaved; access to money for a paid worker;[53] and accommodation and administrative support for staff.[54] There were some internal doubts about the exact pattern of the future relations between the two organizations. One paper circulated inside Victim Support noted that the proposed boundaries between the two organizations were a little uncertain. It was unclear, for instance, whether the self-help offered by POMC would be a complement or alternative to the work of Victim Support, and, if a complement, would Victim Support be obliged to reduce its service? But there were no doubts that self-help for the bereaved should be explored and that POMC was a perfectly suitable partner for the purpose. Victim Support noted:

POMC is a service-providing organisation and is not currently involved in campaigns—for example on the death penalty—and they are unlikely to adopt policies which would be contrary to those of Victim Support. They would wish, however, to reserve the right to make their own representations to the government or the press on issues relating to murder... In the past,

[53] An earlier application for funding by POMC to the Home Office had resulted in the organization being referred to Victim Support as the supervising body in the field.
[54] Taken from H. Reeves, 'Self-Help Groups—Discussion Paper and Proposal', MS, June 1993.

Victim Support has supported the group in making such representations, and indeed our own policies have been influenced by the views of POMC.

Victim Support eventually contracted to ensure that funding conditions were met; administer the three year project's money; employ, supervise, and manage the project's staff; service and report to a new Steering Committee composed of POMC and Victim Support representatives; and maintain the database owned by POMC.

For its part, POMC would change its name to signal a shift away from a narrow concentration on the parents and children of its title.[55] 'SAM' (Support After Murder) had been mooted by TCF in January 1990[56] when the two bodies separated, and the name was resurrected in 1993 when the alliance with Victim Support was under discussion, finally ('after long and hard deliberations') to become SAMM (Support After Murder and Manslaughter), a name that 'more fully describes our aims and objectives'.[57] The new SAMM would be an independent charity run by an elected committee. The old POMC would provide details of current and future members to compile a computerised database;[58] and it would field three members to represent it on the joint steering committee of the new body.

Money

The raising of money proved to be remarkably easy. A financial management firm had approached Victim Support on behalf of an individual client who, a member of the firm observed:

said that he would like to make a grant to Victim Support...and...provided it met his own personal interests, and those were primarily to do with a balance of responsibility between State and the criminal in making appropriate compensation or restitution or whatever, and he thought that a dimension needed to be added to the Victim Support process which took

---

[55] It is interesting that the American POMC was also to amend its name for precisely the same reasons, becoming the National Organization of Parents of Murdered Children, Inc, For the Family and Friends of Homicide Victims.

[56] Minutes of POMC committee meeting, 14 Jan 1990.

[57] Indeed, from the first, Jane Cooper, SAMM's first co-ordinator, actively encouraged people other than the parents of murdered children to become 'supporters' in an effort to signal that transformation. She also sought to enlist such people on to the new SAMM executive committee. One such member was to be Norman Black.

[58] Although such a database did already exist in the early form of a card catalogue of members' names and addresses.

greater account of that and was willing to make funding available for the purpose. I raised the possibility to Victim Support and their view was that they had done pretty well as much as they could in that field and it was primarily a matter for the State, that their priorities lay elsewhere and so on. I went back to him, he was disappointed, but said that he would nevertheless consider making a contribution of a different order. They came back with a couple of proposals, I think three or four in fact, and we decided upon a training manual which they wished to take up and... the SAMM proposal. We agreed we would do both, as it turned out.

Helen Reeves observed of that original proposal: 'it was about getting compensation to victims and I said no, that isn't something we would do, but what we did was put up two proposals and he accepted them both, which... meant that he was paying for one completely and half paying for SAMM...'

The anonymously-donated 50 per cent subsidy for SAMM was to be matched by another charitable trust, the Lankelly Foundation. 'Our trustees, like any group of people, have a variety of opinions, a spectrum of opinions about how offences and offenders should be dealt with by society and... I think there was a feeling that we were not paying enough attention to the victim, and the cry "what about the victim?" was heard,' said one of its staff. Yet the foundation had not appreciably funded Victim Support in the past because 'there are problems with Victim Support's organization itself... one of the problems is that a very, very high percentage of its funding comes directly from the Home Office.' On the one hand, there was a reluctance to put money into supporting the headquarters staff of a large national organization and allowing the government to take credit for whatever was accomplished. On the other hand, there was a reluctance to support one or more of the innumerable and seemingly interchangeable local victims' support schemes, between which it would be difficult to choose (known to the charity as the scout hut problem[59]). The Didcot-based foundation *had* funded the Oxford victim support scheme but it had done so partly because of its sense of responsibility for a geographical neighbour ('I went out to the victim support group in Oxford. They were in a windowless room, totally reliant upon volunteers apart from the co-ordinator's post, and there just seemed to be a very gross inequality between the rim and the hub so to speak.').

[59] How, it was asked, could one choose between the merits of a scout hut in Surrey and a scout hut in Hertfordshire?

SAMM had the virtue of being neither rim nor hub: 'it was going in to Victim Support, because it was actually dying—the self-help group, Parents of Murdered Children, POMC. I think they were saying that they really needed to get into some kind of a structure.' The Lankelly Foundation confirmed its willingness to fund POMC/ SAMM in July 1994. And the Home Office agreed to let Victim Support use £10,480 of its remaining annual grant to equip and furnish offices for SAMM, a sum that Helen Reeves described as 'a little bit of money left in our local funding budget that we would have to give back to the Home Office.' So it was that financial plans for the first year of the new SAMM could proceed with £12,000 from the Lankelly Foundation, £21,688 from the anonymous donor and £10,000 from local funding. It was possible to move to advertising the posts of a 'project worker' and a part-time secretary.[60]

The new secretary would be required to respond to general enquiries, establish the database, revise the 'existing poor information of membership', and provide information about SAMM's work to its members. The new project worker would 'improve the networking of members and membership', develop a code of practice, plan new, local self-help groups under the aegis of SAMM, and travel about the country to visit those new groups as they began work.

Jane Cooper

Jane Cooper had been appointed project development officer to the Families of Murder Victims Project in October 1987, and she had not only become a part of the small homicide group that straddled POMC and Victim Support,[61] but had also come in some measure to represent them to the wider world. She had made a substantial contribution to the preparation of Victim Support's National Training Guidelines for Work with Families of Homicide Victims. She had fielded questions from the mass media, participated in the training of Coroners, the police, and bereavement groups, and given evidence to the Broadcasting Standards Council and the House of Lords Select Committee on Murder and Life Imprisonment. She

---

[60] The post was advertised in the *Guardian* on 30 Mar 1993 and interviewing took place at the end of May.
[61] For example, she and Peter Dalrymple had attended POMC's ritual pre-Christmas lunch in 1990.

had, she said, 'learned an enormous amount from people like David [Howden] and the family members . . . it helped me get beyond the taboo of murder because I just met such lovely, normal people and I think that was immensely important for me.' In short, she had not only become something of an authority on how to support and act for a group of the bereaved, but also a near-insider herself. Ann Robinson said of her: 'we've seen some pretty horrendous things happen to us [survivors] . . . but I think Jane is a very special person because she has been very, very involved for a long time and she's probably as close as anybody can be without actually having gone through it.' She was widely recognised as understanding, sympathetic, and kindly, an informed woman who gave herself unstintingly, and who received plaudits from her colleagues.[62] But she was above all a professional within the voluntary sector, eligible for appointment because of her command over a particular set of transferable skills and her practical experience in Victim Support, and not because she was herself a survivor of homicide.

Jane Cooper asked Ann Robinson if she wanted to be the new co-ordinator, volunteering to withdraw her application if she did, but Ann Robinson 'had had enough by then', she had 'burn-out', and declared she did not want the post. So it was Jane Cooper who was appointed to the new co-ordinator's position in July 1994.

The old and the young Turks

Despite its show of unanimity, there were reservations amongst some members of POMC about the new alliance, the new name, and the new appointment. How could there not be? The dynamic of fusion and fission was still in play, and it was hard to relinquish an autonomy, achievement, and identity so recently won. POMC's second co-ordinator, Jill Palm, said: '. . . it was only when Victim Support took us under their wing really that anything significant was done. [The old POMC lot] thought [Victim Support] wanted to muscle in, take the glory.' And June Patient commented:

There are people in the group that don't agree with going in with Victim Support—that Victim Support is taking us over—but I don't believe that.

[62] Frank Green, the second chairman of SAMM, was publicly to say of her: 'I would like to . . . pay tribute and thanks to someone who has become a special friend, Jane Cooper . . . without whose help and support I could not have come this far.' Talk given at Victim Support national conference, July 1995.

We need them. We could not have carried on because there was only a few of us raising money, at the time anyway.

The reservations were inevitably most pronounced amongst the more radical members of POMC, those who were becoming identified with the new Victims of Crime Pressure Group, later to be called Justice for Victims, which had become active in the summer of 1993, and whose history I shall give in two separate chapters. After all, at the core of POMC was a social group which had won its independence from TCF, another large organization. It was as if, having achieved that liberty, POMC was about to be engulfed once more within what was defined as an inhospitable bureaucratic environment, an environment which seemed to deny the difference and distinctiveness of the survivor, and there were predictable tensions between the claims of *Gemeinschaft* and *Gesellschaft*, informality and formality, organic and mechanical organization.[63] Gill Pennicard would talk later of SAMM 'not being user-friendly. There are all rules and regulations.' The very title, 'POMC', was an object of sentimental attachment for a few.[64] More general (but not very general perhaps) was the sense that there would be a loss of the intimacy and intersubjectivity, of the fused identities and corporate autonomy, that had been so characteristic of POMC. A longstanding and critical member of POMC said: 'there are always people who are going to be against it, always. There are people who want it to be a little, tight, close-knit thing. But you can't do that. You have to grow.'

Most marked in her ambivalence was Gill Pennicard who hesitantly conceded that the transformation had been inevitable: 'I don't think [POMC] had the resources. I think, I assume, that it helped, because of the resources, and that there was a place for an office. I think, maybe, they couldn't have been on their own. I honestly don't know.' But she also held that much had been lost in the transition. There was, she said, the sheer weight of the history of individual complaints from survivors about the competence of Victim Support:

[63] See T. Burns and G. Stalker, *The Management of Innovation* (Tavistock, London, 1961).

[64] The first annual report of SAMM remarked that the name of POMC 'became widely known and the support it offered highly respected. Therefore, it was not without some regret that the name was changed...to Support After Murder and Manslaughter at the 1994 AGM. However, it was felt that, in order to move forwards towards being able to provide help for more people, our name ought to reflect the wider group...'

'I know from speaking to lots of people that they didn't like Victim Support. It would have been more likely the person they met, the person wasn't accommodating, or wasn't helpful, or wasn't, really and truly, any good at her job.' There was the new involvement of an organization epistemologically disqualified from understanding the lot of the bereaved: 'I always used to think that [Victim Support] would be good regarding practical help, helping people to fill in forms or to find out about the court and whatever. Some of them would be very good but then they really and truly have chosen to do this. Other people that are put in the position of having a loved one murdered are not . . . Nobody, unless they have been in the position or a similar position can know. . . . There is a certain bond straight away with people that know, whereas they would have reservations about someone who is just like, I'll say, a do-gooder for want of a better word. . . . They can be kind and compassionate but nobody can properly understand unless they're in a similar position.' And there was the eclipsing of the old, intimate, and cohesive London group by a new national organization:[65] 'I always classed London, because of it starting in this area, as the trunk of the tree, and Liverpool, Leeds, Scotland, whatever, the branches, and recently, as such. Now, when we go to the committee meeting, it is now a national executive, and London is nothing. But you see, it used to be that it was based, as I say, like the trunk of a tree in London. That we had meetings and all people . . . all people would be involved, able to come . . . There would be no group without the people. The people should be the priority and myself, I just have, as I say, my reservations.'

Her views were significant. For the more radical and impassioned members of POMC, Gill Pennicard, the last co-ordinator of POMC, was an iconic figure, an insider, 'one of us', a fellow-survivor, a strong personification of the compassionate survivor, who gave herself wholly and at all times, prepared to speak at great length and expense to others on the telephone, and particularistic rather than universalistic in her relations. Her apparent downfall, her eventual failure to become the first co-ordinator of the new SAMM (although she had not actually applied for the post), would come to serve as a token of all that had been lost. Joan Bacon said:

[65] 'A government organization', Joan Bacon would call it.

People all over the country used to contact her. She was the co-ordinator...
she was a link, was there practically all time, and was happy to receive the
calls from the people till 2 in the morning.... She was there 2 in the morning,
4 in the morning, 10 o'clock at night, whenever you 'phoned.'

A laudatory letter from the secretary of the Stoke group of POMC
said that Gill Pennicard had been 'the first person to speak to
people, and offer her help and support, and a listening ear to them
after suffering the trauma of having a loved one murdered....I
know I speak for many people when I say thank you Gill for all
your kindness, help and support you have given to so many.'[66] It
was echoed in the minutes of the very last AGM of POMC in March
1994. The secretary, Janet Bamford, reported:

The lobbying of members M.P.'s seems to be bearing fruit on behalf of the
Victims of Crime Pressure Group—I managed to attend one of these meetings and it appears that some headway is being made with the Government
and members injustices are being heeded....On behalf of the Committee
and members of the group, I would like to give a special thanks to Gill
Pennicard for all her hard work, especially via the telephone, during this
past year. Normally, Gill is the first contact new members have with the
group and her compassion and sensitivity have helped many bereaved
members in their pain and turmoil. May she continue her good work for
many years to come.

Jane Cooper was iconic too. To the reformers, her replacement of
Gill Pennicard signified a shift towards formalisation, accountability, growth, proper financial control, universalism, and a profession-
alisation of administration. And there the contrast was drawn.
Pennicard and Cooper became social representations that were
used to mark different ways of doing the work of POMC and
SAMM. Pennicard had served POMC. Cooper was employed by
Victim Support (and some POMC activists had believed that any co-
ordinator would be employed by SAMM). Pennicard represented
the old locally-rooted POMC, Cooper the new national and more
cosmopolitan SAMM (Joan Bacon said 'the London office isn't a
London meeting place, but is only a place where the committee
meetings are held'). Pennicard had been bereaved by homicide.
Cooper had not. 'She's not like us. She doesn't feel things the way
we do,' said one of the more radical members of SAMM Merseyside
of Jane Cooper.

[66] Letter from Sheila Stanyer and all at Stoke, SAMM *Newsletter*, Winter 1994.

In brief, Pennicard was an emblem of the old POMC, Cooper of the new SAMM, and, thought a chairman of SAMM, Cooper could be seen as a personification of all that the old Turks considered wrong with the new organization (just as Pennicard symbolised all that the young Turks considered wrong with POMC). No doubt, those representations performed additional symbolic work as they came to encapsulate much wider distinctions between organizational forms. No doubt they were to be injected with much extraneous symbolic matter. But Thomas's dictum, already cited, still held: the contrasts were defined as real, and they were real in their consequences. Despite the introduction of a relation of loose-coupling between SAMM and Victim Support, despite the insertion of a structural buffer between the two organizations, the tensions between a cool bureaucratic institution and the hot, seemingly autonomous, organic self-help group, between knowledge which was rationally-generated and knowledge which was experientially-grounded, had not disappeared. Neither would they disappear in the future. The old Turks continued to meet in Gill Pennicard's house, calling themselves the London group and forming a kind of POMC over the water.

The old and young Turks of POMC–SAMM began to espouse two rather different histories of the past. For some, the period of the dominance of the Essex–London axis was a Golden Age, and the alliance with Victim Support marked a fall. There were to be claims made later that POMC had been misled ('duped' was Joan Bacon's word), and that the members had been encouraged to believe that Victim Support would provide funding but without any new entangling relationship. Instead, the activists maintained, the cost of transformation had been subjection to a 'takeover'.

For others, the period of dominance had been a time of stagnation from which POMC was liberated by Victim Support. Different constructions generated different, politically-telling teleologies that coloured analyses of SAMM, Victim Support, and Justice for Victims, and of the roles which their principals had played in delivering or abandoning the old POMC. Confusion abounded as the different narratives clashed. It was to be particularly difficult in later months for the newer members of SAMM to decipher quite what to make of the past, and much was said in cryptic form at public meetings. Praise for Pennicard's or Cooper's style of doing things, for instance, could convey much more than simple respect for a woman. It was code for a complete politics of action. So it was that Frank Green, the second chairman of SAMM, felt obliged to tell a SAMM conference at the end of 1995: 'I think that it is a valid criticism that at times, communications have stretched to breaking point and beyond, consequently there are some misconceptions about what SAMM is, and how it operates. . . . I would like therefore to outline something of SAMM's history, and let you know where we are . . . where we are going.'[67]

The launch

The launch of SAMM (or the re-launch of the ailing POMC as some described it) at the end of September 1994 was attended by some 150 people, of whom 80 were the bereaved themselves, tickets having been issued on a 'first come, first served basis'. It celebrated its founders,[68] the new partnership with Victim Support (Helen Reeves's speaking notes talked of how '2 organisations could do business'), and the new-found strength, cohesion, and prominence of the survivor. It objectified in public view the scale of the social movement that was in the making. Anne Viney, Assistant Director of Victim Support, and responsible for liaison with SAMM on the new project steering committee, remarked:

The launch . . . was tremendously powerful. There were about 100 there and the level of ownership of the event was very, very high. People came who got up at 5 in the morning to travel down from the North East. They stayed after Royalty had gone, the minister had gone, the tea and coffee were all finished. There was nothing to stay for except each other. It was the first time for a long time that they had had such a big national meeting, and there was evidence there of a lot of pride and a lot of ownership . . .

The launch was addressed not only by the heads of Victim Support and SAMM, Helen Reeves and David Howden, but also by the patron of Victim Support, the Princess Royal;[69] David Maclean, a

---

[67] Speech delivered to SAMM Conference at Warwick University, 19 November 1995.

[68] David Howden talked of 'two special ladies, our Founders—June Patient and Ann Robinson. Without their courage and determination in those early days many hundreds of victims would have received no help at all, or had the therapeutic benefit of just being with others who can understand a little of how they feel . . .'

[69] The presence of so august a figure could signify powerfully in the world of the bereaved. A SAMM member, unable to attend the launch, wrote: 'You as a member of

Home Office minister; and, by fax, by Nick Ross, the broadcaster. It thereby advertised something of the stature of Victim Support, the new partner of SAMM,[70] and the added reach of SAMM itself. It was intended to attract public notice (the press was told that: 'The launch will be attended by over fifty members of SAMM, many of whom will be willing to speak about their own personal experience'[71]) and it was indeed reported widely, in the *Police Review*, the *Evening Mail*, the *Evening Standard*, the *Daily Express* and elsewhere. SAMM reported that the launch had secured 'a great deal of publicity, and this publicity has continued. The group and the experiences of SAMM members are often highlighted in newspapers, magazines and specialist publications, as well as on radio and television. The SAMM office receives constant requests for interviews with relatives…'[72]

The launch signified the organization's change of ambition and membership: the SAMM committee was to conclude that: 'since the launch…many new members who have lost a relative other than a child have contacted us. This surely justifies the decision to make the change [of name].'[73] Within eleven days, Jane Cooper reported, SAMM had received forty-seven enquiries from families and requests for information from police, social workers, probation officers, victim support schemes, and bereavement groups.[74] Within less than three months, SAMM had been joined by 100 new members and twenty telephone calls were being received every day. Ruth Fuller, a survivor who staffed the SAMM office, said in April 1995: 'we've had so many new members come in. One man I've been talking to, his father killed his grandfather twenty years ago and

the royal family give us strength to carry on…I thank you with all my heart for what you are doing…'

[70] In a survey of all the English daily and Sunday broadsheet newspapers between 1992 and June 1996 conducted by Amanda Goodall for this book, Victim Support featured 127 times, POMC 13 times and SAMM 11 times. What is significant is that, in those stories, Victim Support was discussed 80 times without reference to any other group, POMC 5 times, and SAMM only once. On the other 10 occasions, SAMM was described in the context of its partnership with Victim Support. I shall show in the next chapter that reporting peaked in 1994, the year of SAMM's launch, when Victim Support played a major part, but the focusing of press interest does point to the role played by Victim Support in lending SAMM prominence.

[71] David Howden having established in advance which members would be prepared to speak to the press and which would field the telephones during the launch.

[72] 1994 SAMM Annual Report.

[73] ibid.

[74] Minutes of SAMM/Victim Support Steering Committee, 12 Oct 1994.

that man at forty years of age is now having problems, his marriage is breaking, and he said it's so good talking to someone after all those years. . . . They're coming to us because of the change of name and the publicity we're now getting through Victim Support, through radio, through television.' And the launch was accompanied by the imposition of the rational forms of management which Victim Support embodied, there being for the first time a set of carefully-specified positions instead of what Frank Green, SAMM's second chairman, came to call the 'wishy-washy descriptions and people thinking they know what they're doing' of the old POMC.

SAMM was not to be re-born in a featureless or calm environment. Neither could it effortlessly determine its own progress. To the contrary, it was launched into a turbulent world where it was to be jostled and shaped continually by boisterous infant neighbours and relations who had been conceived at very much the same time and who were themselves struggling for a place in the sun. It would be impossible to understand its future course without stepping back to survey the geo-politics of that world, and that will be the central task of the next three chapters.

7

The Campaigning Survivors: Justice for Victims, Activism, and the Mass Media

Introduction

Although SAMM and Victim Support may have been the most substantial organizations supporting homicide survivors in England and Wales in the mid-1990s, they were not alone. In and around their boundaries, reflexively defining themselves against the foils that SAMM and Victim Support were thought to provide, but working with their own nuanced logic as well, was a scattering of other groups which also strove to give meaning to violent death and its aftermath. I have already listed some of their names, but, viewed from the vicinity of SAMM and Victim Support, the chief organization was Justice for Victims. Justice for Victims was minute, containing at its nucleus some four people, whilst SAMM's members could be numbered in the hundreds, but SAMM was to acquire some part of its own form (or formlessness) in its encounters with that body, constituting itself in the contrasts that it offered, just as Justice for Victims was constituting itself, and any history must therefore acknowledge its influence. Accordingly, I shall discuss Justice for Victims in this and the next chapter.

Justice for Victims

Justice for Victims may have claimed to speak for homicide survivors at large, and it was certainly to attain significance in the politics which grew up around them, but, by some measures, it was always very small. Like TCF, POMC, SAMM, and other survivors' organizations on both sides of the Atlantic, it made no formal count of its members, arguing that bereavement from violent death alone conferred qualification for acceptance. Indeed, 'membership' did not

denote a recognisable and well-defined position at all. Neither was
Justice for Victims a discrete, well-bounded entity which one could
join in any conventional sense. One of its central members, Joan
Bacon, was to say: 'we haven't got a register at all. We haven't even
got an office.' Different people were mentioned from time to time in
connection with its activities, some surfacing on one occasion alone,
apparently never to return. For instance, in one of the very first
actions mounted by the group, fifty people were said to have
marched to Downing Street with a 10,000-name petition. Three of
those marchers were given prominence in one newspaper report,[1]
but their names were never again conspicuous in the history of
survivors' organizations. Precisely who and what Justice for Victims
was, and whom it represented, were thus somewhat loose, almost
metaphysical matters on occasion. Was it the tiny group at its core,
the fifty (or seventy or a hundred) who were willing, quite literally,
to march under its banners, the 300 claimed in a newspaper article[2]
or the thousands who signed its petitions? Any answer must inevitably be contingent, a matter of self-definition rather than the fulfil-
ment of clear criteria of eligibility. What *is* clear is that the most
visible face of Justice for Victims was a tight, cohesive, mutually-
supporting, quasi-familial, London-based cluster of four people—
Derek Rogers, Sandra Sullivan, Joan Bacon, and Ann Virgin, two of
whom, Joan Bacon, and Ann Virgin, were indeed related through a
common bond to Joan Bacon's son, Martin.

Not only was membership vaguely defined, but the group changed name more than once,[3] had no constitution or formal structure,
and was small enough to be untrammelled, adaptable, and fluid.
Joan Bacon pronounced: 'if you want to get anywhere, you can't be
constrained by a constitution ... so you don't have a constitution.
You don't have money. You don't have funds. You have a few of
you. It only needs four, you know, to make changes.' Justice for
Victims could well be used to exemplify Mosca's (or Pareto's or
Michels') observations about the strength and influence that can be
wielded by an organized, enterprising, and energised minority.[4]

---

[1] 'Mothers for justice', *Daily Mail*, 21 Apr 1994.
[2] The *Guardian*, 28 Dec 1995.
[3] Thus it had also called itself the Victims of Crime Pressure Group and Murder
Survivor Victim Families.
[4] See, for example, G. Mosca, *The Ruling Class* (originally published in in 1896,
McGraw-Hill, New York, 1939).

Quite why this particular group, rather than any other, should have undergone what was, in effect, a third stage in the process of fusion and fission that punctuated the history of homicide survivors, is not clear. They themselves attributed it to qualities of personal strength, to will and determination (Joan Bacon said: 'we're all knocked down but some people have got maybe an inner strength that can fight more than others'), yet such qualities must surely have been shared by others and they were clearly shaped by time and place. Just as TCF had broken away from the mundane world of those who were not bereaved by the death of children, and POMC had differentiated itself from TCF, so members of Justice for Victims cast themselves as a separate entity within and against POMC and Victim Support, and the timing and substance of their experiences were of consequence in framing their comparisons. The four core members had public histories of acute grief that were endured at very much the same time, and just when they were thrown together in and against Parents of Murdered Children. Let me proceed by sketching their biographies.

Derek Rogers' daughter, Lynne, had been murdered in September 1991 by Scott Singleton, a man previously unknown to her, who had lured her from Catford in South London to Charing Cross railway station on the pretext of offering work. Singleton could have been indicted at an early point had it been possible to obtain an impression of his teeth to match bite marks for forensic purposes, but it was impossible to do so without his consent.[5] Rogers said: 'shortly after my daughter's life was taken, they arrested a suspect and held him for seventy-two hours. In the end, he had to be released because he was asked to give an intimate sample and he had the right to refuse to and he did. . . . You've got criminals out there. You've got the ability to catch them with this system, and they're not going to use it. This is what we mean about the criminal justice system. It's a farce!' To be sure, an impression was eventually obtained from a dental laboratory, and Singleton was convicted in July 1992, but all those delays and uncertainties proved to be an added burden to Rogers. He had felt bereft, unsupported, and ill-informed. He conceived of himself as irrevocably changed: 'I don't want to go back to being normal—I don't want to laugh or joke.'[6] He had received assistance from

[5] See the report of the appeal case in *The Times*, 22 June 1994.
[6] 'Crime Limited', BBC Press Service, n.d.

Victim Support, although, like many another traumatised survivor, his memory of the event was confused: 'I wasn't aware of it but a victim support volunteer told me later on that she was there from more or less day one of the police investigation.' But he had also wanted much more: 'There should be somebody with the authority to go between the victim, the police and the local authority to tell you your rights, to make sure your bills don't pile up.'[7]

Sandra Sullivan lost her 23-year old daughter in 1992. Katie Sullivan had been killed by a schizophrenic woman for whom she had been caring whilst working in a MIND hostel. Her killer had not been taking her prescribed medication, and Sandra Sullivan was bitter about the poor supervision that had led to her daughter being placed so at risk ('nobody admits to any fault, nobody resigns, nobody is made accountable. The people who allowed Katie to lie alone, bleeding to death, have not lost a day's work.'). She was bitter about the way in which Katie herself had been tended medically after the attack:

Not even an ambulance for her, two and a half minutes from a hospital. A helicopter that took about 25–35 minutes. They couldn't tell us because the computers had gone wrong. Her things were slung in a shoebox and slung at my son who went to the hospital, her toothbrush, everything in a shoe box and then slammed the door on him . . .

Sandra Sullivan had felt symbolically excluded from the subsequent trial at the Old Bailey, and was to become involved in an altercation with security guards in the courtroom when she protested at the conditions under which she and her family were obliged to attend ('we were attacked . . . for nothing at all'). She was bitter when she was dunned as an executor for her daughter's community charge in January 1993, long after the death. She was bitter at the prospect of being denied a voice in any tribunal that might sanction her daughter's killer's release from Broadmoor Special Hospital (she had been told by the Prime Minister that a 'mental health review tribunal sits

---

[7] 'What Price Justice?', The *Sunday Telegraph*, 25 Sept 1994. Victim Support would challenge his complaints about the support he had received. Helen Reeves had appeared on *Crime Limited*, a programme broadcast in July 1994 about Rogers's bereavement, especially to say: 'Each member of every family that's been bereaved will have completely different needs, and these will change from time to time. They may be practical, they may be emotional, they may need information or contacts with other professions. We're willing to stay and share their grief as best we can. What we can't do, of course, is make the grief go away and we can't turn back the clock. A tragedy has occurred and no one can put that right.'

in private unless the patient requests a public hearing.'[8]) Sandra Sullivan also had her criticisms of Victim Support (although the Scheme concerned had not received an official complaint):

There is nobody there to help you pick up the pieces and Victim Support don't do it. The counselling was inadequate.[9] They don't know how to begin to counsel. They are counselling you as though you'd lost a video but you've lost a child.... They don't listen to the ones who know. We're experienced. We can tell them how to do it. I did have someone but my friend had to get her and she came about three months later and she kept saying 'if that's right for you'.... She wouldn't look at me. So I said to her 'quite frankly, do you like my jumper?' and she said 'if that's right for you'. She should have said 'what the hell has that got to do with it?' but she wasn't listening. So I said, 'you are like an iceberg. Go!'

And the outcome was that she came to realise that 'victims had been oppressed and silenced for years'. The journalist, Valerie Grove, reported that Sandra Sullivan 'could never have imagined what eloquence rage would give her. When someone knocks at the door to tell parents their child is dead, their lives are changed forever.'[10]

Sandra Sullivan was to become exceptionally active in the survivors' cause, speaking on their behalf whenever she could, telephoning and writing to the bereaved when their names were published in the press or conveyed to her through the survivor's informal network, sometimes giving them comfort, sometimes, it seems, in the words of one survivor so approached, 'terrifying [them] because of the dire things she said would happen'.

Joan Bacon was the mother, and Ann Virgin the partner, of Martin Bacon, 'a chancer, a successful and happy young man who loved life and drove a red Porsche'.[11] Martin Bacon was killed in November 1992 in an incident outside a public house in which he had been attacked with an iron bar in a *melée* with three men who had accused him of shouting an insult. He had fallen backwards and injured his brain, and, instead of dying instantly, had been admitted to hospital and released to die six days later. Because of the complexities of the medical evidence,[12] because there had been delays in

---

[8] Letter of 11 Oct 1993.
[9] One difficulty, of course, is that Victim Support claims to provide support but not counselling.
[10] *The Times*, 23 Sept 1994.
[11] Joan Bacon, quoted in the *Evening Standard*, 27 Jan 1994.
[12] See the *Evening Standard*, 27 Jan 1994.

reporting the assault, only one solitary defendant, David Kerry,[13] was convicted only of an assault occasioning grievous bodily harm with intent a year later. He was sentenced to ten years but released on appeal after only eighteen months (Joan Bacon recalled 'this was at the appeal court and [the judge's] words were, and they're the last words I hear, and they keep going over and over in my head, again and again and again, "unsafe verdict" . . . The words that I just keep hearing are "unsafe" and what I feel was that it was unsafe that he was out in the first place . . . He was the murderer and he's walked away scot-free!'). Joan Bacon's and Ann Virgin's lives virtually collapsed. Joan Bacon said of Kerry: 'he has come into our lives, absolutely blasted our lives apart, totally!'

In her subsequent distress, and in her grief for her mother who had died of cancer in April 1993, Ann Virgin herself was to be dismissed from her employment in May 1993. Joan Bacon was later to write graphically about the transformation which the two women had undergone:

Total frozen shock, giving way to horrors of such magnitude, mind exploded and fragmented unable to comprehend that a complete stranger has reached into the very heart of a good solid family and taken a precious and valuable life . . . Try to imagine what it is to have your life wrenched and broken all aspirations and sense of well being destroyed, your loved one referred to as the deceased (a diminished statistic)!! and the realisation that you will never be the same. Then experience what it means to survive, only to be used and then ignored by those you thought would be there to help you. The very system you thought was in place to be fair, to protect those who obey the law whilst punishing those who break it has disastrously failed—then discover secondary victimisation![14]

The formation of Justice for Victims

It will have been noted that the core members of Justice for Victims had all been bereaved at much the same time, in the early 1990s, when Parents of Murdered Children was not only established and independent but moving towards an ever-closer partnership with Victim Support. It should also be noted that they were distressed and angry, and I have already argued that anger can be a fiercely

[13] Who, to compound matters, in Joan Bacon's and Ann Virgin's view, had only just been released for a previous offence of violence.
[14] 'A "Civilised Society"?—1994', MS.

accusatory practice which not only unites its subjects but divides them from the objects of their rage. Members of Justice for Victims were to define themselves in contrast to POMC, perhaps because, as very recent survivors, they were pragmatically motivated to confer particular significance on an organization that loomed so large in the survivors' world. Dewey once remarked: 'The singular object stands out conspicuously because of its especially focal and crucial position at a given time in determination of some problem of use ... which the *total* environment presents.'[15] It was just so with POMC. It lay visibly before them, presenting, in effect, the thesis against which, in their turmoil, they could construct themselves as the antithesis. Justice for Victims confronted what appeared to be a settled pattern of support which failed to resonate the intensity, turbulence, and rawness of their own grief, a pattern which was summarily dismissed, in what was to become their stock phrases, as 'tea and cakes' or 'tea and sympathy'.[16] They were to formulate a distinctive way of symbolising the world which was at once similar and dissimilar to the interpretations of other survivors.

Derek Rogers, Joan Bacon and Ann Virgin came together at a POMC meeting in the summer of 1993, and they were critical of what they saw: POMC seemed to be pacific, but they would be politically activist; POMC was private and discreet, but they would be public and bold; POMC was regulated and shackled, but they would be unconfined. Joan Bacon recalled:

[Ann Virgin and I] went to a first meeting [of POMC] in Islington. ... It was unbelievable. This meeting was being held above an undertakers! It was the only room they could get! ... I was almost exploding because people there were saying what had happened to them, what had gone wrong, and I can remember, it was a Sunday afternoon, and it was sunny, and I remember thinking 'nobody out there knows we're up here!' Mike Bennett [of the Police Federation] was talking at that meeting and he was saying how things can only get worse—and it just tipped me over the top. ... Derek was sitting there but I didn't know him [then]. Following on from that, I thought we've got to get out there and let people know that we're here and how we're being treated and what the hell is going wrong. And I spoke to June Patient on the telephone and she was very very supportive and I can remember at

[15] J. Dewey, *Logic* (Henry Holt, New York, 1938), 67.
[16] The words were Ann Virgin's. Record of meeting between Victim Support and Victims of Crime Pressure Group [Justice for Victims], 8 Dec 1993. She employed them again, for instance, in her criticism of the SAMM launch. See the *Independent*, 1 Oct 1994.

that meeting I was so angry, and she came over and put her hand on my shoulder and she said [with irony] 'Joan, you're not allowed to be angry!' She was saying what the hell do they expect, of course you are angry but they won't listen to you if you are angry, the establishment, anybody, people, they won't listen, anybody that you want to speak to, anybody that wants a quiet life. Anyway, I phoned up June and I put to her what I felt, that we should all get out there and get up to the Home Office, and let them see, because that is the place where the rules are made, that's where it all comes from. She was in total agreement and she actually called a meeting at her house—she invited Derek and Sandra.

Derek Rogers's own recollection was:

I remember that first meeting at June Patient's, and I was sitting in the armchair and Joan and Ann were sitting by the side of me, and when they started speaking, they were talking about what I had wanted to do: face the Home Office, which, as a single person, you're going to get nowhere. With Joan and Ann there, that's what started it off. I think we are lucky, that basically the four of us have all got the same strength and we give each other strength to go on.

Sandra Sullivan too had begun to make her own contacts with other survivors. A member of POMC had been introduced to her by the police. She had then met June Patient and her husband who, in turn, passed her on to Joan Bacon and Ann Virgin and the nascent Justice for Victims group: 'I thought this was very interesting and then I started listening to you two and I thought I'm not mad, there are two more people who think like me.' If the formation of TCF was the first, and that of POMC the second, the coming-together of what would be Justice for Victims was the third epiphany and the third process of fusion within and about the boundaries of POMC.[17] Each member of Justice for Victims lent objectivity and authority to the others' grief, and a strong primary group was there forged.

[17] I have used the word 'about' because other members of POMC felt drawn to the emerging Justice for Victims, even though they did not or could not engage fully in its activities. Pat Green, the co-founder of SAMM Merseyside, for instance, had travelled to the old POMC in London only twice because: 'it is a long way to go, and that's where I met Sandra and Joan and Derek and Ann, and you know, I just looked at them and I thought there's other people in this, because I had never met anybody who was experiencing the same grief as I was experiencing.' Although she was not to be a vigorous member of the southern-based Justice for Victims, she did lend its inflection to what was to become SAMM Merseyside. Gill Pennicard said of her group: 'Liverpool really and truly is *the* group.' SAMM Merseyside was to become the most militant SAMM group.

Getzel and Masters described support groups for people bereaved by homicide as substitute families,[18] and that certainly was an impression conveyed by Justice for Victims. The members of the group were intensely dependent on one another; they became what Denzin would have called emotional associates,[19] moving as one in sympathy with each other; generating a shared field of emotional experience; taking one another's memories and making them their own; becoming the bearers of a particularly inflected subculture within POMC and SAMM; and always and everywhere defining themselves as a unity. Sandra Sullivan once informed a meeting of an earlier encounter she had had with a criminal justice agency, 'they wanted me to go alone. I wouldn't. Because they thought I would be receptive. You need at least four or five of us.'

Their cohesion would certainly strike others. For example, a member of the Criminal Bar Association with whom they had had a meeting recalled that: 'they were a group of people who had experienced extreme tragedies and I felt that the grief had brought them together and they were very, very supportive of each other. I got that impression very, very clearly.'

If the contrasts with POMC were one source of dialectical opposition, those with Victim Support were another. It was inevitable that the association would come to bulk large in the pragmatics of bereavement. At stake, and mediated by the survivor's analogical reasoning, were all the matters close to the survivor: symbolic ownership of the crime, symbolic ownership of the organizations dealing with the aftermath of the crime, and the moral balance which should not only award a proper gravity of response to homicide but also give a parity of support to victims and offenders. Justice for Victims proclaimed that it was almost everything that it considered Victim Support not to be.

Victim Support was resented largely because it was seen to stand continuously as a professional intermediary between victim and victim, and between victim and State. Derek Rogers said: 'We've attended a number of conferences and Helen Reeves is always there.' Victim Support was defined as ill-qualified because of its lack of existential authority, the authority which counted in the

---

[18] G. Getzel and R. Masters, 'Serving Families who Survive Homicide', *Social Casework*, Mar 1984, Vol 65, No 3, 143.

[19] See N. Denzin, *On Understanding Emotion* (Jossey-Bass, San Francisco, 1984), 58–9.

radical activists' world and which, it was held, could be vested only in survivors (Noreen Caulfield told a meeting at the Home Office in October 1993:[20] 'Victim Support is totally inadequate for murder/manslaughter Victim Families...Counselling for victims should be provided by victims who have experienced the same crime and it's (*sic*) effects.')

Victim Support was said to be quiescent because of its financial dependence on the State and the Home Office, whilst Justice for Victims was free and unbridled ('The Victim has nothing—Victim Support—by its very Government funding—is gagged—a very silent Government ploy to keep the ever increasing number of victims swept silently under the carpet'[21]). Victim Support was said to be intellectually compromised because many of its staff had had a professional experience of working with offenders in the criminal justice system,[22] whilst the sympathies of Justice for Victims were undivided ('if you like, the victims' organizations and the offenders' organizations are the same people travelling from one side to the other. For me, they're the professional do-gooders and do-gooders do good for what they think is right and not for the people they should be representing.'). Victim Support was said to lack a proper sense of urgency whilst Justice for Victims was mindful of the crisis which survivors faced (Joan Bacon said of a meeting with Helen Reeves in the House of Commons: 'she's a politician, she talks. She said "I'd like to put you in the picture—ten years ago..." We're not interested in ten years ago! We want to hear *now*!'). Victim Support was said to lack the *gravitas* suitable to an organization involved with homicide: supporting survivors was too important a task to be entrusted to volunteers, thought Ann Virgin.

Justice for Victims still mourned what it took to be the loss of POMC's independence (Sandra Sullivan said: 'They want to swallow us up. So that's why we're cagey.'[23]). It was as if the field had already been taken by groups practising the politics of acceptability.

[20] Much of the content of this paragraph borrows from Minutes of Meeting held at Home Office, 18 Oct 1993. Victim Support itself felt aggrieved that it had been excluded from that meeting. There was an evident contest for the ears of officials and politicians.

[21] 'Justice for Victims', leaflet, Apr 1993.

[22] The point was made by Ann Virgin at a meeting held at Victim Support, 16 May 1994. In fact, reflected Jane Cooper, that observation applied to only two senior members of Victim Support, Helen Reeves and, earlier, to Peter Dalrymple.

[23] That was a view robustly contested by the senior officers of SAMM and Victim Support. Frank Green, the second chairman, remarked in May 1996: 'I mean people

But there was more to the rejection of the new formalisation of the politics of the survivor. It was difficult for the members of Justice for Victims, committed to expressive action as they were, to accept absorption within the dull and impersonal routines of a relatively large and bureaucratically-administered organization. Expressivity tends to be locked into the intimate, the concrete and the here-and-now, and it requires the physical or near-physical presence of significant others. Just as the older London group of POMC had been a locus of sentiment which was pitted ideologically against the new cosmopolitanism of the national SAMM, so Justice for Victims celebrated the small[24] and personal in the face of what was represented as the impersonality and scale of SAMM.

What came powerfully to drive the new group was the sense that they had not only acquired a moral standing borne of extraordinary suffering (Sandra Sullivan would say at meetings: 'we have lost children and we need help!'), but also an immediate understanding of homicide denied almost everyone else. Justice for Victims had the existential authority of those who had been through the fire. Consider a confrontation on a *Kilroy* television programme in May 1994 when Ann Virgin rounded on Michael Mansfield, the barrister. Employing one of the central binary oppositions of the survivor's world-view, Virgin had contended that the spectators and defendants in a criminal trial may have had choices but that the victim had been offered none. When Mansfield retorted in the usual measured and unbending language of the courtroom, 'you may have that assumption,' Ann Virgin's own riposte had been simple: 'I'm the expert. I *know*!' I remarked that members of Justice for Victims tend to move about *en bloc*. With Ann Virgin in the studio was Sandra Sullivan, who had added: 'We're giving you our experience. Will you *please* listen. I'm from Justice for Victims. I'm *for* Justice for Victims. . . . We should have a voice because we know what we experience.' And with her too was Derek Rogers, who had added: 'I've had personal *experience*!'

Members of Justice for Victims protested that, acting as what was in effect a 'Government department', Victim Support held regular

even now still come to me and quote the fact that, you know, we're part of Victim Support, or they've taken over, Victim Support manages, and that's clearly not the case.'

[24] See A. Katz and E. Bender (eds), *The Strength in Us: Self-Help Groups in the Modern World* (New Viewpoints, New York, 1976), 113.

meetings with the Home Office from which they themselves were excluded. The standing and experience of Justice for Victims were taken to confer a right to enter any forum which discussed survivors' affairs, and they voiced a deep resentment that they were being managed and discussed at second hand by professionals who claimed to possess an expertise in their suffering. So it was that Ann Virgin was aggrieved that her representations to the Home Office and the Lord Chancellor's Department had only led to her being directed to Victim Support even though 'we are the ones who know what we are talking about.'[25]

Justice for Victims was to be especially incensed when, on 21 February 1995, European Victims Day, Victim Support staged a one-day conference titled 'Justice for Victims', the very title which the group claimed as its own. Alun Michael, a Labour front bench spokesman on home affairs spoke at the conference. So did David Howden. So did the Director of Public Prosecutions and the Chief Constable of Sussex Police. Justice for Victims protested outside the meeting.[26] Derek Rogers remembered:

We found out . . . that Victim Support were holding a conference [using] our title. We got in touch with Anne Viney to find out are any victims being invited and I was told that David Howden would be the representative for SAMM . . . We got Joan in there, we'd fought for that. We should have been invited. They were using our name and we stood outside . . . Helen Reeves came out and said 'there are two spare seats inside, if you would like to come in', and we said, 'unless you can take us all in, we'll stay out here.' When you get in there all they want is the people who think they know talking to other people who think they know instead of listening to us that do know . . . What we're finding out is these conferences are happening week after week after week, and the people that don't know about them are excluded, the people that should be there.

Justice for Victims despatched a fax to David Maclean,[27] the Home Office minister, complaining:

[25] Record of meeting at Victim Support, 16 May 1994. Anne Viney recalled: 'Victim Support explained that we were having discussions at the Central Criminal Court to make sure that the provisions of the Victim's Charter . . . were being provided. These were inter-agency discussions, not concerned with supervising the Witness service.'

[26] One co-ordinator recalled that Justice for Victims had mounted a protest outside the conference and then asked Victim Support to look after their banner. 'We're not allowed to have much to do with them', she said.

[27] David Maclean was Conservative MP for Penrith and the Borders since 1983, and Minister of State at the Home Office since 1993. He was described as a

It is vital as discussed with Michael Howard[28] [the Home Secretary] and yourself that not only 'people who think they know' but people who 'do know' are allowed a voice and representation. . . . It is transparently apparent that the debate on '*victims rights*' and '*how the voice of the victim can be heard*' will not take into account first hand knowledge and experience of victims themselves and no victim will in fact be *heard* at this conference (emphases in the original).

Anne Viney's own account is quite different:

Victim Support staff who were at this conference have commented that this version is inaccurate. Firstly, there was of course the question of a conference fee, which was necessary in order to finance the events. Members of Justice for Victims who had not been able to pay turned up on the day and were offered access to spare places as, by that time, it was clear that the event had financially broken even. The places were originally refused, and then accepted and Victim Support staff looked after the banner whilst they attended the conference!

Justice for Victims as an activist organization

Justice for Victims protested vehemently at what they saw as their ostracism and, impatient with institutional encumbrances, they took to the streets.[29] In a revealing interchange between Anne Viney of Victim Support and an angry survivor on that selfsame *Kilroy* programme of May 1994, Viney was accused of being a member of 'an anti-campaigning group! We don't see you on marches!' Her reply had been: 'You'll see me at the Home Office discussing what can be done.' And in that exchange may be glimpsed the spaces, physical and political, that the two organizations understood themselves to occupy. Victim Support took its

'super-loyal new middle-brow Thatcherite'. A. Roth, *Parliamentary Profiles* (Parliamentary Profiles, London, 1989).

[28] Michael Howard was Conservative MP for Folkestone and Hythe since 1983. He had been a barrister, having been called to the Bar in 1964, and a Recorder in 1986, before becoming an MP. In Parliament, he had served as PPS to the Solicitor-General 1984–5; Under-Secretary of State at DTI between 1985–7; Minister of State, Local Government, 1987–9; Minister of State, Water and Planning, 1989–90; Minister of State, Housing and Planning, 1989–90; Secretary of State for Employment, 1990–2; Secretary of State for the Environment, 1992–3; and Home Secretary from 1993.

[29] See J. Lofland, *Crowd Lobbying: An Emerging Tactic of Interest Group Influence in California* (Institute of Governmental Affairs, University of California, Davis, 1992), 3.

position to fall within the institutional confines of authority, Justice for Victims fell without, on the streets and pavements, holding placards. Joan Bacon recalled:

June Patient then held this next [POMC] meeting at her house and I said 'I just feel that we should get up there and get outside the Home Office and let them know...In July [1993] we all met up outside the Home Office and there were quite a few families there and we marched on the pavement to the House of Commons and we lobbied our MPs. We did it again in October,[30] people travelled down from Strathclyde, from Stoke on Trent, and we did exactly the same thing again. We handed in petitions as well—we'd been out weeks before getting petitions—to Number 10.

Vigorous political activity was in part to become the groups' instrument for reasserting control, balance, and meaning in the anomic aftermath of violent death. It was a project devised to restore sense to the world.[31] Joan Bacon recollected how it had begun, when, in March 1993, she and Ann Virgin had 'started a petition ["Rights for the Wronged"[32]]. I suppose it is anger, everything is so bizarre, you just grasp on to anything like reality or normality that you can. That's the only way I can see it now. It's to get some control over a situation that you've got no control over at all. So we started the petition up.' And Ann Virgin recalled in similar vein: 'That was all we could do really. Just something that we felt we could do to keep sane and to keep them where they were because at that point they had been arrested and it was a mad attempt. Anything that we typed and wrote and got somebody to sign, we felt that it was helping to keep them there, keeping the offenders inside.' Neither had campaigned or organized a group before but what moved them, Joan Bacon said, was 'anger, pure anger'. Out of that anger, and in conjunction with another mother, Noreen Caulfield, who played an active role towards the beginning, they had founded the Victims

[30] The October petition, still in the earlier name of the Victims of Crime Pressure Group, demanded 'recognition, rights and justice'. It declared: 'The Government have failed us and will continue to do so. We the general public have a right to be protected by Government against the criminally motivated.... Every loud campaign and appeal is heard for the convicted criminal...We must, together, address this imbalance.'

[31] See K. Weick, *Sensemaking in Organizations* (Sage, Thousand Oaks, Calif, 1995), 45.

[32] The petition opened: 'Whatever the outcome of any trial—we are victims for the rest of our lives—we have been given our life sentence', and then proceeded to make a list of demands, some of which have already been listed in my earlier description of the binary oppositions of the moral world of the survivor.

of Crime Pressure Group, later to be renamed Murder Victims Families and, later still, Justice for Victims.

Intensive campaigning became a vehicle for the validation,[33] objectification, and articulation of deep feelings, a non-verbal medium to express the inexpressible, a demonstration of an understanding that was more experiential than cerebral. Indeed, a disciplined reasonableness could very well have looked like a betrayal of the authenticity of the survivor's pain. Justice for Victims declared in one of its leaflets: 'We have tried being polite, we have tried to be logical. We have tried to let justice takes its course!! We have held our anger, our emotions in check—we have tried to see—what we are told we must see. We have tried above all to be the reasonable, tolerant, honest people we once were, we have tried so very hard to hold onto this. We have been tried too much!!!!!!' Andrew Puddephatt, then Director of Liberty, a civil liberties organization with which Justice for Victims was to have dealings, commented: 'it's rage verses reason really. It's Outrage and Stonewall.'

What was on the verge of institutionalization in POMC's new partnership with Victim Support was summarily dismissed by Justice for Victims as formalistic, estranging, and constricting. If violent emotion and language are in opposition,[34] if certain feelings can never be expressed, Justice for Victims resorted to the hot symbolism of graphic display in deliberate contrast to the cool disciplines, conspicuous rationality, and meticulous etiquette of the respectable pressure group. Multiple distinctions marked Justice for Victims's distance from the central project of SAMM under the tutelage of Victim Support: the distinctions identified by Weber between *Wertrational* and *Zweckrational*; between the rationality of values and the rationality of instrumentalism, the informal and the formal, the hot and the cold, the personal and the professional,[35] the freedom of the alienated and the conformity of the rule-governed. Joan Bacon said of Anne Viney:

[33] See N. Denzin, *On Understanding Emotion* (n 19 above), 223.

[34] See P. Ricoeur, *Political and Social Essays* (Ohio University Press, Athens, 1974), 89–90, 99.

[35] See A. Gartner and F. Riessman (eds), *The Self-Help Revolution* (Human Sciences Press, New York, 1984), 22, 109. Justice for Victims complained that, whilst Victim Support staff were salaried, victims themselves received no money from Victim Support (record of meeting between Victim Support and Victims of Crime Pressure Group, 8 Dec 1993.

She said 'I am experienced as well',[36] which took my breath away, because I thought, 'I'm so sorry', and then I realised she was talking about academic experience and not real life experience! I can only say those people are very bland, very cold. They have a politician's veneer. They're clinical.

Justice for Victims employed the stock techniques of the angry pressure group: petitioning, marching, demonstrating, questioning, heckling, lobbying Members of Parliament, attending party political conferences, and writing letters. They borrowed from the example of other groups in Britain and overseas (for instance, by organizing memorial services for victims that were modelled on the pattern of an American homicide survivors' group, the Stephanie Roper Foundation). They offset their small numbers and powerlessness by mounting dramaturgical and dramatic displays[37] that were intended both to capture the attention of others and to work demonstratively for themselves.

Take as an example the 'March against Murder and Violence' that was staged on 11 September 1995, the third such march organized by Justice for Victims, and one that followed what by then had become a conventional pattern. The march was advertised as an 'express[ion of] the public anger and discontent at the current complacency reflected by the Courts, MP's, Parole Boards and the Home Office and their policy of releasing back into society those who take human life.' It assembled outside the Home Office, a major symbolic location, at 12.00 pm, and members of the group distributed leaflets setting out a 'statement of policy' to passers-by and officials, leaflets that called for preventative policies against murder, a Minister for Justice, a Bill of Rights for victims, the introduction of victim impact statements, victim contributions to parole and trubunal hearings, an accountable judiciary, and an accountable membership of the 'secret panels who release and put unsuspecting society at risk...' To the palpable disappointment of the marchers, the demonstration was attended by very few press, certainly fewer

---

[36] Anne Viney was to observe later: 'The point I was trying to make is that, in dealing with tragic events all kinds of experience are relevant. No one expects Police Officers to have suffered from every crime they have to deal with, and yet they are expected, we hope, to be able to deal humanely with victims of crime. Victim Support's experience is drawn from many years of designing, delivering and redesigning services to victims of crime...'

[37] See J. Lofland, *Protest: Studies of Collective Behavior and Social Movements* (Transaction Books, New Brunswick, NJ, 1985), 9.

than hitherto, only a single cameraman-reporter from a small commercial satellite channel, Channel 1 News, and a reporter from GLR News being present. One marcher said afterwards: 'it's just despicable! You've got to go around begging! There was no coverage, none!' A seasoned Ann Virgin observed that media interest depended on what else was in competition for attention at the time, and 11 September was the first day of the Trades Union Congress annual conference.

Some sixty people left the Home Office at 12.40 pm to process past another symbolic location, Downing Street, where personal letters were handed in (but not a petition—Ann Virgin said that Justice for Victims had come to realise that 'they don't read petitions'), to arrive finally at 1.55 pm at yet a third symbolic location, the Law Courts. Most of the marchers dispersed in Temple Gardens, scattering into small conversational knots, but a few broke away to lobby counsel as they entered and left the Law Courts in the Strand until later in the afternoon.

The marchers had carried red roses donated by Ann Virgin in memory of the dead, and they had paraded under the banners of Justice for Victims and SAMM Merseyside, banners that proclaimed 'It's time the courts backed the police. Kent demands that we stop cossetting violent criminals. March against murder and violence'; 'Life to mean life for murder'; 'The law of the land has let us down'; and 'Too many murders in Gloucestershire'. Sandra Sullivan, the mascot of the march, had been armed with a megaphone in the vanguard and, egged on by cries of 'Go on Sandra! Give it to them Sandra!', she shouted out a running tirade as much, it seemed, for the delectation of the marchers as for the occasionally bemused spectators:

We are Justice for Victims! We want our rights! We want murderers locked up for life so they can't kill again! Keep Britain safe! Give us back the old Britain! Give the police more power. Keep the murderers down! We want justice for victims, justice for the families of murder victims, justice for the families of victims! We are victims! We want rights, dignity, respect and above all murderers locked up for life. Stand up for victims! Keep murderers in prison. Stop the murders that are happening now! Write to your MP! No bail for prisoners!

It was on such marches and demonstrations, advertised formally in the newsletters of POMC and SAMM, and informally in survivors's social networks, that the 'membership' of Justice for Victims grew and coalesced. The more activist survivors came together on the pavements of London. Ann Virgin recalled how:

Brigitte [Chaudhry of RoadPeace[38]] came on one of the marches, and that's how we met her. It started off at the Home Office, that was when the petition was handed in.... There was people from Strathclyde [the Watsons and FOMC] and this was a result of an insertion going into the POMC newsletter that went round the country....

And Derek Rogers added:

On the second [march], it was the people that came down from Strathclyde, Stoke-on-Trent, Manchester, Blackpool. I mean people turned up there. It was obviously what people wanted, but all they needed was pulling together.

Justice for Victims and the mass media[39]

Justice for Victims may have been numerically small, but, for a while, much of what it did and said was publicised nationally, and the magnifying lens of the mass media lent it an imposing scale in the politics of survivors. It was as if it had acquired a media-conferred hyper-reality that inflated every action, and, in that hyper-reality lay its political and phenomenological importance. What did it matter that Justice for Victims numbered only four or so activists when they appeared to have acquired such a national stature? An article on the work of the Oxford University Centre for Criminological Research in *Oxford Today* certainly took it that that stature had been achieved, alleging, as it did, that 'fringe organizations like Justice for Victims... have hijacked the public agenda.'[40] Indeed, some of the staff of Victim Support began briefly to sense it had itself been somewhat eclipsed, and they were puzzled and piqued that such a little object could have obscured a national institution. It was as if they had prepared a path which others had

---

[38] She herself observed: 'I met Sandra Sullivan years ago and we are friends. I know them all... When Justice for Victims started they asked me to support them from the word "go".'

[39] All the quantitative work, a number of the citations and some of the argument of this section are based on analysis produced by Amanda Goodall, to whom I am very grateful.

[40] 'Victims' Rights', *Oxford Today*, Hilary Issue, 1995, Vol 7, No 2, 24.

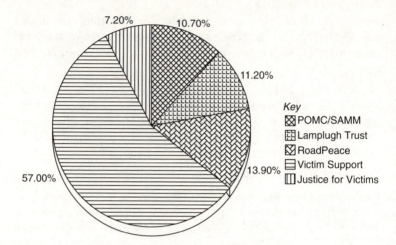

Fig. 7.1   Coverage of victims' groups in broadsheet newspapers: Jan 1992–June 1996*

*Graph prepared by Amanda Goodall, showing the coverage of six victims' groups by reports in the *Guardian*, the *Independent*, *The Times*, and the *Daily Telegraph* newspapers, their Sunday editions, and the *Sunday Times*

then seized. Helen Peggs, Victim Support's press officer, observed: 'I believe that Victim Support had managed to establish a public vocabulary on victims' rights, and by doing so, we opened the door for *Justice for Victims* and the other groups. I don't believe that they would have merited such media (or political) attention had we not paved the way for them. In short—we [had] made "victims" a fashionable issue.'[41]

In fact, as Fig. 7.1 shows, Victim Support did remain paramount in its coverage by the press. To be sure, Justice for Victims had only been established in 1993, settling on its name a year later, and Fig. 7.1 misleads. Perhaps the situation is more helpfully conveyed by Figs. 7.2 and 7.3 which show the individual and total numbers of reports of some of the new groups that appeared in the broadsheet press during the period. It is evident that they confirm the sovereignty of Victim Support, the largest, most authoritative and best staffed of all the victims' organizations. They confirm too, the rise in reporting that attended the emergence of so many new groups in 1994.

[41]   Letter to author, 9 Sept 1997.

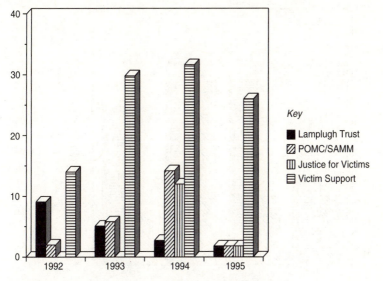

Fig. 7.2   Annual press coverage of victims' groups: 1992–95*

*Prepared by Amanda Goodall and based on reports in the same broadsheet newspapers as Fig. 7.1. Note the surge of interest in 1994, not only in Justice for Victims, but also in SAMM. 1994 was the year in which both organizations were launched.

Crime is central to the project of the mass media,[42] and it is stories about violence and killings[43] that are at its very core. Murder and manslaughter are assumed to be objects of abiding public interest. They have a pathos, immediacy, urgency, and horror that lend themselves to ready dramatisation, and they are continually being translated into news, entertainment, and 'human interest' stories for public edification. They are, moreover, thought to exemplify truths about the condition of society, and the exceptional homicide will be pored over incessantly for the moral, personal, and political lessons it is thought to impart about the way we live now.[44] There

[42] See R. Ericson, introduction to *Crime and the Media* (Dartmouth, Aldershot, 1995), p. xi. In his earlier work on crime reporting in Toronto, conducted with Baranek and Chan, Ericson discovered that 'crime stories constituted just under half of all news coverage in newspapers and popular TV, well over half of all news coverage on quality TV and approximately two thirds of all news coverage on radio.' R. Ericson *et al, Representing Order* (Open University Press, Milton Keynes, 1991), 341.

[43] See J. Ditton and J. Duffy, 'Bias in the Newspaper Reporting of Violence', *British Journal of Criminology*, Apr 1983, Vol 23, No 2.

[44] See J. Lull and S. Hinerman, 'The Search for Scandal' in *Media Scandals* (Polity Press, Cambridge, 1997), 3.

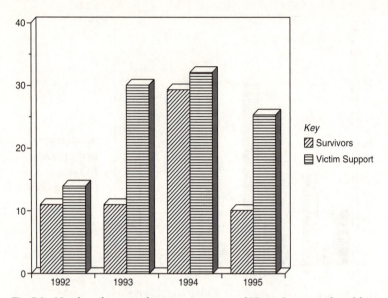

Fig. 7.3   Number of reports of survivors's groups and Victim Support in broadsheet newspapers: 1992–95*

*The newspapers covered are the same as those in Fig. 7.2. The survivors' groups are the Lamplugh Trust, POMC/SAMM, and Justice for Victims.

are professional commentators who will seize on just such an occasion as a spectacular murder to impart whatever parables they may wish to emphasize about the state of society.[45] The murder of James Bulger in England, the massacre of schoolchildren in Dunblane in Scotland, and the killings by Paul Bernardo and Karla Homolka in Canada,[46] and by Jeffrey Dahmer in the United States have all served as 'news hooks' for prolific interpretive work about everything that was deemed to be rotten about society.

Yet, paradoxically, it tends not to be the causes,[47] demography, history, or broad structural trends of homicide that are analysed by journalists. They do not care, for instance, to be reminded that child murders by strangers are rare events which are not markedly on the

[45] See J. Katz, 'What Makes Crime "News"?', *Media, Culture and Society*, 1987, Vol 9.
[46] See N. Pron, *Lethal Marriage* (Seal Books, Toronto, 1995).
[47] See G. Barak (ed), *Media Process and the Social Construction of Crime* (Garland, New York, 1994).

increase. Rather, in common with wider reporting practices,[48] it is the impact of homicide as a personal tragedy that is salient, and the media are swollen with stories about horrible murders and beautiful victims, tearful appeals and sad funerals, dragnets and manhunts, trials and convictions. Homicide, in short, is a calamity collapsed into a succession of poignant scenes with their attendant heroes and heroines, villains and victims (Jon Silverman of the BBC remarked that: 'victims have quite a big impact in telling a criminal justice story...there's nothing more emotive than showing a victim'[49]). In its own quest to be reported, Victim Support was also abundantly aware of the media's preference for the personal over the structural narrative, although it would be quite chary always about serving up individual victims for interview. Helen Peggs, Victim Support's press officer, said: 'human interest stories were of interest to the media, policy issues or campaigns were not. For example, we could get attention for the way in which a family of a murder victim had been treated, but not for the way in which the criminal justice system treats families of murder victims.'[50] It is in this manner that professionals working in the media create a continuing demand for a supply of subjects to animate, illustrate, simplify, personify, and illuminate their narratives about homicide,[51] and they are assisted by what Plummer called the 'coaxers, coachers and coercers'[52] whose job it is to elicit personal histories of mishaps, problems, deviants, and deviation.[53]

The personal distress of victims has become a matter of public education and entertainment. With every crisis, with every extraordinary murder, survivors would be hunted down by the staff of the mass media to tell the world how it feels and looks to be bereaved. After the murder of James Bulger in February 1993, for instance, said John Baldock of TCF: 'there was tremendous media coverage, all wanting to know this, that and the other. They

---

[48] See J. Galtung and M. Ruge, 'The structure of foreign news', *Journal of International Peace Research*, 1965, Vol 1.

[49] Interview with Amanda Goodall.

[50] Interview with Amanda Goodall.

[51] See R. Graef, 'We're all hurt by TV's cheap thrills', *Evening Standard*, 9 July 1996; and P. Schlesinger and H. Tumber, *Reporting Crime: The Media Politics of Criminal Justice* (Clarendon Press, Oxford, 1994), 99.

[52] K. Plummer, *Telling Sexual Stories* (Routledge, London, 1995), 21.

[53] See E. Nelson and B. Robinson, '"Reality Talk" or "Telling Tales"?: The Social Construction of Sexual and Gender Deviance on a Television Talk Show', *Journal of Contemporary Ethnography*, Apr 1994, Vol 23, No 1, 52.

contacted a lot of the people who were originators of POMC, like Ann Robinson, Gill Pennicard and June Patient, and there was a resurgence of all their stories in the magazines.'

Organizing that hunt is the idea of the story, and the stories that count are furnished by an occupational solipsism, news being what other newsmen and women discuss and report.[54] Charlie Bunce, the producer of one television studio programme, *Esther!*, said: 'The ideas [for programmes] come from me and the people that I'm working with. It might be kicked off by something you read in a newspaper or it might be an abstract thought...' The news will be explored by trawling through other stories produced by colleagues (the same producer remarked that, in the first instance, he had researched a programme on the grieving process by turning to 'the primary source [which] was newspaper cuttings of things that had happened'). What else can journalists resort to but just such a pseudo-environment of media-generated images?[55]

News is self-reproducing. And it is also self-silencing. There is an engrained professional impatience with the too-obvious repetition, with news which does not look new at all, which merely parrots that which has been exposed already, and, without palpable change or structure, without a dramatic crisis, and often on the basis of only dimly-articulated criteria, newsmen and women will endow the public interest of any event with only a very limited half-life.[56] Even stories about a murder can pall after a time. Duncan Campbell of the *Guardian*, said:

I think for a journalist the difficulty... is that once you're done a story about somebody's particular tragedy once, that's more or less it for them. If you're doing a story about a miscarriage of justice, somebody wrongfully imprisoned, you can carry on doing it as you get new evidence until the person gets out. There is an end point to the story.... [But if] it's a one-off story... I think what a lot of victims find hard is that having told their story once, people move on.

There is thus a perpetual oscillation between a propensity to define a phenomenon as news because professional colleagues have already

[54] See W. Breed, 'Newspaper Opinion Leaders and Processes of Standardization', *Journalism Quarterly*, Summer 1955, Vol 32; and G. Gerbner, 'Institutional Pressures Upon Mass Communicators' in P. Halmos (ed), *Sociological Review Monograph* (University of Keele, Keele, 1969).

[55] See D. Boorstin, *The Image* (Weidenfeld and Nicolson, London, 1961).

[56] See A. Downs, 'Up and Down with Ecology: The Issue Attention Cycle', *Public Interest*, 1972, Vol 28.

reported it as news, and a propensity to regard that phenomenon as no longer newsworthy because professional colleagues have already reported it as news. It is as if news can be sustained only in its changes and contrasts, and it may well take form in dialectical distinction to other, established stories that appear to be in decline.

In part, the new groups, and Justice for Victims amongst them, were to rise up as part of just such a media-engendered cycle in the mid-1990s. Most were new and brash. They touched on core news values and they sought attention. They engaged in dramatic confrontations with members of powerful institutions. And, as I shall show, they were the beneficiaries of a particular movement of professional taste. Although it had been their campaigning that made them visible and audible in the first instance,[57] their prime value for journalists and producers did not reside in their identity as *groups*, in the ideology which they were attempting collectively to impart,[58] or in their general judgements about victims and the criminal justice system. Judgements of that kind could be supplied with greater authority by other organizations, and by Victim Support above all (Terry Kirby of the *Independent* said: 'one would

---

[57] An audibility and visibility that were enhanced, in part, by the larger growth of talk about victims and victimisation, a growth amounting, in some eyes, to fashionableness. In America, where there has been something of a backlash against victims' groups, books were beginning to emerge with titles such as that of C. Sykes's *A Nation of Victims: The Decay of the American Character* (St Martin's Press, New York, 1992). Sykes began by saying, on p. xiii: 'it is almost impossible to debate any issue of weight without running up against the politics of victimization.... Portraying oneself as a victim has become an attractive pastime.' My own view would be that membership of homicide survivors' groups should not be classified as an attractive pastime.

[58] Indeed, for some, and particularly the more liberal or radical journalists, what was thought to be that ideology was not well-regarded, and it acted as a disincentive to report the new groups' activities. One journalist remarked that: 'for a period in the 80s, in the late 80s and early 90s the Home Office was... it's part of the jargon and language of the Government and particularly of the right, that somehow concern for victims became of interest. Journalists, I think, unconsciously found it difficult to distinguish a genuine concern for victims with the sort of language of the Right in terms of retribution, revenge, vigilantism and all those kinds of things.... I'm talking very much from the perspective of the collective centre broadsheet newspapers. This is an instinctive shying away from following the Government's agenda. The government was always banging on about we've go to do more for the victim, the instinctive shying away—"we don't want to do anything, we won't go with what the Government says we should write about". And this kind of uneasiness that it was rather open to the vigilantes and that kind of thing. It kind of acted as a bit of a sort of dampener on it and I think that it's difficult to actually kind of put a finger on, but I think that kind of made the victim thing not perhaps take the profile that it should have done.'

treat Victim Support probably with...less scepticism than a single issue [group] because they have had to prove themselves.... [Besides,] the evidence of single issue groups is often anecdotal [and their] agenda is often slightly uncomfortable.').

Instead, the new groups were approached most commonly in their role as willing and convenient sources of individuals who had interesting stories to tell about matters that had become of topical importance. Charlie Bunce, the producer of the *Esther!* programme remarked:

What we are keen to do is use [the groups] as a point of contact because it would be silly not to, but at the same time remember that the programme is not about pressure groups, it is about people with an involvement, and it would be silly not to go to the groups, it would be silly not to talk to them and often, though not always, to include them in the programme. But the group itself is not what is of interest to us.

The staff of newspapers and television and radio programmes tend to work to very short deadlines, and often to deadlines of only a few hours. If they want a head to talk or an individual to quote, they will almost certainly want that person in a hurry (John Baldock, of TCF and formerly of POMC, remarked: 'when I'm contacted by journalists or somebody from radio or television, it's always a question of "can you come to meet us at the drop of a hat because we've got this important programme...?"'). Any organization that can rapidly and effectively supply a stock of rare subjects will be able to join with journalists in a symbiotic relation. Duncan Campbell said of the new survivors' groups:

Some of them like Diana Lamplugh are a highly organized, very efficient organization and a lot of sponsors and things like that and a lot of press releases and so on. The other, newer ones are less experienced but they also will announce their arrival normally with a press release, usually they will give you half a dozen contact numbers and that means when you get an incident that happens at the end of an afternoon, or somebody who has been released from prison or one of those kind of situations, and you need a comment from a victim of a relative, or somebody who has been a victim of a similar thing, you've got six people, and you can say 'so-and-so of Support after Murder and Manslaughter or so-and-so of Justice for Victims...' You will hope to have a bank of people who can speak on behalf of victims of different kinds of things—victims of schizophrenics who have been released into the community, victims of drunk drivers, relatives of victims of murder and so on. . . . The alternative, if you are working on a kind of day-to-day story, you cannot dig around through the cuttings trying to find a relative, because most of the time those relatives don't want to talk, and the reason that you go to these people is partly because they are prepared to talk about it and therefore you're not intruding.

The journalist's professional commitment to neutrality and balance is practically accomplished by the method of aligning spokesmen or women from opposing positions. For every quotation from a politician of the left, there will be one from a politican of the right. So too with victims and survivors. They can act as a counterweight to others in the construction of a narrative, supplying a tacit interpretive gloss. So it was that Terry Kirby, a crime reporter for the *Independent* for eight years, would turn to the survivors' groups not only to add human interest, objectivity, and diversity, but also to comment in a way that he could not do himself:

I didn't write about [the groups] generically so to speak. I didn't write about them as a whole—'there is this new phenomenon' that sort of thing at all. The occasions when one would write, one would research them when you were writing, would be the occasions demanded by way of a news story . . . What obviously you need on newspapers . . . is that you need someone else to say the things that any impartial, or not necessarily impartial, but any commentator might feel the right to say but you can't say it yourself, you can't editorialise in a news report, or you try not to. What you simply do is to find someone who can make a comment about it to highlight it.

There are rather few homicides in England and Wales and few enough survivors prepared publicly to talk about themselves. But individual survivors like Pat Green *did* want to be heard: speaking on television and radio was a way of memorialising the dead and advertising her group: 'if I keep saying to the press, "no, I don't want to speak to you", I'm not going to get anywhere, am I? I'm not going to get a voice and I'm not going to be recognised.' A number of survivors wanted to write books about themselves. They wanted others to write and broadcast about them. Indeed, more than one approach to SAMM would chronicle the television programmes that were made, or nearly made, about the writer's case. And, collectively, the survivors' groups also wanted to be heard, because, in being heard, they might break out of their marginality and impotence, and become 'empowered'. They would keep a tally of how often they had been approached by the press as a measure of their success and impact on the wider world.[59] They would supply their members with the telephone numbers of television and radio corporations and companies. And, however rudimentary their division of labour may have been on occasion, one of the very first specialist roles they would assign would be that of press officer.[60]

The new survivors' groups were therefore well placed. They represented an accumulation of scarce people with interesting stories to tell, stories, moreover, that few had heard in the mid-1990s.[61] Jill Palm, POMC's second co-ordinator, recalled that they would ask: 'have you got a family with a 7-year old child that's been raped and murdered? Could you put us in touch?' And her successor, Gill Pennicard, said: 'When, if I had anybody' phone, they would say "do you know of anybody?" and I would always say I knew of people who needed to speak out and that it would have helped them to do so... and then I would give them their telephone number when I had spoken to them [to obtain their permission].'

The merging of those trends, the fascination with the human interest personified by the suffering survivor, the use of key figures for vicarious interpretation and balance, and the turning away from a settled pattern of professional reporting, was exemplified in a documentary series, *Crime Limited*, which was shown on BBC television in 1994, the *annus mirabilis* of the new survivors' groups. *Crime Limited* had been instigated at the suggestion of Victim

[59] When the principal speakers at the launch of SAMM were formally thanked by letter, they were told that: 'the occasion generated considerable publicity for us'. Indeed, the cover of the following SAMM Newsletter was decorated with a collage of newspaper cuttings about the launch. SAMM's second bid for lottery funds in February 1996 made the claim that the organization's success was demonstrated by the level of press coverage it had attracted. It is not therefore surprising that the progress reports and minutes of POMC and SAMM committee meetings should have been regularly punctuated by their co- ordinators' assessments of the intensity and scale of media interest in the organizations. The SAMM Annual Report for 1994 reflected, under a separate heading, 'Media', that: 'Publicity is a central way of reaching out to people who are not aware of SAMM. It is also an important vehicle for people affected by murder and manslaughter to have a voice to express their personal experiences of the aftermath of murder, and to bring to the public's notice their concerns about their treatment within the criminal justice process.'

[60] The role of press or publicity officer was as much intended to control disagreeable reporting as to promote useful reporting. Unpleasant representations of survivors' experiences can be deeply wounding. See the report on the making of unwelcome television dramas about homicides in the *Sunday Times*, 26 Feb 1995,

[61] Recall how the press notice accompanying the launch of SAMM had offered the lure to reporters of 50 members of SAMM being available to talk about their personal experiences.

Support,[62] and it sympathetically re-created the life stories of Derek Rogers, David Hines, the Watsons,[63] and other survivors. The producer said 'some of them were [secured through] cuttings, a couple were cuttings, some were from Victim Support, some were cases that we knew, some were through other organisations—Justice for Victims.'

Crime Limited, said Ann Virgin, was 'the first time ever a programme was working from the victim's view'. It was in that sense a clear response to what was considered to have been the earlier surfeit of dramatised reconstructions of murders and serious crimes.[64] Donna Taberer, its producer, argued that it had emerged out of:

[62] Helen Peggs, the Press Officer of Victim Support said: 'for a long time we've had a relationship with the people who make *Crimewatch* and we've said to them "why don't you cover victims' issues? Why don't you try and take something which is from the victim's perspective?" It's the BBC at their most ethical and public service minded, and about three years ago they started this series called *Crime Limited* . . .'

[63] The Watsons exemplified several truths, thought Donna Taberer: 'The daughter was 15 and they had a 14 year old son and there was no counselling, nothing offered for the son. The family was in disarray and a year later the son committed suicide and said "I want to be with my sister". That was looking at how there was just nobody there for her and she was in a slight way comparing what was on offer for the perpetrator, once convicted, and what was given to her family. It also looked slightly at the media and how they treated her. Because it was a fellow pupil or a young girl who ended up in prison, lots of stories came out about this—the dreadful time that the young girl would have once she was in prison. It sort of fabricated all the stuff, saying that the daughter who died was a bully and she absolutely wasn't, and that it was a tiny nick of the heart—and so all those sorts of things, but she was dead and the 14 year old son took the papers and went to a lawyer and said "they have said these disgusting things about my sister" and they said "go away, she's dead, there's nothing you can do about it".'

[64] In time, that response was to generate its own counter-response. Donna Taberer said: 'If you look at the BBC over the year . . . we're not doing another Crime Limited . . . I think there was too much. I don't ever think ours were wrong but others were wrong and there is just too much . . . We discussed whether we would do another—obviously all the people involved, Justice for Victims will tell you that they really wanted another series and I had a file as another series and had to go and do one piece of research following the first series—all very strong journalistic cases and all cases with issues that we hadn't raised. So I could have made another series the week after it finished [based on say Justice for Victims cases?] No, based on letters that came to the programme . . . I think it was a matter of how much people can take of it. We said 'what sort of person would have sat down and watched eight programmes about murder and manslaughter?' if you weren't Derek Rogers and Justice for Victims and you had gone through it could you really seriously watch all eight? Most of us on the team, we were all really proud of it, but our spouses and friends couldn't watch all eight. You literally couldn't cope with it.'

The discussions around crime programmes. Obviously there was a lot of discussion around crime programmes on ITV, a lot of people from the BBC were critical of those—those were purely shock horror murder Michael Winner types which were purely reconstruction for the hell of it...I think we were being told that crime programmes were awful, exploitative and the rest of it...We weren't doing Michael Winner-type programmes, but we were dragged down by it.... It was just felt that it wasn't the timing for it and there wasn't the appetite for it. People didn't want crime reconstructions from that point of view, which was just—here's a true life crime programme.... So what we were looking at it would be what the victims wanted to say, what they wanted to bring out, and it would be an issue so it wouldn't just be 'I have had an awful crime happen to me', it would be 'I have had an awful crime happen to me or somebody I know and something needs to be done about it'.

Publicity can be self-fuelling. When broadcasts such as *Crime Limited* were released, they generated an interest that led to more reporting, more programmes, and more interest. Taberer remarked that: 'people wanted to talk to [the subjects of *Crime Limited*] and they wanted to hear about the problem...magazines like all the *Bellas*[65] and the listings magazines because it's current prime copy for them....So suddenly there were people who wanted to hear their stories.' Justice for Victims and other survivors were courted and reported, and being reported, they were regarded as even more self-evidently newsworthy.

Figs. 7.4, 7.5 and 7.6 make the general point clearly. They display the broadsheet newspapers' coverage of a number of victims' groups between 1992 and June 1996. What they reveal would apply *a fortiori* to 'talk shows', discussion programmes, and the like, which were more heavily invested in the reproduction of human interest stories. Victim Support was treated by the broadsheet newspapers as an authority on matters touching on criminal justice and criminal justice policy, but it did not supply victims who could narrate their own life-histories. The survivors' groups were themselves regarded in some measure as commentators on aspects of criminal justice (there being thirty-nine such stories); they were treated as interesting in their own right (sixteen stories centred on the survivors' groups and the services they provided);

---

[65] According to an interview conducted by Amanda Goodall with the deputy editor of *Bella*, victims of crime have become the magazine's 'stock-in-trade'.

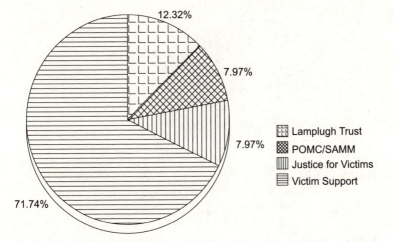

Fig. 7.4 Broadsheet newspapers' reporting of groups as experts on criminal justice policy: Jan 1992–June 1996.

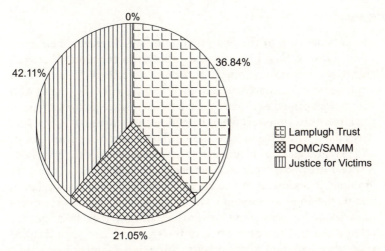

Fig. 7.5 Broadsheet newspapers' reporting of survivors' experiences as victims: Jan 1992–June 1996.

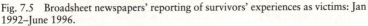

but they were also reservoirs of interesting people who could be approached for personal narratives (nineteen such narratives were relayed).

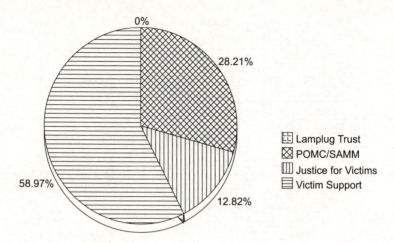

Fig. 7.6   Broadsheet newspapers' coverage of services and campaigns conducted by groups: Jan 1992–June 1996.

Kilroy

Let me now turn to the one programme which exemplified those trends most starkly. I have already alluded to encounters between Justice for Victims and others on *Kilroy*, the television studio programme which was orchestrated by Robert Kilroy-Silk, a man who had himself played a critical role in criminal justice policy matters in the House of Commons when he had been a Labour MP.[66] *Kilroy* was a daytime television 'chat show' which centred on diverse social and psychological problems, including crime. Most of the principals of this history had appeared on one or more editions of the programme. In a sense, it was to act as a crucible for the consolidation and public objectification of some of the new groups, and survivors took an ambivalent stand towards it. It was, they held, both a celebration and an aggravation of their griefs. They often disliked it but they had risen to prominence through the fame it bestowed.

The content of *Kilroy* was shaped reactively. What was discussed on the programme was a response which targeted and amplified what other media had already defined as reportable and interesting. One of its producers, Brian Wesley, recalled:

---

[66] I discussed his role in *Helping Victims of Crime* (Clarendon Press, Oxford, 1990).

I think it's a self-fulfilling prophecy...we were news reactive...we were reacting because we had to be because otherwise there would be no interest in talking about it. So it had to have been in the public ethos for 48 hours or whatever...and the whole thing, as I say, programmes like the Kilroys and newspapers and current affairs programmes and...the reactive groups are part of an organic process...Then crime is one of the key issues really and since the principle of the programme is that the people who take part must have—whatever we are talking about must have—touched their lives in some way, then you are obviously looking at criminals and victims.

Kilroy was conceived to be an entertainment programme, animated, in part, by the tensions of a contained conflict[67] ('there has to be conflict, there has to be a divergence of opinion, but that could well be debate rather than a row'), and composed of those people who had actually undergone the experiences or problems under scrutiny ('we always used to have a kind of policy that we didn't want spokespeople—the only kind of spokespeople were either to set an agenda or to sum up when there were particular factual things that we needed. So, we wouldn't for instance, with great respect, we wouldn't get a criminologist...'). Programmes about crime would turn, *inter alia*, to those who had become expert and interesting through their own suffering and, 'obviously if you're going to get people who've been involved as the victims of crime then you are going to come across the victim support groups and so on.' The staff of Victim Support itself were awarded low authority on the programme: 'we used to hate people saying "I am here to represent Victim Support" and Robert always used to say 'well [on air sometimes] the victims are here, and they don't *need* anybody to speak on their behalf.' *Kilroy* actively sought out victims who were willing to tell their own

[67] The standard opening shots of the programme were a montage of members of the audience shouting, laughing, weeping, gesticulating and arguing, all with great emotion. A somewhat critical piece on the show remarked that: 'The files kept by newspaper libraries are fat with tales of bust-ups, reunions and revelations, super-intended by Mr Kilroy-Silk...They are the lifeblood of the programme and the principle [*sic*] means by which the Kilroy brand maintains both its place at the top of the ratings and its bad (ie. good) reputation....Programme makers justify [their] stunts by arguing that they are using first-hand experiences to tackle difficult issues head on. This argument seems like a disingenuous excuse to exploit people for the sake of ratings.' (P. Foster, 'Talk show to freak show', *The Times*, 23 July 1997)

stories in a public forum that was centred on anatomising problems of human interest.[68]

The first such victims were procured from TCF for general programmes about bereavement and about grieving children: 'out of that,' said Wesley, 'came a crime thing—people who are bereaved because of murder—or drunk driving was a classic (we were always doing something about drunk driving).' *Kilroy* focused on child murders in December 1994 (the catalyst being Myra Hindley's assertion the day before that 'she had paid for her crime and wanted her freedom'. *Kilroy*'s supporting copy announced that: 'The families of her victims are, of course, absolutely outraged. What kind of suffering do child murders leave behind?'). *Kilroy* focused on 'victims fighting back' five months later[69] in direct response to the publication of the second *Victim's Charter*.[70]

Surviving homicide was an area of political activity, Wesley remarked, in which social networks proliferated: 'they all knew each other, so all those groups started springing up', and, for pragmatic reasons, given the scarce supply of available survivors, it was easier to return repeatedly to the same groups for contributors: 'one of the things is you can't actually 'phone up somebody who has recently been bereaved. . . . We tried to get different people each time but then, when the story came round again, we did it again.' In the second programme on 'victims fighting back' were Pat Green, Derek Rogers, Sandra Sullivan, and Ann Virgin.

The one outstanding difficulty for the producers was the embeddedness, particularism, and concreteness of the stories that were told: Wesley said: 'we want people who have experienced the subject we are talking about, whether it be crime, victims or whatever, you actually need the specifics to go on to the general, and they find it impossible to go on to the general argument. In fact, they are a group of singularly obsessed people who happen to have a common

---

[68] It was just so with other studio programmes. There is an apparent immediacy in the victim's or the survivor's narrative that is thought to be lacking in that of the professional intermediary. What was sought were people with a disingenuous appearance who would speak directly about personal suffering. One who had worked on the *Esther!* Programme said: 'what we don't talk about particularly on the programme is . . . campaign[s]. What it is very much about is that personal experience . . . The experts are actually in my view the people who have been through whatever it is.'

[69] The copy advertising the programme declared that: 'British crime victims are fighting back against a legal system that they claim ignored them and pampers the criminal. The victims of crime fight for greater justice.'

[70] Discussed at length in the next chapter.

cause but they can't make a common cause, in my view.' The difficulty for the participants was that, whilst an appearance on *Kilroy* and similar programmes gave them publicity and a catharsis, it could also turn them into something of a public spectacle.[71] Gill Pennicard thought: 'all they want to do is know people's business, they want to see the people sad and they want to see them cry, they want to see them happy... they like all this and I think that it's wrong, I think it's not a positive thing.' The participating studio audience would be large, the programme of forty-five minutes brief, and bidding for attention could be correspondingly fraught. One survivor who was there talked about the 'competitive grief' that was on display and wondered 'how much pain you can subject yourself to, sitting with these families...' People in mid-flow, publicly testifying perhaps for the very first time, could find themselves being interrupted as Robert Kilroy-Silk orchestrated first one voice and then another. Ann Robinson recalled: '[Kilroy] would try to keep the views balanced but he would actually stop people and go back to somebody... some of the programmes were very frustrating. You weren't allowed to say very much at all. You were cut off short.'

On *Kilroy* and kindred programmes, members of Justice for Victims and its kindred groups became transformed into public figures. Wesley observed: 'I think perhaps more than most we did actually [give them an identity] because we made them realise that if they shouted loud enough, somebody would listen.' They offered themselves in part as the representatives of campaigning organizations, it was as individuals that they were courted, and their organizations acquired prominence in consequence.

It is conventional for such programmes to end with a display of help-line telephone numbers, and June Patient remembered after an appearance on *Kilroy* how: 'you'd be bombarded with telephone calls. It was unbelievable how quick the people would call.' An observer from Victim Support reflected:

---

[71] Ann Robinson recalled: 'we were being portrayed as the poor pathetic little people who were out of our minds with grief, and *what* we were saying wasn't really relevant, and that made me very angry.' Her successor, Jill Palm, said: 'they get everybody fired up. They asked me to go on [one programme involving a confrontation with prisoners] and I said "no", because it's just for other people's entertainment... I'd get really worked up and really nervous and then you'd have all the hassle of television and, at the end of the day, you'd think "well, people have watched that, and you're completely out of their minds the next day. They don't care".'

Kilroy researchers are like vultures picking off other press stories, finding names and checking people out and they got together a whole group of people for a programme about a year ago and I think that is where people like Road Peace and Justice for Victims met each other and I think the media decided that there was this thing going on about angry victims and that there was a story there and so we kept getting article after article after article. . . . Crime stories always go in waves and it was a wave on its own of angry families of murder victims.

Conclusion

Within the confines of the newly-emergent POMC, a POMC that was moving towards a liaison with Victim Support, there emerged a small, vigorous group that engendered what was, in effect, a radical subculture inside the larger culture of homicide survivors. Its beliefs and actions were simultaneously at one with those of other survivors and yet opposed to them. The group had firmly established itself inside POMC and its successor, SAMM, but it also defined itself by its resistance to what it thought were the supine qualities of the support group and the alienating formality of Victim Support.

It would have been easy enough to disregard Justice for Victims. Its members were so few and ill-equipped. But such was the intensity of their feelings, so animated was their campaigning, and so fascinating as individuals were they and others like them to the mass media, that Justice for Victims was to become enlarged out of all proportion to its numbers. Helen Peggs of Victim Support came to conclude: 'I was very bemused at the time by the reactions of the media to these new groups. I noticed that the media quickly gave them an identity and an authority. Some of the groups seemed to have no real identity outside of their media coverage and within a short space of time I noticed that even the more respectable media had a tendency to quote them as though they were experts in victimology, often in preference to Victim Support or to academics.'[72] Members of Justice for Victims were to grow to such a political stature that they and their group could affect the development not only of its *Doppelgänger*, SAMM, but also an array of much larger institutions in the criminal justice system. And it is with those politics, the exchanges between Justice for Victims and practitioners, officials, and Ministers, that the next chapter will be occupied.

[72] Letter to author, 9 Sept 1997.

8

The Politics of Justice for Victims

The demands of Justice for Victims

Most of Justice for Victims' demands were probably not very different from the manifest desires of many other survivors and of SAMM members at large. They were extrapolated from the survivor's analogical reasoning, and they could probably best be summarised as a call for *respect*,[1] a key word in the survivor's lexicon. By *respect* was meant an amalgam of different gestures: the symbolic and practical incorporation of survivors into society and the criminal justice system, the restoration of moral balance between good and evil, and a public recognition not only of the families' unwarranted suffering but also of the lives of the victims that had been so wantonly lost. Sandra Sullivan said: 'No respect [was] shown any of our children. That's why we go on really. It's just the lack of respect shown to them in their graves. They've lost their lives forever. They can't feel the sun. The murderers can feel the sun. That's why we do it. The utter disrespect!' Let me amplify.

First, respect meant a recognition of the family's symbolic property in crime and conflict.[2] Crime was not merely an offence against the reified community but against identifiable individuals who had a stake in what happened to them and the transgressor. Sandra Sullivan said:

We don't want it to be considered a crime against the State. It's a crime against us, and that's a major thing.

---

[1] For instance, in a report of a meeting with the Criminal Bar Association, Joan Bacon was reported to have said that 'all victim's families sought was respect for their needs'. Notes of a Meeting with Representatives of 'Justice for Victims', 19 May 1994.

[2] Joan Bacon said: '[We want] recognition... Because, as far as I'm concerned, all the way through, they've lost sight of what had happened, [as if the crime] had nothing to do with it whatsoever, but it had everything to do with it.'

Second, it meant public acknowledgement that good people had been devastated by evil, that something was seriously amiss in the moral order. Joan Bacon said:

We want recognition in the courts separately, to be treated as good families. We've always been tax payers, hardworking people. We're the salt of the earth. We're the people in the middle that are keeping those at the bottom and keeping those at the top with our taxes.

They wanted longer sentences ('life meaning life') and more extensive and aggressive punishment to signify the heinousness of crime, and by 'crime' they almost invariably meant serious offences of violence.

Third, respect meant the maintenance of a proper balance between victim and criminal ('what we have to do is balance', said Joan Bacon). A leaflet declared:

The present legal system is unbalanced—the scales of justice are not protecting the law abiding. The criminal element is utterly protected with all rights. Victims are disregarded, silenced, forgotten people, we demand rights and expect justice!![3]

There had to be a restoration of proportion to the management of the relations between crimes, criminals, victims, and survivors. Members of Justice for Victims argued that homicide and its aftermath were grievous matters, different in kind from any other crime, and they required their own appropriately grave response. So major was the present imbalance, it was said, that the Government should establish a task force to investigate survivors' needs and then staff a new Ministry of Justice at the heart of a new victim justice system. If victim support volunteers were to be despatched to survivors at all, they should have been subject to very rigorous selection and training,[4] but, better still would be the recruitment of professional counsellors equipped to respond to the very special needs of survivors just as criminals were supplied with their own psychiatrists and welfare officers.

Any concession to the wrongdoer should be matched by a concession to the wronged. Members of Justice for Victims said that they were entitled to a bill of rights laying out claims equal to those afforded the criminal and prisoner. They wanted the legal

---

[3] 'Victims of Crime Pressure Group', n.d.
[4] Jane Cooper observed: 'they are'.

representation and legal aid which were extended the defendant. They wanted to meet counsel as defendants did. They required legal advice, a crèche, transport and hotel costs to carry them through the ordeal of the trial. They wanted victim impact statements and the calling of character witnesses to testify about the dead as the defendant could call character witnesses to testify about the living. They wanted an end to the 'character assassination' of malicious mitigation pleas in court. They wanted to be consulted and informed about the release of persons detained for murder or manslaughter.[5] They wanted any consideration of the effects of sentences on prisoners' families to be counterbalanced by a consideration of the effects on victims' families.[6] They wanted blame to be attributed and responsibility assumed when things went wrong. Ann Virgin said: '"Answerable" and "Accountable" are the two words we use all of the time, at all of our meetings . . .'

Such claims to respect are important. Indeed, the psychoanalyst, James Gilligan, built a lengthy thesis around the claim that attempts to preserve respect are the prime motor of violence in violent men.[7] Dignity, face, and self-esteem are strong values in the survivors' world too, and, when they are threatened, theirs can also be an irate response. The demand for respect may be accompanied by a politics of anger.

Political encounters with Justice for Victims

It was perhaps ironic that the anger and vigour of Justice for Victims did make their stamp. Justice for Victims may have been small in numbers, it may have defined itself as marginal, impotent, neglected, and excluded,[8] it may have taken to the pavements, but it did succeed in creating a great noise both figuratively and literally, and the noise it made was enhanced by the swelling media attention which I discussed in the previous chapter. Justice for Victims was noticed in many quarters and after only a very

[5] Minutes of Meeting with the Parole Board, 31 Aug 1994.

[6] Evidence to the Home Affairs Select Committee on the Mandatory Life Sentence, 7 Feb 1995.

[7] J. Gilligan, *Violence: Reflections on a National Epidemic* (Vintage Books, New York, 1996).

[8] Sandra Sullivan said at a meeting with officials and a Member of Parliament at the Home Office in October 1993, 'the victim is kept underneath, downtrodden and silenced. . . . We have to keep fighting for everything!'

short time. In Dahl's language, its 'intensity of preference'[9] won political attention in the years of the Conservative Home Office under Michael Howard, a Home Secretary described as 'clever-cautious [and] Rightwing'.[10] They may have been few but their passion was manifestly great.

Within a short while, Justice for Victims managed to gain audiences with almost all the powers of the criminal justice system: meeting, for example, in 1993 with officials of the Crown Prosecution Service and with the Commissioner of Metropolitan Police;[11] with policy officials at the Home Office on 18 October; with Members of Parliament and officers of Victim Support at the House of Commons on 8 December; and, in 1994, with Members of Parliament and David Maclean, the Home Office minister, on 20 April; with Victim Support on 16 May; with the Criminal Bar Association on 19 May; with the Parole Board on 31 August; with Liberty on 9 September; and with the Home Secretary on 19 September. They even secured an audience with groups whom Victim Support itself had struggled hard to meet, and such access to the powerful was a trophy indeed in the wary world of criminal justice. A senior official of Victim Support remarked; 'it's not just David Maclean, for goodness' sake!...The Crown Prosecution Service has met them, and what's more, the working party of the Judicial Studies Board dealing with human awareness has met them as well. It has taken us years to have a say with the Judicial Studies Board!'

Some small part of their success must be ascribed to the sponsorship of insiders and near-insiders, and, in particular, of two Labour Members of Parliament, Ron Leighton,[12] who was Noreen Caulfield's and the Manwaring family's Member, and Neil

---

[9] See R. Dahl, *A Preface to Democratic Theory* (The University of Chicago Press, Chicago, 1956), 48–9.

[10] A. Roth, *Parliamentary Profiles* (Parliamentary Profiles, London, 1989).

[11] Sandra Sullivan recalled: 'we met with Paul Condon and he was so supportive—I wasn't satisfied with the murders through care in the community so he brought a psychiatrist, he brought a policeman, an ex-psychologist who has now become a policeman, and Derek put the DNA, all the different things forward—we had a very long meeting, about 2 hours, and we mentioned all the things we wanted and when we went to go he made it very clear, he shook my hand for a very long time, and he kept looking into my face and saying "don't give up".'

[12] Labour MP for Newham North-East since 1979. He was to die within a few months of playing such an active role in the affairs of Justice for Victims. He had had no formal parliamentary or occupational expertise in criminal justice matters. Leighton was described in Roth's *Parliamentary Profiles* (n 10 above) as, *inter alia*, a 'traditional Left Newham-protector'.

Gerrard,[13] the Member representing Joan Bacon and Ann Virgin, who was to take over Leighton's role as mentor after his death in 1993.

Leighton had written to the Prime Minister on 4 September 1993 asking him to receive a petition from the Victims of Crime group on their march of 18 October and to the Home Secretary to meet their deputation.[14] He had met with sixty-one bereaved families at the House of Commons and had then accompanied members of the group to a preparatory meeting with officials in the Home Office on that day in October 1993, a meeting that would lead to other meetings with Ministers. Joan Bacon said: 'it was Ron Leighton that made the openings.... [He] was a man of the people and he wasn't in it for himself.... Ron Leighton's perspective was saying these people must be helped; these people need to make a fresh start and these people must be helped. You can't just wipe them away, they need special attention.'

Protesting that they too had had their civil liberties breached,[15] members of Justice for Victims had also approached Andrew Puddephatt of Liberty (formerly the National Council for Civil Liberties) who promised to provide Liberty's 'expertise and campaigning help' in attempting to formulate a Charter of Rights for victims,[16] draft a Private Member's Bill, and accompany them to their meeting with the Home Secretary later in the month. Those sponsors, the

[13] Neil Gerrard was Labour MP for Walthamstow since 1992. He had been a teacher in secondary education and lecturer in computing in further education before becoming a Member of Parliament.

[14] For its own part, Justice for Victims had earlier approached the Prime Minister about receiving its petition, and Noreen Caulfield had approached her MP, Ron Leighton, to support what was being done. Joan Bacon observed that 'we had set all the wheels in motion'.

[15] Writing about their 'lack of rights and civil liberties', Justice for Victims said to Liberty in August 1994: 'We are severely damaged people who through no fault of our own are without any recognition, rights, or respect...The reason we are here is to find out from you what our Civil Liberties are...'

[16] See *agenda*, Dec 1994. The proposed Charter of Rights declared that: 'Liberty believes that victims and their families need enforceable rights to ensure that the criminal justice system at the very least treats them equitably and fairly.' It then proceeded to lay out those rights: 1. An adequate system of damages comparable to common law damages; 2. An enforceable right to be informed about the progress of any criminal proceedings; 3. A right to have a person appointed by the State whose role it would be to provide information about investigations and to represent families during those investigations; 4. A right to be informed about these rights; 5. A right to an adequate system of legal aid; and 6. A right for victims and their families to be free from discrimination. (Draft of 12 Sept 1994)

Members of Parliament and Andrew Puddephatt were to act, in Anselm Strauss's words, as 'status coaches', as competent insiders who would guide the learner as 'he moves along, step by step. [The learner] needs guidance not merely because in the conventional sense he needs someone to teach him skills, but because some very surprising things are happening to him that require explanation.'[17]

In effect, the coaches saw it as part of their role to school members of Justice for Victims in the manners, language, and etiquette of the politics of criminal justice. Puddephatt said that he had taken it to be his duty to introduce the group to influential insiders[18] and assist them in their encounters: '[I was] trying to bring it into the framework, not co-opting to the establishment, but bringing it into the framework where real change can happen. It's always about getting things happening...I helped them practically with the press and I helped them with the grant application.'

But there was always to be something of a gulf between the hot, emotional, self-referential, particularistic, and embedded language of Justice for Victims and the considered, cold, universalistic rationality of the official and the politician,[19] between the communicative actions of Justice for Victims and the strategic actions of the policymaker,[20] and the two groups would often leave meetings professing

---

[17] A. Strauss, *Mirrors and Masks* (Free Press, New York, 1959), 110.

[18] For example, he raised the issues troubling Justice for Victims at the meeting of the Parliamentary Labour Party civil liberties group on 6 December 1994, arguing that civil libertarians should co-operate with victims. He tried to float the idea of a Private Member's Bill, the Victims of Crime Bill, in that month. Again, Liberty's undated submission to the Royal Commission on Criminal Justice contained a section on the rights of victims to information and to speedy compensation.

[19] Margaret Lockwood-Croft of Disaster Action, the federation of disaster survivors, whose member groups have met with signal success in some of their campaigns, advised her fellow-survivors at a meeting: 'you've got to be icy cool and cold, because you will never get anywhere otherwise. You've got to put it over in a calm way.' Her colleague, Pam Dix, reflected: 'sometimes I really do have to hold myself in check. I do a lot of work on the supportive side for Disaster Action. I do a lot of the training for police officers and social workers, and there are many occasions in which I feel I really have to hold it back because I must not alienate them...'

[20] The terms are borrowed from Jürgen Habermas, who gave them a slightly different emphasis from my own, arguing that: 'We call an action oriented to success *strategic* when we consider it under the aspect of following technical rules of action and assess the efficacy of influencing the decisions of a rational opponent....By contrast, I shall speak of *communicative* action whenever the actions of agents involved are coordinated not through egocentric calculations of success but through acts of reaching understanding.' *The Theory of Communicative Action*, Vol 1 (Heinemann, London, 1981), 285–6.

that they had not understood one another at all well. Neil Gerrard remarked:

There is anger there, that there's not always a very clear articulation. They're not lawyers, they're often people who have had no contact with the criminal justice system before. So they're not necessarily terribly aware of the way that the system works and so I think sometimes, to perhaps Home Office officials or to people who are concerned regularly with the criminal justice system, what they're saying may appear a bit vague and a bit unfocused [but] I think they're learning and I think through working with people like Liberty. I think Liberty are actually being quite helpful in starting to get them to focus and they've produced this charter with Liberty and I think Liberty have actually done quite a good job there in sort of distilling out something that is a bit more focused.

The most important target for any criminal justice pressure group in England and Wales was the Home Office,[21] the very centre of power of the criminal justice system, a centre that was under the control of Conservative Government throughout the formative years of the new organizations, and Justice for Victims were to meet both David Maclean, a Minister, and Michael Howard, the Home Secretary. An official charged with victims policy at the Home Office at the time said that Justice for Victims were awarded attention because, 'to be blunt, they were the ones that were very persistent, kept coming to Ministers, kept demanding attention one way or the other', and, a colleague reflected, 'we have ministers who already may have been concerned about the treatment of victims and who were therefore obviously more likely to listen. . . . I think . . . Ministers would take the view that obviously victims as a whole need perhaps more consideration than they've had in the past. Families of murder victims are obviously in a particularly sensitive and difficult position.' To be sure, the issues raised by survivors' groups were recent and not the most pressing for Government. Homicide survivors were not numerous and their organizations were weak: 'they're a small group. There are proportionally very few people in that situation and Ministers recognise that as well, so I don't think they'd want to get it out of proportion.' Indeed, of the thirty copies of news releases and Ministerial speeches touching on victims that were distributed by the Home

---

[21] See P. Schlesinger and H. Tumber, *Reporting Crime: The Media Politics of Criminal Justice* (Clarendon Press, Oxford, 1994), 70.

Office between 1982 and 1996, only one mentioned homicide and homicide survivors, and that was David Maclean's news release of 20 April 1994 after his meeting with the Justice for Victims group. Again, the 1992 and 1997 Conservative Party election manifestos and their companion documents[22] made reference to only one voluntary organization for victims, Victim Support. Yet, given the strong emphasis Ministers attached to law and order issues, officials reasoned in the mid-1990s, it would have been difficult to deny the group the opportunity to come to the Office to express its views. Ministers themselves were said to be aware of Justice for Victims (then called Victims of Crime) and they were anxious to be seen to respond.

Before that meeting with the Minister in April 1994, there were doubts about the group's representativeness, but officials were aware that its members felt strongly about a terrible experience undergone without support or recognition. They could defend themselves, they thought, although Justice for Victims might not prove to be satisfied. The group was known to have a deep sense of loss and bitterness and needed someone on whom to vent their feelings. It would not be an easy encounter.

There was a gulf between the stocks of knowledge possessed by the two groups. On the one hand, officials and politicians had a working knowledge of the criminal justice system derived from meetings and briefings, conferences and conversations, reports and texts. They were masters of the general principle that had been abstracted from the empirical instance and worked into the precise rhetorical forms of the policy paper and speech. On the other hand, survivors had learned much from the harrowing details of their own and others' very particular and intense confrontations with bereavement, they could testify most eloquently about their own hurts, they had what was often a profound hermeneutic knowledge,[23] but they knew rather little of what passed for general analytic principle in bureaucratic settings, the methods for establishing such principles,

---

[22] For example, 'Protecting the Public From Crime', *Politics Today* (Conservative Research Department, London, 31 Jan 1997) and 'Law and Order: Key Facts', (Conservative Research Department, London, Jan 1997).

[23] SAMM, for example, was to inform the Home Affairs Select Committee inquiry into the Mandatory Life Sentence in written evidence that its 'experience . . . concerns the *individual personal experiences* of its members who have lost a family member through *homicide* and the impact that the criminal justice system . . . has in the aftermath of the crime' (my italics).

or the fund of substantive knowledge that insiders possessed about the law and workings of criminal justice. One member of Justice for Victims was to confess to a meeting: 'when I went to the Home Office, I was really upset because I wouldn't learn unless I asked, but I didn't know what to ask.' It was redolent of Bernstein's contrast between restricted and elaborated speech codes, between speech that was socially and emotionally embedded, and speech that depended principally on its syntactic complexity and vocabulary for the generation of meaning.[24]

Encounters between Justice for Victims and powerful insiders could be discordant. The one group was distressed, driven by vivid images of particular personal griefs, and diffusely angry;[25] the other preferred to rely on a careful consideration of practicable proposals that flowed from professional and departmental mandates, duties, rights, and competences and that were governed by broad rules of administrative procedure. A Home Office official said: 'it has been our experience with Justice for Victims that they do make demands which on the whole are unreasonable—they're not unreasonable from their point of view, but, as far as we're concerned, they're going to be difficult to implement and often have much wider implications than they themselves realise. But that's a problem that everyone faces in all sorts of problems. It's not just with victims' groups.' David Maclean, the minister, captured the point well at his meeting at the Home Office with Justice for Victims of 20 April 1994:

[PG] [Pat Green] There isn't any advice given to us.

[DM] [David Maclean] If you say there is no advice given then we want to plug that gap if we possibly can.

[SS] [Sandra Sullivan] We want as many rights as the criminals, we deserve more, definitely more than the criminals.

[DM] I said that as a general proposition, but let's see how we can turn that acceptance of the general proposition into hard practical advice of the sort that Neil [Gerrard] is asking for.

---

[24] See B. Bernstein, *Class, codes and control: Theoretical studies towards a sociology of language* (Routledge and Kegan Paul, London, 1971).

[25] A member of Justice for Victims was to write to Helen Reeves after a meeting held at the House of Commons on 8 Dec 1993: 'The meeting did get a bit "angry" at times and you were not able to finish giving us your information regarding the specialist training given to volunteers who deal with murder victim families...' (Letter of 16 Dec 1993).

The frequent complaint made by the one group was that they tended to be misunderstood or dismissed peremptorily by the powerful (one complained of how committees had 'talked down' to him in the past). The frequent complaint of the other was that Justice for Victims' demands were too concrete, emotional, imprecise, unfocused, *ad hoc*, and *ad hominem* to prepare the ground for intelligent policy-making. A person who had attended a meeting at the House of Commons with Neil Gerrard and others in December 1993 recalled that: 'the meeting was all over the place with people weeping in corners and people shouting. It was terrible. I think in a way one of the problems is that bereaved angry people can be very frightening...' Joan Bacon's own memory was that, 'to be honest, to be confronted with reality, they were at a loss'. Another observer commented on the meeting with Michael Howard in September 1994: 'Obviously they can't negotiate, they don't have the negotiating skills so they didn't.... So they started shouting at him basically from the moment that they sat down.... It was all quite heavy stuff really. It is a difficult thing to be on the receiving end of, and Michael Howard is not a person who has empathy, he is probably the worst single politician you could have in that I can think of.' One of the members of the Justice for Victims group who had been present was herself quite blunt about the tenor of that meeting: 'Michael Howard? Oh he's a moron.... He was... well he sat there, his civil servants were sat there and Joan laughs every time I say it, they were just like a load of cardboard cutouts.... They just talk a load of lies.... They just say "well, we're doing this or we're doing that", and they're not doing anything! It's just political jargon. And, so we tell them "you're not doing anything".'

Let me turn to two illustrative encounters in greater detail. The first was the preparatory meeting with officials at the Home Office on 18 October 1993 which Ron Leighton had engineered. Even before it began, officials wondered whether it would be possible to hold a 'sensible discussion' with Justice for Victims. The meeting began with a discussion of Justice for Victims' allegations about the deficiencies of Victim Support and then proceeded to the manner in which details of the Criminal Injuries Compensation Scheme were conveyed to potential claimants and to other, more general reforms in criminal justice:

CS [Christine Stewart, C4, Home Office] Things are now happening, the RCCJ [Royal Commission on Criminal Justice] recommend that saliva and hair roots should be non intimate samples for all recordable DNA.

DR [Derek Rogers] Does this include dental impressions?

AS [Ann Scott, Police Department, Home Office] It is not possible to take dental impressions without consent. There will be no particular benefit over that. We can get most from saliva or hair.

CS Advances are being made in forensic medicine with regard to non intimate samples. We cannot take dental samples at present if they object it would be difficult without co-operation.

PG [Pat Green] The person who murdered my son is walking free and was never brought to trial because he kept his right to silence.

CS The Right to Silence is going to be altered.

DR They object—They have the right to object to dental impressions—without this evidence the killer of my daughter would still be free.

CS If they refuse samples no account can be taken of this.

JB [Joan Bacon] When will the RCCJ recommendations be implemented. With the present upsurge of the judiciary wanting to protect the criminal and not wanting to sentence them, how far can Government go.

CS Parliament will be discussing legislation probably in the next session.

JB The institutionalised disinterest and inhumane treatment of murder/manslaughter victim families is a national disgrace.

One of the Home Office officials present at that meeting reflected:

There were all sorts of issues across a whole range of criminal justice matters actually stemming from their own personal experiences I think. So, effectively, there would be a list of demands which reflected their individual circumstances—things to do with taking DNA samples—all this stemmed from Derek Rogers' own case—through to policy on releasing sentenced prisoners, use of bail, right of silence . . . release of bodies from coroners, that sort of thing. A whole range of, on the whole, fairly practical sort of issues stemming really from the circumstances of their own cases, problems that they've had which then become issues for the group. More recently they have started to focus a little bit more, and the position still obviously stems very much from their own personal experiences, but it's not quite as diffuse . . .

Again, at their meeting with the Criminal Bar Association on 19 May 1994, Justice for Victims had raised points about the allocation of places in Court to members of the victim's family, the manner of the judge ('there was little the Bar could do'[26] said the chairman of the Criminal Bar Association), the payment of expenses to the family ('this was a matter wholly for the Government. The Bar could not help'), the role of defence counsel in defending obviously guilty defendants ('all barristers... had a duty to defend their clients and it was not for them to put themselves in the place of the Court'), the Bar's attitude towards sentencing, and the like. A lengthier excerpt from the Criminal Bar Association's record of that meeting, covering the first item, conveys some of its character:

Mrs Bacon (JB), Mrs Sullivan (SS), and others stressed that, above all, families of victims were seeking respect for their needs. At the moment, very little notice was taken of them, e.g. places to sit in the well of the Court were not often available and when they were, defence counsel often objected to the presence of families. Public galleries were cramped and crowded with tourists. Mr Rogers (DR) said that he and members of his family had had to queue to get into the gallery and a daughter had had to stand throughout on one occasion. RF [Richard Ferguson, the chairman of the Criminal Bar Association] said that the provision of places in court was a matter for the authorities and for the Judge, not for the prosecution or defence. Having said that, he could see no reason why families of victims should not have places in Court in most circumstances...

One of the members of Bar present felt as if there had been no proper interchange at all:

I don't know whether they were asking [questions]. I think they were telling... and they had a point of view to get over and they got their point of view over, and I hope that we were courteous and tried to put a balanced point of view, but I'm not sure they really wanted to know what we felt. They didn't want to know how we believed the system should work. They just wanted to tell us what they felt, and I think really, because they have felt such enormous tragedy they can't give a balanced view of the criminal justice system.

Ann Virgin's own recollection was:

We felt that Richard Ferguson was quite a half-decent chap, and we had a long discussion. They allowed an article that Joan wrote to go into the Bar Council's booklet, and they sent us a brief outline of the minutes of the meeting, and they did seem to understand. Since then, we've seen them on

---

[26] These and following observations are taken from 'Notes of a Meeting with Representatives of "Justice for Victims"', 19 May 1994.

television programmes as well, and we've got a complete opposite opinion of them. It's definitely for the criminals. They couldn't give a damn about the victims' families. So I think we were hoodwinked a bit there. Nothing came of the meeting.

The information pack

At his meeting with Justice for Victims on 20 April 1994, David Maclean had not wished to offer the group funding (money for the support of victims in the voluntary sector principally went to and through Victim Support and it would continue to do so), he would not sanction the replacement of Victim Support by Justice for Victims as the national organization for victims ('it would be absurd to reinvent the wheel when there's only a spoke missing'), and he would not sanction victims and survivors exerting an influence over sentencing policy. But he had wished to emphasise the Government's commitment to victims and he did seek to 'propose a constructive way forward'. It will be recalled that amongst the points made to him had been Pat Green's complaint about the paucity of advice tendered to the families of murder victims,[27] and that Maclean had offered to 'plug the gap'. Not only had survivors a great appetite for information, they also sought, on the basis of analogical reasoning, a counterpart to the materials supplied prisoners on reception. Derek Rogers had complained at the meeting that 'the prisoners information pack...is a glossy folder with leaflets telling you everything, and I think it was Christine Stewart who picked up a small leaflet [at the earlier meeting in October 1993] and said "have you received one of these?"—it was an A4 piece of paper about the police,[28] it talks to you about having your bike stolen and compensation and that is what they gave to victims' families!' The Home Office printed and distributed the prisoner's

[27] The complaint amplified an earlier submission prepared by Joan Bacon to the Minister in anticipation of the meeting: 'I had produced a report...what I wanted to do was get a foot in the door of the Home Office whichever way. I didn't want a meeting that you go away from—end of story. I produced an agenda, a target with objectives [and a] report saying [we need] a victim information pack....I faxed them through and he [Maclean] took from that....Really, we're asking for the same as the prisoners have, for the same entitlements.'

[28] The leaflet to which he referred was a folded A4 sheet of paper titled 'Victims of Crime: How you can help the Police to help you'. Published in 1989 by the Home Office, it discussed criminal injuries compensation and compensation orders, civil proceedings, and the work of the Motor Insurers' Bureau.

pack and it was only fitting that it should do so for survivors too:[29]
'We want an information pack—like this (referring to Prisoners
Information Pack), there are many, many rights there for criminals.
Nobody gave us a pack when we lost our children...', Sandra
Sullivan had said at the meeting.

So it was that three recommendations were made: an 'information pack' would be prepared for homicide survivors; Justice for
Victims would be included on a steering group evaluating Victim
Support's work with survivors, a review that had arisen from an
earlier proposal from Victim Support to the Home Office, and
which will fall outside the scope of this book;[30] and Justice for
Victims would meet the Home Secretary himself at a later date in
response to its request, later endorsed by Liberty, to discuss a
proposed charter of rights for victims.

Not only would the information pack give practical assistance
and act symbolically as a counterweight to material already offered
the criminal, but, in David Maclean's words, it would entail the
provision of 'victim input' into its drafting. Justice for Victims[31] had
initiated the project and SAMM and Victim Support were to be

[29] Joan Bacon remarked: 'we're balancing with the prisoners' information pack so
that a victim will have an information pack. Both published by the Home Office and
funded and we can have our name on the back like the Howard League and Penal
Reform [Trust] have got.'
[30] Invitations to tender for the contract to evaluate the services offered by Victim
Support were publicised in August 1994. The project was 'part of a normal review
needed in a service delivery organization', a 'normal audit' of service. It had arisen as
a result of an internal memorandum from Anne Viney to Helen Reeves recommend-
ing the review as a useful development 'alongside the new partnership with SAMM'.
Anne Viney called it important because it was an opportunity to 'listen to the
consumer'. Supervising its implementation initially was a steering group on which
sat John Southgate, former Chair of Victim Support; Jane Cooper and Ron Rodgers
of SAMM; Joan Bacon of Justice for Victims; Victim Support staff; and researchers.
When Jane Cooper left SAMM, the SAMM membership then became Ron Rodgers
and Derek Rogers. Membership was offered to Justice for Victims by Victim Support
at one of their meetings. One part of the brief would be to discuss with Victim
Support's National Office its current policies and practices in response to bereavement; make contact with the co-ordinators of victim support schemes; and conduct
group interviews with SAMM members and individual interviews with police officers. Another part entailed a small proportion of homicide survivors, a group of 10,
being referred for 'in-depth interviews' about their psychological state. An official of
the Home Office, the Government department responsible for funding the project,
took it that part of Victim Support's impetus to review its work stemmed from the
'criticisms that were being levelled at them by people like Justice for Victims who
were very scathing in their comments about Victim Support'.
[31] The Justice for Victims members were initially to be Ann Virgin and
Derek Rogers, but different people would attend the various meetings. The SAMM

invited to join them and Home Office officials in a specially-convened Working Group that would meet first in September 1994. It was a nice acknowledgement of the survivor's experiential expertise, an immediate engagement of survivors in the policy process,[32] and a recognition of the political importance of Justice for Victims[33] (and of SAMM and Victim Support). It allowed Ministers to say with perfect propriety that they were heeding the needs of homicide survivors.[34]

David Maclean had sought an inexpensive practical gesture and it had presented itself. An information pack might allow the group to feel they have contributed something and take the 'sting out of their complaints'. Ministers would have amply demonstrated that they had listened.[35] Maclean was to tell Neil Gerrard that Justice for Victims had 'identified a lack of relevant information as a major problem for families...I agree...we should do something about this.'[36] And it should be noted that Justice for Victims itself, in pragmatic style, had also resolved to make a practicable gesture: Joan Bacon said:

members were Jane Cooper and Gill Pennicard. Victim Support fielded only one representative, Anne Viney.

[32] The subsequent Home Office news release of 20 April 1994 contained a quotation attributed to David Maclean: 'We also need the involvement of the families themselves when trying to help others in the same position.' Justice for Victims had originally considered that they were not represented in sufficient strength, and had considered declining the invitation to participate, but they had done so at the urging of Neil Gerrard.

[33] One newspaper called it a 'major coup'. H. Nowicka, 'A fight for justice by the bereaved', the *Guardian*, 28 Dec 1995.

[34] It was in this fashion that David Hines of NEVA could be told by a Home Office official that, although the Home Secretary did not have time enough to meet him, he 'is well aware of the problems faced by families and friends of homicide victims. Both he and...David Maclean met members of the organisation "Justice for Victims" last year. As you may know that organisation is in the forefront of those representing families of homicide victims....The Ministers were accordingly able to hear at first hand of their particular needs and concerns. As a result of those meetings the Home Office has set up a small working group to consider the needs of homicides victims' families, with a view to producing a pack of information that will be geared specifically to their needs....' (Letter of 21 Feb 1995).

[35] On the *Crime Limited* programme devoted specifically to Derek Rogers's case, and shown in July 1994, David Maclean was to be seen saying: 'Now I believe VS do a very, very good job, but I'm also conscious that the group that met me are in a very special position. They have suffered someone close to them being murdered. We're going to set up a Home Office working group on which they'll be represented. There're special information needs there and we're going to look into them.'

[36] Letter of 3 May 1994.

That day when we went to see David Maclean . . . that day that we went in to see him, I knew I wasn't going to come out with nothing, and the only thing I could think of . . . I thought well, you know, my God, they've got packs for this, packs for . . . and I thought, but there was nothing, as you know, absolutely nothing, nothing at all for us, and when I came out of that meeting and that was agreed, he couldn't do anything else. I mean, we weren't asking for anything unreasonable. It was such a basic thing. . . . I mean I knew that you had to give them something that they couldn't refuse.

The information pack was eventually published in November 1995. It was the product of much discussion (which some had found unfocused and diffuse: Jane Cooper reflected that they were: 'quite difficult meetings, they go off at lots of tangents', and Christine Stewart said, it had been 'difficult to get the tone right'). It had been difficult to hit upon a literary style which was clear, uncluttered and satisfactory to the official and the politicians, on the one hand, and to survivors, on the other. Officials and politicians had their sensitivities about the possible responses of the criminal justice agencies (there were fears, one official said, that earlier drafts would read like 'a slap round the face . . . The consideration we have to bear in mind is that this is going to be published by the Home Office—obviously prepared in consultation with other people—and there are other agencies involved—the police, the CPS etc., who understandably would not want to be painted in quite the light that Justice for Victims would like to see them painted.'). Survivors' had had their own sensitivities about content and form. They had wanted a 'very blunt message' said an official: ' "Don't expect the police to help you", that sort of message.' And time was also spent on what proved to be a fruitless search for an acceptable synonym for the crude word 'body'. Should it be 'the deceased' or 'the dead person' or the 'loved one'? Eventually, remarked an official, 'we stuck with body because a body is a body.'

What resulted was a handsomely-produced collection of documents, published in a first edition of 5,000. It was intended to be distributed by the police, enveloped in a royal blue folder emblazoned with the Royal Crest and the seal of the citizen's charter, and fulsomely acknowledging the help of Justice for Victims, SAMM, and Victim Support. It contained information, the writing on the sleeve announced, that the bereaved 'might find helpful. We have prepared it with the help of people who have been through the same experience as you.' It contained no new statement of policy, said

Christine Stewart, one of the officials on the working group, but an explanation of 'what currently happens because that was really what people were saying. They would also like all sorts of new things to happen, but as much as anything else, the message that we were getting was that they found themselves in this awful situation and they hadn't a clue what was going to happen and what to expect.'

Within the folder were specially-drafted pamphlets on the workings of the criminal justice system of England and Wales and on 'Coping when someone close has been killed' (there had also been disputes about that wording—Justice for Victims preferred the term 'loved one', but others wondered whether everyone who was killed had been loved). 'Coping when someone close has been killed' covered the components of grief: shock, anxiety, emotional outbursts, panic, depression and loneliness, physical symptoms, guilt, anger, and hope. It was an anglicised version of an American leaflet in use in the Old Bailey Witness Service and supplied by Jane Cooper. It covered the funeral and the reactions of family and friends (the bereaved being warned that family members 'may find it difficult to talk openly about their feelings because they are scared of upsetting you and each other'). It dealt with being alone, and with resuming normal life. There was a special section on children, and the adult's need not to overlook them in one's own distress. There were other pamphlets from the Benefits Agency on what must be done and the help that can be given after a death; on legal aid; on being a witness at trial and the work of the Crown Court Witness Service; on the Criminal Injuries Compensation Board and the work of the coroner; from Victim Support on murder and manslaughter; and from SAMM and Cruse.

Justice for Victims and the Labour Party

Relations between Justice for Victims and the Labour Party, the party of opposition during the 1980s and early 1990s, ran parallel to those of the Government. The Labour Party was also moving cautiously towards a greater recognition of the place of victims in the criminal justice system. Alun Michael, shadow Minister for Home Affairs, said at the Victim Support conference of 21 February 1995 that he and other members of the All-Party Group on Penal Affairs were persuaded that: 'the whole criminal justice system should become more victim focused. This is not only right because victims are the injured party, who for too long have been given insufficient priority. It is also important because confidence in the criminal justice system is eroded when victims are dealt with in a thoughtless and insensitive way.'[37] Similar sentiments had been voiced by politicians of all parties on both sides of the Atlantic for fifteen years. What the Labour Party acknowledged was the need for information, separate waiting rooms in courthouses, and other measures to which Conservative Home Secretaries and Lord Chancellors had themselves already acquiesced (indeed, given the longevity of the Conservative Government, all the major reforms in the treatment of victims had occurred under its administration). Like the Government, the Labour Party awarded primacy of place to Victim Support: Victim Support was the body with which they would do business and would continue to do business should they come to power.

Justice for Victims had had talks with local Labour Members of Parliament in their dual and overlapping roles as constituents and members of a pressure group.[38] Being confronted by the pressure group, the MPs had shown no uniform response. Only a very small number proved to be overt allies. Ron Leighton had evidently been moved to act as a sponsor until his death (Joan Bacon called him the 'only MP of those whole 600 that gave us an assistance...'). So, more cautiously, had Neil Gerrard. Another, Ron Davies, MP for Caerphilly, had accompanied Justice for Victims on their first march to Downing Street to advertise his support for more robust sentencing.[39]

But most Labour politicians were wary and pragmatic, and particularly those who were official spokesmen on criminal justice matters. They took Victim Support to be the only authoritative body representing victims. Victim Support had proved itself politically, and that was how matters should remain. Andrew Puddephatt of Liberty recalled how he had spoken to the Labour Party's civil liberties group who had: 'definitely pushed me towards Victim Support and away from them [Justice for Victims] in the coded

[37] A. Michael, 'Putting the VICTIMS at the heart of the Criminal Justice System', text of speech delivered at a Conference organised by Victim Support.

[38] Jane Cooper and Frank Green of SAMM, it should be noted, had also had their meeting with Jack Straw, then Shadow Home Secretary, in the summer of 1995.

[39] See *Daily Mail*, 21 Apr 1994.

way that MPs can. They said "we think you should talk to Victim Support and make sure they are fully involved".' And that was to be the general tenor of advice within the Labour Party, just as it was in the Conservative Party. In September 1995, for instance, George Howarth, Shadow Minister for Home Affairs, warned a meeting of SAMM Merseyside, a body that was tantamount to a Justice for Victims local group: 'from a tactical point of view, to get into an argy-bargy with Victim Support would not help from your point of view. It would be better if you worked out what you can do and what they can do. It would be better to sort out your enmity. Victim Support has a lot of respect. To get their opposition is not going to help your case.'

Members of Justice for Victims met with Tony Blair and Jack Straw, the two successive shadow Home Secretaries during the period of this research. They were as little impressed as they had been with Conservative Ministers. Opinions differed. A member of SAMM Merseyside reflected: 'I didn't like Tony Blair. He doesn't believe in punishment—no joy with him.' But after a meeting with Jack Straw, Ann Virgin said: 'he gave us answers that we would have liked, that we would have asked him for...'

But there was also an evident reluctance by the Labour Party to concede what Justice for Victims most fervently demanded: enforceable rights to information and better treatment, and, more importantly still, their recognition *as* victims. When SAMM Merseyside wrote to a local Labour MP, Frank Field, requesting that he table questions in the House of Commons about why murder victims' families were not: 'recognised as victims in the criminal justice system, and why [they] are treated with such lack of respect within that system', his reply had been: 'I am not...willing at this stage to table a Parliamentary Question along the lines that you list. I am concerned about the general tendency in society to seek financial redress for so many events which, while deeply distressing, are not ones that should be put at the door of the taxpayer.'[40]

The second Victim's Charter

That was a hesitancy shared by Government. The politics of victims' rights were just beginning to come to the fore, partly encouraged

---

[40] Letter of 27 Nov 1995. Reprinted in *SAMM Newsletter*, Winter 1995.

by Government,[41] partly by bodies such as Justice[42] and Victim Support,[43] but also treated with some ambivalence by that selfsame Government, and with particular ambivalence in the context of homicide survivors. At stake were at least four linked issues: money, the conferment of justiciable rights, the financial and legal liability of the State for the risks and misfortunes of its citizens, and the legal standing of the 'secondary' victim of crime. The rights of victims proper have always been tenuous enough. After all, victims have no status in law unless they appear as *alleged* victims to tender evidence at trial or as the recipients of compensation from the offender or the State.[44] And the principal reason why there had been such a very long delay in putting the Criminal Injuries Compensation Scheme on a statutory footing in England and Wales, a delay that yawned from August 1964 to December 1995, was a nervousness that any legislation might possibly be taken to imply that victims of violence had a claim in law against the State because of its failure to protect them, a responsibility which Governments were loath to assume. But the eventual passing of the 1995 Criminal Compensation Act did hint at the provision of some rights. So too did the *Victim's Charter*, published first in 1990, and one of a large portfolio of such citizen's charters introduced at about that time.

There is an interesting ambivalence in the wording of the charter. The first edition of 1990 was subtitled 'A Statement of the Rights of Victims of Crime',[45] the second of 1996 'A statement of service standards for victims of crime'.[46] The foreword to the first edition spoke of 'an integrated approach, considering the rights and

---

[41] At a conference with the highly significant title of 'Victims' Rights?', held in June 1996, Ian Chisholm, head of the Criminal Procedures and Victims' Unit at the Home Office, was reported to have said: 'Victims' rights issues have been recognised in much of the present government's legislation. . . . . ' *Victims' Rights?*, St Catharine's Conference Report No 53 (King George VI and Queen Elizabeth Foundation of St Catharine's Cumberland Lodge, Windsor, 1996), 1.

[42] Justice had established the Committee on the Role of the Victim in the Criminal Justice Process in 1995. See also *Increasing the Rights of Victims of Crime*, Parliamentary All-Party Penal Affairs Group, London, 1996.

[43] See *The Rights of Victims of Crime* (Victim Support, London, 1995).

[44] The very word 'victim' does not appear in the standard English legal dictionaries: *Osborn's Concise Law Dictionary* (Sweet and Maxwell, London, 1993); *Harrap's Dictionary of Law and Society* (Harrap, London, 1989), and *Words and Phrases legally defined* (Butterworths, London, 1990). It was otherwise with American legal dictionaries.

[45] *Victim's Charter* (Home Office, London, 1990).

[46] *The Victim's Charter* (Home Office, London, 1996).

expectations of the victim of crime', the foreword to the second edition spoke of 'what sort of service victims of crime should expect'. No doubt the latter version adopted some of the new political language of service, customers, and markets[47] that had emerged after the *Citizen's Charter* White Paper of July 1991, but there had been a notable wobble that left the precise status of the victim unresolved. It was a wobble deliberately introduced as a result of a closer scrutiny of the use of the word 'rights' in the first charter. The conventional legal view is that Governments can create enforceable rights only through legislation, and that there is no such entity as a justiciable right without a corresponding duty laid on the person or agency against whom a claim may be made.[48] There have indeed been instances where the rights stipulated in charters have been incorporated in legislation, but without such a piece of express law-making the 'rights' of the first charter had no more substance or power than the standards of the second.[49]

However, it was quite possible to construct another argument, and it was that argument which had been put to the Interdepartmental Victims Steering Group that met twice a year with representation from Victim Support. Sir Louis Blom-Cooper, the distinguished lawyer and chairman of Victim Support since 1994, had attended meetings of the Steering Group in 1995 when the second charter was being drafted, and it had been his judgement that the wording of the first charter had been 'dangerous' for the Government because, in the context of the aims and objectives of the Steering Group, 'it would not be sensible to use a word that suggested a legally enforceable right' that might be taken to judicial review.

The Home Office's own view, said an official who had also served on the Victims Steering Group at the time, was that the word 'rights' had been excised because it tended only to raise false expectations. 'Service standards' was the more appropriate phrase. Indeed, the Group had originally conceived themselves to be working on a

---

[47] See N. Lacey, 'Government as Manager, Citizen as Consumer: The Case of the Criminal Justice Act 1991', *Modern Law Review*, July 1994, Vol 57, 534.

[48] I am grateful to Colin Scott and Lucia Zedner for their advice in this area.

[49] See A. Barron and C. Scott, 'The Citizen's Charter Programme', *Modern Law Review*, July 1992, Vol 55, 529, where it is argued: 'the precise status of these documents is difficult to ascertain. Formally they are of no legal effect, being merely aspirational, but they could be characterised as customer service contracts or customer guarantees and, as such, they clarify the standard of service which the customer is entitled, in principle, to receive.'

'statement of service standards' rather than on a revised charter, but, in the framework of the larger growth of charters that had started in 1991, it had seemed more appropriate to make it a 'proper charter' and 'we didn't want to mislead people'.

The second edition none the less still *hinted* at rights. Having told the victims who might read it about what they should expect, it proceeded to lay out 'what you can do if you are unhappy about the way you have been treated; the information you have received; or decisions which have been made'. There was a new complaints procedure that might at least lead to an 'issue being made' and to a demand for explanations and justifications for actions that had been taken by departments and agencies. It could be argued that, although there had been what could be construed as a retreat, there is probably only a very fine line between the explicit but non-justiciable rights[50] of the first edition and the weakly-enforceable standards of service[51] which a Government had prompted victims to expect in 1996. Perhaps the issue is practically immaterial, neither 'rights' nor 'standards' have content in law, and standards are a vague enough entity anyway,[52] but it did seem that victims might have received some tentative administrative recognition.[53]

[50] And that non-justiciability seems to be a feature of many so-called rights. See, for example, Ezzat Fattah's analysis of the UN Declaration of Basic Principles of Justice for Victims of Crime and Abuse of Power ('The UN Declaration of Basic Principles of Justice for Victims of Crime and Abuse of Power: A Constructive Critique', in E. Fattah (ed.), *Towards a Critical Victimology* (Macmillan, London, 1992), 418). Rights and principles are enforceable only if a specific legal duty is laid on a person or institution, and much rights talk is little more than a rhetoric of ideals and aspirations.
[51] The victim's charters did nevertheless set the responsible agencies to work in examining whether they had met the standards stipulated and what more was needed to constitute compliance. In the case of the probation service, for example, see J. Wynne, 'Victim Charter Enquiries', *Mediation*, Spring 1997, Vol 13, No 2, 11.
[52] See J. Black, *Rules and Regulators* (Clarendon Press, Oxford, 1997), 20. Black said: 'Standards are seen as allowing a more "purposive" approach [than rules], so affording flexibility in their application and conferring greater discretion, but also entailing uncertainty and dangers of discrimination and partiality...'
[53] The matter is reviewed by Helen Fenwick in 'Procedural "Rights" of Victims of Crime: Public or Private Ordering of the Criminal Justice Process?', *Modern Law Review*, May 1997, Vol 60, No 3. Fenwick writes about a drift to the recognition of victims' rights in England and Wales, but concludes that they are not currently enforceable. Indeed, she has some evident difficulty in finding an exact form of words to cover the position: 'At present, procedural and service rights for victims...exist on a quasi- or non-legal basis since they are contained in various Home Office documents, including the Victim's and Court's Charters. Both Charters are part of the Citizen's Charter, and therefore appear to share its obscure legal status. It

The Home Secretary announced: 'Since the first Victim's Charter was published . . . we have listened to the views of victims and learnt from their experiences. . . . We are doing all we can to make sure that the criminal justice system treats them with respect and gives them what they need.'[54] Amongst eighteen new standards of service catalogued in the new edition was one that alluded to the information pack: 'If a member of your family has been killed as a result of a crime . . . the police will give you the relevant information pack to help you.' Survivors themselves were beginning to be listed as recipients of service under the Victim's Charter.

There was to be more. Aspects of three of those new standards in that second charter were to be 'piloted . . . to test their practicality and impact on the criminal justice system':[55] the standards being those which touched on the personal allocation to victims of a named police officer whom they could contact about their case; and those which laid out that: 'The police will ask you about your fears about further victimisation and details of your loss, damage or injury', and that: 'The police, Crown Prosecutor, magistrates and judges will take this information into account when making their decisions.'

What, in effect, those new provisions and their evaluation represented was a hesitant redefinition of the victim and his or her place in the conflicts and practices of the criminal justice system, and they were examined with some attention by victims' groups. The first pilot experiment would entail the limited introduction in Sussex, Merseyside, and three other police divisions of written victim impact statements. Victims would be asked by police officers about the financial, physical, and emotional effects of crime, and the statements they made would be available at all stages of the trial before and during prosecution and before the imposition of a sentence.[56] Impact statements could have great practical and symbolic import. They could serve as the victim's (and survivor's) catharsis; a recognition of the harm done to the person; an acknowledgement

may possibly have some quasi-legal status but, as a White Paper, it clearly has no legal status. While the Victim's and Court's Charters tend to be couched in prescriptive and, in places, in very precise language, they do not provide victims with legal remedies if their provisions are breached' (at 323).

[54] News Release: 'New Charter Standards for Victims of Crime', Home Office, London, 18 June 1996.
[55] Accompanying letter from R. Cohen, Home Office, 18 June 1996.
[56] See *The Times*, 18 June 1996.

that crime was more than a dispute waged solely between an offender and the State, the Crown, or the community metaphysically conceived; and an opportunity personally to testify on behalf of oneself or those who could not testify for themselves. Justice for Victims had flagged victim impact statements as one of its recommendations in a short paper prepared for its meeting with officials on 18 October 1993.

The second experiment, known colloquially as the 'One-Stop Shop', would entail the systematic provision by a number of police stations of information to victims about the progress of their cases. And just such a dearth of information had been the frequent complaint of victims and survivors. Justice for Victims itself had emphasized the need to 'set up a specific department within the Home Office fully equipped to deal with murder victim family enquiries'.

The *Victim's Charter* and its pilot projects could be read as an inventory not only of practical measures taken by the Government but also of its definitions of victims. That was important. Justice for Victims and its confederate, SAMM, wished to ratify homicide survivors not as lesser, secondary, or indirect victims but as victims *tout court*. Jane Cooper, SAMM's co-ordinator, said a few weeks after the launch of the new *Charter*: 'the one thing I questioned was calling families of murder victims "secondary victims" because I wouldn't do that, because I think they're victims in their own right.' So too with the other groups. Justice for Victims was not called Justice for Secondary Victims or Justice for Survivors, and NEVA (The North of England Victims Association), Victim's Voice, and the rest all employed the unadorned word 'victim'. Indeed, when I chaired a meeting of Justice 'on the role of the victim in the criminal justice process' in March 1996, the very first question put to me and the others present by Paul Lamplugh of the Suzy Lamplugh Trust and David Hines of NEVA was whether we would recognise the secondary victims of homicide as victims for purposes of discussion, and the meeting did so agree to recognise survivors.

What is significant is precisely how those experiments attached to the new Victim's Charter were, for the time being, to define victims. In effect, they prescribed who was, and who was not, a victim for purposes of practical policy-making, and they made it clear that survivors were *not* regarded as victims. To the contrary, homicide survivors were excluded. They were not the immediate victims of homicide: those victims were dead and beyond reach, and they could not make enquiries, testify, or prepare statements. If Government, the Home Office and other bodies were beginning, very cautiously, to assimilate the victim into the criminal justice system, they unequivocally rejected the claims of those whom SAMM and Justice for Victims represented.[57] That was to be the chief complaint of Victim Support, which not only had a direct interest in supporting survivors, but also an indirect interest through its partnership with SAMM. Victim Support released a press statement and a briefing paper at the time of the the second Charter's publication:

...there are no plans to include all victims or all stages of the process.... The families of homicide victims are omitted although in many areas other arrangements already exist to keep them informed.... Victim Support believes that all victims should have the opportunity to make...a [victim] statement.... Families of homicide victims are specifically excluded in spite of Victim Support's experience that they are the group which would most like to make such a statement.[58]

It was that emphasis which many of the subsequent newspaper reports of the Charter were to note and repeat in their own accounts.[59] Thus the *Sunday Times* of 23 June 1996 declared that the 'Voice of the victims will be reduced to a whisper', and its claim was illustrated by a colour photograph of Joan Bacon who was herself captured by the one word, 'distressed'. The newspaper observed that attention to the fine print of the new charter would reveal serious omissions, including, in a paraphrase of Victim Support's own announcement: 'Most seriously, perhaps, the people who would most like to be able to make a statement to the courts about the effect a crime has had on their lives—the families of murder victims—will still be denied that opportunity.' Joan Bacon was quoted as saying:

We have really pushed for a victim impact statement and I am distressed to find the charter does not cover it.... At the time of the trial I drew up a letter to the court. I wanted to explain what my son's life had meant and

[57] Also excluded were most victims of domestic violence, assaults classified lower than 'grievous bodily harm', criminal damage under £5,000, and theft.
[58] 'The Victim's Charter 1996: A Briefing Paper by Victim Support' (London, 1996).
[59] For example, whilst *The Times* of 18 June 1996 announced: 'Victims will report on crime effects', the heading in *The Times*'s report of the following day was 'Murder families denied a say in victim impact statement'.

how our life had been shattered by his death, but the judge refused to look at it. It was as if our feelings counted for nothing.

The Home Office official responsible for drafting the charter reflected on the difficulties which those exclusions had occasioned and how Victim Support had 'majored' on them in its press release:

It was the lawyers really who made it rather difficult . . . It's made very clear to the victim that if you want to opt in to making a statement, they may be subject to cross-examination by the defence. Because that statement is part of the trial papers, and that is one of the great difficulties in this area, is the conflict between the ideal needs of victims and the trial process evidentially. . . . We drew the line, and this was mainly driven by the legal interests, the line around direct victims who could therefore give direct evidence, not hearsay evidence. . . . That is a major difficulty because there's no doubt that it is victims, or families of homicide victims, who are the most upset . . . Criminal justice process works in terms of evidence and [a homicide survivor's statement] couldn't be used as direct evidence in the way a statement by the victim can.

It was plain that all that work to redefine and assimilate the survivor, all those meetings with Ministers and others, had met with only partial success by the summer of 1996. Survivors remained ambiguous and unresolved entities who lay beyond the margins of the social world of the criminal justice system. Some matters had not changed markedly in the twelve years since 1984, when Ann Robinson, speaking for the newly-founded POMC, had complained: 'we're not really recognised as victims . . . ourselves. I don't think society realises the emotional devastation, the trauma. We're victims ourselves.'[60]

Justice for Victims as outsiders and insiders within SAMM

For quite different reasons, the place occupied by Justice for Victims within SAMM was also structurally ambiguous. I have remarked that neither SAMM nor Justice for Victims exacted fees, enforced discipline or expelled members.[61] Membership was entirely elective, a matter of how the bereaved chose to define and place themselves at any time. Pat Green of SAMM Merseyside and Justice for Victims

---

[60] From the videotape of an unnamed, undated studio talk programme of 1984 in Ann Robinson's private possesion.

[61] The SAMM constitution does, however, base membership on the inquest definition of unlawful killing.

said: 'we don't pay' dues, 'all those members of Justice for Victims are members of SAMM as well.' June Patient said: 'There's no difference [between SAMM and Justice for Victims]. We're the same people. It's just that they've started a group and want justice. They want fair sentences. That's all.' Gill Pennicard said: 'they're just separate. There's a separate things of Justice for Victims and it is . . . more campaigning, but then the thing is you can belong to any one [group] you wish and you can wear different hats.' And Joan Bacon herself said: 'it's like Liberty have their charitable arm and their campaigning arm. SAMM is the charitable arm, we are the campaigning arm.'

There was an antinomy. On the one hand, SAMM and Justice for Victims were held together by the common sympathies of the bereaved, which, no matter their differences, united them against the rest of the world (Ron Rodgers, then vice-chairman, and about to become chairman of SAMM, told the SAMM Annual General Meeting in 1996: 'we've all been very badly hurt by outsiders, and by all sorts of people, and the last thing we want to do is hurt one another, because if we carry on hurting one another, it will finish SAMM completely'). Members of SAMM and Justice for Victims were supposed to be bound together by the moral injunction not to revictimise a fellow-survivor, an injunction encapsulated in the survivor's word 'respect'. (It was, it must be admitted, an injunction frequently disobeyed. Frank Green felt impelled to reflect after a SAMM meeting in November 1995, a meeting so acrimonious that it had had to be prematurely terminated: 'Often we suffer through the ignorance of those who just don't think about what our bereavement is like. The sad thing is that we almost expect it from those who have not experienced our sort of pain, but at times it feels like we are guilty of the same. If we can't get it right, how can we expect it of those who do not share our experiences?'[62])

Members of SAMM and Justice for Victims were unified, as the early Protestants had been unified, by an elementary democracy born of an immediate understanding of powerful truths. Theirs was an equality of knowledge of pain. What need had they of bishops, experts, or chairmen to tell them what to know? How could one survivor, extolling experiential understanding as all survivors do, reprimand another for speaking in personal truth?

[62] 'Summary of SAMM Conference 1995', *SAMM Newsletter*, Winter 1995.

How could he or she claim, in the woundingly condescending words of the expert, to know best? There may have been differences but there could be no hierarchy of experiential authority.[63] Gill Pennicard said: 'I think that everybody's point is valid, and I think that there are some people that can be stronger with regards to speaking to media, and stronger with regards to campaigning, and there are some people that are, that can only cope with life by being an ostrich—it's all different.' One is reminded of Lawrence Friedman's description of the political creed of individualism which presumes the individual's irreducible sovereignty, freedom, and uniqueness.[64] To dictate to another would have been an imposition indeed, and it was quite impossible to expel members of Justice for Victims from SAMM during the period of my fieldwork. Indeed Frank Green described SAMM publicly at its national meeting in Warwick in November 1995 as a 'place where people can experience joy and pain together without *judgement or recrimination*' (my emphasis).

On the other hand, the relations between Justice for Victims and SAMM were irremediably laced with adversariness. If anger needs its objects, if meaning is accomplished by continual juxtaposition, it seems that members of Justice for Victims required their close antagonistic alignment with SAMM and Victim Support for symbolic sustenance. Theirs was a more florid, confrontational style which ensured that they kept themselves within striking range but also at bay, the outsiders within the gates, the unassimilated who made a virtue of their estrangement, the *Steppenwolf* of the victims movement, people whose travails had secured them a liberation from conventional restraint, the permanent critics. Members of Justice for Victims were, in effect, at once inside and outside POMC/SAMM, supporters and opponents, locked in a dialectical embrace from which they could not free themselves. Frank Green a former chairman of SAMM, said of them: 'they want retrospective change, and they want it today. Well, they want it yesterday, and that doesn't happen... They're very unforgiving people. They'll never forgive [Victim Support] for getting it wrong all these years, so I think there'll be mistrust for a long, long time.'

---

[63] See A. Katz and E. Bender (eds), *The Strength in Us: Self-Help Groups in the Modern World* (New Viewpoints, New York, 1976), 114.

[64] See L. Friedman, *The Republic of Choice* (Harvard University Press, Cambridge, Mass, 1990).

The scale of the two groups was wholly different: one was large (with perhaps 900 members) and its composition was diffuse, the other was very small (with perhaps a dozen members, four of whom were especially prominent) and it was united, and there were ensuing differences of control and co-ordination. A member of Victim Support commented of SAMM: 'as a service delivery organization, your job is to treat everyone the same. You can't insist that [it contains] only nice people.' The structures of the two groups were different. One was laden with a full set of legal, financial, and administrative responsibilities, the other was not. One was constricted in a fashion that did not affect the other.

As prodigiously energetic radicals, a number of the members of Justice for Victims were more than mere fellow-members of SAMM. They were repeatedly elected or co-opted to positions at its heart,[65] but they expressly did *not* wish to occupy SAMM's core administrative positions, to become its chairman (or chairwoman) or treasurer, not only because that would have carried with it the burden of dull instrumental work in the service of *Zweckrational* but also because, like many another radical group,[66] theirs was a stance strongly wedded to the principle of continual struggle. Their preferred role was that of a permanent opposition within the organization and its executive committee.[67] Joan Bacon said: 'I'd rather be a troubleshooter.... You know you can get too bogged down in the running of things, and no, I'd rather be the one that raises issues.... I wouldn't like to be bound by rules, and I feel that being on the committee [of SAMM] I'm not, because if I want to

[65] Thus SAMM's very first Committee, in 1994–5, consisted of David Howden as Chair, June Patient as Vice-Chair, Arthur Linsely as Treasurer, and Janet Bamford as Secretary. Amongst its other members were Gill Pennicard, Sandra Sullivan, Mike Sullivan (Sandra's husband and a *Sun* crime reporter), Frank Green, and Derek Rogers. In 1996, Janet Bamford, Gill Pennicard, Derek Rogers, and Sandra and Mike Sullivan were still on the Committee, and they had been joined by Joan Bacon.

[66] In February 1917, for instance, and on a much grander scale, the Soviet leaders were reluctant to take power. According to O. Figes: 'They had spent so long in hostile opposition to all governmental authority that many of them could not suddenly become—or even think of themselves—as statesmen. They clung to the habits and the culture of the revolutionary underground, preferring opposition to government.' *A People's Tragedy: The Russian Revolution 1891–1924* (Pimlico, London, 1996), 332.

[67] It was nevertheless true that SAMM's second chairman, Frank Green, was elected to the chairmanship of the committee as a Justice for Victims nominee, having been advised by a fellow-member of his local group in Stoke about the autocratic ways of his predecessor, but his view of the way in which power was exercised at the centre of SAMM changed after 'only a couple of meetings'.

say anything, I say it under my own steam, or I say it under Justice for Victims anyway. . . . I've got no respect for authority now.'

In 1995, Justice for Victims, appointed as SAMM Committee members, were awarded editorial control over the SAMM newsletter[68] and they were to report and advertise their marches and other events there, although marching was formally foreign to SAMM (one activist member of SAMM Merseyside asked angrily at a national meeting of SAMM: 'why can't we march under the SAMM banner? I took one and was told I couldn't march under the SAMM banner. That banner is going to stay with me until the day I die!'). The newsletter was increasingly to be given over to campaigning during their editorship and the style of their control was to be actively disputed.[69]

So it was that there, in the centre of SAMM, the two positions, the supportive and the campaigning, the universalistic and the particularistic, were arrayed and contested, the authority of office always being vested in the young Turks, and opposition to authority in the members of Justice for Victims on the committee and in the rank and file of SAMM. Of course, it would not do to argue that the ranks of the two groups were completely closed or that affiliations were always unequivocal. There was some evidence of movement back and forth between the positions as the politics of SAMM and Justice for Victims unfolded. But the metaphor of the young and old Turks does remain helpful in elaborating this narrative.

On one level, the presence of Justice for Victims was deemed not unhelpful to the young Turks. It was a goad (Jane Cooper wrote in one of her very first memoranda as project worker that: 'any developments within SAMM must keep in mind and not ignore the current climate around many recently affected by murder. There are, as you know, a range of very vocal, articulate and convincing victims who feel that little appropriate help is available and their

---

[68] The editors were Sandra Sullivan, Derek Rogers, and Joan Bacon.

[69] For example, the Spring 1996 issue of the newsletter was withdrawn by the chairman of SAMM because it was deemed too upsetting in its attacks on the Home Office and the London office (staffed, it will be remembered by Jane Cooper and a secretary, neither of whom had been bereaved by homicide, and neither of whom was therefore 'one of us'), and because it advertised a Justice for Victims march without using the title of the group, making it seem, in the judgement of the chairman, as if it were parading under the guise of SAMM. SAMM was to receive letters complaining of the 'more political, angry and aggressive stance' and the loss of the commemorative poems and the softer tone of the older newsletters.

needs are not being met. This is a challenge.'[70]). But, on another level, it also embodied the things that the young Turks felt SAMM could not itself be, standing, as it did, for the activist functions disallowed SAMM by its charity status. At SAMM Committee meetings, according to one chairman: 'Justice for Victims tended to act as a caucus... always urging SAMM to do more, to shout more, to campaign more.' SAMM's young Turks came to define themselves in their contrasts with the model formulated by Justice for Victim: they would not march *as* SAMM; they would not take 'stronger action' about the release of convicted criminals (Frank Green, the chairman, said 'we need to work within the law'); they would not publicly advertise SAMM[71] (they could not afford to do so and they feared that, even if it was supposed that they could, as an organization with meagre resources, they would be swamped);[72] and they would not bring test cases in the courts because that was not part of SAMM's role.[73]

It was the attempt to close the separation, to make SAMM over into the image of Justice for Victims, or *vice versa*, that particularly disconcerted the protagonists. SAMM could not become a campaigning body, and Justice for Victims could not abstain from campaigning. It was as if the unwelcome intimacy of the relation, the enforced proximity of SAMM and Justice for Victims, their inability to separate and carry the dialectic of fission to its conclusion, had led to a freezing of conflict and a resulting confusion that was never resolved during the period of my research. The process of fission had been arrested in stasis.

For Victim Support, the third party and SAMM's partner, it would perhaps have been best if SAMM had managed to contain that conflict and remain both a supporting and campaigning organization. Anne Viney, the Assistant Director of Victim Support, and responsible for the liaison with SAMM, observed in November 1995:

I suspect that SAMM could turn out to be large enough and healthy enough to hold that conflict of purpose... the difficulty if you split it is that you will then get people who also want help and support going to the campaigning organization, and it's very difficult to say 'well, what do I feel like today?

[70] 'Ideas re. SAMM develop a national self-help network', undated MS.
[71] Although it was listed in all the appropriate agency directories.
[72] Although SAMM was listed prominently in the Home Office information pack.
[73] Minutes of SAMM Committee Meeting, 19 Nov 1995.

Do I feel like a campaigner or do I feel like...?' You know. Because the central thing is the shared experience and the experience has a number of aspects.

For Justice for Victims, SAMM was a potentially powerful source of change, but, in its present guise, it served as little more than the enfeebled paw of Victim Support (Derek Rogers said in March 1995: 'we know David Howden has gone through hell, the same as we have, but...he is saying the things Victim Support want him to say, and he is wheeled out as the spokesman every time and that angers some of us in SAMM.').

For the senior officers of SAMM, the young Turks, Justice for Victims was an ambiguous entity. On the one hand, it could be interpreted as playing the part of the enemy within. There were suspicions of what visiting members of Justice for Victims—defined by some in the national office and on the executive committee as a fifth column—might do with information and addresses lodged in SAMM's files and database. There were fears that Justice for Victims would use names tendered in confidence to mount its own independent recruiting drive. But Justice for Victims was also useful as an expressive political force in a tacit division of labour. Take the views of two successive chairmen of SAMM.

The first, Frank Green, said of SAMM:

We should be strong on the emotional support which is our first and foremost *raison d'être*, and a pragmatical campaigning group second. Justice for Victims is obviously a very different group, and what's always irked me is that Justice for Victims has a place. You know, I've said to Joan and I've said to Derek...Justice for Victims is important to SAMM. You need the two approaches, but it's always irked me that there seems to be this fifth column approach to get, to take over SAMM, and to use it for overtly campaigning issues to the detriment of the emotional support.

Ron Rodgers, the third chairman of SAMM, reflected:

It's to a great extent...it's like shoving a boulder around this is. We're all in it. We're all around this damn thing, off pushing in different directions and we're stood in the middle of a swamp so we're going to get nowhere.

But he also reflected:

We've got two strings to the bow. Why the hell are we trying to make just one string out of two? Why should we do that? Let's have the two strings, we can fire two arrows then instead of just firing the one.

More than once, a new chairman of SAMM would enter office pledged to resolve what was probably an insoluble structural conflict,[74] only to retire disappointed at the end of his term, vowing that the sole solution was to complete the process of fission and detach Justice for Victims altogether. Frank Green remarked on the eve of his own retirement:

I've said for the last few months anyway, in any new organization you get growth, division, growth, division and so on, until you end up with a comfortable number of groups that that field will accommodate, each perhaps having a different direction or a different approach, and I think an ultimate split is necessary. . . . I was always frightened of its happening to some extent, I suppose in part because I didn't want to be the person at the helm when it happened . . . but I think that one of the things that would facilitate that is a debate on what SAMM is, and I think that has to happen, because there seems to be two opinions

Interestingly, just such a decisive process of fission did take place in Scotland where Parents of Murdered Children's offshoot and Justice for Victim's counterpart, FOMC (Families of Murdered Children), mutated into a number of groups, including the rather more pacific and support-oriented PETAL (People Experiencing Trauma and Loss). Margaret Watson, co-founder of FOMC, said: 'it's just they've got different ideas, I don't know how their meetings are run, I don't enquire but at first Kate [Duffy, co- founder of PETAL] said she would like to be an offshoot of our group [but] she's got her own ideas. So she wants to get independent and that's good.' PETAL left FOMC in October 1995.[75] Said a member of the staff of the Scottish Association of Victim Support Schemes who liaised with the new groups:

FOMC have traditionally been very aggressive towards any sort of outsiders whether that's me, whether that's the social work department, anybody from the establishment. They have taken on a more campaigning role. [PETAL] the other group, the largest of the [other] groups, have been more conciliatory in tone. They've actually made a point of that and they've absorbed into the culture. . . . [The debate has been on whether] the emphasis

---

[74] In June 1995, for instance, one of a number of special committee meetings was called by the chairman of SAMM. The letter of invitation began: 'It seems as though there are a few disagreements working into the executive, which worries me that it will create divisions which could be very damaging to the committee and as a result SAMM itself.'

[75] See *Motherwell People*, 7 July 1995.

should be on the support function rather than a campaigning function . . . and it's been a process of osmosis. People have split off and . . . found their own level and gone about things in their own way. I think they're all angry, but, if you want a frank opinion I think the PETAL people have a more realistic view about actually how you get things done.

Interestingly, too, North American homicide survivors' groups passed through very similar processes of fusion and fission in their time, but there the fission had been accomplished by a firm expulsion of the activists. For instance, what claimed to be the largest victims' advocacy group in Canada, CAVEAT (Canadians Against Violence Everywhere Advocating its Termination) had been founded in 1992 by Priscilla de Villiers, a woman whose nineteen-year old daughter had been murdered by a man released on bail. It chose to define itself (as indeed did SAMM) as '**nationally recognized as a serious, responsible, and intelligent** advocate for justice reform and victims' rights'.[76] Dawna Spears of CAVEAT told me that it had been realised from the first that they would 'get nowhere' unless they spoke 'reasonably and calmly' with the officials of government and the criminal justice system. A tight discipline was exercised over members: only delegated members of the executive were authorised to speak in CAVEAT's name and only on specified subjects. Bereaved Families of Ontario, Ontario's counterpart to TCF, laid down 'strong parameters' and insisted that its members must follow its 'mission statement' in any utterances they made. If a member proved to be 'so needy that they are stopping others getting to terms with their grief', he or she would be 'counselled out' and removed from the group to be exposed to a spate of individual counselling.[77]

Similarly, Parents of Murdered Children, SAMM's American cousin founded in 1978, claiming 100,000 members in 300 chapters in 1995,[78] defined itself strictly as a support group which would tolerate no overt political campaigning and no discussion of the contentious problems of handguns, religion, or capital punishment: 'our founders fortunately had the foresight to exclude political

---

[76] 'How CAVEAT is Working to Protect You from Violent Crime', n.d, emphases in original.

[77] The words were those of Lesley Parrott, the Chair of Bereaved Families of Ontario, at a meeting at the Ministry of the Attorney General on 12 Aug 1997.

[78] In common with survivors' groups elsewhere, it levied no membership subscription and membership was notional, based on the number of those who wished to receive its newsletter and remain on its database.

activity... This philosophy works well, giving the bereaved space needed for grief work and not isolating anyone who disagrees with a political stance.'[79] Parents of Murdered Children mounted copious campaigns about victims' rights and against such matters as specific parole applications and the exploitation of murder in entertainment. However, Nancy Munch, its executive director in 1996, said: 'we do not touch political issues or lobby. We are not a political organization. We offer support for survivors. You don't change the system, you change the people.' And that last phrase was an established part of POMC's *credo*.

Overt campaigners would be obliged to leave POMC. 'They use the organization. We tell them if they want to campaign they can do it, but they can't take the organization over... We've shut a couple of chapters down. They tried to get into California and two other states, and they've been expelled', said Munch. One of those chapters, in Pleasant Hill, California, was run by Jean O'Hara and Valerie Richards. Richards recalled:

We see Parents of Murdered Children as a first stage victims' group. In other words, it covers the trauma/grief support. Once, we've found out, and from my own experience and [my co-founder's] experience, once victims are at a point through the healing-grieving process, they have seen so many injustices done to them, secondary victimisation, that they want action. They want something done. And in order to facilitate their healing, we provide that for them.... [Families and Friends of Murder Victims] are a two stage group. We do have the support meetings and the hotline and so forth for the trauma/grief support. That is our primary function. The secondary functions are the programmes and the education and we're working on legislation to stop some of these atrocities.... POMC did some things to Jean O'Hara my co-founder, accused her of taking some political stands which she did not do. They accepted word from one person and it was like a Salem witch trial... We didn't seek the split. It was more or less we were forced into it because of the circumstances. But now that I look back I'm glad it happened this way because we can now do what we want to do.

So too with another California group, Citizens Against Homicide:[80]

I think [POMC] have a function. To be perfectly honest, I can't read their newsletters because their main function, from my point of view, is grief,

[79] National Organization of Parents of Murdered Children, Inc, *1995 Annual Report* (Cincinnati, Ohio).
[80] The group did not consider itself to be a politically-campaigning organization, but did differentiate itself from POMC in its stress on a pragmatic activism.

and . . . their newsletters are so maudlin, I mean, I can't read 'em. . . . They're full of poems. All the loved ones and all their anguish is coming out in print, and to me, that is probably very necessary, and I'm not going to say they're not a worthwhile organization, because they are and some people need that grief. But there . . . comes a time when you have to get on with your life, and you have to do something positive. And so we let the grievers go to Parents of Murdered Children. When they've had enough of that, and they want to work on legislation and go to the Capitol and testify, or help us with the parole [appeals] . . . then they come to us because we do not sit around and cry and grieve.

Conclusion

That was how Justice for Victims was to remain as a political force during the time of my fieldwork: few in numbers, significant in a fashion that was quite out of proportion to its size, heeded but not quite fully effective in the making of its demands, the outsider which could neither be dismissed nor accommodated. That, too, was how the structural link between Justice for Victims and SAMM was to remain, and it is tempting to apply very different metaphors to their relation. They were bound together step by step in a kind of *apache* dance in which the partners enacted a choreographed conflict. They were Siamese twins, together yet apart. They were partners in a Strindbergian alliance which was neither fully one entity nor two. And that, after all, was how Justice for Victims had begun, as an affirmation which was also a negation of the world view embodied in POMC and SAMM, formulated within and set against POMC.

Two of the three national SAMM conferences that took place during the two years of my fieldwork broke up in disarray as quarrels erupted between different factions. For instance, after a prolonged and angry outburst at a meeting attended by some seventy SAMM members on 'The Criminal Justice System on Trial' in November 1995, an outburst about the indignities suffered by one woman and her family from SAMM Merseyside, an outburst that dwelt in particular detail on the horrors of the autopsy and organ donation, members fled the room in tears, and the meeting was first adjourned and then terminated by the chairman who said: 'it can't go on like this, I'll have to end it. Too many people are worked up.' Members of Justice for Victims took the woman's outburst to be eloquent testimony to the depths of survivors' pain, the magnitude of their need and the impotence of Victim Support:

'she wouldn't be like that if she had help', said one. It was a stark proof of their case. Other members of the conference drew other inferences. Some remonstrated: 'we're supposed to be a compassionate organization. You can't fight murder with anger and aggression.' Some evinced regret. One member from the Stoke branch of SAMM said 'it's such a shame that we created about what we created today. To fight amongst ourselves like we've done is disgusting. I've found as a trade unionist that if you ask for everything at once, you get *nothing*, if you ask for it little by little, you get somewhere.' Frank Green, the chairman, was to talk later on the verge of his retirement:

I suppose what I'm feeling... is that I am too falling into this trap of the 'us' and 'them'. I mean, one of my principal things in... taking on the chairmanship was to actually try and consolidate an organization which I felt in many ways was probably on its knees twelve months ago... in that there was such a fractious feeling.

9

The Evolution of SAMM

Introduction

In this, the final chapter on a substantive theme, I shall trace some patterns in the early evolution of SAMM after its launch and within the environment of groups and political processes that I have described. I cannot and will not examine every detail of that history. Rather, I shall chart some prominent developments as they bear upon the larger themes of this book.

SAMM was POMC reincarnated, and POMC's purpose and ideology remained intact. The wording of a leaflet describing SAMM's work and organization was no more than the lightest adaptation of an earlier POMC leaflet, only the titles having been changed,[1] and SAMM itself was portrayed word for word in the earlier language of POMC as an organization which would supply 'understanding . . . support, information and advice, being an ear to listen and a shoulder to lean on and by being a safety-net at times of severe emotional crisis.'

SAMM presented itself in terms that will have become quite familiar. It was a grouping of ordinary people who had been beset by extraordinary misfortune (Jane Cooper, its first co-ordinator, called them 'very normal people, having very natural reactions to a very abnormal event'[2]). Indeed, so very extraordinary was their ill fortune that it was thought to fall quite outside the reach of mundane and professional knowledge, and survivors were initially at a loss to understand or cope with what had befallen them. Only those who had passed through the same experience could have any conception of the devastation inflicted by homicide, and they became

---

[1] The only addition was a new paragraph which explained how, in February 1994, the name of the organization was changed 'to more fully reflect the activities of the charity and sadly respond to a wider need'.

[2] Talk by Jane Cooper at Victim Support National Conference, July 1995.

experts *faute de mieux*, the only ones who 'know what murder is really like'.[3]

Survivors suffered not only grave problems of alienation, grief, desolation, confusion, impotence, and anger, but also all the added indignities and exclusions inflicted by a protracted process of criminal investigation, newspaper and television reporting, inquests, trials, and tribunals. They were survivors who had endured and victims who were oppressed. Frank Green told a member who resigned from SAMM in protest at its use of the word 'victim' in the place of 'survivor':

I fully understand the concept of establishing the survivor in the client, but I believe we can be victims too. In debate we established the concept of 'a recipient of continued victimisation' to express the problems experienced by such as SAMM members. Particularly with respect to the Criminal Justice system.[4]

It was only those who had become knowing through affliction who could offer useful assistance, and understanding and aid would be supplied 'through the mutual support of others who have suffered a similar tragedy'.[5] With their agency, SAMM could end the survivor's feelings of isolation and powerlessness. It could end the taboo that barred the bereaved from talking about murder, death, victims, and grief. It could end the self-censorship which prevented people from displaying anguish and outrage. It could restore a semblance of normality to the apparently abnormal[6] (the cover of SAMM's first annual report was laden with phrases from members' letters, one of which was: 'I needed to be told that I wasn't going mad'). It could act as a friend and guide (a letter to SAMM reflected: 'I needed to talk to someone, anyone who was removed from the situation, who wasn't going to tell me it was OK and that everything would work out fine, with a little time and patience. I needed someone who could understand the way I felt and would not tell

---

[3] ibid.

[4] Letter of 21 June 1995.

[5] Talk by Jane Cooper at Victim Support National Conference, July 1995.

[6] One of the prime influences in maintaining that definition was Colin Murray-Parkes, adviser to POMC and SAMM, who remarked: 'rather than saying "I'm a psychiatrist coming to tell you how much danger of mental illness you're in because of your bereavement", I was reassuring them saying "I'm not here because I think you're mentally ill, I'm here because I think people often misunderstand about mental illness. Severe anxiety, panicky feelings, are normal. You'd be abnormal if you didn't get palpitations at this time".'

me to get on with life and cope.'). It offered sanctuary and warmth in a cold world ('so important for so many', commented Jane Cooper). A SAMM volunteer remembered of David Howden, he 'gave me a cuddle, and that was the most precious cuddle I've had in my whole life apart from when I was a kid...That was the most meaningful cuddle and that just made me realise that I wasn't going mad and that there was somewhere for me.'

SAMM had inherited POMC's charitable status, and its senior officers and Victim Support maintained always that it could not and should not act as an overtly political organization,[7] although they did take it that SAMM would campaign[8] within the conditions laid down by the charity commissioners.[9] It was 'not fundamentally about the politics of the criminal justice system... SAMM is about its members and helping them through their grief and bereavement',[10] announced its Chairman in 1997. As a charity, SAMM could undertake educational work to 'raise public awareness' about 'the devastating and painful' impact of murder on families and friends; 'take up issues of concern arising out of the effects of

[7] John Davis, the chairman of SAMM in 1997, wrote in the newsletter: 'I suspect 9 out [of] 10 of you reading this are not at all bothered about the politics of SAMM. After all, the vast majority of us came to SAMM for the kind of practical and emotional support which members can offer each other—based upon the common experience of having a loved one killed by homicide.' 'From the Chair', *SAMM Newsletter No 39*, Jan 1997.

[8] Frank Green put it that: 'I am not suggesting that we become political activists, shouting from the roof tops. But I am suggesting, for those who want it that we become active. In local groups giving and receiving the support working within the agreed constitution. And at national level, to carry on with our pragmatic approach, making the system aware of our existence and what changes we need.' Opening speech at SAMM conference, 19 Nov 1995.

[9] *Political Activities and Campaigning by Charities: Revised Regulations* (Charity Commissioners, London, Mar 1994). Those guidelines are inevitably imprecise, emphasizing, as they do, the difficulties of laying down blanket regulations which could cover every contingency, and relying on the guidance of court rulings in particular cases. 'Politics' tends to be defined rather narrowly, referring to actions affecting Parliament, political parties, and Members of Parliament. One general principle is that charities should not have political objects as their chief end, but: 'There is...little direct guidance from the courts on the line to be drawn between activities by charities in a political context in pursuit of their objects which are permissible and those which encroach too far into the sphere of politics' (at 2). Charities are thus not allowed to be political organizations, but they are not precluded from political activity. It is how much activity, and how it is conducted, that count. Political campaigning must be subordinate to other ends; views must be reasoned and reasonably presented, unbiased rather than 'biased', education rather than 'propaganda'; and not favourable or hostile to any specific political party.

[10] J. Davis, Chairman's Report, *SAMM Newsletter*, No 40, Apr 1997, 5.

murder and manslaughter', and promote and support research.[11] Yet
I have also shown that that position was actively contested. In
particular, members of Justice for Victims and its allies, the group
within a group, sought to transform SAMM into a more activist
organization, and they faced resistance in their turn. Chief amongst
their opponents was Norman Black, later briefly to be Chairman and
then Vice-Chairman of SAMM, who said: 'Campaigning isn't really
the function of SAMM. We are not there as a fighting organization—
our function is mainly to listen and speak gently to educate.'[12]

The environment

Part of the work of any new or refurbished organization is to create
and nurture a network of relationships with other groups around it,
constructing an environment which it must tend, which would give
it an identity and to which it must respond. That was no easy task.
Attracting members and sponsors, raising money, taking up 'issues
of concern', and 'raising public awareness' required the manufacture and dissemination of favourable representations of a category
of victims and an organization that were barely recognised in the
1990s.[13] The very idea of homicide 'survivors' was not then in wide
currency in England and Wales, the legitimacy and public standing
of SAMM were uncertain, and SAMM's co-ordinators, chairmen,
and mentors were continually mindful of the 'credibility' of their
association, of how they appeared and sounded to others.

Take the work that was devoted in early 1997 to applying the
advice of the Charity Commissioners to the redrafting of SAMM's
constitution.[14] Members were warned that they would forfeit the
very future of SAMM if they did not approve what was done.[15] Just

[11] Statement of Aims, *Annual Report 1994* (SAMM, London), 1.

[12] In *Woking News and Mail*, 17 Nov 1994.

[13] A survivor said at a meeting of SAMM Merseyside in September 1995: 'none of
these [criminal justice] bodies accepts us as victims entitled to the same representation. We're entitled to legal representation. Victim Support is for the living. It's not for
us. The strongest point is to recognise us as victims.'

[14] *Inter alia*, the constitution established quorums for meetings and for votes (a
minimum of 30 full members) and the code of practice laid down that 'SAMM
members making public statements on behalf of SAMM must keep within SAMM
policies' and 'Members stating their personal opinions should make it clear that this
is the case.'

[15] John Davis, the new chairman of SAMM, wrote very baldly in April 1997: 'In
very simple terms, if the decision made is not to accept the new Constitution, then

after the constitution had been overwhelmingly approved by ballot, by 143 to 10, the new chairman of SAMM, John Davis, told the organization's annual general meeting in May of that year: 'I know that if we hadn't done this work, we wouldn't have Mr Chisholm [head of the Victims and Procedures Division of the Home Office] here because we wouldn't be an appropriate organization for funding.'

Funding was the Achilles' heel of the organization, and being—and being seen to be—such an appropriate organization was clearly of the utmost moment. After the first success orchestrated by Victim Support, attempts to raise money had proved barren. Successive applications to trusts, charities, the Home Office, and the National Lottery were not fruitful, and the expenses of running SAMM had proved not only to be higher than expected but, it was argued, should be higher still. There had been a delay in appointing the part-time secretary, and the position had been filled by more expensive temporary staff until June 1995. There was thought to be a need to translate Silvia Mariani, the secretary who *was* eventually selected, into a full-time position. Salaries had been under-estimated.

At the end of 1995, Victim Support, SAMM's partner, began running into budgetary deficit[16] just at a time when, piling Pelion on Ossa, and despite appeals and pleas, one of the two trusts which had supported SAMM decided not to continue doing so after conducting its annual review. SAMM had responded to the trust's requests for further information by submitting a portfolio of case histories of members who had been supported,[17] the conventional ideographic means by which survivors document themselves, but the trust had not been content. After 'considerable time ... invested by our advisers in assessing the case for continued funding in relation to the serious situation facing SAMM',[18] the trust determined it could no longer offer support. It was administered by business people who 'applied business principles', and they professed themselves dissatisfied with the the financial management of SAMM and the financial

Victim Support will cease to offer us their assistance, the Home Office will refuse our request for finances and with all probability, the national office will cease to operate.' Chairman's Report, *SAMM Newsletter*, No 40, Apr 1997, 5.

[16] The SAMM Annual Report for 1995 showed a deficit of £3417 for the financial year 1995–6.

[17] Minutes of meeting of SAMM/Victim Support Project Committee, 1 Nov 1995.

[18] Letter to author, 17 Sept 1997.

data, statements of aims and objectives, business plans, and performance indicators which it had submitted. There was some evident mutual misunderstanding between SAMM and the trust. On the one hand, Victim Support and SAMM were confused about what precisely was required of them. The trust was anonymous, it could be approached only through an agent, and communication was difficult: 'we've been told that he wants human interest stories. We gave him them, and now he wants a strategic plan', said an officer of SAMM. On the other hand, an officer of the trust proclaimed simply, that 'comment...distorts the reality'.[19]

Victim Support did agree in March 1996 to support SAMM financially until the end of the three-year project period,[20] a commitment of some £69,000, but the shock of losing funds from one of the trusts was great and it concentrated the minds of those running SAMM. At the very least, the national executive committee thought for a little while that they might actually become personally liable for shortfalls in expenditure, and attention to the forms of accountable administration became a matter of paramount interest. All three chairmen between 1994–1996 feared for the association's very survival.

In short, SAMM was intended by the young Turks to appear as an authoritative and responsible organization, and that intention had to be realised in language and gesture. Other groups stood before SAMM as examples of what to do and of what *not* to do (Frank Green told the 1995 Victim Support Annual Conference: 'we've got away from ranting and raving. We've got a certain amount of *kudos*.'). The young Turks were ever alert to signs of rejection and acceptance, knowing that they and their organization would rise or fall with the responses of powerful others.

Matters had begun well enough at the launch in September 1994 and had continued to prosper with the further conference on Justice for Victims in February 1995. To those who noticed such things, the blessing of the Princess Royal, a Home Office Minister, and Victim Support would certainly have conferred some legitimacy on an *inconnu*.[21] But SAMM was not widely known. How could it have

[19] Letter to author, 17 Sep 1997.
[20] Minutes of meeting of SAMM/Victim Support Project Committee, 20 Mar 1996.
[21] Indeed, I have already remarked that POMC had been formally acknowledged well before the launch when, with Victim Support, it had presented oral evidence to

been so? Homicides are rare and the new survivors' groups were small, poor, and very new.[22] SAMM was not widely trusted. Members of criminal justice agencies, penal reform groups, and, indeed, Victim Support have long feared an insurrection of angry victim-vigilantes, and SAMM itself was regarded with some suspicion at first. It was even eyed warily by a number of victim support schemes despite its sponsorship by their national association.[23] In November 1994, for instance, Jane Cooper received a letter from the chairman of a northern scheme saying:

A lady claiming to represent this organisation [SAMM], in this area, has recently approached [our] scheme, with the aim of establishing a long term link. She states that SAMM is an organisation within Victim Support, and working under its umbrella in offering support to the families of murder victims.... I would be grateful if you could clarify the relationship between Victim Support and SAMM, and provide any information about training or other relevant matters to enable our Management Committee to make any necessary or appropriate decisions.

It was important for SAMM and its members to be heeded and consulted—to be 'respected'—and SAMM was meticulous in keeping a tally of the organizations which had approached it for advice and which had received its overtures.[24] The tally was regarded as a direct and useful measure of the organization's influence, and it was presented whenever SAMM gave a public account of itself. Thus an undated information sheet produced by SAMM talked of how its

the House of Lords Select Committee on Murder, Manslaughter and Life Imprisonment in early 1989. Ruth Fuller, who had been one of those to address the committee, remembered: 'I was one of the lucky ones who went to that and it's good to have those experiences. I'd rather have my boy back, but that was a brilliant experience in my life. You feel as if you're actually doing something to change all that out there.'

[22] In America, by contrast, homicides are not rare, and the survivors' movement has made much more of an impact. The co-founder of Citizens Against Homicide reflected: 'I think the victims' movement here has gained a lot of notoriety and a lot of worth, because there are so many of us. You see every day we grow.' To be sure, the sheer scale of homicide was not the only reason why the survivors' movement was more prominent in the United States, a country with a tradition of populist democracy and a polity dominated by conceptions of rights.

[23] The co-ordinator of a southern victim support scheme declared at a workshop at the July 1995 Victim Support Annual Conference that 'no-one has heard of SAMM and the police haven't heard of SAMM...'

[24] In its second bid for funding to the National Lottery, for instance, a bid entered in February 1996, SAMM cited the 'Acknowledgement of SAMM's activities in Government reports and changed policies or procedures', and 'Level of press coverage' as proofs that it was attaining its stated goals.

representatives had attended the annual general meetings of TCF and Victim Support, contributed to victim support volunteer training programmes, met with Members of Parliament, and given interviews to 'serious' newspapers and magazines. Jane Cooper's talk to a seminar at the 1995 Annual General Meeting of Victim Support catalogued how Victim Support and SAMM: 'are represented on a Home Office Working Group producing an information pack for those bereaved by homicide, and we are being consulted about and monitoring the implementation of the Probation Services' procedures to consult with victims and their families over the sentencing process and release'. Successive SAMM annual reports noted how often SAMM members had assisted in training the police or victim support volunteers or had spoken to organizations such as the Crown Prosecution Service,[25] the Home Office's C4 division [later the Victims and Procedures Division], and official committees such as the Home Affairs Select Committee on Mandatory Life Sentences. Frank Green told a national meeting of SAMM in November 1995 that 'it is a measure of our success that we are now recognised, respected and consulted as we are.' Frequent and intimate contacts thus seemed to confirm SAMM and its members as experts in their own sphere. They demonstrated that SAMM was making a mark on the world. To be noticed was to be successful. To be reported was to acquire a public existence.

Yet there were dilemmas. So small an organization, staffed only by a chairman, a project officer, a part-time secretary, and occasional volunteers working from two small rooms in Victim Support's headquarters building in Brixton Road could not maintain an elaborate division of labour, and certainly no dedicated press officer. From the beginning, David Howden, the first chairman, had done 'his best'[26] to publicise the organization, and his successors and colleagues had done likewise, but they were limited in what they

[25] See *CPS Journal*, July/Aug 1995, 4, in which there is a brief description of David Howden talking to the 40 staff of Anglia headquarters. The Branch Crown Prosecutor had heard Howden speak at Victim Support 'Justice for Victims' conference in February 1995 and 'was sufficiently impressed about his story to think that my staff could learn something from him ... [I wanted him] to make the staff more aware of the problems that victims and witnesses face during the course of prosecutions. It was to heighten awareness. . . . [His] story was so horrific, is so startling, that I have to say that I thought that he would highlight the concerns of victims and witnesses in a very dramatic fashion . . . if he did nothing else I think he made people more aware, more sympathetic to their needs.'

[26] *Annual Report 1994* (SAMM, London), 4.

could do, and those limits were considered providential by many. Too conspicuous a public identity might only have resulted in a flood of applications for urgent assistance which SAMM, in its infancy, could not meet.

The activity of manufacturing a presence came to be restricted for very practical reasons. There could be no public advertising,[27] no press campaigns, no press in attendance at SAMM's national meetings, and no general courting of the media[28] in the first few years of SAMM's life lest the organization collapse under the sheer weight of unsatisfied demands for its attention.[29] More prudent was a policy of phased growth. In effect, SAMM resolved to move step by step, beginning by acquiring the forms of a rational and responsible organization, attempting to win strategically-placed practitioners[30] and voluntary groups,[31] campaigning about quite specific problems to the press[32] and regulatory agencies,[33] and constructing a web of local branches and groups capable of bearing the load of present and future members. It was the standard way of many new voluntary groups, based on conventional recipe knowledge, and it was dressed in a conventional language of 'networking', 'standards', 'codes of practice', and 'good management'.

---

[27] That was a decision recorded in the minutes of the SAMM Committee meeting of 18 June 1995. Jane Cooper, the project worker and co-ordinator, asserted that she could 'barely cope as it was'.

[28] Jane Cooper said to the SAMM Annual General Meeting of March 1995: 'we didn't do a press release.... On the one hand it was quite an internal meeting and I think we couldn't actually handle media interest because there was so much work to do.'

[29] Jane Cooper even came in time to believe that the launch had been too prominent: 'we shouldn't have had a high profile launch, you know. That should have been a bit later.'

[30] For example, copies of the annual report were sent as a matter of course to chief constables. Again, Jane Cooper was to write to Judge Stephen Tumin, then Chief Inspector of Prisons, about how best she could distribute information about SAMM to members of the judiciary.

[31] Inquiries had been received from CRUSE, for instance, in March 1995 about forging contacts with SAMM in the West Midlands.

[32] For example, letters were written by the co-ordinator and chairman of SAMM to support the BMA's demand for a reduction in delays in releasing bodies for burial (*Independent on Sunday*, 25 June 1995); to deplore the lack of public sympathy for the victims' families in the agitation over the imprisonment of Private Lee Clegg (*Belfast Telegraph*, 10 July 1995); and to protest at the sale of a video showing public executions (The *Independent*, 22 June 1995).

[33] For example, Frank Green wrote in October 1995 to the Independent Television Commission to complain about an advertisement containing the phrase 'I could murder a curry'. It brought back bad memories, he said.

For obvious genetic reasons, the design to be followed by SAMM was that of TCF, and it was TCF's example that was pursued in the construction and co-ordination of the new groups. Many of those who organized the new groups had themselves been members of TCF and had observed its methods (Margaret Watson of FOMC had done so. She said: 'obviously I've been to quite a few [meetings] and I knew what happens.'). It will be recalled that TCF had proceeded by matching survivor to survivor for mutual support by telephone and personal meeting, on the one hand, and by bringing survivors together in local groupings for collective support and mutual aid, on the other, the whole being administered by a national office in Bristol. That had been the pattern imprinted on POMC and it was inherited by SAMM in its turn. Jane Cooper informed a meeting of SAMM in March 1995: 'one of the models that I've looked at is the Compassionate Friends who have a whole sheet with county contacts and even more contacts within a county and generally they put phone numbers and they are usually people's personal numbers. Equally, Compassionate Friends has a national office.'

The other sources of recipe knowledge were also plain. The preface to an undated workplan drafted by Jane Cooper stated that it was 'based on a model used by a number of voluntary organisations and is particularly useful as it will be used as a model for SAMM's own workplan and possibly for local branches'. Those other voluntary organizations were not named, but it will be recalled that Jane Cooper had been sent to a seminar run by the National Self-Help Support Centre of NCVO in June 1988; had acquired NCVO materials in her office in January 1995 (including 'Taking Stock— Issues for Self-Help Groups' and 'Self-help Groups, Getting Started—keeping going'); and had consulted the NCVO in 1994 about the proposed contract between SAMM and Victim Support. Frank Green had attended the annual training conference of NABS (the National Association of Bereavement Services) in July 1995.

The closest and most important source of all was Victim Support, SAMM's partner and mentor, ensconced on the SAMM/Victim Support Joint Steering Committee, wholly conversant with the language and forms of organizational rationality, and enlisted precisely because of its managerial experience and knowledge of the world of criminal justice. Victim Support offered SAMM the template which it had itself adopted, a model that reiterated the themes of training, standards, consultation, codes, and transparency. Helen Reeves would remind SAMM members publicly about the necessity of constructing a 'really stable organization...of service providers', with a stress on 'consistency, good service and safe[ty] [secured by] a code of practice', and on the 'good management' of training and leadership ('that's absolutely vital if you want to stand up and say "we are an excellent organization and we can be trusted".'[34]).

The relations between Victim Support and SAMM were tangled. To the young Turks, Victim Support remained SAMM's patron, saviour, model, guide, and partner.[35] It gave legitimacy[36] and access to sources of influence and money[37] (Ian Chisholm, the man in charge of the Victims and Procedures Division of the Home Office in the mid-1990s, said: 'we have tended to operate through Victim Support in dealing with the smaller groups...'). It sometimes spoke directly for homicide survivors, acting for them in the vexed problem of revisions to the criminal injuries compensation scheme, for instance.[38] It was the employer of the project's staff. It was quite usual, Jane Cooper told a Northern Ireland Victim Support Workshop on Victims of Violent Crime in January 1995, for charities to collaborate in such a fashion so that 'larger groups [can become] the launching pad for developing ones'.

[34] H. Reeves, 'The Future Partnership between SAMM and Victim Support', SAMM Annual General Meeting, 24 May 1997.

[35] Jane Cooper described that connection as one that would enable SAMM to 'benefit from the administrative and organisational structures of VS and its more developed experience as a voluntary organisation, employer and manager...' Talk given at Victim Support National Conference 1995.

[36] A former chairman of SAMM reflected that: 'what Victim Support has given SAMM is a credibility within the system. Because of that link we were seen as a credible organization, and an acceptable organization. Otherwise we might have always been seen as something of another Justice for Victims, notwithstanding that we're not, we might have been seen in that context. So they were useful in that context.' It will be remembered that officials had reminded the Home Secretary in August 1994 that SAMM had been guaranteed by Victim Support and was therefore to be regarded as worthy of his patronage. It was that endorsement, in part, which led to David Maclean attending SAMM's launch a month later.

[37] For example, it was agreed at the meeting of the SAMM/Victim Support Joint Steering Committee of 1 November 1995 that Victim Support would give SAMM the names of suitable trusts to approach for money and that the two organizations should confer regularly about raising funds. Victim Support was willing to allow SAMM to use its name and promise to underwrite SAMM when any such approaches were made (minutes of SAMM/Victim Support Joint Steering Committee of 20 Mar 1996).

[38] Thus, in September 1995, it campaigned vigorously over anomalies in Criminal Injuries Compensation that had arisen as a result of the Home Secretary's decision unilaterally to change the formulae for awards.

But to the old Turks, Victim Support remained the shadow organization that had harnessed POMC and rendered it alien.[39] The old
Turks, members of Justice for Victims and the core of the 'London
group', were not wholly reconciled to the intervention of Victim
Support in their affairs. They continued to champion their own
special claims to knowledge, understanding, and territory;[40] and
they signalled their disapproval by such gestures as conspicuously
refraining from applause when officers of Victim Support spoke at
conferences and by disagreeing with the proposal that SAMM
national executive committee minutes should be received by Victim
Support.[41]

Locally, relations between SAMM and Victim Support were
transacted through links between victim support schemes and the
SAMM national office or SAMM groups where such groups existed,
referrals, advice, and information travelling back and forth between
the two organizations. Victim Support could attend to practical
matters and emotional support in the immediate aftermath of
bereavement, helping with advice about the criminal justice system,
criminal injuries compensation, and the mass media. SAMM could
become involved 'at a point where people with similar experiences
are needed'.[42] Anne Viney said:

If our workers are well trained, we can support families after a murder. We
can help them through the criminal justice system, particularly with the
witness service. We can help them with some of their practical problems
that may arise afterwards. What we can't offer them is that other person
who has shared—not shared—but the other person who has had a similar
experience, and that's what SAMM offers.

Physically, those relations were intimate indeed. Victim Support and
SAMM were neighbours in the same building, and there was much
informal and formal commerce between the two organizations.
SAMM staff would use Victim Support photocopiers and meeting
rooms. They would consult with Victim Support staff. They would

[39] June Patient reflected: 'there are some people who say, "no, they're not doing the
right thing. The things that are going out to the people are cold . . ." But I still say, and
I emphasise, that we need [Victim Support].'
[40] Their hostility met with hostility in return. One chairman of SAMM observed
that he would ask the old Turks: 'how much did you do to help victims before your
own experience?'
[41] Minutes of meeting of SAMM Committee, 23 July 1995.
[42] *Victim Support*, Winter 1994, 11.

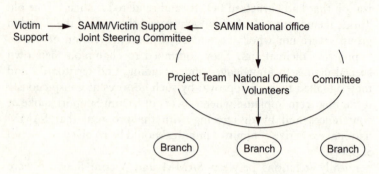

* Adapted from Frank Green's speech to SAMM Conference, 19 Nov 1995

Fig. 9.1   The formal organization of SAMM*

* Adapted from Frank Green's speech to SAMM Conference, 19 Nov 1995

gossip together as they passed in the corridors and on the stairs. Ruth Fuller, a SAMM volunteer, passed through Victim Support daily on her way to the SAMM office: 'I think they're a brilliant organization. They're so kind. When I come in that door, it's like coming home. It's a lovely place to be.'

Formally, as Fig. 9.1 shows, relations were mediated at the national level by the structure adopted in the trial three-year development project,[43] already described in Chapter 6, that was overseen by the SAMM/Victim Support Joint Steering Committee. Victim Support was the employer of the project worker and custodian of SAMM's money; the SAMM committee was the governing body of the charity; and the two organizations each fielded three members[44] on what was, in effect, a buffer committee devised not only to signal Victim Support's semi-detached relation from an independent SAMM, but also SAMM's financial and managerial

[43] The project had diffuse goals. One role of the project was to test a form of trial marriage. In Helen Reeves' words, it was designed to 'work out whether there is any permanent relationship that we could work out'.

[44] At times, said Anne Viney, fewer than three people represented Victim Support, 'because we really only need two of us and we didn't want to over-pack it with Victim Support people'.

accountability through the medium of a larger and better-known Victim Support.[45] It was a cumbersome arrangement for a small organization, and it was made more cumbersome still by endemic tensions, some members' mistrust of Victim Support,[46] and the absence of an overlapping membership after David Howden, weary of SAMM's internal wars, left the executive committee in 1996.[47] The Joint Steering Committee was sometimes represented as little more than an obstruction to effective communication.[48] Ron Rodgers, who became SAMM co-ordinator in June 1996 remarked:

The executive committee and the Steering Committee are at loggerheads, and in some ways I can understand why because we've got none of them on the committee, but that's not the problem as far as I'm concerned. The biggest problem is it seems is... it's the SAMM committee that do have the power to sign a constitution but the Steering Committee is SAMM's committee's link with Victim Support...

Membership

Because of its apprehensions about the consequences of unregulated growth, an expansion of the membership did not at first bulk very large in the manifest aims and objectives of the new organization.[49] There was more interest in securing the structures and practices which could receive the new members when the time came.[50] Frank Green, for example, observed at the Victim Support Annual

[45] The aim, said Anne Viney, was to 'inject an element of charity management experience into what happens'.

[46] A member of the SAMM executive committee, simultaneously a member of Justice for Victims, declared that SAMM was controlled by Victim Support through the Steering Committee. For its part, Victim Support insisted that 'it was not for us to say' what policy directions SAMM took. Its sole responsibility was for the limited, three-year development project. 'Where we will contribute', said Anne Viney, 'is to the policies and procedures on running the self-help network.'

[47] Frank Green observed: 'you effectively had a broken link between the executive committee and the members mandated to be its representatives on the steering committee.'

[48] After receiving a letter from the SAMM Secretary in February 1995, it was agreed at the meeting of the SAMM/Victim Support Steering Committee of 1 March 1995 that there should be discussion between Anne Viney of Victim Support and the Chairman of SAMM about 'improving lines of communication'.

[49] It did not, for instance, feature in a 'SAMM Project Action Plan' drafted in April 1996. However, the encouragement of new referrals did appear in an undated 'Victim Support/SAMM project brief'.

[50] The character of those aims is captured by 'Ideas re. SAMM develop a national self-help network', an undated *aide-memoire* written by Jane Cooper. It declared,

Conference in 1995: 'we're still very young. We could go out and make a great splash, but we probably couldn't cope with the members we attracted and we wouldn't want to turn them down. That would be catastrophic.'

Seen from the central vantage point of the small group of staff of SAMM in their national office, expansion was effectively divided into discrete stages. First would come the creation and consolidation of a national web of local groups and branches, and second would follow a drive to promote a rise in the number of new members which those groups could attract and support.[51] Of course, one form of growth was little more than an aspect of the other, and cultivating groups and recruiting members were practically inseparable activities. Besides, the founding of new groups often took place when critical masses of new members coalesced to form new, territorially-based clusters.[52] But there was a somewhat stronger emphasis placed on structures, constitutions and practices than on recruitment. And the numbers of members did rise inexorably and without any vigorous prompting from the national office.

The basis of membership was a statement, later to be signed, as an agreement to 'keep within SAMM policies that the new member has been bereaved by an unlawful killing'. SAMM's constitution held that those names were members for purposes of attending and voting at extraordinary general meetings and annual general meetings, but there were no dues to pay, no count taken of the membership of local branches, and little effective policing of who was and was not 'really' bereaved (although once or twice approaches were refused because they did not convince SAMM chairmen that they were from *bona fide* survivors).

Membership was thus notional, and the numbers quoted in different sources differed markedly. It was commonly accepted that

---

inter alia, that: 'the SAMM/VS partnership aims to build an existing good practice and develop to structure of the network. It is not to set up a new service ... I would want to see a process established that can identify ways to explore both the structure and the service.' Frank Green said at the 1995 Victim Support national conference: 'it is essential to ensure that we are on a professional programme aimed at fully supporting the corner stone of our organisation, the branch network, which Jane is working hard to develop.'

[51] See *SAMM Annual Report 1994*, 7.

[52] Members might have to travel very far to come to meetings. I met a man who had travelled 50 miles to attend the meeting of SAMM Merseyside in September 1995. One may imagine the incentives that existed to establish a more local group.

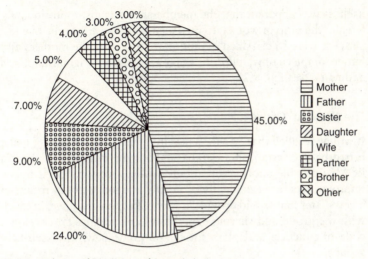

Fig 9.2   Relation of SAMM member to victim*

*Based on table in *SAMM Annual Report 1996/97*, 25

there had been some 300 members in the last days of POMC, and 250 members at SAMM's launch in September 1994. Figures of 100[53] or 200[54] more members were reported to have joined by the end of the first year. Membership was then said to have climbed steadily by some 50 a month to reach a figure given diversely as 650[55] and 700[56] by the Spring of 1995; 750[57] by November 1995; 700[58] again by early 1996; and 900 a year later.[59] Perhaps little of that variation matters very much, and enumerating members was never an easy exercise. Nevertheless the numbers certainly convey an impression of change and growth that transformed SAMM into the largest organization of its kind.

The computer database was set up in 1994, but it took time to design and more time to enter information, and it was only in 1996 that the system became effective and SAMM was able to analyse

[53] In letter to Lankelly Foundation, 23 Dec 1994.
[54] Figure given in 'Response from SAMM to Home Affairs Committee on Mandatory Life sentences', 18 Nov 1994.
[55] Given in *SAMM Annual Report*, 1994, 1.
[56] Given in letter from David Howden to the Home Secretary, 3 Apr 1995.
[57] In speech delivered by Frank Green to SAMM conference in November 1995.
[58] Given in SAMM's second bid to the National Lottery, 13 Feb 1996.
[59] Figure given at the SAMM AGM, 24 May 1997.

itself. It was apparent that the membership was disproportionately female (the ratio of women to men members was 2:1) and white (87 per cent were so classified[60]); and that most were the mothers and fathers of the victims, reflecting the organization's original emphasis and name (see Fig. 9.2).

The National Office

It will be recalled that SAMM's development project had supplied a broad brief to establish a database about the members of the old POMC; provide information about SAMM's work to its members; improve links between members directly and indirectly by means of a newsletter that would provide 'a way of keeping members in touch with the group and sharing experiences and feelings';[61] develop a code of practice; and plan, form, and guide new, local self-help groups.

Even before the formal launch of SAMM in September 1994, former members of POMC were told that the new organization had secured rooms in the quarters of Victim Support in London and that Jane Cooper was taking stock of what she was about to co-ordinate. She sought names and addresses for the new database,[62] lists of those who were prepared to support other members and speak to the mass media or other bodies, and volunteers to assist in staffing the office.

By the summer of 1995, four SAMM members were serving as volunteers who worked on a rota and acted as a complement to the one and a half staff of an office that was open from Monday to Friday. The numbers fluctuated (in 1996 there were seven volunteers, but only two were left a year later[63]). Being able to talk on the

---

[60] *SAMM Annual Report 1996/97*, 25. In 1997, Ron Rodgers did have talks with Pat Ekpo, the mother of a young black man murdered in South London, and other black parents about their relations within and with SAMM, an organization recognised to be predominantly white. A largely black survivors' group was in the process of being established in Clapham, but its role was uncertain. See 'Pat Ekpo Story', *Victim Support Magazine*, Spring 1997.

[61] Talk by Jane Cooper at Victim Support National Conference, July 1995.

[62] A database with mailing addresses was complete by September 1995, but an adequate database displaying more copious information was long in the preparation. For reasons that were difficult to ascertain, it only just became functional at the time I quit the field in the summer of 1996.

[63] Volunteers were 'thin on the ground' said the co-ordinator, Ron Rodgers, in May 1997. Some had found paid employment. 'In three years, your life changes, so there's only a finite time you can put in and I can't put too much pressure on them.'

telephone or in person to a sympathetic co-ordinator or fellow survivor was a matter of great moment to many of the bereaved.[64] Quite characteristic was a letter received by Jane Cooper from the parent of a murdered man in January 1995: 'You have been in contact with my daughter —— and she has found it a great help to talk with someone who understands, she had taken three years to get to the point of being able to even talk to the rest of the family about our son —— [who was] shot in November. . . 1991.' Another survivor wrote in March 1995: 'I felt you were the closest friends in the world. I needed you and you were there.' And yet another wrote in October 1995: 'it took a lot of tears and despair before I could contact you and I am now so grateful. Thank [a volunteer] for being such a good friend.'

The congested SAMM national office was to become something of a small social world for volunteers and members, a friendly place to which one could go to be useful and learn what was afoot. It was a place for meetings and gossip. It was a stopping point for members visiting London. In February 1995, for instance, a woman from Somerset 'dropped in' for conversation. She was being prepared by the Old Bailey Crown Court Witness Service for a forthcoming trial, and she always 'called in' when she was in London.

A discreet and oblique recruitment of new members did take place from the first, sometimes locally and sometimes nationally, sometimes methodically and sometimes in *ad hoc* fashion. Although it was not unusual for SAMM chairmen to write personally to the families of the victims of murders which had received publicity in the mass media, in the main, the staff and branches of SAMM waited for others to approach them. The flow of communication was intended to be inwards, towards the local group, not outwards from the local group and National SAMM. Those relations are laid out clearly enough in Fig. 9.3, a chart based on an early SAMM draft code of practice. There was, said a member of the SAMM committee in 1997, a doctrine: 'that we don't go out and find members. Members find us.'

Two thousand leaflets had been printed and distributed to victim support schemes and police stations in November 1994, and it was those agencies that were to become the principal source of referrals.

---

[64] More complicated problems of compensation, money, and the law and the like might well be fielded by the staff of Victim Support in their offices which adjoined SAMM's own.

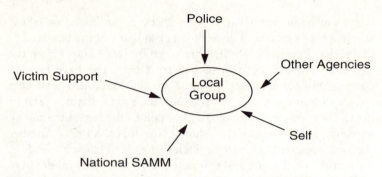

Fig. 9.3   SAMM referral system

Bereaved people wrote and called, and, in the typical instance, they would receive a long and sympathetic hearing before being referred on to a SAMM member in their vicinity and being offered a place on the newsletter mailing list, SAMM's sole register of its 'membership'. Referrals and enquiries to the national office were made at an average of forty-two a month for the first six months of SAMM's life and they continued at much the same rate thereafter. They flowed from existing SAMM members,[65] other bereavement support groups, the police,[66] Crown Court witness services, and victim support schemes[67] (see Fig. 9.4), and their numbers would be enlarged whenever there was focused media coverage of SAMM[68] or of murders and atrocities such as the Dunblane massacre,[69] survivors at large coming to learn about its existence when homicide, and organized responses to homicide, were in the public news. They flowed, it would seem, through a succession of filters. Joining SAMM, believed Ron Rodgers, were the families of notorious

---

[65] For example, one grieving mother wrote to Jane Cooper in June 1995 to say that she had distributed copies of the SAMM newsletter amongst her relatives. Such actions could lead to a proliferating membership as information travelled through informal networks.

[66] By early 1995, a SAMM leaflet had been included in the information pack distributed to all probationer police officers in the Metropolitan Police, for instance.

[67] In the month between early November and early December 1994, for instance, the office received 33 new enquiries, 28 needing support, 15 from agencies and 13 from Crown Court witness services. Minutes of SAMM/Victim Support Steering Committee meeting, 7 Dec 1994.

[68] Thus David Howden had appeared on Channel 4 television in October 1995 and a 'high number of contacts' was said to have ensued. Minutes of meeting of SAMM/Victim Support Steering Group, 1 Nov 1995.

[69] Minutes of meeting of SAMM/Victim Support Steering Group, 20, Mar 1996.

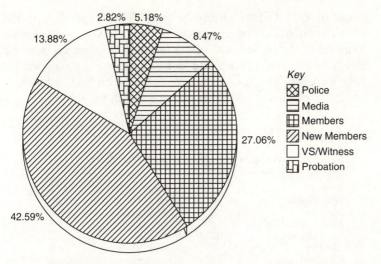

Fig. 9.4   Telephone calls received in National Office: July 1995–Jan 1996*

*Source: *SAMM Annual Report 1995*

murder cases and other families with whom Victim Support, TCF, and other bodies could not cope. SAMM was something of an association of last resort, the association to which others would turn when all else failed.

Those making enquiries were also disproportionately women. I examined the 37 'cases' of which SAMM had kept details between 1 December 1995 and 22 February 1996. Of these, 29 emanated from women, 6 from men, and one was a joint enquiry. Three enquiries were made in the immediate aftermath of the homicide, 12 within six months, and 11 were made after an unspecified length of time. Almost all the enquiries were from members of the victim's nuclear family: there being 11 parents, 10 sisters, 5 children and 2 brothers of the victim. And almost all stemmed from POMC's old heartland: 12 from London, 10 from the South-East of England, 6 from the North and 4 from the Midlands. In the 15 instances where the nature of the enquiry was made apparent, the bulk were people 'needing support' (10). The rest variously 'needed to speak' (1); sought information about SAMM (1); or wanted to re-open a case. In 9 cases a SAMM contact was assigned, and 27 were sent information about SAMM and the newsletter. Again, the original stamp of POMC may clearly be seen. Those approaching the SAMM national office in one of its earlier phases were female members of the victim's immediate family who stemmed from the area in and around London and looked for emotional support. Yet there were also enquiries from beyond the South East of England, and it was there that SAMM was charged with expansion.

Local groups

Table 9.1   Members of SAMM by area: May 1996[70]

Avon	23	Lothian	2
Bedfordshire	8	Merseyside	40
Berkshire	10	Mid-Glamorgan	3
Buckinghamshire	5	Middlesex	15
Cambridgeshire	12	Midlothian	2
Cheshire	19	Norfolk	8
Cleveland	5	North Yorkshire	2
Clwyd	2	Northamptonshire	12
Co. Durham	7	Northern Ireland	2
Cornwall	5	Nottinghamshire	10
Cumbria	4	Oxfordshire	9
Derbyshire	6	Powys	3
Devon	16	Shropshire	3
Dorset	9	Somerset	7
East Sussex	7	South Glamorgan	4
Essex	44	South Humberside	3
Gloucestershire	9	South Yorkshire	16
Grampian	2	Staffordshire	17
Greater Manchester	11	Strathclyde	14
Gwent	3	Suffolk	8
Hampshire	24	Surrey	25
Hereford & Worcester	7	Sussex	10
Hertfordshire	14	Tayside	2
Highland	3	Tyne and Wear	15
Humberside	4	Warwickshire	5
Isle of Wight	3	West Glamorgan	5
Kent	39	West Midlands	38
Lancashire	33	West Sussex	6
London	160	West Yorkshire	12
Leicestershire	7	Wiltshire	6
Lincolnshire	2	Yorkshire	14
		Total	827

The first local SAMM group (see Table 9.1) had been founded in Stoke-on-Trent in the Potteries in 1992 when SAMM was still

[70] Taken from the Minutes of the Meeting of the SAMM/Victim Support Steering Committee, 15 May 1996.

POMC[71] (that was Frank Green's home group). There were other former POMC groups in London (where it had an ambiguous existence as the home of the old Turks and the ghost of the old, unreformed POMC); and in Scotland (where it hived off to become FOMC).

At the outset, SAMM announced in an information sheet that it sought to promote the founding of more groups 'to help others to benefit from the personal therapy of personal contact with others who are bereaved'. Within months of its launch, SAMM's local network had indeed undergone a slow growth that was perhaps not so very slow given the infrequency of homicide and the sparseness of survivors. The distribution of groups was to reflect the geographies of population density and homicide (it was only to be expected that the areas of greatest population would also be those with the largest numbers of homicides (Spearman's *rho* = .72) and that the areas with the most homicides would have the largest numbers of members (Spearman's *rho* = .56)[72]). But it probably also mirrored the way in which information about SAMM percolated from person to person through informal networks, moving out from their epicentre in Essex and the environs of London.

Local groups were founded in Merseyside in December 1994 (where the group was as much a provincial satellite of Justice for Victims as of SAMM[73]); in the South-East (the home group of Norman Black, which was formed in November 1994 after five local murders were thought to justify the establishment of a local group[74]); Leeds (whose first meeting was also held with five members in November 1994); the 'South' (founded in September 1995 and meeting in Weymouth, the home group of Ron Rodgers, later co-ordinator and, briefly, chairman of SAMM); and the Midlands, founded in November 1995. By the end of 1996, sixteen groups had been established and two more appeared to be in the offing.[75] By the Spring of 1997, there were seventeen groups, three new groups having been formed and two former ones having lapsed for want

---

[71] For a description of the first meeting of the group, see P. Whent, 'What Friends are For', *Police Review*, 18 Dec 1992.

[72] I am indebted to Andri Soteri for calculating these correlations.

[73] See *Liverpool Echo*, 24 Aug 1994.

[74] See *Woking News and Mail*, 17 Nov 1994.

[75] Minutes of Meeting of SAMM/Victim Support Joint Steering Committee, 6 Dec 1996.

of volunteers to lead them.[76] New groups were then being formed in Truro, Cardiff, Hull, Bedford, and Manchester. But there were still gaps. There was no group in Cumbria or Lincolnshire and London had only 'one and a half' groups, Gill Pennicard's 'London' group based in Upminster, and a group struggling to attain viability in Clapham.

A local meeting

The groups which I observed in 1995 tended to have an informality of style, a looseness of procedure, and an unfocused agenda. They were new, and they subordinated form and formalism to the apparently spontaneous expression of emotion and airing of current preoccupations. To do otherwise, it seemed, would cramp expression, censor people who were only too sensitive to the slights of censorship, and impose an alienating structure on those who sought *Gemeinschaft*. So it was that, at the December 1995 meeting of SAMM's oldest group, the Staffordshire group, three years old and attended by twelve members, minutes and apologies for absence were taken for the very first time; a bank account was only just about to be opened in the group's name; and the group's formal name (SAMM Stoke-on-Trent) was at last agreed. There was uncertainty about other matters. There was no constitution and it was not evident whether the chairman could vote at all times or only when the membership was evenly divided.

Yet there were lesser, idiomatic conventions in use. For example, the cost of hiring the room for the meeting (£7.50) and of paying the expenses of members who had attended a national meeting of SAMM in November was raised by a raffle held amongst the members at the meeting, and such raffles were a standard source of securing funds. Again, at the end of the meeting, everyone exchanged Christmas cards, a friendly consolidation of relations at a time of exceptional strain. Formality was creeping in, but I was told that some members had threatened to leave if the group's proceedings became too rigid because it would then lose its extempore character.

The group's secretary reported a problem at the outset: a forty-five-year old man had been murdered, and she had been in contact

[76] *SAMM Annual Report 1996/97*, 17.

with the family who were distressed by the manner in which the case had been reported by the press (a member said 'typical!'); there had been allegations about the victim's involvement with drugs, yet no drugs had been found in the house. 'I don't hold with drugs,' said the secretary, 'but you've got to think of the family.' An older member of the group concurred: 'the thing is, when you come, you're just family. We don't judge.'

Next there were announcements about forthcoming events, including a memorial service for victims organized by Justice for Victims which would take place a few days later. The sponsorship of the service was not made explicit, and, indeed, local groups did not appear to discriminate with any interest between projects initiated by SAMM and by Justice for Victims: at a distance from London such distinctions seemed to become blurred, and the projects were all supposed to work for victims and survivors.

There was discussion of that perennial theme, the efficacy of Victim Support, and members agreed that 'no one can train people to feel like we do' but disagreed about whether, in the words of one critical woman, 'they're no good to us'. Frank Green, simultaneously a member of the local group and chairman of SAMM proper, a young Turk, put the pragmatic view: 'they can be very useful first aid in the first place, but after that, they need us. They aren't going to go away. We might as well teach them how to do it right.'

There was discussion about how to make the local group better known to the newly-bereaved. The secretary had devised a technique of approaching those families whose names had appeared in the local newspapers, making use of her contacts with local undertakers to pass her letters on ('and as often as not I get no reply. But they would reply when they were ready.'). There was discussion about the crippling impact of bereavement (one member said: 'all I wanted to do was go to bed and never wake up', and another said: 'you don't know what's hit you') and about the pains of ostracism. There was discussion about the coldness of employers who gave the bereaved no time off from work to attend trial, and it was agreed that: 'once we're up and running properly, we could contact people early, and we could do something about it. We could go to the employer and explain.' There was discussion about the distinctiveness of mourning those who had been killed rather than those who had died from other causes.

There was little evidence of a structured programme or of a clear orchestration of talk. Rather, people spoke when they were moved to do so about matters that preoccupied them. What seemed to be significant was that survivors were together, commiserating with one another, understanding one another's suffering, convening regularly, and thereby lending organization and purpose to their distressed lives, and the actual content of the speech that animated them at any particular time appeared to be a secondary matter. It was a moment of companionship in an indifferent world.

Near and far

Local SAMM groups were differentiated: a member of the East Anglian branch reflected: '—— [another group] don't know what anybody else is doing. We don't know what other groups are doing.' Groups could be independently-minded. There may have been attempts to regulate[77] and co-ordinate[78] what they did, but a number of the groups nevertheless clearly regarded themselves as

[77] For example, SAMM's constitution, signed in March 1994, laid down that a local branch should have broad control over its own money and affairs, but that it must also pursue the objects and policies of the national association; be 'subject to such conditions as may from time to time be laid down by the [National] Committee'; and be prevented from publishing statements contrary to the objects and policies of the national association. Again, an undated draft 'checklist' of decisions that must be taken in establishing a new branch asked whether contact had been made with the SAMM co-ordinator, Jane Cooper, to discuss founding the branch; whether initial guidelines had been read; whether an inventory of local members and agencies had been compiled; and the like. The guidelines were slow in the writing and groups persisted in complaining they had not received them. Seen from SAMM's national office, effective regulation was nigh impossible. David Howden, the chairman, and Jane Cooper, the coordinator of SAMM, complained to me in January 1995 that it was difficult to keep track of what was happening because so many uninspected dyadic relations were being formed between members.

[78] Even before the launch at the end of 1994, Jane Cooper visited branches, and held 'workshops' for co-ordinators. Further workshops took place in March and November 1995. Local branch newsletters were circulated by Jane Cooper to members in the vicinity. Further, members of fledgling groups would be introduced to those from better-established branches. For example, Ron and Christine Rodgers, the co-founders of the local branch in the South, were taken to a meeting in Sheffield in September 1995 and they 'looked at Stoke, and we looked at Merseyside, and they seemed so professional, and the way that things should be done and within the local area, so the person can come along and talk to them, or they can nip out and see them. So that's what we wanted. That's how we decided we were going to form ourselves.' Later, under John Davis's chairmanship in 1997, the SAMM newsletter would contain news of local branch activities and local branches were requested to supply standard items of information about their doings to the national office.

quasi-sovereign. A member of SAMM Stoke-on-Trent told a meeting in June 1995: 'we've been told that we're autonomous in our local SAMM branch.[79] We do our own thing', and the founder of another group said: 'I just know SAMM stood for Support after Murder and Manslaughter. It doesn't stand for anything else for me. I mean, they tell you you can't campaign under a charitable organization, but I know you can. Nobody can stop you having a voice.... If we're restricted, if we're told "we can't do this and we can't do that", we will change our name.' Indeed, by 1997, SAMM was told that a number of groups were acquiring independent charitable status.

The principle of mutual aid was, after all, embedded in the here-and-now of the little community of survivors rather than in the more abstract, remote, and impersonal notion of a national organi-zation (one member of SAMM Merseyside said: 'we're special in Liverpool. We care about each other.'). The thought of many mem-bers was itself anchored in the concrete, local, and particular rather than in the abstract and impersonal. It did not deal in general principles but in particular hurts.

The groups themselves were small, intimate, and quasi-familial,[80] the site of shared identities, subjectivities, and strong feelings, a forum where pain and sorrow could be displayed without overt criticism (Frank Green reflected that: 'I have a place where amongst friends, I can shout if I want to, curse the system when I want to, cry when I need to and no-one judges.'[81]). They had formed voluntarily and in opposition to the alienating rationality of other systems and procedures. They could become emotionally potent, acting as a catalyst of the fusion and fission which was repeatedly to join and sever people in the world of survivors. They were centres of paro-chial loyalty (one woman said at the 1996 SAMM annual general meeting: 'we raise our own [money], and we keep our own. We don't send any down South [to London].'). They embodied their very own distinct histories, rhetorics, and styles, and they frequently did not know how other groups did things.[82]

---

[79] It was not clear by whom they had been told that.

[80] A member attending the very first meeting of SAMM South East in October 1995 reported in the group's first newsletter of November 1995: 'I felt really comfort-able amongst so many people I didn't know, but it didn't take long at all before I felt that I had known everybody for ages.'

[81] Talk given to Victim Support Annual Conference 1995.

[82] Although the co-ordinators of SAMM had requested minutes and other papers from local groups for dissemination.

The groups were reservoirs of expertise and moral influence, and they were reminded continually of their authority: Jane Cooper told their leaders in March 1995: 'my work I firmly believe must always be led and and informed by you all', and later, in November of that year, she said: 'my role as national coordinator is to try to support the groups, both before and after they start . . . But it is you who are unfortunately the experts and intuitively know the value of mutual support. Often I can only support you at a distance—and often I feel I have an impossible task as it is potentially so vast.'[83] And local groups could not be subject to ready dictation[84] in a moral world which laid great stress on 'respect',[85] the rights of individuals, personal experience, the imperative to avoid the 'revictimisation' of those who had already suffered enough, and the need, in Jane Cooper's words, to 'reflect local circumstances.' A member of the SAMM committee in 1997 was to observe that the bereaved were united by a common suffering which made it nigh impossible to expel or discipline fellow-survivors.

In short, the groups could stand as redoubtable centres of local independence. Some allied themselves closely to SAMM and its project as the young Turks conceived it. Others as adamantly associated themselves with Justice for Victims and the old Turks. Others took no clear position at all. And many did not appear to phrase the issue of allegiance in national terms at all, but picked out their own distinctive stance from between the polarities of activist campaigning and support. SAMM's chairmen more than once concluded that the local groups had little appreciation of the history and doings of SAMM.[86] What were the micro-politics of SAMM and Justice for Victims to the members, embedded as they were in the immediacy of

[83] SAMM Conference, 19 Nov 1995.

[84] A common problem in the voluntary sector is the political relations of centre and periphery. Strong, evangelically-minded organizers who give their time without monetary compensation to aid those immediately about them (who, indeed, subsidise organizations) do not take well to regulation from afar. Some diplomacy is required of anyone at the centre. Frank Green remarked at the national meeting of SAMM in March 1995: 'obviously each SAMM group should run how it needs to run with its own members in mind, but in order that things are done properly, a simple set of guidelines is proposed, really, to some extent, to help people who are setting up a group perhaps for the first time.'

[85] An *aide-mémoire* for the workshop of SAMM groups in November 1995 stated: 'Probably the most important response people want will be one of respect: an acknowledgement of them as someone who is going through distress and crisis.'

[86] Frank Green wrote, for example: 'the problem seems to have been that whilst doing [many] things and achieving measures of success, I believe beyond any other

their own groups and communities? How else could one account for a woman writing to thank SAMM for the memorial service which Justice for Victims had organized in December 1995?

It was not then perhaps very remarkable that the members of local groups sometimes applied the logic of binary oppositions, of 'us' and 'them', to associations that seemed to be at once phenomenologically near and distant, the associations with which they had an intimate relation. It was precisely in that conception of otherness that they acquired their own sense of identity. Victim Support, the seemingly remote partner of SAMM, was thus conceived to be alien by a number of members. So too was SAMM's national office itself. Indeed, I have observed that not all the old Turks had been reconciled to the very idea of SAMM. There were still strong sentimental attachments to POMC. One woman from Liverpool shouted at SAMM's 1996 annual general meeting: 'POMC did alright until it was taken over by SAMM and then it went crap!!' And old Turks on the executive committee evinced unhappiness when references to POMC were erased in the opening paragraph of SAMM's revised 1997 constitution.

The project co-ordinators

Seen from afar, a handful of people working in a small space in an undistinguished building sometimes seemed to take on the appearance of a well-financed, powerful, and occasionally indifferent Leviathan set down in a distant national capital. SAMM Merseyside complained that Jane Cooper had not found it a place from which to work, for instance (although it was to find its own base with the aid of Joan Jonker of Victims of Violence[87]). And that sense of remoteness was compounded in the sentiments of some survivors. Remember that, to the old Turks, Jane Cooper was not only not 'one of us', but she was paid a salary for what she did, her payment came from Victim Support, that shadow organization, and her motivation was conceived to be professional rather than existential, calculating rather than freely-given. No matter how hard she might work, no matter what she accomplished or how she accomplished it, she remained an

organisation in our field, the Executive Committee, which acts as the national voice, has not communicated this well enough to us as members.' 'Summary of SAMM Conference', *SAMM Newsletter No 36*, Winter 1995, 6.

[87] See my *Helping Victims of Crime* (Clarendon Press, Oxford, 1990), 187–93.

outsider to Justice for Victims and some of the more activist members of SAMM. Not only was she one who had not been bereaved by homicide, but she bore with her the twin stigmata of association with Victim Support as her employer and as member of the allegedly obfuscating SAMM/Victim Support Joint Steering Committee, and she was not allowed fully to participate in all the doings of SAMM and its national executive committee.[88] To the young Turks, of course, it was quite otherwise: Jane Cooper was always esteemed by the chairmen and volunteers of SAMM with whom she worked. But I have already explained how the smallest matters could become ideologically-pregnant in the internal rifts of SAMM.

Acting as a professional manager, bound by the directives of the charity commissioners and by legislation, Jane Cooper continued to symbolise the new pragmatism to some and the new structural alienation of SAMM to others. There were those in Merseyside, for example, who claimed not to understand why she had not marched with Justice for Victims (and Ron Rodgers, her successor, was to be accused in like fashion when his time came). How could she (or he) profess to care about victims if she did not march? There were problems of access to the database which she guarded. The Old Turks wanted the names and addresses of SAMM members but, under the Data Protection Act, and for reasons of safety and reassurance[89] it was impossible for Jane Cooper to disclose the names of

---

[88]   So it was that objections had been raised to Jane Cooper representing SAMM on the Home Office Working Party that produced the information pack, but the SAMM/Victim Support Joint Steering Committee affirmed its support (minutes of meeting of SAMM/Victim Support Joint Steering Committee, 14 September 1994). Jane Cooper was allowed to attend meetings of the SAMM national executive committee on an 'ad hoc basis' and 'by arrangement only' (minutes of meeting of SAMM/Victim Support Joint Steering Committee, 9 November 1994.) She was allowed to attend the 22 January 1995 meeting of the SAMM national executive committee, but only for 30 minutes in order to present a report. In the event, she was not available to attend. That exclusion was to be removed in time.

[89]   Quite a few members were terrified at the prospect of killers being released from prison on leave or at the end of their sentence. Indeed, they were sometimes threatened by prisoners with reprisals or revenge. A number had changed their name and address (the common advice given by the police when a fixed sentence was given for manslaughter) and for them, in the words of a woman at the 1997 SAMM AGM, confidentiality was 'quite literally a matter of life and death'. One woman wrote to a member of Justice for Victims in a state of alarm because the man who was subsequently to be convicted of the murder of her daughter had been given bail and 'is still allowed to walk the streets with very few restrictions. I do not even feel safe in my own home as he knows my address and has called me on my telephone the day after he murdered my daughter.'

those who had written to SAMM without their express consent, and the database itself was 'password protected'.[90] 'We can't give out names and addresses to a [local] organizer because of data protection. And because I've done very simple guidelines, it's too bureaucratic, and so that in fact [I'm accused of] creating barriers for people...'[91]

In the guidelines issued to new groups, Jane Cooper had tried to disabuse new leaders of the idea that the London office was a massive bureaucracy by inviting them to visit her in her cramped quarters, but the dialectic of fission and the sense of distance could be too powerful on occasion. Even the well-disposed founder of one local branch called the London office 'so damn far away'.

Jane Cooper was, in fact, being worked very hard ('totally unrealistic[ally], given the pressure', were her words.) Account after account made it clear that developing guidelines, codes, and workplans; organizing volunteers; trying to establish a database; visiting new groups; raising 'public awareness'; 'networking' and 'developing links with other agencies'; approaching victim support schemes about referrals; attending conferences; speaking to the press and other mass media; preparing reports; attending committee meetings; and answering the incessantly-ringing telephone,[92] imposed a strain. She was as much office manager as project co-ordinator. Although it had been agreed that she should be 'out of the office more', there was not always a colleague to staff the office and telephone in her absence, and she became tethered to Cranmer House. In her very first report, she said frankly:

[90] So it was that Jane Cooper would inform group organizers that she could not 'hand out' membership lists, and that initial contacts about new members had to come from the SAMM office. To some organizers, that represented an attempt to hoard precious information and enforce dependency. To Jane Cooper and the SAMM executive committee, it was a matter of complying with the law. Frank Green said: 'one of the burning issues that that group seems to push for time and time and time again is "we want a list of all the members". Now, why do they want a list of all the members except to write to them and start pushing propaganda, and I'm not prepared, I was never prepared to allow that to happen.'
[91] What she could do instead was distribute information about local meetings.
[92] The minutes of the meeting of the SAMM/Victim Support Joint Steering Committee of 26 July 1995 recorded that the 'office is under great pressure and the lines are always busy'. Listening frequently and at length to the newly-bereaved in their raw grief was harrowing indeed (as a member of Victim Support reflected, a typical telephone call would begin: 'can you help? My child has just been murdered').

I intended at an early stage to conduct a review of the membership by contacting members on the mailing list ... Due to a heavier daily pressure of work than we had anticipated, from people affected by murder, from a wide range of people and organisations enquiring about our service, and from the media (television, radio, newspapers and magazines), I have not been able to begin this in an organised way.'[93]

Jane Cooper befriended a number of members, allowing them to stay with her when they visited London, blurring the lines between work and non-work, becoming absorbed into the wider informal life of SAMM, and sometimes finding it difficult to distance herself from the pain around her.[94] Yet she continued to be treated by a few activist members as an outsider who had not really been fully blooded,[95] an icon of the alleged problems of the new SAMM. She was subject to criticism in conference, committee, and the newsletter that had come under the editorship of Justice for Victims at the end of 1995.[96] She became enmeshed in the civil wars of SAMM itself ('it's not just the immediate stress, it's the stress of [other] people ...'). And the work grew in volume all the while. Frank Green observed at the opening of SAMM's first conference in November 1995: 'When the project first commenced this level of growth was not envisaged. It has brought about pressures on the office ... It should be noted that, essentially, Jane and Silvia's specific tasks are to work on the development project, but often due to ... requests for information from individuals, and other pressures on the office, in support of the organisation as a whole, they work far beyond that which they are required to do.'

Jane Cooper was responding to events rather than innovating herself ('it just all the time was reactive, and I feel ... a lot of frustration about that'). By the beginning of 1996, those accumulating

---

[93] 'Report of the Co-ordinator', *SAMM Annual Report*, 1994, 8.

[94] There were signs that, far from being an outsider, she had 'gone native' in SAMM. For instance, she delivered a most impassioned criticism of the criminal justice system at the Victim Support Annual Conference of 1995.

[95] However, it should be noted, as I have observed, that many members had taken great comfort from Jane Cooper. She was herself to say: 'the bits that I enjoyed most were starting off groups, and generally I was very well received, and probably, apart from Merseyside, not made to feel that I couldn't help because I hadn't gone through a murder. I mean, it's rather ridiculous because you know some of my best friends, I probably have more friends who've had a murder in their family than anyone else in the country...'

[96] Gill Pennicard pointed out that the newsletter team were there in their role as members of SAMM, not as members of Justice for Victims.

pressures proved too great. She suffered exhaustion ('I just got tireder and tireder and realised that so much of the stress was the work...'). Finally, induced by the attempted suicides of two people close to her,[97] she took sick leave and did not return to work in the SAMM office (although she did assist SAMM in its fundraising), being replaced in June by Ron Rodgers,[98] himself a survivor, the former Vice-Chair and recently elected Chairman of SAMM.

Within a year, Ron Rodgers himself was under a like strain. The volunteers working in the office had evaporated away, leaving him and a part-time secretary to contend with new referrals (there were twelve such referrals in the week beginning 26 May 1997 alone), the founding of new groups, the preparation of reports, and all the other matters that had so worn away at Jane Cooper. Above all, there was the persistently nagging telephone: 'I applied to be a co-ordinator, not a glorified telephone answering machine.' Rodgers had become an emblem of the 'establishment' as Jane Cooper had been before him. However, unlike Jane Cooper, what he *could* claim was that he had also been bereaved by murder and that he had won his spurs as they had done. He was 'one of us' and 'I can shout just as loud as they can because I'm just as much an insider as they are.'

Coming together

Various discontents and divergences could be multiplied when the various branches assembled in their occasional national meetings. The membership of SAMM was quite diverse. One chairman conjectured that it suffered from a twofold problem: it had undergone a long and unhappy exposure to the criminal justice system and was generally angry about the way in which it had been treated, and it 'shared absolutely nothing else in common'. Members were not united by class, belief, or politics and they found it difficult to establish communal ground about almost any issue other than the oppression of the survivor. The consequences were palpable.

---

[97] Her own parents had committed suicide just before she became SAMM's co-ordinator, a matter which she discussed publicly in a training video 'No Chance to Say Goodbye: Traumatic Bereavement and its Management', Jo Marcus Productions, no place, no date. The later attempted suicides were consequently especially harrowing.

[98] The appointment was formally announced in June 1996. Minutes of meeting of SAMM/Victim Support Joint Steering Committee, 12 June 1996.

First, SAMM did not and could not purport to speak with a single voice on policy matters, claiming instead to consist only of a collection of individuals with discrete opinions. The mechanism adopted where evidence was solicited was to channel members' views through the project co-ordinator who then collated them,[99] but only very rarely was there a corporate SAMM voice.

Second, it was transparent that SAMM nationally (and locally) was an aggregate of people and of small groups of people joined only by their grief,[100] confusion, rage, and alienation.[101] Coming together they could experience solace and solidarity: it was that which constituted the value of support in self-help, and it was valuable indeed. But there could be discord as well, a discord fuelled by a diffuse anger and its companion sense of the otherness of those lying outside the small, quasi-familial, local clusters which offered survivors their symbolic refuge. Members of Victim Support, the criminal justice system, the press, and SAMM itself were readily made alien.

It was not difficult to be cast as an other. Geographical, structural, and symbolic spaces were littered with the boundaries and markers which the survivors laid down; political positions and arguments were themselves located within the landscapes that were thus defined; agreements and disagreements came to reflect the *who* and *where* of argument as much as its *what*; and suspiciousness was rife. Take a controversy about the very definition of a SAMM member and the right to regulate membership that were debated in an exchange between the platform and the floor at the national meeting of SAMM in March 1995. It was not a particularly acrimonious exchange, SAMM had been exposed to greater conflicts in the past. Yet it did exemplify an endemic wariness not only about the motives of the central staff and executive committee of SAMM, on the one hand, but also about the

---

[99] That was the technique adopted in the submission of evidence to the Home Affairs Committee on the Mandatory Life Sentence, for example. Jane Cooper prepared a draft distillation of members views which was then reviewed by the SAMM/Victim Support Joint Steering Committee (minutes of the meetings of SAMM/Victim Support Joint Steering Committee 12 Oct 1994 and 9 Nov 1994).

[100] See G. Getzel and R. Masters, 'Serving Families who Survive Homicide Victims', *Social Carework*, Mar 1984, Vol 65, No 3, 142.

[101] The minutes of an early meeting of the SAMM/Victim Support Committee, held on 12 October 1994, reflected that: 'SAMM members hold a range of different views. It was generally felt that SAMM aims to contain and encourage diverse views on many issues.'

identities and purposes of local members and of the volunteers who sought to work in the national office,[102] on the other. Recall that, at that time, SAMM at its centre knew very little about itself and its members, and that there were few formal procedures for controlling entry to the association. Recall too that, for their part, members were cautious about bureaucracies, rules, exclusions, and rejections:

Frank Green: 'Item four, that SAMM should compile a membership application form to be completed by applicants for membership of the charity. Such a form to elicit information to determine whether the applicant is eligible for membership and such other information as it would be helpful to know to be able to identify ways in which the applicant might be able to help SAMM in its work. The wording of the form to be up to the SAMM committee to decide, having sought and considered such representation as it considers appropriate. This is proposed by Sebastian Wilberforce. As seconder, Colin, can I ask you to speak on this.'

Colin Caffell: 'Sebastian has been very very careful in wording this whole thing. There's not much I can add to it. One point was made to me this morning is that it should be a registration rather than an application form. One thought I had about that is I think one of the reasons Sebastian used the word "application form" is that it might help to identify some people who may be better served by another type of self help group—for example, people who have been bereaved by an unlawful road death, which may not be as appropriate to be in our group. I'm not sure but I think that was some of the idea behind it. Basically, it's just to make sure that people who are involved with the group don't bring us into disrepute, that's the other point away from that.'

Gill Pennicard: 'I just think that it sounds to me, the wording, I may be wrong, but I think it sounds like a means test, I don't think we should shut the door to anybody, however their views are, whatever.'

Frank Green: 'Would you accept the wording "registration" rather than application?'

Gill Pennicard: 'To me it sounds like a means testing, everybody has had doors kicked in their faces, the system, whatever has happened in their life—we should not shut the door to anybody.'

---

[102] So it was that the SAMM/Victim Support Joint Steering Committee agreed at its meeting of 12 June 1996 that only 2 or 3 volunteers in the national office should be given the password that would provide access to the membership database, that they should sign an agreement guaranteeing confidentiality, and the like.

Voicing their discontents with Victim Support, the criminal justice 'system',[103] the officers and staff[104] of the national committee,[105] and with one another, members of SAMM frequently injected rancour into conferences and committee meetings. Indeed, despite routine pleadings for mutual 'respect', compassion, and forbearance made by chairmen at the outset of every conference,[106] despite a routine expectation that anger (and a tolerance of anger) was an inevitable concomitant of public meetings,[107] all but one of the national meetings I attended between early 1995 and early 1997 was terminated prematurely because of its disorderliness. Colin Murray-Parkes said in March 1995:

One of the things that fascinates me and worries me is what I call the cycle of violence—the vendetta—I turned up in the middle of the AGM of SAMM last week and person after person was getting up to express their rage at someone. It was the police, it was the law, it was the murderers, and resolution after resolution was being put and passed with very little thought as to the consequences of what this might be and whether it was actually going to do good or harm and the poor chairman was having a terrible job—it was an unenviable position for him to be in.

Rancour could become so pronounced that a number of members of the less activist local branches proclaimed themselves appalled and

---

[103] Revealed, for example, in resolutions moved at SAMM meetings. One resolution, proposed by members of SAMM Merseyside at the annual general meeting in March 1995 urged: 'That SAMM investigate the practice of barristers both prosecution and defence, conniving together to exploit the law, using all the legal technicalities and loopholes in the law to get the charge of murder reduced to manslaughter. We the victims want peace of mind, such illegal practices do not help. The only one to gain is the murderer who is given an option he can't refuse.'

[104] The Spring 1996 issue of the newsletter, edited by members of Justice for Victims, was to be withdrawn by Frank Green because, amongst other matters, it was deemed to be overly critical of the staff of the national office in London.

[105] David Howden, the first chairman of SAMM, declared that: 'it was all the rows that wore me down in the end.'

[106] Typical were the opening observations of Frank Green whilst chairing a difficult conference in November 1995: 'I think it is important to acknowledge that I have...seen incidents of such anger and contempt between members that my sadness has been overwhelming. **We have a right to be angry, we have a right to feel pain and express it.** But the concepts of compassion and understanding for each other within this organisation, set down by Ann and June so many years ago should never be compromised.' (Emphasis in original)

[107] Frank Green, who had chaired some of the stormiest meetings of SAMM, observed stoically: 'it's socially unacceptable to talk about what's happened to us, so we shelve our feelings...We don't all see eye to eye. We're all normal. We understand.'

did not return to future meetings. A member of the Southern branch observed during the 1996 SAMM annual general meeting that his fellow-survivors had been driven away by what they had seen and heard at an earlier meeting: 'it's very unrepresentative,' he said, 'it's alright to have anger, but they [the old Turks] are going to be the end of SAMM. I'm here because of the "S" in SAMM, the support.' And his remarks were echoed by the founder of another new branch. Even the more activist members voiced their distress. At an especially stormy meeting, one said to me: 'it's very destructive. We ought to be attacking them [members of the "system"], not each other!'

Alienation thereby compounded alienation: the spectacle of the estrangement of some leading to the estrangement of others. A member of the executive committee observed after a meeting in November 1995, 'we stand up and complain about the insensitivity of other agencies and individuals and their treatment of us and their use of language, and we're doing it amongst ourselves!' Acrimony could appear perilously close to a form of symbolic violence at times, and it could be made additionally frightening by lurid stories of deaths, post-mortem examinations, abuses, and injustices. Participants themselves sometimes came to assume roles that, in one another's eyes, closely recapitulated those of perpetrators, witnesses, and victims,[108] and it was not uncommon for members to flee the room in tears.

What was done in the national meetings was, in effect, done to the body of SAMM itself. SAMM achieved great things but it seemed always to be at war with itself, a war that was carried out in the local groups and between the groups and the London office, within the executive committee[109] and between that committee and the SAMM/Victim Support Joint Steering Committee. Some members of the executive committee confessed that they would wonder at the disparity between the compassion shown in their local branches and the rank hostility of meetings in London, and vowed after every meeting that it would be their last. One woman said after her first committee meeting: 'it was awful.

---

[108] See J. Herman, *Trauma and Recovery* (Pandora, London, 1994), 217, 219.

[109] Anne Viney of Victim Support observed that 'quite a lot of the flak is coming from within the committee and whoever takes on the role of chair has a very difficult job to do, because, however you try and avoid it, you become an authority figure, and then, once you've done that, people throw mud at you.'

It was dreadful. It was the most unpleasant experience...!'
And successive chairman came dourly to prophesy that SAMM
would destroy itself. There was talk of the young Turks breaking
away to form their own organization. One said bitterly in the
wake of the November 1995 meeting: 'next year will be the
last year and that will be it'. And another, Frank Green, summarised
his own impressions of the meeting:

Two words were often used in connection with SAMM's activities: political
and campaigning. Both of which seem to be interchangeable within the
context that they are being used and it appears that they mean different
things to different people. To some it appears that there is a call towards
party politics, to others, a channel for activity within the political system in
general. Some say that SAMM is getting too political, others that we are not
political enough. I am concerned to see that a dangerous division is not
brought about...[110]

SAMM never ceased to be at war with itself.[111] The composition
of the executive committee was to be angrily disputed in 1996.
The membership of the newsletter's editorial board was angrily
contested. The content of the newsletter under the editorship of
SAMM members aligned to Justice for Victims was occasionally in
contention, especially when it criticised the staff of the national
office. The decision of Gill Pennicard to field members' complaints
about SAMM was contested.[112] There were disputes centred on the
divulging of information about members.[113] There were disputes
about the relations between centre and periphery, and between
SAMM and Victim Support. All of those quarrels were, at bottom,
disputes about the never-to-be-resolved issue of the fundamental
identity and aspirations of SAMM itself. And the social structure
of the survivors' world ensured that they were organized in and

[110] 'Summary of SAMM Conference 1995', *SAMM Newsletter No 36*, Winter
1995, 5.
[111] In July 1995, for instance, Frank Green was to write to members of the
executive committee urging them to be forbearing in their manner towards each
other.
[112] A notice had been placed in the withdrawn newsletter of Spring 1996 which
announced that, as the SAMM Office: 'is the first point of contact for new members—
and an essential line for many. We realise the importance of getting it right. Please let
us know of your personal experience in contacting the London office. Please let Gill
Pennicard know if you have any opinions on this.'
[113] One pragmatic member of the executive committee observed: 'to actually put
the names and addresses of folk in there. I mean, I was miffed, and a lot of other folk
were miffed. They should not have done that!'

around the cohesive groupings of the family and local branch, the survivors' principal formations. Quarrels could become clan wars.

The executive committee was 'hung', split between the pragmatists and the activists throughout much of 1996. We 'never got anywhere', said John Davis, the chairman of SAMM and a Police Chief Inspector who came to office late in the year.

In September 1996, there was, in Ron Rodgers's words, 'one final meeting before everything fell apart'.[114] Group facilitators or leaders were invited to London to mediate their differences, and, it was reported, such was the level of anticipatory anxiety that 'people were being physically sick before coming'. That was to be a bitter confrontation indeed, and it again broke up in disorder and threats of physical violence ('total chaos' was the term one protagonist used). The opening paragraphs of the minutes convey something of the meeting's character (the themes and names should be familiar enough by now):

June Patient	Stated that SAMM had gone wrong from the outset. Funding was only achieved by Victim Support; too much control was exercised over the Newsletters. SAMM from the outset had been controlled by Victim Support.
Joan Bacon	The last Newsletter had been agreed and then not published.
Anne Viney Victim Support	There was no Victim Support involvement in this decision. Frank Green had already blocked it because of some of the contents.
Marie Ellis Merseyside	We work on our own. Working with Victim Support but not under their control.
Pat Green Liverpool	All of the problems are within the central office.
Joan Bacon NEC	We can stand alone just as Merseyside has.
Sandra Sullivan NEC	We did not have any of these problems when we were Compassionate Friends. None of the other agencies pass any details on to us because of the confidentiality issue.

---

[114] It was one of a number of such meetings. An earlier crisis meeting of the same sort had been held in June 1995, for instance.

Irene Ivison Sheffield	There is always the complaints procedures to deal with internal matters.
Des Sadler East Anglia	How will the organisation function without a central-office? Who will provide the links between the groups; who will organise AGM and Conferences?
Joan Bacon NEC	The local groups can meet locally and arrange all that.[115]

The two factions were evenly represented on the executive commit-tee and the outcome was a stalemate that stalled its work. Figure 9.5 makes a number of the committee's structural properties clear: first, there were alliances based on family; second, there were alliances based on political affiliation (for example, Justice for Victims and its allies were always well represented on the committee); and third, there was a progressive shift in the balance of power over time from the old to the young Turks. In November 1996, an EGM (extra-ordinary general meeting) of the committee was convened at Stoke. Bernie Davis, who was to become a member of that committee at that time, recalled:

There was nothing being done, and the committee was totally split, and no decisions were being taken.... Really, the committee wasn't going any-where. They decided that the only real way forward was to have an EGM, and the purpose of the EGM was for everybody to stand down and have a re-election. The whole thing was bizarre because ... one party said 'we'll never stand down' ... [and] the others were saying, 'if you don't stand down, we're not'. So you've got the bizarre situation where we're having this EGM to select a new committee but nobody's going to step down.... John [Davis] said 'you can actually solve this problem now by co-opting', and they wouldn't co-opt [at first].... But the decision was taken by the members that were there that it was going to be, that no decisions were actually going to be voted on, but the people that were there would go on the committee, because they'd got no other choice.... There were only four nominations to go on the committee. There was the three of us [John and Bernie Davis, and Desmond Sadler, all from East Anglia]. [Another] put in later.... We've got a working majority trying to go forward now...

One family bloc of young Turks there aligned itself with another, John and Bernie Davis joining Ron Rodgers, Ron Rodgers's wife, Christine, and Jeffrey Rodgers's former girlfriend, Hazel Spencer. Together, they contributed to a shift in what one called 'the weight

[115] 'Questions + Answers session, SAMM Regional Groups Meeting', 7 Sept 1996.

1994

Young Turks and their affiliates	Old Turks and their affiliates	Non-aligned*
Officers		
David Howden (Chair)	June Patient (Vice-Chair)	
Arthur Linsley (Treasurer)	Jane Bamford (Secretary)	
Committee		
Lilly Collett	Gill Pennicard	
Frank Green	Sandra Sullivan	

1995

Officers		
Frank Green (Chair)		
Ron Rodgers (Vice-Chair)	Janet Bamford	
Kate Gane (Treasurer)	(Secretary)	
David Howden (Publicity Officer)		
Committee		
Arthur Linsley	Joan bacon	
Valerie Kavanagh	Gill Pennicard	
Michael Yorath	Derek Rogers	
	⌐Mike Sullivan	
	⌊Sandra Sullivan	

First Committee

1996

Officers		
⌐ Ron Rodgers (Chair)		
Norman Black (Vice-Chair)		
Kate Gane (Treasurer)		
David Howden (Publicity Officer)		
Committe		
Maxine Meadows	Joan Bacom	Moria Windass
Simon Phillips	Irene Ivison	Clare Pearce
⌐ Christine Rodgers	Derek Rogers	
⌊ Hazel Spencer	Sandra Sullivan	

**Second Committee
(After November 1996)**

Officers		
⌐ Ron Rodgers (Co-ordinator)	Janet Bamford	Graham Hawkins
Joan Davis (Chair)		(Treastee)
Bernie Davis (Treastee)		
Des Sadler (Secretary)		
	Joan Bacon	
Committee	Irene ivison	
Maxine Meadows	Gill Pennicard	Moria Windass
Simon Phillips	Derek Rozers	
⌐ Christine Rodgers	Sandra Sullivan	
⌊ Hazel Spencer		

—— = family
Connection

* Members who were unaligned or whose position was not Clear

Fig 9.5   Composition of the SAMM committee

of the voting to go forwards, and not to go down the road of campaigning, which was what we were trying to achieve, really'.[116] A member of the winning faction remarked: 'since then, there's been a lot of work done. Every time there's a show of hands, [Justice for Victims] has been outvoted.' By the summer of 1997, a new agreement had been drafted between SAMM and Victim Support, and SAMM had adopted a Code of Practice.

For Justice for Victims, it had been a terrible time. They had been ousted from the executive committee. They had lost the secretaryship. They had resigned from the editorial board of the newsletter after group leaders had protested at the public disclosure of their names and addresses (number 38, 'long delay[ed] ... due to circumstances outside of [the board's] control',[117] and published in the summer of 1996, was the last to appear under their names). For Justice for Victims, in Joan Bacon's phrase, SAMM had become 'a quango directed by Helen Reeves'. And another member concluded sadly: 'the story lies more in the beginning than in the end. We don't even recognise the group now. It's all rules, codes, regulations.'

The small, forty-two strong, 1997 AGM ended peaceably, and that was in part because the radicals of SAMM Merseyside had been 'let down' by their transport and were not present, and in part because Ian Chisholm of the Home Office, a very embodiment of 'the system', addressed at the meeting as 'Minister', had served to catch the flak which might otherwise have been directed at the committee (which, said John Davis, the chairman, 'hadn't really been the intention'). Four members of the meeting did roundly criticise Chisholm for failures of sentencing and compensation and for the lack of parity between victims and offenders in matters of legal aid. (The question of legal aid had arisen because newspapers had carried the mischievous story that a Tunisian, sentenced to life imprisonment in the Wolds prison, had secured help to go to law because he had been denied his breakfast during a prison officers' strike.) One of the four, Sandra Sullivan, was to protest: 'a prisoner is allowed to sue. Where do you stand? ... Basically don't victims have rights? Victims can't afford help and they don't get legal aid.

---

[116] Gill Pennicard held that a system of proxy voting introduced by John Davis had also contributed to the outvoting of Justice for Victims.

[117] *SAMM Newsletter No 38*, Summer 1996. The 'circumstances' were the row about the publicisation of a Justice for Victims march and criticisms made of the staff of the national office, a row that had led to the withdrawal of the first draft issue.

When is the Home Office going to wake up and support us?!'
Sandra Sullivan told him that when members of SAMM had visited
the Home Office, they had been informed that: 'we're not here
for you'. Chisholm was asked questions about the release of
Myra Hindley ('do you want us to commit a crime in order to get
help?!').

To be sure, familiar criticism was also directed at the SAMM
executive committee for not being more activist. The committee
was accused of censoring the newsletter ('everybody's got a right
to their views and none of us are criminals!'). It was accused of
being indifferent to victims' rights. It was said to be indifferent to
campaigning. When John Davis, the chairman, declared: 'we're not
here fundamentally to go on campaigns; we're here to support
members; there are other organizations out there that will take
[issues] up', Sandra Sullivan asked: 'if you don't take up cases,
why should people come?' When John Davis observed: 'we've all
been damaged, we've all been scorned, and one of the consequences
is we've become less tolerant of others', Sandra Sullivan demanded:
'why do we love to fight? Why aren't the rights there?' But, in the
main, SAMM did abstain from devouring itself at that meeting in
May 1997.

Conclusion

SAMM's civil wars had not come to an end by the time at which I
write in the summer of 1997. SAMM will probably not become an
adamantly activist organization, but it was not allowed to forget the
possibilities of activism. Neither was it given wholly to support and
advice, and it was not allowed to move unequivocally in that direction. There were no plans to expel dissidents or to carve a unitary
SAMM into segments that could work apart and at a safe distance
from one another. Neither was Justice for Victims likely to become a
more detached or less determined organization. Rather, like Mexico's governing Party of Institutionalised Revolution, SAMM will
continue to be beset by its internal contradictions.[118]

[118] Although the beginnings of a tighter discipline were becoming evident in 1997.
One instance was the refusal of SAMM to accede to a request from Norman Brennan
of the Victims of Crime Trust, a British Transport police officer who was not a
member of SAMM, to distribute to its members a letter deemed by John Davis to
be libellous.

SAMM will continue to be storm-tossed, blown around by chance changes in funding, sponsors, or the balance of power and factions on its committees. People would join the organization, make their mark, but then leave or retire to play a lesser role, tired, disappointed, or wishing to 'move on'. David Howden, a gentle man, was just such a one. So was Frank Green, a constitutionalist and a pragmatist. They were largely lost to SAMM, and their immediate influence was lost with them. John Davis observed in June 1997: 'it's still on a knife edge ... because it's in the nature of SAMM that a lot of people will not stay long. They'll take out of it what they need and they'll move on.'

More important, perhaps, there is no likely end to SAMM's endemic contradictions, the cross-currents that tugged continually at the association. Ron Rodgers, once a naval man, adopted an apt boating simile in May 1997 to capture its progress: 'things are still very fluid. It's like being in a rowing boat on a river. One moment, you're floating smoothly and then you hit unexpected eddies.'

10

Conclusion

I'll say that madness, a certain kind of madness, often goes hand in hand with poetry. It would be very difficult for predominantly rational people to be poets, and perhaps it is just as difficult for poets to be rational. Yet reason gets the upper hand, and it is reason, the mainstay of justice, that must govern the world.[1]

For decades penal reformers and policy-makers in England and Wales were haunted by the spectre of angry victims of violence, the victim-vigilantes who would storm out like latterday *sans-culottes* to wreak a terrible revenge[2] and undo all their liberal reforms. 'The road from victims' rights to the chamber of death is short', wrote Joe Rogaly portentously: 'If you doubt it, ask Timothy McVeigh.'[3] Criminal injuries compensation was devised in part in the 1950s and 1960s to appease those victims, who, like Orestes, were thought to be bent on a 'blood-hunt, [a] persecution, [driven by] a fiend of vengeance...' Yet no victim had ever effectively expressed a public wish for monetary restitution.[4] The reparative justice movement of the 1970s and 1980s was motivated in part by a desire to 'demystify' and assuage the angry victim's apprehensions about an offender who was thought to have grown over-large in a fearful imagination. But victims manifested no obvious wish for reparation and mediation. It was almost as if, in their own fearfulness, reformers had constructed a new monster, a twentieth-century harpy, who could spoil all their work.

---

[1] P. Neruda, *Memoirs* (London, 1978), 41.

[2] See for example, C. H. Rolph, 'Wild Justice', *New Statesman*, 18 Jan 1958.

[3] 'Keep the rod of justice in the right hands', *Financial Times*, 7,8 June 1997. (McVeigh was the man convicted of the bombing of a federal government building in Oklahoma City. The penalty for his crime was determined by the jury in his trial in Colorado). Rogaly predicted that the introduction of victims' rights and victim impact statements would bring about the demise of justice.

[4] See my *Helping Victims of Crime* (Clarendon Press, Oxford, 1990), ch 2.

In fact, very few 'angry victims' of violence did ever actually make their presence felt in the world of the politics of criminal justice. They were not consulted, polled, or investigated until the mid-1970s (indeed the very idea of talking to them occasioned some political nervousness). They did not themselves come forward. Perhaps they had been too immobilised by the impact of crime to become activists; perhaps they remained isolated from one another and lacked a consciousness of themselves as a collectivity; perhaps talk about victims' rights was, and, despite the vacillations of the wording of the *Victim's Charter*, still is premature in the United Kingdom where rights are not easily won or bestowed;[5] and perhaps they identified themselves by some other term than 'victim', choosing to call themselves 'disabled', 'blind', or 'handicapped' instead. And those victims of violence who did eventually come to define

---

[5] Rights do not seem to play much of a role in states which provide extensive social services and/or lack a written constitution. See M. Joutsen, *The Role of the Victim of Crime in European Criminal Justice Systems: A Crossnational Study of the Role of the Victim* (HEUNI, Helsinki, Finland, 1987) 281–2; J. Shapland, 'Fiefs and Peasants: Accomplishing Change for Victims in the Criminal Justice System', in M. Maguire and J. Pointing (eds), *Victims of Crime: A New Deal?* (Open University Press, 1988); and E. Viano, 'Victimology: A New Focus of Research and Practice', in *Victim's Rights and Legal Reforms: International Perspectives* (Antigua Universidad de Oñati, Gipuzkoa, Spain, 1991), 21. Yet there are fewer legal rights for victims in the United Kingdom than in many other jurisdictions (see H. Fenwick, 'Procedural "Rights" of Victims of Crime', *Modern Law Review*, May 1997, Vol 60, No 3, 333). Those rights that are conferred or advocated elsewhere, by the Council of Europe, for instance, tend often to be as imprecise as their counterpart in the UK. For example, on inspection, the Council of Europe Committee of Recommendations Nos R (83) 7 (on participation of the public in crime policy) and R (85) 11 (on the position of the victim in the framework of criminal law and procedure) are legally as obscure as anything in this country. They tend to recommend the extension of greater sensitivity and sympathy in the criminal justice rather than precise, enforceable rights. British and European victims certainly enjoy fewer rights than in America, where rights generally play a much larger part in discourse and procedure. Dworkin observed that: 'The language of rights now dominates political debate in the United States' (R. Dworkin, *Taking Rights Seriously* (Duckworth, London, 1994) 184). Victims' rights have been entrenched in a growing number of laws in America since the first, passed in Wisconsin in 1980. By 1989, 42 states had 'victim bills of rights' which share the common features of i) the non-justiciable right to treated with dignity, respect, and compassion; ii) the right to be present at bail hearings, sentencing, probation revocation hearings, and parole hearings; iii) the right to protection from intimidation (although it is uncertain what protection can really be afforded); iv) and the right to compensation or restitution. Those rights can be exercised in the normal case only if they do not interfere with the rights of the accused, and they cannot create the basis of an action for monetary damages against the state, county, or muncipality. (I have taken this information from F. Weed, *Certainty of Justice: Reform in the Crime Victim Movement* (Aldine de Gruyter, New York, 1995), ch 1).

themselves politically adopted a language which pointed away from crime, victims, and the criminal justice system. They were caught up in the feminist politics of the 1970s and 1980s which portrayed the victims of rape, incest, sexual abuse, and domestic violence as the survivors of patriarchal oppression, and that was a different sort of politics altogether.

Ironically, when the time came, those who were to be called 'angry victims' took another guise and were barely acknowledged as victims.[6] Instead of being the direct victims of violence, they were the 'indirect' or 'secondary' victims or survivors who had been bereaved by homicide. If victims proper had had a hard enough task of being recognised and placed,[7] those 'secondary' victims of crime were a marginal group indeed.[8] They did not even have an agreed name.

Homicide survivors were to encounter one another within the structures prepared by the politically catholic self-help and mutual aid movements of the 1960s. Again and again, they described their meetings as a revelation or an epiphany. Ann Robinson, first of the line of those who experienced that epiphany, was to say:

> It's just so therapeutic to be able to talk to other parents who want to hear about your child and your feelings, who are willing to listen. You can share experiences. The empathy

[6] They were nevertheless greeted with some trepidation by penal reformers in the 1990s just as their spectre had created anxiety in the 1950s. The Howard League Policy Co-ordinating Group, meeting on 5 September 1995, noted in its minutes that one of its members had been 'confronted with victims' groups which felt that the Howard League, and other similar organisations, largely ignored victims only championing offenders' rights. . . . it was thought that the Howard League ought to consider victims more, and have a more coherent policy on victims' issues.——feared that the way that victims' groups were becoming increasingly vociferous and hard line and they were going to become increasingly attractive to "the Right".'

[7] In a paper written for Justice in March 1996, David Faulkner, the lately retired and influential former Deputy Under Secretary at the Home Office treated almost every aspect of the victim's status as problematic and open to assessment. Nothing was fixed or certain. Faulkner wondered whether the victim should be regarded as a citizen, or as a passive recipient of rights, as a consumer of public services or as one who should 'have a stronger voice and more decisive influence in . . . investigation, prosection and sentencing . . .'

[8] It should be nevertheless noted that some moderately authoritative bodies do explicitly recognise survivors as victims. The 1985 United Nations Declaration of Basic Principles of Justice for Victims of Crime and Abuse of Power stated in its annex that: 'The term "victim" also includes, where appropriate, the immediate family or dependants of the direct victim and persons who have suffered harm in intervening to assist victims in distress or to prevent victimization.'

that is there within that room is almost tangible, and to be able to listen to each other and perhaps hear different emotions that people have—you suddenly realise 'oh yes, I felt like that!' or 'yes, I'm feeling like that' or 'oh well, maybe I'm not going mad. Maybe it is natural'...[9]

Individuals who had hitherto been separated by grief, confusion, fear, and rage came together and they experienced in that encounter a shaping, affirmation, and collectivisation of a powerful passion that created an emotional field, identities and identifications, sensibilities and motives, and boundaries between the 'us' of the survivors and the 'them' of the world outside. And what was the quality of that passion? It was not simple anger, although 'anger' was the word most commonly employed to describe it. 'Anger' was at best an approximate term which could be applied only rather clumsily to a cacophony of tumultuous and ineffable feelings that fused body and mind; past and present; individual, situation, and collectivity together in one inchoate compound. The turbulence of deep mourning led to strong bodily sensations and emotions which not only acted as the content, context, and object of reflection, but also gave intensity and physicality to feeling and thought. Bereavement after homicide did not permit much calm, disembodied contemplation about the facts of unnatural death, victims, survivors, and criminal justice.

At the existential centre of all that intensity, the 'I' of the survivor worked as a charged and self-referring symbolic process that was continually preoccupied with itself and its own reactions. It was a self sporadically swamped by its own feelings; it was anger with which the survivor had to reckon; and many (but not all) no longer took anger to be shameful. Survivors had, it was claimed, a right to their anger, they had earned it, it gave them strength, and strong feelings were no failing in an indifferent and cruel world.

It had once been believed that the chaos of an empty Utgard encircled the orderliness of the inhabited world of Midgard. Using different similes, the survivors' own cosmology was not very distant from that of its Norse antecedent. For a while, survivors sensed that they had been cast out from the familiar and taken-for-granted world to confront the meaninglessness beyond. What they craved above all was the return of causality, meaning, and order to a

[9] 'All Things Considered', BBC Radio Wales, 13 December 1987.

disordered universe—in short, an end to estrangement. Part of the project of the new groups, The Compassionate Friends, Parents of Murdered Children, Support After Murder and Manslaughter, Justice for Victims, Victim's Voice, and the rest, was to attack alienation by giving that inner turmoil an outer cladding of structure, stability, communality, and direction. Different words were employed to convey what was sought—accountability, answerability, respect, and rights—but the theme was always clear: symmetry, purpose, and sense had been lost and had to be regained.

Survivors felt as if they had been shouldered aside and excluded from processes that should have incorporated them. Inquests, trials, tribunals, consultations, and investigations should have been central, defining phases in their own and others' lives, and in the larger work of sense-making that had to be undertaken in the aftermath of death. But survivors had lost control over what was done to and for the victim, and it rankled. It compounded their alienation and emphasized their powerlessness.[10] If the solitary, weak, and inexperienced mourner could not reclaim control, if, as Judith Herman claimed, the traumatised person was often dismissed as flawed,[11] something might be done with the aid of a group possessing numbers and a suprapersonal name. Groups could seem objective and authoritative in a fashion denied to individuals, and it was a result that the organizations that were so founded came to labour under a heavy weight of meaning and expectation.

Organizations could be expected, first, to give comfort, support, and moral validation to those who imagined at times they had lost not only their bearings but their very reason. They supplied meaning, structure, purpose, and identity. Organizations could be expected, second, to represent sentimentally and politically all the afflictions, wrongs, and indignities that individuals had suffered, and they were looked upon as a vehicle to restore balance and correct injustice. They became political and moral instruments. Organizations could be expected, third, to become symbolic objects

[10] It rankled particularly in the case of the individuals and organizations whose losses were not fully acknowledged as criminal. Chief amongst them were those campaigning for the families of road deaths. There is a span of stances towards those deaths, the labels being applied stretching from 'homicides' to 'accidents'. Currently, in 1997, the Home Office is not prepared to sanction its funding to Victim Support being used to support those families, although the organization received 1,306 referrals in 1996 (I am grateful to Anne Viney for this point).
[11] J. Herman,' *Trauma and Recovery* (Pandora, London, 1994), 115.

in their own right, standing as a kind of metonym for the survivor and his or her pain, and members sometimes believed that they rose or fell with the respect which their group was awarded. And organizations could be expected, in turn, to take highly stylised positions in a larger dialectic of affirmation and negation. So it was that TCF, POMC, and, indeed, Victim Support, were not only understood to support and champion the survivor, giving him or her a role, but, playing 'performative roles',[12] they also provided the dispositions and contrasts by which survivors and their groups could be recognised and defined.

Out of chaos there emerged a new identity, a grammar of binary oppositions, analogical reasoning, and the choreography of fusion and fission—the repeated coming-together and splitting apart that marked the early history of the new groups. It was almost as if the groups could not establish character and purpose without the dramatic distinctions which shared emotions and an accusatory anger engendered. One cost of social and moral affirmation was negation, and groups were continually setting themselves against one another and against many of the outsiders whom they encountered in their campaigns. So very preoccupied with meaning were the activists of the 1980s and 1990s that they transformed their own fragmentary environment into a highly-coloured, bitterly-contested, and expressive moral map.

What was integral to that dialectic was the sustenance which it supplied: it was not always easy for groups who defined themselves conflictually to move too far from one another because they would then have had to forfeit some part of the process by which their own character and cohesion was accomplished. The affirming and the negating were too integral to one another, too much parts of a single signifying process, to permit ready severance. Like sets of twin stars the groups circled one another, and like twin stars, possibly, they threatened one another's ultimate extinction.

I asked in the Preface whether the new groups constituted the beginnings of a social movement. Perhaps the answer should be that their members, people in great need, had come together within the interstices of an extant organization, The Compassionate Friends. But it was not they who had devised the orginal structural formulae

---

[12] See J. Austin, *How to do Things with Words* (Oxford University Press, Oxford, 1976).

for self-help or mutual aid. Those formulae were already in place. Without The Compassionate Friends, it may be conjectured, it would have taken very much longer before the homicide survivors' groups would have begun to emerge. Indeed, they might never have emerged at all. Survivors were often too lonely and destitute to coalesce. Many had waited in isolation for decades for a POMC or a SAMM to appear, and Victim Support, the prime mover in the area of services for victims, had had little success in promoting self-help. Perhaps, eventually, there would have been an importation of formulae from the United States, but North American influence was actually remarkably slight during the thirty or so years covered by this book, registering yet further the extent to which bereavement can inflict isolation. Once they *had* appeared in the bosom of The Compassionate Friends, the English groups began to evolve around the central dialectic which has been the theme of this book. They came to make up a loosely-coupled network of competing moral entities that continually grappled with one another in a struggle for resources, attention, intepretive authority, and identity.

Central to all those signifying processes, indeed lending them their animation, was the telling and retelling of narratives that were at once personal and communal, original and conventional. At the outset of any support meeting on either side of the Atlantic, it was customary for old and new members to recite their personal history, beginning, perhaps, with 'my name is——and two years ago my son was stabbed to death in a supermarket...', or 'my name is——and ten years ago my daughter was raped and murdered'. In effect, individual and collective themes were compressed into biography, the survivor's very self being retold to document hurts, griefs, and achievements. Because survivors tended to take a large part of their identity from the new organizations, such a biography became simultaneously a tale about an individual and a tale about a group, the one collapsing into the other, providing reference points for identity.

Those stories had force and poignancy. They concentrated in the main on the survivor as a person benighted by bereavement, as a self built around the stark facts of homicide. They constructed a new master status to which other pieces of biographical material were thematically subordinated. Enveloped within them were narratives of injustice, misunderstanding, alienation, and anger, on the one hand, and of new, albeit limited, possibilities of transcendence, visions, and purposes, on the other. They were repeated in public and private, again and again, honed, as it were, in the telling. The outcome was that each person assembled a situationally-contingent self devised to make sense of the impact and aftermath of catastrophe, and the self that emerged was shaped in an environment of other stories told by other survivors.

There was something sacramental about that process of baring hurt, alienation, and humiliation. It marked the passing of a threshold, an emotional *rite de passage*. Those who participated translated it into an offering, a gift of their innermost self to the collectivity, and it powerfully cemented the group together in a special sharing of truth. Indeed, it is significant that one of the most frequently-discussed projects upon which Victim's Voice chose to embark, a project that was mooted first in September 1995 but not achieved during the period of my fieldwork, was the compilation of what was called a 'Founding Members' Casebook'. Publishing a collection of autobiographies was taken to be the most potent way of underscoring the purposes and character of Victim's Voice. Each member would offer a brief history of his or her case, pointing to the problems that had arisen and the attention which was required. Underlying it, one may suppose, was a quieter and more plaintive message: 'this is who we are, look how we have suffered, look how we still suffer, look how we have entrusted ourselves to you. How can you deny us?'

I have likened some part of what was done to alchemy, to a passage through the fire of the chemical furnace that so changed the survivor that it was difficult to convey sentiments to others who had not undergone a similar crossing. No doubt others, such as rape and incest survivors, have also worked with a like reasoning, but the fervour of many survivors tended to be quite incandescent and it affected almost all their dealings with outsiders.

The political language which emanated from the groups was not always the measured and dispassionate discourse of the audiences to whom it was directed. Neither could it depend for its legitimacy on the impersonal authority of office or professional expertise. To the contrary, in many instances its mandate was personal, moral, and existential and it flowed from the unique experiential understanding of the survivor to take the form of bald demands delivered with a pitch and level of personal engrossment foreign to Whitehall, the Bar, and the more private recesses of Westminster. After all, survivors were often irate, frightened, alienated, and bewildered people who were beset by images of violence, people who sometimes looked on passion as the natural and outward sign of authentic feeling. Consider an exchange that took place between Lord Longford, Myra Hindley's champion, and Ann West, the mother of one of Myra Hindley's victims: he 'asked me if I would like to "take wine" with him,' said Ann West; 'I told him that it would choke me.'[13] Michael McConville, an astute and sympathetic observer of the new survivors' groups, reflected:

> The frustration of victims is so intense that they do shout. There's enormous anger which has to be directed somewhere. They see the locus of the problem in the politicians who maybe say 'well, research actually shows such and such', trying to adopt a sort of academic approach or a rational approach to this, and victims are not tolerant of that, or some victims are not tolerant of that.

So endemic had that angry style of talk become, so lacking in influence was it known to be to the officials who were its target, that a choice was forever before survivors.[14] On the one hand, as one member of Victim's Voice argued, 'we must be calm and reasonable because those committees think of us as unreasonable.' On the other hand, there was the argument, conveyed in the retort of a member of Justice for Victims, that: 'you'll only have to wait another forty years'. A survivor remarked to me at a local meeting of SAMM that he well understood that it was probably right to adhere to a policy of appearing reasonable in negotiations with officials, but 'when I start talking, I do get so emotional'.

Mindful of the stereotyping that undermined their standing, survivors who did moderate their language would sometimes advert to the fact. Take the emphasis adopted by Disaster Action in its response to a Law Commission consultation paper that:

> It is sometimes the case that the media portray bereaved families, who call on the criminal justice system to take action, as people who seek simple revenge. Disaster Action would like to make it very clear that this is not the motive behind this

[13] A. West; For the Love of Lesley (Warner, London, 1993), 108.
[14] For a discussion of that choice as it was phrased by the survivors of the Hillsborough disaster, see The Independent, 7 Apr 1995.
[15] 'Response to the Law Commission Involuntary Manslaughter Consultation Paper' (Disaster Action, London, 1994), 2, 3.

> particular submission or indeed of any comments that we make about the issue of criminal accountability... Disaster Action's policy on corporate accountability has nothing to do with vengeance and all to do with equity.[15]

In the main, rewards were attached to talking the native language and observing the local customs of the policy-maker and politician. Distinctions between acceptable pressure groups and the rest are well enough known inside and outside Whitehall (in the Home Office, for instance, store is placed on whether an organization is what officials would call 'house-trained'). Ministers were certainly advised by their officials in August 1994 that they should pay more heed to SAMM than to Justice for Victims, and that they should attend SAMM's launch to promote an association that was reasonable in the face of competition from one that was not. Although the campaigning Justice for Victims might have overshadowed SAMM in the summer of 1994, it was said, SAMM was the more constructive, rational, and cohesive association whose propriety was guaranteed by Victim Support.

A consequence was the emergence of a series of dilemmas for the new groups. One way of being a survivor may have been more fulfilling, demonstrative, and cathartic, but the other seemed calculated to achieve clearer instrumental gains. One way may have looked as if it got to the heart of grief, but the other enabled officials and politicians to 'do business' with the groups. One entailed the appearance of acting in good faith, the other sometimes the appearance of acting in bad faith. But good faith and bad faith, authenticity and inauthenticity, were increasingly difficult to disentangle when so much was conveyed in premeditated performances in staged settings. How could one judge between the real and the feigned in the world of expressive politics? After all, the very decision to appear 'natural' and spontaneous could vitiate itself.[16]

It was not an easy predicament for expressive organizations preoccupied with meaning. Neither was it a predicament that could be resolved lightly by abandoning old strategies and adopting new ones. To be sure, members of SAMM, Justice for Victims, and kindred groups could stand back and comment on themselves and others' performances and protestations. But styles of performance were not a strictly instrumental or impersonal matter at all. They

---

[16] See E. Goffman, *Interaction Ritual* (Doubleday Anchor, New York, 1967).

were not easily dispensable or malleable. They went straight to the core of identity. Public behaviour proclaimed who one was, how one memorialised the dead, how one grieved, how one made sense of the past and the future, how, in short, one had organized a new self to contend with the disorganization of *anomie*. The self that ensued may have been a bit ramshackle at times, it may have been displeasing to the survivor on occasion, but it *was* an existential structure to which one could cling. To change was not only again to lose structure but also to deny a new self and the dead it commemorated.

And there was another predicament of equal proportions which remained unsettled during the time of my fieldwork. Part of the palpable strength of self-help and mutual aid was the way in which they brought the lost and grieving together in an emotional communion that generated a sense of intersubjectivity and amplified sentiment. Survivors found in their unity and fellow-feeling a liberation from alienation. It allowed them to redefine their responses as normal and proper in the appalling aftermath of homicide. It enabled them to reconcile themselves to their anger. It gave them a history and a language with which to speak about the unspeakable. But it also tended to freeze them *as* survivors, for it was as survivors, and as survivors alone, that they had an identity, membership, and role in the group. 'Moving on', 'getting over it', and allied phrases which represented grief as a moral career with a determinate ending subverted the group's very world-view and were resisted by many. Within the group, at least, grief tended to be represented as a permanent condition that could not be shaken off, and there was no recognised role for ex-survivors, the survivors who had ceased effectively to be survivors, no acceptable words to describe how surviving itself had been survived. Rather, people were obliged inconspicuously to slip away from the groups, saying merely that they were 'burnt out' or had 'had enough', that a new spouse would not tolerate their remaining active, or that they had been neglecting their family. It was almost as if, in leaving, they had somehow failed.

The experience of shared emotions, validated anger, and objectified injustice could lead to a restless and strong impulse to campaign, to move away from the 'tea and sympathy' of the drawing room and into the streets. Activists often deprecated quieter styles of action as no action at all, and within the centre of the support group there could consequently grow the seeds of a destructive contradiction: communality engendered an anti-communality that threatened to tear community and its supports apart.

The groups did not cope well with those internal conflicts in England and Wales. To the contrary, the officers of TCF, POMC, and SAMM were to be repeatedly preoccupied with the management of rifts that consumed their time and attention and arrested the organizations' smooth development. It seemed difficult for the one strain to triumph over the other so completely that an organization could take a straight and unambiguous course towards a militant politics or towards support. To the contrary, many groups fed off their conflicts. It seemed as difficult to contain antagonism or use its arguments for reflexive self-examination. Rather than responding purposefully and with a single mind to the grievous needs of the bereaved, a number of groups have actually been bedevilled by a succession of wasteful civil wars.

Perhaps the only practicable answer will lie in the North American stratagem of divorcing the protagonists so completely that each can pursue a discrete role, style, and identity. But that remedy will have its own costs. No one organization can supply all that a survivor needs. Although the American groups did resolve an effective division of labour, allowing survivors to move from group to group for different purposes, there are fewer survivors in England and Wales, they are spread thin, and organizations in those countries cannot afford to squander their numbers and strength by creating too many divisions.

Yet, for all that, and despite its tensions, SAMM will remain a source of very great comfort to the bereaved. Indeed, it will be the only such source to many. SAMM will make apparent the suffering, incomprehension, and isolation that have been concealed for too long. It will give purpose and direction to those who once had none. It will work with Victim Support so that families can receive practical assistance. Together with a number of the other new organizations—and RoadPeace, the Suzy Lamplugh Trust and The Zito Trust[17] above all—it will continue to give advice and training to

---

[17] The Zito Trust is now managed, in its founder's words, 'purely... by staff and trustees who have not been a victim of homicide or a victim of a mentally disordered offender'. Jayne Zito herself left her position as Director to become Patron: 'I am involved with promoting good practice within [the] field of support and have found agencies very interested in how best they can improve their response to... trauma.... We refer specifically to the "situational stress factors" that exaggerate the secondary victims' experience and distress' (letter of 29 Sep 1997).

those in and about the criminal justice system who find it difficult to comprehend the dreadful aftermath of homicide and violent death. With those other organizations, it may bring about the introduction of greater rights to information about cases and decisions and, perhaps most important, the symbolic and practical incorporation of secondary victims into a criminal justice system which they fear all too readily excludes them.[18] It may even bring about a legal and administrative redefinition of victims and victimisation.

There is already evidence of a beginning. Home Office officials and politicians, and members of the Bar, the judiciary, the Parole Board, and the Crown Prosecution Service, have certainly indicated a willingness to talk to and about survivors. There is an allusion to homicide survivors in the second *Victim's Charter*. There is a new conversation about victims' rights, although quite what it portends is not clear. The Zito Trust has already secured money from the Department of Health and there is a probability that Home Office funding will underwrite SAMM in future. Victim Support has brought about the inauguration of police family liaison officers and the Crown Court Witness Service. There is the information pack. A victim's family may be allotted space in the well of the courtroom and away from the 'public' and the offender's family and supporters, but only at the discretion of the judge. Secondary victims are being treated more sympathetically in entertainment and the mass media, no longer fleeting figures who suffer no pain but substantial actors in their own right.[19]

And there are the self-help groups themselves. At the local level, particularly, and away from the stormy politics at the centre, SAMM groups offer advice, solace, and companionship where little was to be had before. Perhaps Ann Robinson, one of the two women who started it all, should have the very last word. The achievement of SAMM, she said in late 1997, lies in 'the fact that there is now help available, support available, in more parts of the country. There's nothing so valuable as to be in a room with people who allow you to express your feelings and your pain.'

[18] For The Zito Trust's campaigns to incorporate secondary victims in mental health tribunals see *ZT Monitor*, June 1997, No 1.

[19] Robert Reiner, who is currently collaborating in a major analysis of shifts in mass media representations of crime and criminals in the United Kingdom since the war, would maintain that one of the principal transformations has been the growing acknowledgement of the victim as one who is critically affected by criminal events.

Index